THE
HERMENEUTICS
OF CHARITY

THE HERMENEUTICS OF CHARITY

Interpretation, Selfhood, and Postmodern Faith

EDITED BY JAMES K.A. SMITH
AND HENRY ISAAC VENEMA

Studies in Honor of
JAMES H. OLTHUIS

Brazos Press
Grand Rapids, Michigan

Published by Brazos Press
a division of Baker Publishing Group
P.O. Box 6287, Grand Rapids, MI 49516-6287
www.brazospress.com

Printed in the United States of America

Library of Congress Cataloging-in-Publication Data
    The hermeneutics of charity : interpretation, selfhood, and postmodern faith / edited by James K.A. Smith and Henry Isaac Venema.
        p.   cm.
    "Studies in honor of James H. Olthuis."
    Includes bibliographical references.
    ISBN 1-58743-113-0 (cloth)
    1. Postmodern theology. 2. Hermeneutics. I. Smith, James K. A., 1970– II. Venema, Henry Isaac, 1958– III. Olthuis, James H. IV. Title.
    BT83.597.H47 2004
    230p.046—dc22   2004010940

For Jean,
for years of being-with

James H. Olthuis,
Senior Member in Philosophical Theology,
Institute for Christian Studies, 1968–2004.

Contents

Acknowledgments

This collection of essays to honor Jim Olthuis was made possible by many helping hands—a community of scholars eager to honor Jim's legacy, working together in a spirit of love and grace that we've seen modeled by Jim on so many occasions. We want to express our deep appreciation to each of the contributors for their work on these essays, prompt and punctual submissions, and their patience with us as we've shepherded the book to press. It has been a pleasure for us to work with all of you.

This book could not have been possible without the very tangible support of the Institute for Christian Studies (ICS) in Toronto, Ontario—Jim's institutional home for over thirty years. In particular, we have appreciated the support and encouragement of Bob Sweetman, then academic dean while we launched this project, and Harry Fernhout, president of the Institute. Thanks also to other staff and students at ICS who have helped us pull together information and data on Jim's work, particularly Michael DeMoor's work on the bibliography under the auspices of the Faith and Learning Network at ICS. The book bears the imprints of an institution's labors of love.

Thanks also to Rodney Clapp and Rebecca Cooper at Brazos Press for their support of the project. We are thrilled to honor Jim with a book from Brazos—a press that embodies so many of Jim's own concerns and passions.

Seleena Lindsey from the office of faculty services at Messiah College, Grantham, Pennsylvania, provided invaluable assistance with the preparation of the manuscript, and both Messiah College and Calvin College, Grand Rapids, Michigan, granted us reduced loads, which enabled the completion of this project. Our thanks to our home institutions for taking seriously the labors of integral Christian scholarship.

Finally, the entire book is constructed as a tribute to a mentor and dear friend who has left an indelible mark on each of us. As student after student will happily testify, Jim's care and compassion, love and embrace have made an impact rivaled only by his scholarly acumen and critical theoretical insights. But behind, beside, and in front of him has been his wife, Jean, to whom we dedicate the book, for years of "being-with."

—m—

Chapters 1 and 7 originally appeared in James H. Olthuis, ed., *Knowing Other-wise: Philosophy at the Threshold of Spirituality*, Perspectives in Continental Philosophy (New York: Fordham University Press, 1997). They are reproduced here with the kind permission of the series editor, John D. Caputo, and Fordham University Press.

Contributors

Steven Bouma-Prediger is John H. and Jeanne M. Jacobson Professor of Religion at Hope College, Holland, Michigan, and author of the award-winning book *For the Beauty of the Earth: A Christian Vision for Creation Care* (Baker) and *The Greening of Theology* (American Academy of Religion).

Constantin V. Boundas is professor of philosophy at Trent University, Peterborough, Ontario, and an internationally distinguished scholar in contemporary French philosophy, particularly the work of Gilles Deleuze. He is the author of *Gilles Deleuze and the Theater of Philosophy* (Routledge) and editor of *The Deleuze Reader* (Columbia University Press).

John D. Caputo is David C. Cook Emeritus Professor of Philosophy at Villanova University, Villanova, Pennsylvania and Watson Professor of Religion at Syracuse University and a leading international figure in continental philosophy of religion. His most recent books include *On Religion* (Routledge), *More Radical Hermeneutics* (Indiana University Press), the award-winning *Deconstruction in a Nutshell* (Fordham University Press), and *The Prayers and Tears of Jacques Derrida* (Indiana University Press). He is editor of the Perspectives in Continental Philosophy series from Fordham University Press.

Jeffrey Dudiak, the first student to complete his doctorate under the direction of Jim Olthuis, is Assistant Professor of Philosophy at King's University College, Edmonton, Alberta. He is best known for his insightful work on Levinas, most notably in *The Intrigue of Ethics* (Fordham University Press).

David Goicoechea is professor of philosophy at Brock University, St. Catharines, Ontario. A leading Nietzsche scholar, he is the editor of *Joyful Wisdom* and author of *The Nature and Pursuit of Love: The Philosophy of Irving Singer* (Prometheus Press).

Hendrik Hart is emeritus senior member of systematic philosophy at the Institute for Christian Studies, Toronto, Ontario. A fellow student with Jim Olthuis, and a longtime colleague, Hart has written books including *Understanding Our World, The Search for Community in a Withering Tradition* (with Kai Nielsen), and a collection of essays on *Rationality in the Calvinian Tradition* (all University Press of America) edited with Nicholas Wolterstorff and Johann Van Der Hoeven.

Richard Kearney, formerly of University College Dublin, is Charles B. Seelig Professor of Philosophy at Boston College, as well as an accomplished poet. An

11

important bridge to contemporary French thought, Kearney is the author of *The God Who May Be* (Indiana University Press) and *On Stories* (Routledge), and editor of an important collection of interviews with French thinkers, *Dialogues with Contemporary Continental Thinkers* (Manchester University Press).

J. Richard Middleton is associate professor of biblical studies at Roberts Wesleyan College, Rochester, New York, and one of the leading voices on Christian faith and postmodernity. With Brian Walsh, he is the author of *The Transforming Vision* (InterVarsity) and *Truth Is Stranger Than It Used to Be* (InterVarsity).

Julie Robinson is a former student of Jim Olthuis. After having graduated with a master's degree from the Institute for Christian Studies, she moved to Edmonton, Alberta, where she is a full-time mom and a part-time poet. She is a member of the Edmonton Stroll of Poets' Society, and has published in the Canadian literary journal *Descant*.

James K.A. Smith is associate professor of philosophy at Calvin College, Grand Rapids, Michigan, and Director of the Seminars in Christian Scholarship. A former student of Jim Olthuis at ICS, Smith focuses his work on philosophical theology in the continental tradition. He is the author of *The Fall of Interpretation* (InterVarsity), *Speech and Theology: Language and the Logic of Incarnation* (Routledge), and *Introducing Radical Orthodoxy: Mapping a Post-Secular Theology* (Baker Academic).

Henry Isaac Venema is associate professor of philosophy at Messiah College, Grantham, Pennsylvania. Also one of Jim's former students, Venema is the author of *Identifying Selfhood: Imagination, Narrative, and Hermeneutics in the Thought of Paul Ricoeur* (State University of New York Press). His research is in the area of religion and hermeneutics/deconstruction.

Brian J. Walsh is CRC chaplain at the University of Toronto, Ontario, and teaches theology at Wycliffe College, Toronto. A groundbreaking voice on the frontiers of Christian faith and cultural critique, Walsh is author with J. Richard Middleton of *The Transforming Vision* (InterVarsity) and *Truth Is Stranger Than It Used to Be* (InterVarsity).

Merold Westphal is distinguished professor of philosophy at Fordham University, New York City. Westphal's work—including books such as *Overcoming Onto-Theology* (Fordham University Press), *Suspicion and Faith* (Fordham University Press), and *Becoming a Self* (Purdue University Press)—has been instrumental in providing a Christian engagement with contemporary continental thought from Hegel to Levinas.

Lambert Zuidervaart is now senior member in systematic philosophy at the Institute for Christian Studies, Toronto, Ontario, after a long tenure at Calvin College, Grand Rapids, Michigan. His research includes aesthetics and critical theory, and most recently has focused on questions of ontology in the late Heidegger. He is the author of *Adorno's Aesthetic Theory: The Redemption of Illusion* (MIT Press) and *Artistic Truth: Aesthetics, Discourse, and Imaginative Disclosure* (Cambridge University Press) and coeditor of *The Arts, Community, and Cultural Democracy* (St. Martin's) and *Pledges of Jubilee: Essays on the Arts and Culture* (Eerdmans).

Introduction

The Word of Love

Hermeneutics, Selfhood, and the Work of James H. Olthuis

James K.A. Smith and Henry Isaac Venema

According to many published reports, the devil is from Paris. In the circles of Christian theologians and philosophers, the dreaded enemy of "secular humanism" has been supplanted by a more terrifying creature: "postmodernism"—a label that functions as a kind of blob that absorbs anything contemporary that is considered antithetical to Christian faith. And almost invariably the provenance of postmodernism is traced to France, as if postmodernism were a kind of Frankenstein created in the laboratories of Jacques Derrida, Michel Foucault, and Jean-François Lyotard. Many Christian scholars have spent the past decade shoring up the front lines against this Parisian threat.

In this context, the work of James H. Olthuis signals a markedly different kind of engagement with contemporary continental thought. Olthuis has found in French philosophers not enemies but allies. Following his early appropriations of the work of Hans-Georg Gadamer and continental theologians such as Pannenberg and Moltmann, Olthuis's earliest engagements with deconstruction—though critical—were characterized by an openness to the work that the Spirit might be doing in Paris.[1] What could make such a unique engagement possible? We would argue that Olthuis's approach was possible only because he was operating out of the Reformed tradition of Abraham Kuyper and Herman Dooyeweerd—a tradition with two features in particular that

---

1. This is seen in Olthuis's first extended engagement with John D. Caputo in "A Cold and Comfortless Hermeneutic or a Warm and Trembling Hermeneutic? A Conversation with John D. Caputo," *Christian Scholars' Review* 19 (1990): 345–63. It is hard to overestimate how important this essay—and the relationship it engendered—has been for the trajectory of Olthuis's work.

account for Olthuis's development of a "Christian postmodernism."[2] First, the Reformed tradition, following the lead of Augustine and Calvin, has long emphasized a notion of "common grace" that affirms that the Spirit can be at work illuminating hearts and minds outside of the walls of the redeemed, granting insight into the structures of creation even to those like Derrida (who "rightly passes for an atheist"). As Augustine drew the picture, as the liberated Israelites who plundered Egyptian gold for the service of Yahweh, so Christian theologians could make off with the loot of the Platonists. In that respect, we might say that Derrida is to Olthuis what Plato was to Augustine: a philosopher with deep insights into the structure of creation, which Christians could ignore only at their peril.

Second, the continental Reformed tradition stemming from Kuyper and Dooyeweerd has long been suspicious of modernity, in two ways: on the one hand, the epistemology of this sector of the Reformed tradition has long called into question the notion of an autonomous, neutral, "secular" reason, arguing that reason is always already committed by a certain faith, by a certain religious standpoint.[3] When such criticisms began to be articulated by figures such as Derrida, Olthuis and others working in the reformational tradition could claim that they had been "postmodern" for a long time already.[4] As Olthuis himself puts it, the themes of postmodernism—"[u]nderstanding the primordial role of faith in theory formation, insisting that the pretended autonomy of theoretical thought is an illusion, witnessing to the reality of human brokenness, pursuing justice for all (not just 'us') in the public arenas of education, media, and politics—all have been compelling themes of the reformational philosophical heritage for nearly a century, beginning with Abraham Kuyper."[5] The reformational philosophical tradition was in a sense already primed for the advent of postmodernism, and thus was able to engage it as a fruitful ally rather than a dangerous enemy. On the other hand, the critical edge of the continental and Kuyperian wing of the Reformed tradition has focused on a prophetic critique of the ways in which the church too often surrenders its allegiance not to the

---

2. We would make the same claim for the exemplary work of Olthuis's friend Merold Westphal. For his own positive account of postmodernism, see Westphal, *Overcoming Onto-Theology: Toward a Postmodern Christian Faith*, Perspectives in Continental Philosophy (New York: Fordham University Press, 2001).

3. For a systematic unfolding of this claim, see Herman Dooyeweerd, *In the Twilight of Western Thought: Studies in the Pretended Autonomy of Philosophical Thought*, Collected Works B/4, ed. James K.A. Smith (Lewiston, N.Y.: Edwin Mellen, 1999). For Olthuis's most systematic exposition of this point, see "Dooyeweerd on Religion and Faith," in *The Legacy of Herman Dooyeweerd*, ed. C. T. McIntire (Lanham, Md.: University Press of America, 1985), pp. 21–41, and, more generally, idem, "On Worldviews," *Christian Scholars' Review* 14 (1985): 153–65. See also the exposition of Hendrik Hart, "Conceptual Understanding and Knowing *Other-wise*: Reflections on Rationality and Spirituality in Philosophy," in *Knowing Other-wise: Philosophy at the Threshold of Spirituality*, ed. James H. Olthuis, Perspectives in Continental Philosophy (New York: Fordham University Press, 1997), pp. 19–53.

4. It was of some interest that Malcolm Bull described Abraham Kuyper as the first postmodern. See Bull, "Who was the first to make a pact with the Devil?" *London Review of Books* (May 14, 1992): 22–24.

5. James H. Olthuis, "Love/Knowledge: Sojourning with Others, Meeting with Differences," introduction to *Knowing Other-wise*, pp. 12–13.

Lord Jesus Christ, but rather to secular nationalisms or destructive modernisms. On this account, the reason for the almost vitriolic criticisms of postmodernism from Christian scholars stems from their allegiance not to Christ, but to modernity itself. Having unwittingly baptized modernist philosophical and political assumptions as "Christian," the church has not been able to recognize its complicity with modernity. Thus when postmodernism launches an attack on the cherished mandates of modern foundationalism, individualism, and nationalism, Christians have too often taken this as antithetical to Christian faith. But in fact, such postmodern critiques are antithetical only to a *modernist* distortion of Christian faith—an idolatrous Christianity that worships at the feet of Reason or the state. The reformational tradition stemming from Kuyper has consistently called attention to these idolatries and thus could affirm the same criticisms when they were articulated by figures such as Lyotard and Foucault.[6] One can see this prophetic critique of modernity in some of Olthuis's earliest work.[7]

This collection of essays, grappling with questions at the intersection of theology, philosophy, and postmodern theory, are engendered by an event: the retirement of James H. Olthuis as senior member in philosophical theology and Ethics at the Institute for Christian Studies in Toronto, Ontario—a post he held from 1968 to 2004. But it would be better to say that this collection is engendered by a *person:* one simply known as "Jim" to his students and friends—a person who has had formative influence in the lives of students who have gone on to make their own impact as Christian scholars, and someone whose exemplary scholarship has been at the leading edge of Christian engagements with postmodernism. The collection includes contributions from Jim's friends (Caputo, Kearney, Westphal, Goicoechea, and Boundas), his colleagues (Zuidervaart, Hart), and some from a circle of his grateful students (Smith, Venema, Robinson, Middleton, Dudiak, Walsh, and Bouma-Prediger).

Olthuis's work, particularly with respect to postmodernism, has crystallized around two themes: on the one hand, questions regarding language, interpretation, and hermeneutics; on the other hand, correlate questions regarding the nature of the human person, selfhood, and the normative structures of intersubjective relationships. In academic parlance, Olthuis's signal contributions

---

6. In this respect, it is becoming clear that the reformational tradition is in common cause with two other recent (and related) theological trajectories: the postliberal theology of Stanley Hauerwas et al., and the Radical Orthodoxy project. On the latter, see James K.A. Smith and James H. Olthuis, eds., *Creation, Covenant, and Participation: Radical Orthodoxy and the Reformed Tradition* (Grand Rapids: Baker Academic, forthcoming).

7. See James H. Olthuis, "Must the Church Become Secular?" in John A. Olthuis et al., *Out of Concern for the Church* (Toronto: Wedge, 1970), pp. 105–25, and idem, "Worship and Witness," in John H. Olthuis, ed., *Will All the King's Men . . .* (Toronto: Wedge, 1972), pp. 1–27. For the work of students that exemplify this Olthuisian trajectory, see Brian J. Walsh and J. Richard Middleton, *The Transforming Vision: Shaping a Christian Worldview* (Downers Grove, Ill.: InterVarsity, 1984) and J. Richard Middleton and Brian J. Walsh, *Truth Is Stranger Than It Used to Be: Biblical Faith in a Postmodern Age* (Downers Grove, Ill.: InterVarsity, 1995).

have been in the field of heremeneutics and philosophical anthropology—a dual focus on the Word and Love, on the word *of* love, in homage to the God who is the Word (John 1:1) and Love (1 John 4:8)—a God who speaks, and when he speaks utters the word of love. As such, we have organized the essays into two parts reflective of Olthuis's corpus.

Hermeneutics, Deconstruction, and Christian Faith

As a scholar working in the Reformed tradition, and influenced by H. Evan Runner's notion of "scripturally-directed learning,"[8] it was almost inevitable that Olthuis run up against questions related to the word—the nature of religious language, the possibility of revelation, and the messy, difficult questions of interpretation and biblical authority. Olthuis was part of the vanguard of Christian philosophers and theologians who recognized the complicity of evangelical models of Scripture and interpretation with the reductionist, stunted models of knowing inherited from Descartes and the Enlightenment project. While more dynamic understandings of Scripture have become more standard in the work of evangelicals such as Clark Pinnock, Donald Bloesch, and Stanley Grenz, already in the late 1970s and early 1980s Olthuis was working out a general hermeneutics that took seriously the reality of human finitude as created by God. Because the reformational tradition already recognized the inescapable role of presuppositions in knowing—and thus was not frightened by the mediation of interpretation—Olthuis was in a position to critically appropriate the insights of Heidegger and Gadamer regarding the conditions of interpretation.[9] In the 1990s, Olthuis continued this engagement beyond hermeneutics and into the arena of deconstruction, particularly in the work of Jacques Derrida and John Caputo. Again, though there were grounds for criticism, Olthuis found in deconstruction themes that resonated with a radical, integrally Christian understanding of language and human finitude.[10]

8. See H. Evan Runner, *The Relation of the Bible to Learning* (Rexdale, Ont.: Association for Reformed Scientific Studies, 1967). On Runner's influence in this tradition, see Hart's essay below.

9. See James H. Olthuis, "Towards a Certitudinal Hermeneutic," in J. Kraay and A. Tol, eds., *Hearing and Doing: Essays in Honor of H. Evan Runner* (Toronto: Wedge, 1979), pp. 65–85, and more fully in idem, *A Hermeneutics of Ultimacy: Peril or Promise?* with D. Bloesch, C. Pinnock, and G. Sheppard (Lanham, Md.: University Press of America, 1986). For an account of the development of Olthuis's work on hermeneutics, see Joshua Lie, "The Hermeneutic Spiral as the Hermeneutics of Reconciliation: The Significance of Connection for Biblical Hermeneutics" (MPhilF Thesis, Institute for Christian Studies, Toronto, 2000).

10. See Olthuis, "A Cold and Comfortless Hermeneutic"; idem, "Undecidability and the Im/possibility of Faith: Continuing the Conversation with Professor Caputo," *Christian Scholars' Review* 20 (1991): 171–74; and idem, "Crossing the Threshold: Sojourning Together in the Wild Spaces of Love," *Toronto Journal of Theology* 11, 1 (1995): 188–205. The latter was Olthuis's Presidential Address to the Canadian Theological Society in 1993. For student works inspired by Olthuis on these matters, see Henry Venema, *Identifying Selfhood: Imagination, Narrative, and Hermeneutics in the Thought of Paul Ricoeur* (Albany: State University of New York Press, 2000), and James K.A. Smith, *The Fall of Interpretation: Philosophical Foundations for a Creational Hermeneutic* (Downers Grove, Ill.: InterVarsity, 2000).

The essays in part one below are organized around these themes related to the word, in particular questions of hermeneutics and deconstruction taken up in relation to Christian faith.

Love, Selfhood, and the Gift of Community

While Olthuis wrestled with questions regarding hermeneutics and language, his work from the beginning has been focused on themes in ethics and philosophical anthropology, eventually blooming in his work on psychotherapy and his own therapeutic practice.[11] These domains of inquiry, however, are not discrete for Olthuis: rather, questions of hermeneutics are ultimately matters of ethics, and one can only properly understand selfhood and community in terms of story and narrative. So one finds in Olthuis's contributions a unique interplay of anthropology and hermeneutics, psychotherapy and deconstruction.

Here again, Olthuis's refusal of Cartesian reductionism—which would reduce the self to an isolated, disembodied "thinking thing"—has been generated by Dooyeweerd's and Vollenhoven's reformational emphases on the multiple aspects of human selfhood. Olthuis's anthropology counters this modernist subject on all three aspects. First, it refuses the rationalist reductionism of Descartes. The human being cannot be reduced to a rational animal, nor a merely economic animal; the structurally *religious* nature of human beings created in the image of God means that their identity is to be found in plurality of ways of being-in-the-world. Second, in addition to the fact that Olthuis's model is nonreductionistic, at the heart of Olthuis's philosophical anthropology is the assertion that human beings are *social* creatures created for loving relation. One can only be human by being-*with*. Thus Olthuis's anthropology echoes the deeply Augustinian theme of the *ordo amoris*: "Who we are is determined by who and what we love."[12] So in contrast to the modernist infatuation with thought and being ("I think, therefore I am"), Olthuis proposes an anthropology of loving be(com)ing: "'I love, therefore I am' is rooted in an earlier 'I was loved, therefore I am.'"[13] As always, Olthuis's thought here is deeply Johannine: "We love because God first loved us" (1 John 4:19). Thus be(com)ing an authentic self requires the beautiful risk of relationship, becoming vulnerable to the Other in order to experience grace and love. Finally, in contrast to a long philosophical tradition from Plato through modernity, Olthuis's biblical

---

11. Olthuis's dissertation at the Free University of Amsterdam was published as *Facts, Values, and Ethics: A Confrontation with Twentieth Century British Moral Philosophy, in particular G. E. Moore* (Assen, Netherlands: Van Gorcum, 1968; New York: Humanities Press, 1969). (Those students who studied with Olthuis in the 1990s still find it hard to believe he cut his philosophical teeth on analytic ethics!) Olthuis's most mature philosophical anthropology can be found at the core of his most recent book on therapy, *The Beautiful Risk: A New Psychology of Loving and Being Loved* (Grand Rapids: Zondervan, 2001).

12. Olthuis, *Beautiful Risk*, p. 74.

13. Ibid., p. 71.

anthropology emphasizes the necessity and goodness of *embodiment* along with its attendant aspects of gender, place, sociality, and artistic being-in-the-world. Olthuis discerns the contrast:

> When "I think" becomes the epitome of being human, the fact that we have bodies, are of a particular gender, live at a certain time, enjoy relationships with others, inhabit certain socioeconomic situations, hold rafts of feelings—when "I think" defines humanness, all these are merely secondary. When, by contrast, "I love" becomes the mark of authentic humanity, relationships with others, with God, and with the creation are not small auxiliary concerns, but rather constitutive features of personal identity.[14]

These themes in Olthuis's philosophical anthropology—the centrality of love, the necessity of relation, and the goodness of embodiment—resonate with contemporary French philosophical influences. In particular, Olthuis has found important resources from what might appear unlikely sectors: Jewish thinker Emmanuel Levinas[15] and the work of French feminists Luce Irigaray and Julia Kristeva. Thus their work has provided a philosophical framework in which Olthuis could articulate his anthropology for a contemporary context. These themes of love, relationality, and selfhood are explored in the essays collected in part two of this book.

The final part of the book provides a further tribute and introduction to Olthuis's work with a narrative of his intellectual development and contributions, followed by a bibliography of his work. It is our hope that this book will introduce more students and scholars to Olthuis's unique scholarly contributions in these fields, as well as introduce them to a reformational tradition of Christian theoretical reflection that has unique resources for navigating the postmodern terrain. The bibliography is followed by what might be the most fitting tribute to Jim's labors: his students. To give a sense of the ripple effect of Jim's thought, we have concluded the volume with a list of the theses and doctoral dissertations that he has supervised. While Olthuis has made an impact as a scholar, his greatest impact (and pride) is found in his students. And while we honor him as a scholar, we love him as a mentor, teacher, and friend.

---

14. Ibid., pp. 69–70.

15. For exemplary work by one of Olthuis's students in this respect, see Jeffrey Dudiak, *The Intrigue of Ethics: A Reading of the Idea of Discourse in the Thought of Emmanuel Levinas,* Perspectives in Continental Philosophy (New York: Fordham University Press, 2001).

A Poetic Tribute

"Love as gift creates a space-which-is-meeting,
inviting partnership and co-birthing. . . .
Love as excess—love without a why—
overflows onto the plains and meadows
of life as a celebrating-with."

James Olthuis,
from "Crossing the Threshold:
Sojourning Together in the Wild Spaces of Love"

In the Beginning:
The Creation of Mother and Child

Julie Robinson

On the first day of this creation
the dark waters of the deep
that surrounded you
gave way to a brightness so commanding
you unfolded like petals
responding to the sun's heat
while the spirit that lurked within me
departed
leaving a strange red trace.
On the first day we learned
separation and difference
and someone said it was good.

On the second day you learned
hunger and disappointment
because milk and honey did not yet flow
and you returned to an inward curl
to cry or hide
while I appealed to angels on high,
whispered in your ear mysteries of Bethlehem,

sang Joy to the World (for it was the season).
And so we passed day and night
wondering that this could be good.

On the third day we learned
that a certain let-down is part of life,
that paradise,
if it existed once,
comes now in fits and spurts
and is often messy.

By the sixth day I was sure
that in the beginning
was desire,
that this mother-child relation happened
not because you bore my image
but because a wild love
flared at every union
as though my emptied self
were a burning mystery.

Part One

HERMENEUTICS,
DECONSTRUCTION,
AND CHRISTIAN FAITH

1

Crossing the Threshold

Sojourning Together in the Wild Spaces of Love
[1993]

James H. Olthuis

In the wake of the eclipse of the divine, darkness . . .
    sacred darkness lingers . . .
lingers endlessly.
Night
Sacred night
Night that is not day
Night beyond
Night
Night
From which we never
Awake[1]

We live in a "time between times," a "place which is no place,"[2] where, as Mark C. Taylor describes it, "sacred darkness lingers . . . endlessly." Like it or not, the Enlightenment dream of a world increasingly controlled by the light of pure rationality is fading fast over the horizon. Control through reason and science has left wide swaths of destruction in its wake: systematic violence, marginalization, oppression, suffering, domination of the "other." It is that sorry history that both lies at the root of the postmodern attack on the totalizing power of reason and gives shape to the postmodern ethical impera-

---

1. Mark C. Taylor, "Think Naught," in *Negation and Theology*, ed. Robert Scharlemann (Charlottesville: University Press of Virginia, 1992), p. 37.
    2. Mark C. Taylor, *Erring* (Chicago: University of Chicago Press, 1984), p. 6.

tive to include the "other" and to make room for the "different." But what now—at the end of reason, after virtue, after philosophy, after God? What if there is neither a religion nor a morality within the bounds of reason alone? Was Taylor right when he recently exclaimed: "Though it continues, theology is as dead as the God for which theologians search"?[3] If the "sacred escapes the strictures of ontotheology,"[4] unattainable by either the *via positiva* or the *via negativa*, is the sacred beyond reach?

The questions are formidable. But they are also exciting, especially for those of us involved in the theological enterprise. The kinds of questions and queries about claims to certainty and warrants to power that postmodernism is raising are precisely the kinds of limit questions[5] that lie at the heart of the theological endeavor. In the modern era the declaration of human autonomy was also the announcement of God's death. But now, paradoxically, since postmodern voices are declaring that the death of God finds its completion only in the death of the self,[6] questions of how to talk of self and God are once more taking center stage. As I see it, new spaces are opening up for theologians to be once again relevant players and significant voices in the public realm.

I suggest that Jacques Derrida's emphasis on undecidability, the secret, and the *khôra* open the way to a new postsecular discourse about faith and God. However, Mark C. Taylor's figure of the erring, serpentine wanderer as a liberated being in carnivalesque release abandons us only to isolation, wounds, and tears, and asks that we give up on any possibility of meeting, healing, and mending. I therefore propose that we replace an ontology of being—with its question, "To be or not to be?"—with a vision of love—with its basic question, "To love or not to love?"[7] In the priority of love, agency returns, not as a self-construction but as a gift to be received and a call to be heeded. I conclude by intimating that sojourning (rather than settling or wandering) in the wild spaces of love is an apt metaphor for a genuine postmodern theology.

The House of Being: Power

In philosophical theology the concept of being has traditionally played a central role, and God has been considered the highest Being and the ground of every being. Since metaphysics needed a centerpiece, a keystone, in its house of being, it may be credibly said that the advent of "God" in philosophy arose less

3. Taylor, "Think Naught," p. 36.

4. Ibid., p. 37.

5. See David Tracy's discussion of "limit" in ch. 5 of *Blessed Rage for Order* (New York: Seabury, 1975), pp. 91–119.

6. For Taylor the "death of God is at the same time the death of the self" (*Erring*, p. 20).

7. Although Jean-Luc Marion, in his *God without Being*, trans. Thomas A. Carlson (Chicago: University of Chicago Press, 1991), makes a similar proposal in respect to God, he continues (questionably, in my view) to see "to be or not to be" as "the first and indispensable question" for every creature (p. xx).

from God than from metaphysics. As Heidegger has described, this concept of God finds its full formulation in the modernity of Descartes, Spinoza, Leibniz, and Hegel with the *causa sui:* "The Being of beings is represented fundamentally, in the sense of the ground, only as *causa sui.* This is the metaphysical concept of God. . . . This is the right name for the god of philosophy."[8]

Heidegger concludes: "Man can neither pray nor sacrifice to this god. Before the *causa sui,* man can neither fall to his knees in awe nor can he play music and dance before this god."[9] In other words, the *causa sui* is only an "idol" of God, and so-called "god-less thinking is more open to him than ontotheologic would like to admit."[10] In another place Heidegger makes the same point. "[A] god who must permit his existence to be proved in the first place is ultimately a very ungodly god. The best such proofs of existence can yield is blasphemy."[11] In a 1951 seminar at the University of Zurich, Heidegger summarized: "If I were yet to write a theology—to which I sometimes feel inclined—then the word *Being* would not occur in it. Faith does not need the thought of Being. When faith has recourse to this thought, it is no longer faith."[12]

But the problem is not simply that as *causa sui* God becomes a prisoner of our concepts, metaphysically chained in the ontotheological abode of being.[13] The category of being itself as the institutionalization of reason, with its claims to full presence, is fraught with difficulty. For at least since Descartes set out to establish the ego as point of absolute certainty, being has been characterized with what Spinoza termed the *conatus essendi:* "Everything, in so far as it is in itself, endeavours to persist in its own being."[14] Since for him all things are modes of God, this *conatus essendi* emerges by necessity out of the eternal and infinite essence of God. Since "God's power is identical with his essence,"[15] power becomes the central concept of modern ontologies.[16] Here theology is the keystone in a theory of absolute power.

Even when the human ego replaces God as the apex of the system, the self-maintaining ontology of power takes center stage, whether as Leibniz's monads of power, Nietzsche's will to power, Freud's libido, Dasein's care (in

8. Martin Heidegger, *Identity and Difference,* trans. Joan Stambaugh (New York: Harper & Row, 1969), pp. 60, 72.

9. Ibid., p. 72.

10. Ibid.

11. Martin Heidegger, *Nietzsche,* vol. 2, trans. David Krell (New York: Harper & Row, 1984), p. 106.

12. As quoted in Marion, *God without Being,* p. 61, who gives the German text of Heidegger, pp. 211–12. Derrida discusses it in "How to Avoid Speaking: Denials," in *Derrida and Negative Theology,* ed. Harold Coward and Toby Foshay (Albany: State University of New York Press, 1992), pp. 126ff.

13. Two recent discussions have been especially helpful: Marion, *God without Being,* chs. 2 and 3, and Theo De Boer, *De God van de filosofen and de God van Pascal* ('s Gravenhage: Meinema, 1989), pp. 49–58.

14. Benedict de Spinoza, *Ethics,* in *The Chief Works of Benedict de Spinoza,* trans. R. Elwes (New York: Dover, 1955), part 3, proposition 6, p. 136.

15. Ibid., part 1, proposition 34, p. 74.

16. "'I think' comes down to 'I can.' . . . Ontology as first philosophy is a philosophy of power . . . a philosophy of injustice" (Emmanuel Levinas, *Totality and Infinity,* trans. A. Lingis [Pittsburgh: Duquesne University Press, 1969], p. 46).

Heidegger), or the striving for being (in Sartre). In other words, as Derrida and Levinas have argued, what has developed is a process of totalizing with reason as the instrument by which an ego or society of egos overpowers and totalizes, appropriates and disempowers anything that is "other" or different.[17] Whatever the details and variety, being is a system of maintenance, control, domination: power-over.[18] One either dominates or is dominated—as Freud, Hegel, and Sartre in particular emphasize.[19] Thus, Paul Tillich defines power as "the possibility a being has to actualize itself against the resistance of other beings."[20] To be a self is to have enemies. Implicitly, if not explicitly, one is always at war. This apotheosis of the self is seen to crest in the idealism of Hegel in which everything becomes itself in and through its own other. In the end, since the "other" has a utilitarian function in relation to the self, relationship to the other is, finally, self-relationship. When an "other" resists this role, failing to mirror the self, when it resists being used and consumed, it must be invaded and dominated.

There is one more telling aspect of this picture that needs to be noted before we continue with the deconstructionist critique. In the world of being-as-power, suffering has no legitimate place.[21] Spinoza again voices the dominant tradition: "Pain is the transition of a man from a greater to a lesser perfection."[22] Pain and suffering are diminutions of being. Pain weakens the power of activity and suffering is powerlessness. Even Heidegger, an archcritic of the ontotheologic tradition, by considering that the essence of pain cannot be painful in a feeling sense, takes the suffering out of pain.[23] Strikingly, some postmodernists do the same. Deleuze and Guattari, for example, champion "the schizophrenic process" in its "potential for revolution"[24] without any attention to the actual psychological pain and suffering of schizophrenics.

17. In *Positions,* trans. Alan Bass (Chicago: University of Chicago Press, 1981), p. 64, Derrida terms this totalizing "motif of homogeneity, the theological motif *par excellence.*" As Kevin Hart (*The Trespass of the Sign* [Cambridge: Cambridge University Press, 1989], p. 32) points out, in Derrida's sense, a theological discourse need not involve God; it only needs something that functions as an agent of totalization.

18. In this context, I cannot resist alluding to Walter Wink's *Engaging the Powers* (Minneapolis: Fortress Press, 1992), where he insists that the heart of Jesus' life and message was challenging the "domination system."

19. For an excellent analysis of the "problem of domination," see Jessica Benjamin, *The Bonds of Love* (New York: Pantheon, 1989).

20. Paul Tillich, *The Courage to Be* (New Haven, Conn.: Yale University Press, 1952), p. 179.

21. Theologically, I think this is one (perhaps *the*) compelling reason why the philosophical idea of the impassibility of God has historically often prevailed over the suffering love of God.

22. Spinoza, *Ethics,* part 3, definition 3, p. 174.

23. Martin Heidegger, *On the Way to Language,* trans. P. Hertz (New York: Harper & Row, 1971), p. 181; and *Poetry, Language, Thought,* trans. A. Hofstadter (New York: Harper & Row, 1971), p. 205. See John D. Caputo, "Thinking, Poetry, and Pain," in *Southern Journal of Philosophy,* 28, Supplement (1989): 55–81.

24. Gilles Deleuze and Felix Guattari, *Anti-Oedipus Capitalism and Schizophrenia,* trans. R. Hurly, M. Seem, and H. Lane (London: Athlone, 1977), p. 340.

Erring

In our day, prefigured by the masters of suspicion, Marx, Freud, and Nietzsche, the imperial self has also been declared dead. More precisely, the self as the child of enlightenment, fully present to itself, self-conscious, sovereign, absolute agent, given power over the world as object, is revealed to be itself a production of this very world and the processes it was said to master. All we have left is a decentered, deconstructed "self," the self as a product and effect of the crossings and interfacings of impersonal cosmic forces.

Mark C. Taylor has given in *Erring*[25] perhaps the fullest description of such a non-self self: postmodern persons are "transitory 'points' of intersection," "'sites' of passage," "erratic markings" (137). A human subject is a "wanderer" (150), an "errant trace" (144), a "drifter" (157) "attached to no home and always separated from father and mother" (156), "deindividualized" (135), "anonymous" (143). "Everyone becomes no one" (142), "always suspicious of stopping, staying, and dwelling" (156). "Rootless and homeless" (156), deprived of "origin, center, and conclusion" (156), "the subject is *always* both 'stained' and 'wounded,'" and the marks are "incurable" (139). The "life of erring is . . . nomadic" (156) and the "serpentine wandering" (150) is "purposeless and aimless (endless)" (157). This "careless wanderer" yearns neither for "completion" nor for "fulfillment" (147), and therefore is not unhappy but free from "anxious searching" (157) and no longer preoccupied with past and future. Indeed, for Taylor, although such liberation means "self-dismemberment" (144), accepting that is "grace," which "arrives only when God and the self are dead and history is over" (157). "Extravagant expenditure" (142), "perpetual displacement" (156), "festive discharge, carnivalesque release" (161) . . . "endlessly" (143).

Let me offer four observations about such a description of the "non-self."

First, along with Taylor, I do not believe there is any hope of resuscitating the Cartesian self or any of its remnants. But it is well to recognize that that is no real loss, for it never existed in the first place, but was an illusory product of reason. Put in the language of psychotherapy, the self of reason is a false self, defensively created out of fear,[26] that needs to be undone and broken through if I am to come to terms with my true self. This suggests that the death of the self of reason and the death of the god of reason reveals not the death of self and God, but the failure of reason. From this perspective, the death of God, and now the self, marks the dethronement of reason and the collapse of its house of being.

---

25. All references to *Erring* (note 2) in this paragraph are included in text.

26. To take a classic example, we have discovered that Descartes's "ideal of the *cogito*, of the *matheis universalis* means *denial*, a defense against the flesh because the flesh is synonymous with anguish; and the clean fission between mind and body is an *isolation*, a setting apart and rendering innocuous of all that which spells dread" (Karl Stern, *The Flight from Women* [New York: Noonday, 1965], p. 101).

Second, the fact that the modern self of absolute agency is an illusion does not demonstrate that there is no such entity as a self. Indeed, I suspect the postmodern non-self will be shown to be as mythical as its predecessor, another adapted, false self. There is still room for an agent self that is not absolute, with no claims to self-authorization and full presence, but a gifted/called self, gifted with agency and called to co-agency by an *Other*. It is true that would demand breaking with the radical immanentism and autonomy of modern philosophy. But this is the very kind of thinking that is precisely being called into question by thinkers such as Emmanuel Levinas. I suspect that as long as postmodernism champions the non-self (as the negation of the modern self), it still, regrettably, hostage to logocentrism.

Third, Taylor's erring wanderer is a scary, sad, desolate figure, nameless, impersonal, and incurably wounded. Can such a postmodern person, without home and without purpose, be called to responsibility? And is not such an anonymous person a difference that makes no difference—a difference that is the same, because there is no longer any uniqueness? Even more troubling, Taylor has only tears—tears and wounds. What about healing, mending, and hope? Taylor seems to collapse a healthy self/other tension (which includes mutually enhancing interactions as well as alienating ones) into a determinism of sorts, in which relations are unavoidably only wounding and tearing.

Fourth, it will not be easy to talk of self and God in new ways because talk of self and God, certainly philosophically and theologically, has been so tied to an ontology of being that to speak of self and God is almost unavoidably to invoke echoes of these illusions. Can nothing be said? Are we left speechless? Is silence the only answer? Echoes of Wittgenstein's "What we cannot speak about we must pass over in silence"? That also was Heidegger's response: "Someone who has experienced theology in his own roots, both the theology of the Christian faith and that of philosophy, would today rather remain silent about god when he is speaking in the realm of thinking."[27] But even then we need to say something, because silence bespeaks sometimes joy, sometimes contempt, sometimes pleasure, sometimes fear, sometimes consent, sometimes renunciation, sometimes impotence, sometimes honor. There is the ultimate silence of death. And there is the silence that has to do with God, with what Pseudo-Dionysius had in mind when he exhorted us "to honor the ineffable with a wise silence."[28]

Derrida: Remaining on the Threshold

Indeed, it is because of the recognized difficulties of the *via positiva* in talking about God, amplified in recent times by the deconstructionist critique, that

27. Heidegger, *Identity*, pp. 54–55.
28. Quoted in Marion, *God without Being*, p. 54.

there is today increased interest in the *via negativa*. The question is even being asked if deconstructionism itself is a form of negative theology. Does all negative theology have a "superessentiality"—a supreme being beyond being—or does it, at least in some versions, have a God who transcends all conceptions of being as presence? Does negative theology use language under erasure in a fashion similar to deconstructionism?[29] Though the verdict is still out, it does seem clear that deconstruction is atheistic in the sense that it de-centers and does away with God as the center of a system[30] (but as Kevin Hart makes clear, only in that sense).[31] Whether Derrida or other deconstructionists have faith in God is entirely another matter. And about that, Derrida is, at least to my knowledge, silent.

It is in what is perhaps his most confessional essay, "How to Avoid Speaking: Denials,"[32] that Jacques Derrida in 1987 directly addressed the supposed connections between his thinking of *trace* and *différance* and negative theology. There is much debate on whether he delivers on his promise or continues to defer.

In the end, Derrida's denials, or denegations, as Taylor aptly translates,[33] seem neither to assert nor to deny. They circle around in a cacophony of sounds. However, strikingly, in and through the verbal clatter, there is the internal desert of silence. In Derrida's words, "We are still on the threshold."[34] And he remains on the threshold, always. That threshold is a "place of passage, this time, to give access to what is no longer a place,"[35] and seemingly he is unable to ever cross over with Eckhart to the "threshold that gives access to God."[36] On the threshold he talks as if having no secret is the secret. "There is no secret as *such;* I deny it. And this is what I confide in secret. . . . The name of God (I do not say God, but how to avoid saying God here, from the moment when I say the name of God?) can only be said in the modality of this secret denial: above all, I did not want to say that."[37]

Derrida then proceeds to treat negative theology in terms of three paradigms—Greek, Christian, and neither Greek nor Christian. He does so, he notes, "to avoid speaking of a question that I will be unable to treat; to deny it in some way, or to speak of it without speaking of it"—the question of the relation of negative theology to Jewish and Islamic thought.[38] That this is an

29. See especially Kevin Hart, *Trespass of the Sign;* and two recent books of relevance: Scharlemann, ed., *Negation and Theology;* and Coward and Foshay, eds., *Derrida and Negative Theology.*

30. For Derrida, "God is the name and element of that which makes possible an absolutely pure and absolutely self-present self-knowledge" (*Of Grammatology,* trans. G. Spivak [Baltimore: Johns Hopkins University Press, 1976], p. 98).

31. Hart, *Trespass of the Sign,* pp. 29, 30.

32. Reprinted in Coward and Foshay, eds., *Derrida and Negative Theology,* pp. 73–142. See note 39.

33. Mark C. Taylor, "nO nOt nO," in ibid., pp. 174–75.

34. Derrida, "Denials," p. 96.

35. Ibid., p. 121.

36. Ibid., p. 128.

37. Ibid., p. 95.

38. Ibid., p. 100.

important void for Derrida is clear not only because he goes out of his way to remind his readers of the omission two more times, but because Derrida is himself a displaced North African Jew. It is in this context that he talks of the "internal desert": "In everything that I will say, a certain void, the place of an internal desert, will perhaps allow this question to resonate. . . a resonant space of which nothing, almost nothing will ever be said."

Derrida pleads silence—almost. For then, in a telling footnote at precisely this point, he begins to self-disclose in a way that almost breaks the silence—but not without the hint of untold secrets and pain, even much pain:

> Despite this silence, or in fact because of it, one will perhaps permit me to interpret this lecture as the most "autobiographical" speech I have ever risked. . . . But if one day I had to tell my story, nothing in this narrative would start to speak of the thing itself if I did not come up against this fact: for lack of capacity, competence, or self-authorization, I have never been able to speak of what my birth says should have been closest to me: the Jew, the Arab. This small piece of autobiography confirms it obliquely. It is performed in all of my foreign languages: French, English, German, Greek, Latin, the philosophic, the metaphilosophic, Christian, etc.[39]

Taylor, in commenting on this essay, perceptively notes: "For many years at least since *Glas,* and I suspect long before, perhaps even from the beginning—Derrida has been struggling with the question of autobiography. . . . I begin to suspect that Derrida's deepest desire is to write an 'autobiography.'" He concludes: "Derrida could (or would) no more write an autobiography than he could (or would) write a theology."[40]

Derrida remains on the threshold.[41] No matter how strong his desire,[42] he cannot cross over and come home and tell his story.[43] He is the exile, the outsider, remaining always deliberately in/determinate and un/decidable. Do his constant deferrals on the threshold deliver us only to a gaping silence? Or does the work of Derrida perhaps open up a silent space before and beyond all metaphysical embarrassments, an interspace of in/finite im/possibility?

39. Ibid., p. 135. Derrida wrote these words in 1987. After this speech was first delivered, I discovered that Derrida in 1991 surprisingly published a very moving, personal text—reflecting on his childhood and his mother's death and including also a commentary on St. Augustine's *Confessions*—called *Circumfession* as part of a dual text written with Geoffrey Bennington under the title *Jacques Derrida,* trans. Geoffrey Bennington (Chicago: University of Chicago Press, 1993). "[T]he constancy of God in my life is called by other names" (p. 155).

40. Taylor, "nO nOt nO," p. 195.

41. The threshold image is just one of the many un/decidability images which flood Derrida's work. Others include the hinge, breast, fold, valley, Plato's *pharmakon,* Mallarme's hymen.

42. In his "Post-Scriptum" (in *Derrida and Negative Theology,* p. 318) Derrida sees a special connection between "desert" and "desire": "One has more and more the feeling that desert is the other name, if not the proper place, of desire."

43. My colleague Brian Walsh alerted me to the catchy line of Amos Wilder: "We cross the threshold into the story-world" ("Story and Story-World," *Interpretation* 37, 4 [1983]: 355).

That this is a real im/possibility is clearly evident in his preoccupation, also in "Denials," with place and space. In his treatment of the Greek paradigm he treats at some length the "absolutely necessary space" that Plato in the *Timaeus* calls the *khôra*,[44] as the place making possible the formation of the cosmos. This *khôra*—place, spacing, receptacle—is not to be talked of "as of 'something' that is or is not, that could be present or absent, intelligible, sensible, or both at once, active or passive, the Good . . . or the Evil, God or man, the living or the nonliving."[45] *Khôra* is "radically nonhuman and atheological . . . radically ahistorical," . . . "nothing positive or negative. It is impassive, but it is neither passive nor active."[46] As "absolutely necessary space," *khôra* cannot be spoken of, but, at the same time, it cannot not be spoken of.

When Derrida moves on from the Greek paradigm to the Christian, he considers Eckhart, who conceives of Being as a place, "[s]olely a threshold, but a sacred place, the outer sanctuary (*parvis*) of the temple,"[47] which gives access to God in what is beyond place. He suggests that Heidegger's viewpoint represents a paradigm neither Greek nor Christian. He calls attention to Heidegger's posing the question as to whether "a *wholly* other place" is a "place of Being" or is rather "*a place of the wholly other.*"[48]

Finally, in his *Post-Scriptum* to the Calgary Symposium, recently published under the title *Derrida and Negative Theology*, he raises the issue of place once more. In negative theology, "[t]here remains the question of . . . the place opened for this play between God and his creation."[49] Is it a place opened or created by God, by the name of God? Or is it "'older' than the time of creation, than time itself, than history, narrative, word, etc.," in order to make both God and his play possible? Is it a friendly place "opened by appeal" or is it a preceding space that remains "impassively foreign, like *khôra*, to everything that takes its place and replaces itself and plays within this place, including what is named God"?[50]

He asks whether we need to choose between the two. He wonders if it's even possible. But—and this heightens the stakes—he immediately adds: "But it is true that these two 'places,' these two experiences of place, these two ways are no doubt of an absolute heterogeneity. One place excludes the other, one surpasses the other, one does without the other, one is, absolutely, without the other."[51]

Although faced with this un/decidability, ever wary of choosing, Derrida, ironically, precisely because his commitment to undecidability goes all the way

44. Derrida, "Denials," p. 104.
45. Ibid., p. 106.
46. Ibid., pp. 106, 107.
47. Ibid., p. 121.
48. Ibid., p. 123.
49. Derrida, "Post-Scriptum," p. 314.
50. Ibid.
51. Ibid. Derrida points out that "what still relates them to each other is this strange preposition, this strange with-without or without-with, *without.*"

down,[52] has to de-fer from the first space, which is primed in a certain way (I call it the with-space of creation,[53] the love-space), and opt for the un/primed second space, the without place, the "'something' without thing, like an inde-constructible *khôra* . . . as the very spacing of de-construction,"[54] the spacing of *différance*. The space is held to be more primordial, more neutral, a kind of nontemporal "abyss without bottom or surface, an absolute impassibility (neither life nor death) that gives rise to everything that it is not."[55]

No doubt Derrida's staying on the threshold faithfully reflects his prefer-ence for un/decidability. At the same time, it may also leave him inadvertently under the bewitching spell of logocentrism. For, when all is said and done, if one tarries silent on the threshold because metaphysical claims to certainty and warrants for power are illusions to be overcome, have we really overcome them? To presume that we need to give up on any sense of a founded or grounded decision because the modernist tradition confuses/conflates giving logical reasons and grounding seems questionable. Grounding is much more and wider than logical grounding. Experiences of empathy, trust, and belonging, for example, are everyday sources of existential grounding.[56]

To repeat: I do believe that Derrida goes a long way in showing that language and metaphysics cannot provide privileged access to self-present meaning. But does that mean access to the mysterious, sacred desert place is impossible? Perhaps there are other ways and means to enter that space beyond or before. Can we can agree with Derrida that another philosophy/theology will not help? Reason is im/potent. But what about an approach that sees access as a non-philosophical/non-theological gift[57] to be received rather than a way to be engineered?

As Derrida describes it, to cross the threshold is, for Meister Eckhart, to use the power of the eye as a sieve. This new eye, for the mystics, is the eye of

52. At the same time, I admit to wondering if Derrida's "choice" for the second space does not precisely call into question whether undecidability can ever go all the way down.

53. In reference to the God-with-us (John I) by whom all things were created.

54. Derrida, "Post-Scriptum," p. 318.

55. Ibid., p. 315. It is important to note that this does not mean ethical neutrality for Derrida. Undecid-ability is a kind of quasi-transcendental condition, calling for decisions. Deconstruction is an intensifica-tion of responsibility, "a positive response to an alterity which necessarily calls, summons or motivates it. Deconstruction is therefore a vocation—a response to a call. . . . It is possible to see deconstruction as being produced in a space where the prophets are not far away" ("Deconstruction and the Others: An Interview with Derrida," in *Dialogues with Contemporary Continental Thinkers: The Phenomenological Heritage,* ed. R. Kearney [Manchester, U.K.: Manchester University Press, 1984], pp. 118, 119). See James Olthuis, "An Ethics of Compassion," in *What Right Does Ethics Have?* ed. S. Griffioen (Amsterdam: VU University Press, 1990), pp. 125–46.

56. For a valuable discussion of logical and existential grounding in the work of Richard Rorty and John Dewey, see Carroll Guen Hart, *Grounding without Foundations* (Toronto: Patmos, 1993).

57. Derrida is now emphasizing that faith is presupposed by any deconstructive gesture. "I don't know, one has to believe" (*Memoirs of the Blind,* trans. Pascale-Anne Broult and Michael Naas [Chicago: University of Chicago Press, 1993], p. 129).

love, an eye that opens up a place beyond words, where words are no longer necessary. There may be homecoming.[58]

But Derrida remains poised on the threshold: although he wants to come home and tell his story, he cannot. He remains on the outside, an exile, displaced, wanting to break through. In her summary comments at the Calgary Symposium, Morny Joy touches the heart of the matter: "The eye of love is foreign to the forays of his deconstruction."[59] For Derrida it seems as if once Reason has been dethroned, there is no other possibility for providing direction and hope. So we remain wandering, sometimes dwelling in the threshold of the temple, but we can never cross over and enter.

But perhaps there is a new eye: a new eye of love that, with the death of the metaphysical concepts of god, espies a space open for God free from onto-theological apron-strings. It is a space prior to the theoretical space defined by metaphysical thought. However, it is also, as a with-space, the space of and for love, not the neutral "without" space of *différence*. The god that appears would have nothing to do with the god of the philosophers.[60] In this space (to play on Paul Ricoeur's famous phrase) "love gives rise to thought," discourse is reborn, not for purposes of mastery or limitation or hemming in with conditions, but for connection. Because God as love (and love as God) is an overflowing, an excess, an emptying going beyond its own limits, a letting go, life and discourse can be connective, celebrative, communicative.

Crossing the Threshold: A Vision of Love

Lingering in this space, and wending my way to a provisional end, I offer a few fleeting glimpses of the far-ranging implications of replacing an ontology of being not with a deconstructed de/ontology, but with a (rediscovered)[61] vision of love.

In the first place, and of fundamental importance, "To be or not to be" is no longer the sum of the matter. Nor is the deconstructionist version on target: "to be *and* not to be, for to be is not to be, and not to be is to be."[62] Rather,

---

58. "Homecoming is not a return to the past but it is a becoming into the future" (Charles Winquist, *Homecoming: Interpretation, Transformation and Individuation* [Missoula, Mont.: Scholars, 1978], p. 9).

59. Morny Joy, "Conclusion: Divine Reservations," in Coward and Foshay, eds., *Derrida and Negative Theology*, p. 263.

60. Marion, *God without Being*, p. 752.

61. Rediscovered, not only because it harks back to the love mysticism of St. Bernard, Meister Eckhart, John of the Cross, or Ruysbroeck the Admirable, but also because the important work of women mystics such as the twelfth-century Hildegard of Bingen and the Rheno-Flemish Beguines of the thirteenth century is coming to light. Eckhart's famous expression about the gratuitous nature of divine love, "without a why," appears for the first time in the work of the Cistercian nun Beatrice of Nazareth, and later in the writings of the Beguines. See Emilie Zum Brunn and Georgette Epiney-Burgard, *Women Mystics in Medieval Europe* (New York: Paragon House, 1989), p. xxxi.

62. Mark C. Taylor, *De-constructing Theology* (New York: Crossroad, 1982), p. 56.

the supreme question is: "To love or not to love." In other words, love replaces being-as-power as the highest category. For in the degree that one is not in love, one is deficient in being. God's love comes as a gift, an overflowing, an "excess," which calls us forth—luring, inviting, sustaining.[63] Being is liberated from its fixation on power and freed for love. As a result, in the phrasing of Jean-Luc Marion, "The fundamental ontic difference between what is and what is not becomes indifferent—for everything becomes indifferent before the difference that God marks with the world."[64]

Instead of the Cartesian self-grounding of "I think, therefore I am," beginning with God's love means "I am loved, therefore I am." The birth of a self and an identity is a bestowal of the love of others, birthed in and through the love shown by others. The human self is intersubjective: in the we there is the I; in the I there is the we. The self finds its center in mutuality. Consequently, the healthy decentering of the modernist self as self-centering need not lead to the postmodern non-self, but to a recentering of the self in relations of love in community.

The passive "am loved" also suggests that whether or not we are existentially able to love is inextricably related to whether we were first loved. Enfolded within the bosom of "to love or not to love" is the question "To be loved or not to be loved?" This pivotal interconnection between receiving love and giving love is one of the important emphases of all post-Freudian psychotherapeutic developmental theories since Erikson. Insofar as a child has not received what D. W. Winnicott calls "good-enough"[65] mothering, the child is handicapped in its ability to genuinely love and care for others. By the same token, healing, restoration, and empowerment of a fragmented self is best nourished in relationships of empathy and love.

The gift *of* love is also a gift *for* love; the gift is simultaneously a call. It is the birth of human agency as response-ability for the gift. Therefore, I love in order to be.[66] The process of receiving identity is at the same time a process of constituting one's identity in relation to others. A self is born not only in and through (receiving) love, but equally, reciprocally, in and through (giving) love to others. The two sides belong inextricably together. In this understanding of identity and agency, not as self-creation or self-certification but as a received empowerment, a call to live out and fulfill, it remains important to talk (in contrast to postmodernism) of a core self of continuity, coherence,

63. Like Marion, I want to carefully distinguish between beginning with a gift given by God from Heidegger's impersonal *es gibt*, in which the gift is the giving without starting from any giver. See Marion, *God without Being*, pp. 102–7.

64. Ibid., p. 88. See Marion's discussion of Rom. 4:17 and 1 Cor. 1:28, where God calls "nonbeings to become beings . . . , [and] calls the nonbeings as if they were beings" (ibid., pp. 88–95).

65. Donald Winnicott, *The Maturational Processes and the Facilitating Environment* (New York: International Universities Press, 1965), p. 145.

66. *"I am to the extent that I am loved, therefore I love in order to be."* According to French feminist literary critic Julia Kristeva, this saying is "for the medieval thinker . . .an implict definition of the subject's being" (*Tales of Love*, trans. L. Roudiez [New York: Columbia University Press, 1987], p. 171).

and agency.[67] This core self—not, it is true, the Cartesian unitary self of reason—expands and contracts in the vicissitudes of its experience. It is crucial in helping us to make sense out of the multiplicity of experiences that both surround us and inhabit us. When we do not have a bounded and gendered core experience of ourselves, instead of being able to celebrate postmodern multiplicity, we suffer from fragmentation of self, sometimes to the point of psychosis or multiple personality.[68]

Indeed, I believe it is a fragmented sense of core identity, or even a lack of such a sense of core identity, that brings many (most?) people to therapy. Those who celebrate the fluid self as "effect" seem, as Jane Flax puts it, "self-deceptively naïve and unaware of the basic cohesion within themselves that makes the fragmentation of experiences something other than a terrifying slide into psychosis."[69] Only when a person has some sense of core self can s/he enter the inter-space and reach out to a neighbor, not only with a sense of dread and fear of domination, but also with hope for connection, enrichment, and expansion.

Is it entirely coincidental that just when many women are attaining a sense of agency and selfhood, postmodernism, largely male and middle-class, questions the very existence of self?[70] It is even more disturbing, speaking psychotherapeutically, to realize that the kind of multiplicity which certain forms of postmodernism champion results from the very patriarchal domination and abuse that it sets out to challenge. No wonder postmodern feminists such as Julia Kristeva and Luce Irigaray treat the issue of multiplicity with more sensitivity than many postmodernists.[71]

Those who think it best to abandon the subject altogether as a fiction, or who see the subject as a position in language or effect of discourse, may be adopting, wittingly or unwittingly, yet another strategy to avoid facing their deeper selves. Is it, asks Flax, yet another way "to evade, deny, or repress the importance of early childhood experiences, especially mother-child relationships, in the constitution of self and the culture more generally[?] Perhaps it is less threatening to have no self than one pervaded by memories of, longing for, suppressed identification with, or terror of the powerful mother of infancy."[72]

67. In his groundbreaking clinical study *The Interpersonal World of the Infant* (New York: Basic, 1985), Daniel Stern concludes that infants between two and seven months form a sense of core self—self-agency, self-coherence, self-affectivity, and self-history.

68. In fact, James Glass, in *Shattered Selves* (Ithaca, N.Y.: Cornell University Press, 1993), critiques the postmodern celebration of multiplicity by demonstrating that for the many people who suffer from schizophrenia and multiple personality, multiciplicity is unadulterated anguish.

69. Jane Flax, *Thinking Fragments* (Los Angeles: University of California Press, 1990), pp. 218–19.

70. See Patricia Waugh, "Postmodernism," in *Feminism and Psychoanalysis: A Critical Dictionary,* ed. E. Wright (Oxford, U.K.: Basil Blackwell, 1992), p. 344.

71. Toril Moi, in her introduction to *The Kristeva Reader,* ed. Toril Moi (New York: Columbia University Press, 1986), p. 13, sees Kristeva doing a "balancing act between a position which would deconstruct subjectivity and identity altogether, and one that would try to capture these entities in an essentialist or humanist mould."

72. Flax, *Thinking Fragments,* p. 232.

Descartes, afraid of women and his body, retreated to the supposed certitude and splendid isolation of his ego. Is the postmodern espousal of the non-self a similar attempt to continue to repress, deny, or dull the pain? Perhaps the postmodern non-self is yet another version of the adapted or "false self" that needs to be abandoned in a dark night of the soul in order that the core or "true self" may emerge from hiding and begin the process of remembering and healing.

Beginning with love as an overflowing, an invitation (not a coercion) that is realized intersubjectively (not individualistically), opens up a new understanding of the spaces between self and other. In the big dichotomies that have defined the history of metaphysics since the Greeks, mind, culture, form, and intellect have been considered "male"; body, nature, matter, and sentiment, "female." And, of special interest here, *techne*, time, and same have connoted the male; physis, space, and the other, the female.[73] The "only way to give language to Nature, to Space, has been through *techne*—through technique . . . as the active, masculine aspect . . . giving a narrative to [female, passive] *physis*."[74] The result has been the master narratives by which those in power dominate and exclude "the spaces of the *ensoi*, Other, without history—the feminine . . . [the] unknown, terrifying, monstrous, . . . the mad, the unconscious, improper, unclean, non-sensical, oriental, profane."[75] The breakdown of these master narratives has generated new ways of recognizing and renaming the other than ourselves—the space, now unbound, coded feminine, outside the logic of modernity, not made possible by its structures, and thus sacred. Kristeva, in fact, calls this sacred place "a place of passage, a threshold where 'nature' confronts 'culture.'"[76]

Buber names this sacred interspace the "the sphere of 'between.'"[77] I prefer the term the "wild"[78] spaces, to emphasize that it is a space as free for love as it has been despoiled by control. "On the narrow ridge, where *I* and *Thou* meet, there is the realm of 'between.'"[79] It is a space "conceptually still uncomprehended . . . not an auxiliary construction, but the real place and bearer of

---

73. According to Kristeva, the connotations of space and the feminine go back at least to Plato's *khôra*, and "the 'other' is the 'other sex'" (*La révolution du langage poétique*, p. 326, quoted in Alice Jardine, *Gynesis* [Ithaca, N.Y.: Cornell University Press, 1985], p. 114).

74. Ibid., p. 73.

75. Ibid, pp. 72–73.

76. Julia Kristeva, *Desire in Language*, ed. Leon Roudiez, trans. T. Gora, A. Jardine, and L. Roudiez (New York: Columbia University Press, 1980), p. 238. For Kristeva, the undifferentiated space shared by mother and child is called *khôra* (p. 133).

77. Martin Buber, *Between Man and Man*, trans. G. Smith (London: Collins, 1947), p. 244.

78. I distinguish my use of "wild" in reference to interspace from Julia Kristeva's discussion in *Tales of Love* (pp. 1, 2) of a love "aptly called *wild* . . . a crucible of contradictions and misunderstandings." For me, love is the primal force both gifting to and calling for good ordering (i.e., good connections). Kristeva's wild, semiotic love is over against and subversive of the symbolic rule of the law of the Father even as it is subject to it.

79. Buber, *Between Man and Man*, p. 246.

what happens between. . . . [I]t does not exhibit a smooth continuity, but is ever and again reconstituted in accordance with [people's] meetings with one another."[80]

Love as gift creates a space-which-is-meeting, inviting partnership and co-birthing, and fundamentally calling into question the deconstructive idea that structures are necessarily always violent. It suggests a new thematization of meaning and truth as good connections, in contrast to both modernity's power, control, judgment and postmodernism's disruption and dissemination of any claim of entitlement to meaning and truth. Narratives are possible, not as grand control devices, but as tales of (broken) love coauthored in community. There are countless narratives of endless suffering and horror, but there are also wonderful tales (small, subversive stories)[81] of meeting, healing, and suffering love in the midst of and in spite of suffering.

This is not an encouragement to retrench and build fixed residences in the domesticity of modernity. Neither does it, in postmodern rejection of the modern, need to mean exile in the desert (expulsion and wandering), perpetual homelessness. Rather, we have an invitation to meet and sojourn together in the wild spaces of love as alternatives both to modernist distancing or domination and to postmodern fluidity and fusion. Connection rather than control is the dominant metaphor. In the interstices of love, Nygren's antithesis of *eros* and *agape* notwithstanding, mutuality can be a sojourn together in which loving self and loving other need not be in opposition but may be mutually enriching.

In making room for a mutuality ethos, a vision of love re-envisions *eros*, not as the urge to unite, but as the urge to connect. Therefore, *eros* would no longer be a nostalgic but feared wish to return to a primal, undifferentiated state, as it is with Freud (and even Heidegger). For Freud, both individual and social history moves from undifferentiation (birth) to differentiation and back again to undifferentiation (death). In this way *eros* (love) and *thanatos* (death), although opposing instincts, end up turning into each other: fusion as the realization of *eros* is the death of the individual self.

With the focus on *eros* as the desire to connect, as the passion for mutuality and right relation, we have the possibility for non-possessive, non-competitive (i.e., non-violent) connecting, co-partnering, co-birthing, in the interspaces of love and creativity.[82] Tragically, such spaces are often the abysses of the wounded, the labyrinths of the lost. But they can also be places of healing and meeting. Tears, no doubt, but also laughter; tears, but also mending.

The priority of love, with its impulse for mutuality over being, with its focus on survival and power, does not mean there will be no conflict; nor does it

80. Ibid., pp. 244–45.

81. De Boer contrasts the Grand Stories of domination with the "small story . . . of Abraham, Issac, Jacob and Jesus Christ" (*De God,* p. 152). Brian Walsh works out the idea of the gospel as subversive in *Subversive Christianity* (Bristol, U.K.: Regius, 1992).

82. See Christian feminist Carter Heyward's inspired revisioning of Eros along these lines in *Touching Our Strength: The Erotic as Power and the Love of God* (San Francisco: Harper & Row, 1989).

suggest a resigned toleration of whatever demons of oppression and domination are afoot. In fact, when we begin from a self created in, with, and for love, choosing not to resist injustice further injures and diminishes the self. Acts of resistance against injustice are acts of love. Beginning with a vision of love means that domination and alienation need not be inevitable. There is also the possibility of mutual recognition, empowerment, and pleasure. Transformation is possible. Healing can be as real as rending. Power need not always be meted out as power-over or power-under. Power relations can be transformed into power-with relations, relations of love.

If I read Foucault correctly, this belief goes along with his treatment of power, and then goes a step farther. For Foucault, when power relations are fixed and no longer in constant struggle, there is no power but violence and slavery. Power relations always imply the possibility of reversal. In my view this possibility of reversal, when seen through the eyes of love, can become not only a continual reversal of who is in control, but also a transformation of the power dynamics of conflict to one of shared connection. Power-with as an alternative to hierarchical power-over also opens up the possibility of ecological partnership with the earth and all its creatures, copartnership in the cosmic family so that the cosmos may be a love-place—a home rather than a deserted and ravaged desert.

Love is the difference that matters. And suddenly suffering has a different place, a legitimate place. It is no longer a diminution of being, a suffering-from, which detracts from who we are, but a very different suffering-with, a voluntary being-with that comforts and heals, enriching and transforming everyone and everything it touches.[83] Love as excess—without a why—overflows onto the plains and meadows of life as a celebrating-with. It seeps into life's cracks and fissures as suffering-with.

Beginning with love as a creative power (making something out of nothing) gives new place to love as forgiveness (making nothing out of something). In the experience of forgiveness there is release, a letting go, a freeing to new starts and new creations. Love turns us to the other, not as diminution of being, but as enrichment, hospitality, and celebration.[84]

Letting be (*Gelassenheit*) is the way of God. Since the way of God is love, this letting be is not simply a Heideggerian releasement to things; nor is it a meditative waiting for and remaining open for the miracle of Being's advent. It is a proactive being-with, especially with those who suffer, and, when appropriate, a robust pursuit of justice for the oppressed and a planetary ecological ethic for all creatures. In other words, such letting be is not ethically neutral, as it is with Heidegger, in which both the "hale" and the "evil" appear equally in the clearing of Being.[85]

83. According to Rom. 8:17, suffering-with goes along with being an heir of Christ.

84. In "Post-Scriptum," p. 317, Derrida notes: "To let passage to the other, to the totally other, is hospitality."

85. "With healing, evil appears all the more in the lighting of Being. The essence of evil . . . consist[s] . . . in the malice of rage. Both of these, however, healing and raging, can essentially occur only in Being,

At the same time, since love cannot be controlled, the *Gelassenheit* of love eschews control. And giving up control demands faith and trust, in spite of. *Gelassenheit* is a surrender of our will to control, a giving over, an Eckhartian abandonment to the cosmic wave of God's love. Such surrender is not forced. It is a voluntary movement of empowerment that releases to the energies alive in other people, in the world, and in God.

In closing, I trade on two of Julia Kristeva's titles. We do not simply have the "powers of horror"; we have also "tales of love." Instead of a Heideggerian *Dasein* facing the otherness of death, we have persons facing each other

> crossing the threshold, despite . . .
> taking the risk, despite . . .
> not trying (always to counter),
> not (always) fusing or fleeing,
> but sometimes meeting-in-the-middle spaces of love,
> not always wandering in labyrinths,
> or falling into abysses,
> yet not smugly settled, serenely ensconced,
> but journeying together . . .
> sojourning in the wild spaces of love, despite and in spite of
>   Zarathustra's laughter,
>   in spite of the killing fields . . .
> Faith is always despite . . .
> We sojourn not alone.
> God tents, tabernacles—sojourns—with us.[86]

> The ways of Love are strange,
> As those who have followed them well know,
> For, unexpectedly, She withdraws Her consolation.
>   He whom Love touches
>   Can enjoy no stability.
>   And he will taste
>   Many a nameless hour.

> * * *

> Sometimes burning and sometimes cold,
> Sometimes timid and sometimes bold,

---

insofar as Being itself is what is contested" (Martin Heidegger, "Letter on Humanism," in *Basic Writings*, ed. D. Krell [New York: Harper & Row, 1977], p. 237). For neutrality as a property of traditional ontologies of being, see De Boer, *De God*, pp. 49–52. In contemporary philosophy Levinas, in particular, protested that such neutrality is in fact oppressive. Paul Ricoeur's *Oneself as Another*, trans. K. Blamey (Chicago: University of Chicago Press, 1992), is also a recent eloquent plea against ethically neutral ontologies. I want to emphasize again that Derrida intends his priniciple of undecidability to intensify ethical responsibility. See John D. Caputo's *Radical Hermeneutics* (Bloomington: Indiana University Press, 1987), chaps. 9 and 10, and *Against Ethics* (Bloomington: Indiana University Press, 1993) for a Derridean ethics of dissemination that contrasts with Taylor's more Nietzschean approach. See also Simon Critchley's *The Ethics of Deconstruction* (Oxford, U.K.: Blackwell, 1992).

86. Lev. 26:11, Rev. 21:3, John 1:14.

The whims of Love are manifold.
    She reminds us all
    Of our great debt
    To Her lofty power
    Which draws us to Herself alone.

Sometimes gracious and sometimes cruel,
Sometimes far and sometimes near
He who grasps Her in faithful love
    Reaches jubilation.
    Oh, how Love
    With one sole act
    Both strikes and embraces!

Sometimes humble, sometimes haughty,
Sometimes hidden and sometimes revealed;
To be finally overwhelmed by Love,
    Great adventures must be risked
    Before one can reach
    The place where is tasted
    The nature of Love.

Sometimes light, sometimes heavy,
Sometimes somber and sometimes bright,
In freeing consolation, in stifling anguish,
In taking and in giving,
Thus live the spirits
Who wander here below,
Along the paths of Love.[87]

---

87. Hadewijch of Antwerp, most of thirteenth-century Stanzaic Poem V, quoted in Zum Brunn and Epiney-Burgard, *Women Mystics,* pp. 113–14.

2

Olthuis's Risk

A Heretical Tribute

John D. Caputo

In the view taken by Jim Olthuis, there is a fundamental beneficence at work in the world, a positive force above, below, and within things, an enveloping, encompassing horizon or milieu of love. This is something he has learned from the biblical tradition he has so deeply assimilated and something that the work of postmodernist thinkers from Levinas to Luce Irigaray have allowed him to articulate in richly phenomenological turns as a matrix of love. His view turns on a community of love as a community of difference, in which the different connect and in that inter-connection are made whole, not simply as community but also as individuals with their individual differences.[1] He pursues the point that faith is not opposed to knowledge but productive of knowledge,[2] that hope is not wishful thinking but productive of the future, that love is not a fuzzy feeling but a deep and powerful force that is productive of who we are. Unlike most of us academic theologians and philosophers, he is not content to talk and write about these things, however sensitively. Instead, as a therapist and counselor, he reaches out to the other in pain to lend a helping hand and provide a helping voice in a therapy of love that renounces the model of therapeutic cure and control—the "fixer"—and embraces the model of caring and compassion—the "helper." He practices a therapy aimed at restoring the joy

1. See James H. Olthuis, "Introduction: Exclusions and Inclusions: Dilemma of Difference," *Towards an Ethics of Community* (Waterloo, Ont.: Wilfrid Laurier University Press, 2000), pp. 1–12.

2. See his "Introduction: Love/Knowledge: Sojourning with Others, Meeting with Differences," in *Knowing Other-wise: Philosophy at the Threshold of Spirituality,* ed. James H. Olthuis, Perspectives in Continental Philosophy (New York: Fordham University Press, 1997), pp. 1–15.

41

of life, as witness the case of "Amanda," one who is worthy to be loved, where previously there was only the death of isolation, fear, and anxiety.[3]

His thought is marked by a boldness and willingness to take risks that can be undertaken only by those who are firm in their faith, and so it is fitting that he has taken Levinas's expression about the "beautiful risk" as the title of a recent work. Life is a risk because of its radical uncertainty, but a beautiful risk because what is at stake is grace and love.[4] He has taken the full measure of postmodern and poststructuralist thought, which he sees as exposing the modernist idols of mastery and control that level differences and turn people into the raw material of method. By way of his study of the Scriptures in connection with the postmodern ethics of alterity, he has seen that alterity, including the alterity of gay and lesbian love, belongs to the uncontainable richness of love and to the polymorphic diversity of the goodness of creation, and he has not avoided the personal risk of saying that.

Olthuis's work "begins with God": "In the beginning" (Gen. 1:1), God created the world, and "God is love" (1 John 4:8). One of the underpinnings, perhaps it is the central one, of his phenomenology of loving faith and faithful knowledge is a theology of creation that goes back to the opening creation narrative in Genesis, that Elohim, having finished the work of creation, looked upon all that he created and declared that it was good. The goodness of creation by a God of love is the first, last, and constant faith—or instinct, or intuition, or commitment, or presupposition—of Olthuis's work. It is the horizon or milieu within which his thought moves and it gives all of his work, philosophical, theological, and therapeutic, its structure and bearings, its tonality and charge. God's loving gift in creating is "the warp and woof" of the world, and the cosmos is a swirl of spiraling "interconnecting energies of love—wild spaces of love in which we are called to do this connecting and reconnecting."[5]

That is why, when Olthuis encounters Derrida's stark account of the wild spaces of *khôra*, he wants, by way of Irigaray, to reread *khôra* not as a kind of cold and lifeless desert night, as Derrida describes it, but as "the friendly with-place of creation," "a friendly space opened by appeal," a "matrix" or a "place evoked by the *oui, oui* of love and justice," a "creational matrix primed toward the good of acts of love and justice," which make of God and *khôra* "kissing cousins."[6] Under Olthuis's hand, *khôra* becomes a "choreography of love,"[7] a divine space in which love dances, a divine milieu or loving matrix,

---

3. James H. Olthuis, "Amanda's Story," in *The Beautiful Risk: A New Psychology of Loving and Being Loved* (Grand Rapids: Zondervan, 2001), pp. 15–22.

4. Ibid., p. 22.

5. Ibid., p. 43.

6. See John H. Olthuis, "The Test of khôra: grâce à Dieu," in *Religion With/out Religion: The Prayers and Tears of John D. Caputo* (London: Routledge, 2002), pp. 110–19. This was originally a feature review article of my *Prayers and Tears of Jacques Derrida* (Bloomington: Indiana University Press, 1997) and *Deconstruction in a Nutshell* (New York: Fordham University Press, 1997) in *International Philosophical Quarterly* 39, 155 (September 1999).

7. Olhuis, *Beautiful Risk*, p. 63.

a welcoming embrace, a mothering womb that loves individual into beings, a centripetal force that sweeps lovers into each other's arms, or even a messianic force that carries us toward the democracy to come, or perhaps the force of the flowing waters of justice in Amos's famous image. To be sure, Olthuis's matrix of love/ *khôra* preserves its undecidability and unprogramability. As a milieu not an enclosing systemic law, it is not a force of inevitability and predetermination, but a supportive horizon that remains fraught with risk and structurally exposed to the possibility of error and violence. That is all very saucily summarized by speaking of "the beautiful risk of dancing in the wild spaces of love with love and compassion,"[8] a phrase that itself dances throughout this text!

There is much to recommend this beautiful manifesto of the goodness of creation and the power of love, to which I am proud to append my signature. Let the word go forth that I accept it. Far be it from me, God forbid, that I should deny such a radiant vision. I am with Jim Olthuis in this friendly with-place. *Me voici, oui, oui.* I buy it!

Not, however as a description or redescription of *khôra,* but as an account of something else, that is, of God, or of God's presence in the world, or of the Spirit of God within us, or the Spirit that blows over the waters, or of the divine milieu. But not of *khôra.* So if Jim Olthuis wants to claim the name of *khôra* for his divine milieu, then we an-khorites will need to go off, heads bowed and disheartened, in search of another name for poor *khôra,* which will not have gone away but simply have been stripped of its name. Poor *khôra,* already poor and barren and nameless enough, will have now been deprived of her very name, which is now given over to God or to God's soft but radiant glow, which is I suppose the sort of thing that happens to this poor Cinderella creature. She just can't catch a break for herself.

But is this Cinderella creature truly a "creature?" Is *khôra* created? If so, then Jim Olthuis must be right and she too belongs to the endless panorama of things that Elohim calls good in the first creation narrative. But what if she is *not* created? Is that not what Derrida hints might just be the case when, in posing "the test of *khôra,*" he wonders whether she or it "is 'older' than the time of creation"? If *khôra* is not created, then she/it is not good, although it is also true that she/it is not evil either, the difference between the two not having been yet drawn or constituted. *Khôra* itself, if there is such a thing, is neither good nor evil, neither/nor, *ne uter,* just neutral.

I have already had the poor grace to have contested Olthuis's reading of the test case of *khôra* once before.[9] But I have in the meantime thought of still another argument against it, which I would like to present here, one that arises from Jim's embrace of the Levinasian "beautiful risk." So in a perverse analogy to the medieval masters who piled argument upon argument for the

---

8. Ibid., p. 15.

9. "John D. Caputo, "Hoping in Hope, Hoping against Hope: A Response," in *Religion With/out Religion,* pp. 144–48.

existence of God, like sandbags stacked one on top of the other to hold back the waters of godlessness, I am using the opportunity of this volume dedicated to celebrate Jim Olthuis's work to add another bag of sand to my attempt to hold back the rushing waters of his divine milieu. I only want to contain this beautiful stream, to hold it within its banks, of course, not dry it up entirely, which would ruin everything. In the end, I actually think I am buttressing what Jim Olthuis is saying about the beautiful risk, because I think the "risk" would actually be threatened by his revisionist account of *khôra*. To this end, I must hold his feet to the fire of the risk in the beautiful risk.

In the text we cited, Derrida, wondering out loud, asks whether *khôra* might be called up by the word of God, which is the option Jim Olthuis seizes upon, or whether it might be, as Derrida puts it, "older than creation."[10] If forced to choose, Derrida himself would say, given his distaste for binarities, I would bet on it, "It is not a matter of choosing between the two." That I think is probably right and probably what I am myself arguing—that the divine milieu (the Olthuis rendition of *khôra*) is opened in the space of *khôra* (the colder look at *khôra*). But to make this argument, I must seize upon the second option—that *khôra* is older than creation—and here offer some evidence in its support, because Jim Olthuis has swept it under his rug of love. The evidence I will adduce for this ungodly hypothesis arises, God forbid, from the Scriptures themselves.

Part of Derrida's idea in coming up with the idea of *khôra* was to pose a counterpart to the *agathon,* a second tropic or pole of unnameability, that is, a sphere of namelessness that is nameless not by excess but by defect, an unnameable "I know not what that is" not beyond being but below it, which never gets as far as being or essence or name. Its correlate in the subsequent tradition is the *prote materia* of Aristotle, the pure nameless "out-of-which" stuff (*ex quo*) whose whole essence, if it had an essence, would be to take its essence from the form that forms it. But *khôra* also reminds us very much of the anonymous rumbling of Levinas's *il y a,* which, it has been pointed out, is itself a kind of phenomenological transcription of the *tohu wa bohu* of Genesis 1:1–2, the formless void upon which God breathed his creative word. So Levinas's *il y a* is in an important way below *ousia* or *être* in a way that parallels (in the manner of a mirror opposite) the sphere of what is beyond it, *au-delà de l'être* to the point that in an interesting text he says that the *il* of *il y a* and the *il* of *illéité* pass into a "possible confusion."[11] There is a kind of parallelism of these two spheres of namelessness in Levinas, as well as in Derrida's reading of Plato's *khôra.* Now the little bit of heresy I want to advocate here is that the same parallelism, between a certain Good and a certain *khôra,* is to be found in Genesis 1.

10. Jacques Derrida, *On the Name,* ed. Thomas Dutoit (Stanford, Calif.: Stanford University Press, 1995), pp. 75–76.

11. Emmanuel Levinas, *Basic Philosophical Writings,* ed. Adriaan Peperzak, Simon Critchley, and Robert Bernasconi (Bloomington: Indiana University Press, 1996), p. 141.

I started out trying to honor Jim Olthuis by being as orthodox as possible, but I failed and now find myself offering up a bit of heresy as my tribute to him. I am sure he will understand and love me no less in my fallen state. Of course, if this is a heresy then the first heretic on this point is the priestly author of the opening narrative of Genesis. In the beginning is Elohim *and* the *tohu wa bohu,* both together not one without the other, in a kind of eerie parallelism. One of the things that strikes us when we read the first creation narrative is that there is no *creatio ex nihilo* doctrine there. Elohim clearly does not create out of nothing but separates water and earth, light and dark, living and nonliving, etc. Creation is separation, differentiation, a kind of divine movement of differing-deferring over the formless void. But the formless void itself Elohim did not create, which is as plain as day (or will be just as soon as there is one). In the narrative, the formless void is as old as God and, to use the words of Derrida, "older than creation," having preceded creation and provided Elohim with the stuff from which to create by providing the chaos and confusion that required ordering and differentiation. So things begin with the two, Elohim and the formless void, in unnerving parallel. (What was it like before Elohim set out to shape up the formless void? What was Elohim thinking about or doing?) The later doctrine of *creatio ex nihilo* was unknown to the Babylonian world to which this story belongs; it is a later doctrinal development that emerged from a debate with second-century-C.E. pagan cosmologists.[12] Indeed, the Elohist narrative itself emerged as a counterpart to the *Enuma elish,* the Babylonian creation myth about Marduk and Tiamat that their Babylonian captors were telling the Hebrews, with which Genesis exhibits numerous parallels.[13]

Now in my heretical frame of mind, I am of a mind to interpret this story literally, to stick to the Genesis narrative *ad literam* as Augustine said, in the sense of taking each literal component seriously and finding its significance. In that case, the uncreated character of the *tohu wa bohu* is an important element of the story signifying a certain ingrained element in things that Elohim must deal with and master, over which he must exert the power of his word but which Elohim does not entirely own through and through. Furthermore, as something irreducible to Elohim, it can from time to time resurface, as when Elohim threatens to return his recalcitrant creatures to the abyss from whence they came. In that sense, the mythic formless void is a figure of the powerlessness of God, of the limits of God's power, for God is working with something pregiven and irreducible to the divine power. I do not mean to resurrect the entirely orthodox idea that it belongs to God's infinite power to be able freely to limit his power in order to allow creatures some space. I mean

12. See Gerhard May, *Creatio ex nihilo: The Doctrine of "Creation out of Nothing" in Early Christian Thought,* trans. A. S. Worrall (Edinburgh: T & T Clark, 1994).

13. For a classic account of the historical-critical basics of Genesis that is still highly regarded today, see Bruce Vawter, *On Genesis: A New Reading* (Garden City, N.Y.: Doubleday, 1977); on creation, see pp. 37–163.

the rather more unorthodox idea that God's power only extends so far, that is, up to the point of the formless void which is of itself, not from God. So God can only do so much. If God created things from nothing, he would be able to dominate them through and through and they would not come unstuck. But the formless void means that there is always a certain resistence to God's power in things, a certain ingrained tendency within the things themselves to return to the disorder, chaos, and formlessness from which things were formed in the first place.

In that sense, the "problem of evil" is not so much God's responsibility, or even ours, or anybody's at all, but the almost inevitable issue of beings that are woven out of chaos. That explains how things can go so wrong so quickly in Genesis. By the time we get to the sixth chapter, these beings made of chaos have made a thorough mess of things. Yahweh/Elohim has come to regret the day he made these creatures and decides to uncreate them, which means to send them all back to the watery deep from whence they came. God did not quite foresee what he was getting into when he made these images of himself, given the unreliable materials of which they are made, and he soon came to the decision that he had made a mistake and the whole thing was a bad idea. The Lord God of Genesis does not match up well with the *omnipotens deus* of the later metaphysical theologies that attributed infinite power and foreknowledge to him, making him a kind of Ideal Standpoint in which every property of mind and will that we can imagine is realized in a timeless, unlimited, and perfect manner. That is a foreign hypothesis to impose upon the first chapters of Genesis. The Lord God of Genesis wrestles with his decisions, debates with his creatures, changes his mind, and gets quite angry when he does not get his own way. The Lord God says, "Let it be so," but sometimes it is not, and then he gets furious.

To be sure, in suggesting an *ad literam* reading I am not suggesting that we take this story in a scientifically literal way but in a literarily literal way. I am not suggesting that we treat the imaginative terms in which a sixth-century Hebrew religious poet tried to come up with a narrative that matched and outwitted point by point the reigning Babylonian myth from the *Enuma elish* as if the poet were trying to paint an *adequatio rei et intellectus* portrait of what actually happened six thousand years ago, *wie est eigentlich gewesen*. The first creation narrative in Genesis is a religious poem meant to sing the praises of Elohim, not a cosmology, either scientific or metaphysical. It is not to be measured by the standards of truth as *adequatio* and absolutely nothing stands or falls on whether there really is or was about six thousand years ago a watery formless void that was differentiated into light and dark, etc. I leave that kind of mindless literalism to the ahistorical fundamentalist repetitions of Genesis and seek instead a mindful, literary literalism, that is, a thinking literalism that takes into account every literal element in the poem, one that, leaving nothing out, seeks to think through its significance. I start by assuming that the opening narrative is a religious poem that makes a point. The main point it makes is to sing the greatness of Elohim who differentiates the land from the sea and light from dark, a power that lies with the majestic power of his word, as opposed to the Babylonian gods who are themselves generated. It is not a theogony explaining how Elohim was created but a cosmogony explaining how Elohim created the world and is not part of the world he created. Elohim is not the moon or the sun or a star, a point that was not entirely obvious in the sixth century B.C.E. and, for a myth, has itself a strongly demythologizing quality. But among the points the narrative is making, embedded in the story, is that Elohim works with the materials that are given him and his greatness is the cool-handed way in which he commands them by the sheer power of his word. But these materials he commands are unmistakably *given* him; he finds them there, pregiven. They are a part of the original scene that is presupposed as the first verse of the first chapter opens, the scene that Elohim encounters when, surveying the chaos from his celestial heights, he decides to bring order where there was previously only confusion.

Thus the first creation narrative describes an anterior, pregiven formlessness, an inoriginate, uncreated, undifferentiated, formless stuff, a kind of pure and perfect "out of which" that of itself is nothing in particular and is, very much as Derrida hypothesizes in one of his alternatives, "older than creation." I take that to mean that there is an ineradicable and neutral givenness in things with which we all must cope, God included. Let me stress that I do not mean to imply that the story is saying that there is anterior sphere of evil and malice that Elohim subdues by his mighty word. The *tohu wa bohu* is not evil but innocent; it does no harm to either man or beast, nor does it cause any eco- logical damage, none of these things having been created yet. It very nicely represents what Nietzsche calls the "innocence of becoming," not because it is beyond good and evil, which is what Nietzsche was pulling for, but because it is beneath them, because, of itself, it does not get as far as either good or evil. The original innocence of the *tohu wa bohu* of the first Priestly narrative is actually older than the innocence of Adam and Eve in the second or Yahwist narrative, which is historically an older story even though the redactors have put it second. Being neither good nor evil itself, the *tohu wa bohu* is but a neutral matrix from which good and evil emerge. The creation story is not a Manichaean story of a rival god, a rival evil principle that a good God must subdue, but the story of a neutral stuff that God forms into something good, which only then presents the possibility of evil as its corruption. It is only upon being made good that things can turn bad, that they thereafter harbor within themselves the power or the potency, the inclination, temptation, or tendency to go bad, to descend into disorder and malice. The formless void is not the disorder of evil, because it is neither orderly nor disorderly, but simply the stuff that Elohim orders, the corruption of which makes disorder possible. Evil is only possible if there is first something good to corrupt.

Now let us return from Genesis to the beautiful risk that Jim Olthuis recommends. The glorious goodness of the world, which is the encompassing horizon of the work of Jim Olthuis, is not thereby denied by what I am saying but in fact made possible. That is because the goodness of things is not denied but reinscribed within a larger and slightly more complicated context, in which order and difference rise up in a certain "triumph" over this neutral stuff. Creation is the triumph of particular and differentiated things over the undifferentiated and indifferent formless void. But this triumph is not once and for all, not a decisive victory that forever subdues and expels the opposing forces, but is a rather more episodic triumph that involves a constant repetition, constantly regaining ground previously won. The other side is always there on the other side of the hill and may at any moment spring on us. The *tohu wa bohu* is not purged or obliterated, expelled or expunged, but differentiated and formed and so it remains embedded in things as that from which they are formed, which means it lingers on in things in another manner, as the very stuff from which they were forged.

In my view, we must—for the very sake of Jim Olthuis's "beautiful risk"—resist the apple that Jim bites, which is to put too kind a spin on the *tohu wa bohu,* to treat it, for example, as a "matrix" in which creation is "engendered," for it does not exactly mother or engender anything and certainly not with motherly care and love. The *tohu wa bohu* does not give birth like a mother, does not love or not love, but constitutes a kind of space or underlying surface on which things are inscribed. The mythic element in Genesis is, in fact, not unlike what Plato called *khôra* or Aristotle called *materia prote* in antiquity, where these notions served a scientific and cosmological purpose and were meant to explain the ontological structure of material being. It also bears comparison to the neutral existence of *il y a* in Levinas, from which determinate existents rise up in a kind of triumph over anonymity, where this notion serves not a cosmological but a phenomenological purpose, providing a kind of phenomenological counterpart or transcription of the way things are forged from the formless void in Genesis. For Levinas, the "existent" is the triumph of definition and determination over the indifference and anonymity of the *il y a,* in a way that very faithfully reproduces the poetics of the first Genesis narrative. Nor is the *tohu wa bohu* entirely unlike what Derrida, in the wake of Plato and Levinas, is calling *khôra,* which is, for Derrida, a surname for *différance,* where it serves a semiological purpose, which means that *khôra* is a figure for Derrida of the indeterminacy within which all determinate meanings and structures are configured.

So it is not too much of a stretch to say that we can string a line from the sixth-century Hebrew priestly author who so profoundly shaped our religious imagination and the recent work of Jacques Derrida. *Khôra* for Derrida is a figure of semiological indeterminacy not of moral evil. So when we say "God or *khôra*" we are not saying "God or the devil," or "good or evil," or "mental health or insanity," or "love or loneliness," or anything of the like. Instead, Derrida's *khôra* is a way of pointing to the fragility of meaning, the instability, contingency, and undecidability of meaning and structure that are always woven out of differential relationships. *Khôra* is not the devil, not the dark menace of insanity, not some sinister Transylvanian specter. The *khôra* effect, the effect of *différence,* simply means that whatever "personal" element we can find in "meaning," by which I mean the Husserlian principle of the meaning-giving act or intention of the conscious agent, there is also an impersonal structure that is not a matrix but at best a quasi matrix (since it is nothing personal) within which meanings are forged. It is in virtue of *khôra/différence* that what is done can come undone, that what is constructed can be deconstructed, which is not a bad thing. For that deconstructability is what keeps things open to revision, amendment, and reconfiguration, which means it keeps the future open. That is not a bad thing, although it can be, if things take a turn for the worse and go from good to bad, which is why Olthuis does not fail to remind us of the uncertainty and unprogramability of the future. That is not the definition of malice, malignancy, and madness; it's just the *risk* that is built into things. The deconstructability of things implied by the notion of *khôra* does not mean that things have gone to the (d)evil, that love has been denied, and madness embraced; it is just a way of explaining the ineradicable risk built into our beliefs and practices.

So the irony is that if Jim Olthuis were to succeed in redescribing the *khôra* as a matrix of love, so that it is not a neutral but a loving milieu in which things are lovingly engendered, nourished, and led into their ends, then he would ruin his project because, while having affirmed the risk, he would have deprived himself of the very means to describe or account for it. As he points out about the beautiful risk, "This may be a dance, but it is dancing along an edge."[14] And what lies over the edge but the abyss, the formless khoral void? Without it, Olthuis would have removed the risk in the beautiful risk that, extending a suggestive expression of Levinas's, he has described so powerfully. While it is true that we are made whole by being loved and being known, the risk that we are not is real, and it is that component in our experience that *khôra* is meant to point to. *Khôra* does not give or promise anything, does not embrace us, love us, or know that we are here, and if you call out to her in the night of solitude or anxiety she/it will not hear. It/she is not justice or injustice, the gift or the economy, hospitality or exclusion, friendship or hatred of the other, but the neutral medium or spacing in which these relatively stable unities of meaning are constituted and remain deconstitutable. But is not justice, if it exists, if there is such a thing, undeconstructable? To be sure, but that undeconstructability is possible only in virtue of *khôra,* which sees to it that what does exist is always deconstructable. *Khôra* keeps the future open and sees to it that the future is indeed a risk, for by deconstructing the law in the name of justice, we are liable to make everything worse. "Justice" is a messianic hope we nourish in an unforeseeable future, a future that is held open by khoral indeterminacy even as the latter also puts it at risk. *Khôra* is not the "'place' evoked by the *oui, oui* of love and justice," which is how Jim

14. Olthuis, *Beautiful Risk,* p. 128.

Olthuis would have it, but the place *in which* the *oui, oui* of love and justice is affirmed and opens things up. The *khôra* is open only with the openness of the indeterminate, not with the openness of the *oui, oui* that is turned toward justice. *Khôra* is the indeterminate, undecidable sphere *in which* we make a decision for justice, which is, as Johannes Climacus says, always a leap. Were that not so, then all the risk would be removed from the beautiful risk, and all the undecidability and unprogramability in things that Jim Olthuis wants to acknowledge would be eliminated.

Let us return to the creation narrative once again. For Jim Olthuis, to love is a risk, a beautiful one, no doubt, but a risk that is for all that beauty no less real. To profess love for the other is make oneself vulnerable, to risk rejection and injury; but to play it safe and not risk love is to lose even more, to lose oneself by being trapped within oneself, riveted to oneself in loneliness and isolation. So true is that, I would say, that it holds not only for human love, but also for divine. Creation must be a risk for God, a venture into the outside in which God makes Godself vulnerable. Otherwise creation is simply a divine display of power, a laser show of lights and explosive cosmic events. To supply such alterity is the crucial role played by the figure of the *tohu wa bohu,* the mythic element that, although it is formed by God, remains nonetheless irreducible to God. Despite the preconceptions that derive from a later metaphysical theology about divine foreknowledge and omnipotence, few things are clearer from the opening pages of Genesis than that the Lord God did not fully appreciate what he was letting himself in for in creating, and that things did not turn out the way he wanted or expected. In creating something *other,* in the image and likeness of himself—that is, beings who, like God, were able to create and reproduce—Elohim exposed himself to injury, rejection, and disobedience. Otherwise he did not create something other, something that would truly break the divine solitude, something that would be a veritable image of himself, something that in response to his creative word would answer *back.* A *creatio ex nihilo* would issue in a world so thoroughly made by God, so through and through a matter of the divine freedom, a world so thoroughly woven from divine power, that it would undermine the possibility of a genuine alterity, of a world that could in truth respond to his address—or fail to. But that is the condition of the beautiful risk, of any beautiful risk, including the one that God takes in creating. Without the *tohu wa bohu,* the world would lack the standing to affirm or reject the divine love, and the divine love would be without risk, which is to say, divine love would be something less than love. Without the *tohu wa bohu,* the world lacks alterity and God lacks exposure to something other, something that is not entirely under his control. If God retains full in command of his powers, then God lacks the power of love, in which one submits one's power to the power of the other. So once again the indeterminate sea of the *tohu wa bohu,* the figure of undecidability and unprogramability, the indeterminacy inscribed in things for better or for worse, is not love itself, or love's milieu or horizon, but the condition of the possibility of love, of the riskiness that a lover requires when he or she makes a leap into the uncertainty of love's churning waters.

Positing the ineradicability of *khôra*, I repeat, is not a Manichaean move meant to pose an opposing evil principle that checks God's every move and leads us all into violence. It does not embrace evil or violence. It simply says that our love of nonviolence is not translucent and unambiguous, but is inscribed in a medium that is such that the worst violence can be perpetrated under the best names we have—like "God" or "justice," "friendship" or "democracy"—so that we are always already structurally exposed to the possibility of violence, not to its necessity. To say *khôra* is to say that our beliefs and practices are inscribed in the warp and woof of differential spacings in virtue of which the very thing that makes them possible also makes them impossible. That means that it is the same thing that makes their relative stability and unity of meaning possible that also makes the absoluteness of their unity impossible. Our beliefs and practices are, as Father Husserl would have said, constituted as contingent unities of meaning. But they are constituted not merely by an intentional act or conscious "word" that says *fiat,* as in Husserl, but by a word spoken in or inscribed within an impersonal web, fitted in or woven from the differential spacing of *khôra,* which sees to it that what is said can come unsaid, that what is done can come undone. That is a hypothesis that Husserl himself entertains under the heading of the "annihilability of the world,"[15] that is, of the inherent possibility inscribed within the contingent strings of unities of experience to come unstrung and deconstitute into worldless confusion. For the conscious speaking subject is not all that there is; whatever the inner motions, emotions, and intentions of the speaking self, the word is uttered in the midst of differential semiotic spacings, which make it possible for the subject to express itself in semiotic systems that make meaning possible. So true is the law of *khôra/différence* that it even applies to divine speech acts; it is even reflected in the priestly author's narrative about Elohim speaking the speech act par excellence, the speech act to end all speech acts (or to start them!), when Elohim breathes his creative word over and into the *tohu wa bohu.*

We have learned from Jim Olthuis that to live and act and love in the world, to be alive at all, to be in play, to be able to play, to dance in the wild spaces of love, is to put ourselves at risk. Life is a risky business, a risky game, that is not for the faint of heart. But it is a beautiful risk, which can be savored by the hardy, the heart-y, those who have the heart to run the risk of loving the other even if there is no payback. To love is to risk rejection, to love one's enemies who may be counted on not to love in return, even to make oneself a fool for the kingdom of God by making a gift without return. The odd thing is that none of that is possible without something like loveless and unloved *khôra,* which provides the risk, without *khôra,* poor nameless *khôra,* which does not even know we are here.

---

15. Edmund Husserl, *Ideas I,* trans. F. Kersten (The Hague: M. Nijhoff, 1983), §49.

3

Philosophizing the Gift

A Discussion between Richard Kearney and Mark Manolopoulos[1]

Richard Kearney

Q: *In the Derrida/Marion debate "On the Gift" (Villanova, 1997) you ask the question "Is there a Christian philosophy of the gift?"*[2] *Do you think either Derrida or Marion or both provide handy directions? Could you summarize or interpret their insights? And whose argument do you find more persuasive?*

RK: They did avoid the question. In Derrida's case that is logical because he will always—reasonably for a deconstructionist—try to avoid tying the messianicity of the gift to any messianism as such, be it Christian, Jewish, Islamic, or any other kind. So it makes sense for him not to engage in that debate per se because he would say: "That's beyond my competence. I'm not a Christian. 'I rightly pass for an atheist.'[3] I respect Christianity. I'm fascinated by their theological and philosophical expressions of the notion of the gift—I learn from it—but it's not my thing." Marion I find a little bit more perplexing

---

1. To Jim Olthuis: risk-taker, hell-raiser, heaven-chaser, and general good guy—who has taught me so much [RK]. The provenance of this conversation was an interview conducted by Mark Manolopoulos (Monash University) at Boston College in the winter of 2001.

2. "On the Gift: A Discussion between Jacques Derrida and Jean-Luc Marion, Moderated by Richard Kearney" in *God, the Gift, and Postmodernism,* ed. John D. Caputo and Michael J. Scanlon (Bloomington and Indianapolis: Indiana University Press, 1999), pp. 54–78, 61.

3. Geoffrey Bennington and Jacques Derrida, *Jacques Derrida,* trans. Geoffrey Bennington (Chicago: University of Chicago Press, 1993), p. 154.

in this regard because he *is* a Christian philosopher. He has talked about "eucharistic hermeneutics" in *God without Being*.[4] Christ is a "saturated phenomenon" for Marion.[5] But Marion is going through a phase—and this was evident at the Villanova conference—where he doesn't want to be labeled as a "Christian philosopher"—and certainly *not* as a Christian *theologian*. He wants to be a phenomenologist. So, being true—at least to some extent—to Husserl's phenomenology as a universal science, he wants to be independent of presuppositions regarding this or that particular theological revelation: Christian, Jewish, or otherwise. I think that's why in his essays on "the saturated phenomenon," Marion goes back to Kant. The Kantian sublime offers a way into the saturated phenomenon, as does the notion of the gift or donation, which—like Husserlian phenomenology—precedes the question of theological confessions and denominations. And I think Marion wants to retreat to that position so that he won't be labeled a Christian apologist—which I think he is. I think he's a Christian theologian who's trying not to be one.

Personally, my own response here would be to say that there are two ways of doing phenomenology—and both are equally valid. One is to begin with certain theological and religious presuppositions. The other is to operate a theological reduction, where you say: "We're not going to raise theological issues here." That's following the basic Husserlian and Heideggerian line. In the *Introduction to Metaphysics* Heidegger says something like: "The answer to the question 'Why is there something rather than nothing?'—if you fail to bracket out theology—is: because God created the world."[6] But if you bracket it out you don't begin with theological presuppositions—and that is what Husserl does, what Heidegger does, and what Derrida does. I think Marion mixes the two, although in the exchange with Derrida I think he's trying to get back to that kind of *pure* phenomenology. He keeps saying: "I'm a phenomenologist! I'm doing phenomenology!" But the lady doth protest too much. Then there is a third way of doing phenomenology *in dialogue with* theology, which doesn't bracket it out but *half*-suspends it. We might call this a quasi-theological phenomenology or a quasi-phenomenological theology. In other words, one acknowledges that there's a certain hybridity, but one doesn't want to presuppose straight

4. Jean-Luc Marion, *God without Being*, trans. Thomas A. Carlson (Chicago: University of Chicago Press, 1991).

5. Jean-Luc Marion, "Le phénomène saturé" in *Phénoménologie et théologie*, ed. Jean-François Courtine (Paris: Criterion, 1992), pp. 79–128; "The Saturated Phenomenon," trans. Thomas A. Carlson, *Philosophy Today* 40 (1996): 103–24. See also *Phenomenology and the "Theological Turn,"* Dominique Janicaud et al. (New York: Fordham University Press, 2000).

6. Martin Heidegger, *Introduction to Metaphysics*, trans. Gregory Fried and Richard Polt (New Haven, Conn.: Yale University Press, 2000).

off which comes *first:* the giving of the gift as a phenomenological event or the divine creation of the world as source of all gifts. This allows for a certain ambiguous intermeshing, intermixing, crossweaving—what Merleau-Ponty described as a chiasmic interlacing. And it seems to me that that's perfectly legitimate. Even though it is methodologically more complex and more ambivalent than the Husserlian move of saying, "Bracket out all political, theological, ideological, cultural presuppositions," it is actually truer to life because life *is* the natural attitude. And the natural attitude *is* infused with presuppositions. And it includes *both* (a) experiences of the gift as pure gift and (b) experiences of the gift for believers as coming from Yahweh or Christ or Allah or the Sun God/dess. And it seems to me that the phenomenology of unbracketed experience, the phenomenology of the natural attitude—which I think Merleau-Ponty gets pretty close to—is what I am practicing in *The God Who May Be*.[7] I'm not writing as a theologian because I don't have the theological competence. I'm writing as a philosopher, but one who, as a philosopher, feels quite entitled to draw from religious Scriptures as sources, just as theologians do, and to draw from phenomenology as a method. I'll draw from anything that will help me clarify the question. And I think by drawing ambidextrously from both, it can open a "middle path" into some interesting questions, even though the Husserlians and the Heideggerians can shout: "Foul! You're bringing religion into this!" and the theologians can say: "Oh, well, you're not a theologian! Did you pass your doctoral exam in dogmatic theology?!" And I just say: "No. I'm just doing a hermeneutic readings of texts—some phenomenological, some religious—and I'm going to mix them. If there be interference, let it be a creative interference. If there be contamination, let it be a fruitful contamination."

Q: *In the Villanova exchange Derrida wouldn't provide a theology of the gift, and Marion doesn't. If you provided a theology of the gift, what would be some characteristics or axioms?*

RK: Well, I repeat, what I'm doing in *The God Who May Be* is not theology as such but a "hermeneutics of religion." It is, I hope, a contribution to the phenomenology of the gift. I usually call "the gift" by other names: (1) the "transfiguring" God; (2) the "desiring" God; (3) the "possibilizing" God; (4) the "poeticizing" God—the creating God qua *poiesis*. They would be my four categories of gifting. *Poiesis* or the poeticizing God engages in a cocreation with us. God can't create the kingdom unless we create the space for the kingdom to come.

7. Richard Kearney, *The God Who May Be: A Hermeneutics of Religion* (Bloomington: Indiana University Press, 2001).

Q: *That's interesting in light of Catherine Keller's thesis that creation* ex
        nihilo *is too one-way.*[8]

RK: What I like about the *creatio ex nihilo*—though I can see that it's
        nonreciprocal—is that it's an unconditional giving. It's not a giving
        because there's some problem to be solved that precedes the giving. To
        use Derrida's language, it comes before economy although it cannot
        continue without economy. As soon as there's history and finitude
        and humanity, there's economy, there's negotiation. And there is,
        to my mind, reciprocity. Here I disagree with Caputo, Derrida and
        Lyotard, and the postmodern deconstructionists who repudiate the
        notion of reciprocity or equity or reconciliation. They see it as going
        back to Hegel or conceding to some kind of economy. I don't think it
        is as simple as that. I am wary of the polarity between the absolutely
        unconditional gift and the gift as compromised by the economy
        (which gets rid of the gift as pure gift). I just think that's an unhelpful
        dichotomy, as I think messianicity versus messianism is an unhelpful
        dichotomy. It's an interesting idea; it's good for an argument. But I
        think it's ultimately unworkable because I don't think you can inves-
        tigate messianicity without messianism; and I don't think you can
        have genuine messianism without messianicity. Now maybe Derrida
        would agree with that. But there's still a difference of emphasis. I don't
        see anything wrong with the mix. Whereas Derrida seems to think it
        is all that is *possible* for us human, mortal beings, but what he's really
        interested in is the *impossible.* I leave the impossible to God and get
        on with the possible. Because that's where I find myself: I'm in the
        economic order. I look to something called "God"—what Derrida
        calls "the impossible"—to guarantee that the economy doesn't close in
        on itself. But I don't hold out God as something that we should even
        entertain as an option for us because God is not an option for us. God
        is an option for God. Humanity is an option for us. If we can be more
        human, that's our business. Our business is not to become God. It's
        God's vocation to become more fully God, ours to become more fully
        human. We answer to the Other without ever *fusing* in some kind of
        metaphysical unity or identity. When I say, "I'm for reciprocity, equity,
        and reconciliation," I'm not for premature Hegelian synthesis. I'm not
        for metaphysical appropriation or some ineluctable evolving "process"
        of integration. I'm not for reducing the otherness of God to being as
        such. But, on the other hand, and this may sound paradoxical, I'm all
        for *traversings* of one by the other—anything that muddies the waters
        and makes the borders between God and us porous. I don't believe
        there's an absolute God out there and then a completely compromised
        humanity here. I think there are constant *to-ings* and *fro-ings.* So the

8. See Catherine Keller's *The Face of the Deep: A Theology of Becoming* (London: Routledge, 2002).

phenomenology of the gift that I'm trying to articulate in terms of poeticizing is a cocreation of history by humanity and God, leading to the kingdom. A new heaven and a new earth. We don't know what that will be because we haven't reached it. We can imagine but we can't pronounce. It goes beyond the sphere of the phenomenology of history because it involves a posthistorical situation. It's an *eschaton.* We can imagine it as an eschatology but it's really something that God "knows" more about than we do.

Q: *What do you mean when you say "giving is desiring"?*

RK: I argue that giving is desiring because desire is not just the movement from lack to fulfillment, or from potency to act, or from the insufficient to the sufficient—these are metaphysical notions of desire. I'm taking the idea of desire as coming from a fullness toward an absence as much as coming from an absence to a fullness. For example, kenosis is a form of desire. And it doesn't come from God being empty and wanting to become full. It comes from God being full and wanting to empty his divinity in order to be more fully in dialogue with the human because, as Levinas says: "On s'amuse mieux à deux." "It's better to be two than one."[9] And it's "better" in the sense of being *more* good, *more* just, *more* loving. It's Eckhart's idea of *ebullutio,* this "bubbling over," this excess or surplus of desire. Not a surplus of being but of desire. Desire is always the desire of more desire. And also the desire for an answer: what's the point in God desiring and having nobody to answer the divine desire? That's why Song of Songs says it all: the desire of the Shulamite woman—representing humanity—for the Lord (Solomon the lover) is a desire that actually expresses itself not just as frustration, emptiness, lack, looking for her lover, but as a desire that sings its encounter with the lover, that celebrates its *being found.* In the Song of Songs, the lover *finds* the Shulamite woman and that is the inaugural moment, as it were, of the song of desire. It's a desire based not on *fine amour* and romantic passion—which is frustration, prohibition, or absence. It's a desire of plenitude—not of presence, because that's fusional. It's a desire of excess not of deficiency. A desire that stems from being taken by God. A response to the desire of the absolute. So that's another form of giving. In other words, the desire of the Shulamite woman is a gift. It's not a subjective hankering. It's a gift; it's a response to a gift. And what's the gift? The gift is desire.

So you've got two desires at work. The traditional view has been to consider the human as desiring the fullness of God because the human is full of lack, insufficiency, and finitude. But what I'm trying to do is to see it as much more complex than that. It's a question of both lack

---

9. Emmanuel Levinas, "Ethics of the Infinite" in Richard Kearney, *States of Mind: Dialogues with Contemporary Thinkers* (New York: New York University Press, 1995), pp. 177–99.

and fullness in God and humanity. There's a lack in God and there's a
lack in humanity. What's the lack in humanity? It's that humanity is
not divine. What's the lack in God? God is *not* human. So, in a way, the
kingdom as a second coming or incarnation is what we're looking for.
But as soon as you have that meeting of the finite and the infinite you've
left history behind—not to return to some kind of fusion or "oceanic
oneness" à la Freud. Let's imagine it hermeneutically, poetically: what
would the kingdom be if the desire of the Shulamite woman and the
desire of the Lover Lord were to meet and mesh in a posthistorical
fashion? The first answer is: we don't know. But if we were to imagine
it—as various religions have done—it would be a dance; it would be
a *perichoresis.* It would be the dance-around of the three persons or of
the two lovers and, arguably, where there are two there is always a third.
So the *perichoresis* is the refusal—even in parousia and *pleroma,* and
eschatology and even in the kingdom—to compromise in terms of a
closed economy. It never closes. The economy is still bubbling, is still
flowering, is still bursting into life and being by virtue of this dance-
around, which, as *perichoresis,* is something I explore in *The God Who
May Be.* The *perichoresis* is the dance-around the *khôra. Peri-chôra.* The
dance-around is each person of the Trinity—whether you interpret that
as Father–Son–Holy Ghost, or God-humanity-kingdom (one doesn't
have to be patriarchal and gender-exclusive in this)—in dialogue with
each other. We're just fantasizing here—which of course most theologians wouldn't allow us to do. They would say: "Well now, is that
according to Saint Thomas or Saint Augustine?" At certain points in
history if you said something like Bruno of Nola, or even Eckhart, you
could be burnt for it. But let's assume we're not going to be burnt in
this day and age for imagining what might go on in the kingdom. Now,
in terms of this desiring relationship with the three persons, there's a
double movement that I'm arguing will or *could* continue—let's imagine—in the kingdom when history has ended as we know it and when
the Shulamite woman who desires God has come face to face with her
lover. The double movement is this: it's a movement of approach and of
distance. The term *perichoresis* is translated into Latin as *circumincessio,*
which is taken from two phonetically similar verbs, (a) *cedo,* "to leave
place," "to absent yourself," and (b) *sedo,* meaning "to sit," "to assume
or take up a position." So there is a double movement of immanence
and transcendence; of distantiation and approximation. Of moving
toward each other and then moving *away* from each other—as in a
dance. A dance-around where each person cedes his/her place to the
other and then that other to its other and so on. So it's not just two
persons. There's a third person in this divine dance whom you're always
acknowledging and invoking. This third person is very important in
Levinas and I think it's very important in certain Christian notions of

the Trinity. Because the danger of two is that two can become one; face to face can become a candlelit dinner, where romantic lovers look into each other's eyes and see themselves reflected in the other. Whereas the third introduces a little bit of "symbolic castration" that safeguards a certain distance and therefore allows for desire. If desire were to reach its end it would end. And a God who is not desiring is a God who's not giving. And a God who is not giving is not God.

Q: *What about the "transfiguring God"?*

RK: The transfiguring God is the God who transfigures us as we transfigure God. The example I use is Mount Tabor. Basically, God transfigures us through creation, through interventions in history—whether it's the burning bush or Christ or the saints or the epiphanies that Joyce and Proust talk about: *that,* to me, is the divine transfiguring the everyday. So presumably if God is giving, God is giving as a constant process and practice of transfiguring. We may not see it. We may not know that it's there. And we may refuse to acknowledge it, in which case it doesn't affect our lives. In a way, that's God's loss, too, because if God's transfiguring goes unheeded and unheard, we're going to have wars, evil, and so on. I'm Augustinian in that regard: evil is the *absence* of God as transfiguring, desiring, poeticizing, and possibilizing—I'll come back to this fourth category in a moment. But transfiguring is not just something God does to us: it's also something that we do to God. And we transfigure God to the extent that we create art, we create justice, we create love. We bring into being, through our actions—poetical and ethical—a transfiguration of the world. It's a human task as much as a divine gift. God gives to us a transfiguring promise; we give back to God a transfigured world—and we can transfigure it in ways that God can't. We can author a poem like a Shakespearean sonnet. God can't do that. But we can coauthor with God a poem called *poesis,* creation, the so-called "real" world. That's a different kind of poem, where God and the human meet each other, complement each other. But either can withdraw from the dance, in which case the other just falls on his or her face. That's the end of it. We can destroy God. That's why I speak of a God who *may be,* which is an interpretation of the Hebrew "I am the God who will be, who may be."[10] If I am the God who simply *am,* I am already accomplished, already there, whereas the God who *may be* is *also* a God of promise, of potential, of the kingdom. At any point we can pull the plug on God. As one of the victims of the Holocaust, Etty Hillesum, says: "We must help God to be God."[11] And that's where we can make a link with people

10. Exod. 3:14.

11. Etty Hillesum, *An Interrupted Life* (New York: Owl, 1991). Cited in Kearney, *The God Who May Be.*

like Eckhart and Cusanus and some of the other church fathers and biblical prophets.

Q: *At first glance the notion that "We must help God to be God" sounds arrogant.*

RK: Yes, but what it's accepting is that *God is not arrogant;* that God does not presume to be able to stop evil. God can't stop evil. Why? Because evil is the absence of God. God has no power over what God is not—namely, evil. God can only be good—unconditionally good in a gifting, loving, creating. That is where the Gnostics and theodicists were wrong: God is not *both* good *and* evil. Even Hegel and Jung made that mistake. God is *not* omnipotent when it comes to evil. God is utterly powerless. And that's terribly important. You find that in the Christian story: Jesus before Pilate, the crucifixion: he couldn't do anything. It's "the power of the powerless" as Vaclav Havel calls it—and he is right.[12] God helps us to be more fully human; we help God to be more fully God—or we don't. If we don't, we can blow up the world and that's the end of humanity, and that's the end of God as the promise of the kingdom because there's nobody there anymore to fulfill the promise. In that instance, God remains as pure *desiring,* of course, as pure *poeticizing*—except God's world has just been broken up by God's own creature. And to revisit the terms of *The God Who May Be,* God remains *transfiguring;* but there's nothing left to transfigure anymore because we've destroyed it.

Q: *You also mention the "possibilizing God"?*

RK: Basically, that means that divinity is a constant offer of the possibility of the kingdom, which can be interpreted in two ways (and you find this in the Scriptures). One is the kingdom as eschatological promise after history, at the *end* of history. The other is the kingdom *now:* in the mustard seed, in the little, everyday, most insignificant of acts. The kingdom is present in the "least of these"—just as Christ is present in the giving of a cup of cold water. That means that in every moment there is the possibility of good and there is the possibility of non-good. There's the possibility of love; there's the possibility of hate, violence, aggression. We're choosing constantly. And every moment we are actu-alizing the kingdom or not-actualizing the kingdom. As Benjamin says so beautifully: "Every moment is a portal through which the Messiah might come." Now what we've got to get away from is thinking that the Messiah comes and then it's all over. If you're a Christian—and I am up to a point: I am a Christian up to the point where the love of "Christians" offends justice and then I'm not "Christian" any-more—you draw from the Christian story and testimony the notion

12. See Vaclav Havel, *The Power of the Powerless* (London: Hutcheson, 1985).

that *each little act* makes a difference. For example, the woman with the hemorrhage: you help her—you don't want to but you help her.[13] There's no wine: okay, we reluctantly change the water into wine.[14] And so on and so forth. You do all of these little things—most of them almost imperceptible—and you don't make a big fuss about it. And when the Messiah comes—even if this happens to be a pretty extraordinary, exemplary instance of the divine in the human—as I believe Christ is—you don't say: "Now it's all over." You *can* say: "Now it's all over for me." But history isn't over. The coming of Christ *wasn't* the end of the world: the Messiah always comes again in history. And the Messiah is always—including the Christian Messiah—a God who is *still* to come (even when the Messiah has already come). The Messiah is one who has already come and is always still to come. And that's why I see the Christian story as exemplary. (But it's not the only story in town. And, in my view, it has no absolute prerogative vis-à-vis other world religions. God speaks in many voices and in many traditions.)

But to return to the Bible, we could take the Mosaic story as well: in the burning bush God came. With Elijah in the cave the Messiah came. But that wasn't the end of it. The Messiah came to John the Baptist too, the voice crying in the wilderness. It always comes *and* goes. And that's the nature of the Messiah: it's already here—the kingdom is already here—but it is also not yet fully here. And it's this double moment that's terribly important because the possible is not just *the Possible*: the telos of universal history coming to an end at the end of time—that's Hegel. That's triumphalism. That's the kind of monotheistic tyranny that leads to religious wars: "We own The Promised Land"; "*This* and only *this* is the Absolute"; all or nothing. In contrast to such triumphalist teleologies and ideologies of power, the divine possible I am speaking of comes in tiny, almost imperceptible acts of love or poetic justice. It is in "the music of what happens," as Seamus Heaney says. Or in what Joyce called "epiphanies," Baudelaire "correspondences," Proust "reminiscences." These are all poetic testimonies to the possible that becomes incarnate in all these little moments of eschatological enfleshment.

Q: *What does "eschatology" mean for you?*

RK: If and when the kingdom comes, I believe it will be a great kind of "recollection" or "retrieval" (*anakephalaiosis* is the term used by Paul) of all those special moments of love; but you can't even see it in terms of past, present, and future because the eternal is outside time, even though it comes *into* time all the time. Christ is just an exemplary figure of it. What does Christ say at the end? He says: "Time for me

13. Matt. 9:19–23; Luke 8:43–48.
14. John 2:1–11.

to go. Don't touch me. *Noli me tangere.* Don't possess me. I cannot be an idol that you possess." The Messiah is deferred. And here I always draw great sustenance from Blanchot's tale of the beggar waiting for the Messiah at the gates of Rome. The Messiah comes and the beggar goes up to him and says: "Are you the Messiah?" And the Messiah responds: "Yes." And the beggar asks: "When will you come?" because the Messiah is always still to come. The Messiah is *still to come* even as the Messiah is *there.* Because we're temporal we're confronted with this unsolvable paradox or aporia—namely, that the kingdom has already come and yet is not here. And that's the way it is for our finite phenomenological minds. No metaphysics and no theology or philosophy can resolve that one. So, to the extent that deconstruction is a reminder of the *impossibility* of ever having the total take on God as absolute, then I'm for deconstruction. But as an endless kind of "soft shoe shuffle" of infinite qualifications and refinements, forever declining any kind of incarnation, I find deconstruction too deserted, too *désertique,* too desertlike, too hard. Derrida's deconstruction is too inconsolable. It's overly uncompromising. Too puritanical—in a way, strangely. It's all about the impossible. But for me, God is the possibilizing of the impossible. "What is impossible to us is possible to God."[15] We actualize what God possibilizes and God possibilizes what remains impossible for us. To sum up: "God is giving" means God is poeticizing, possibilizing, transfiguring, and desiring. That's my *religious* phenomenology of the gift. I also did a *prereligious* phenomenology of the gift in the first part of *Poétique du Possible* published in 1984.[16] And if I were to do that again I would certainly include readings of Proust and Joyce or just everyday testimonies to people's kindness, the small ways in which love and creativity works in the world—irrespective of whether people are religious or not. You can go either way.

Q: *You've answered the question of a "theology of gift" in terms of thinking God as gift. To think creation as gift: briefly, what would that entail for you?*

RK: If we're talking about divine creation—because I think there are two creations going on: divine and human—I don't want to repeat myself but I would probably go back to the idea of *poiesis:* God as *poiesis,* the *nous poetikos* as Aristotle calls it, and the "possest" as Cusanus says.[17] Poeticizing is the act of constantly opening horizons of possibility, gifts of possibility, for human beings to realize. The divine gift as creation is

15. Matt. 19:26; Luke 18:27.

16. Richard Kearney, *Poétique du Possible: Phénoménologie Herméneutique de la Figuration* (Paris: Beauchesne, 1984).

17. Cusanus, *Trialogus de Possest,* in *A Concise Introduction to the Philosophy of Nicholas of Cusa,* trans. J. Hopkins (Minneapolis: University of Minnesota Press, 1980).

powerless to impose that gift on somebody who doesn't want it because that would not be good: that would be evil. If you say to somebody: "I love you," and they say: "I don't want your love," and you say: "Sorry, I love you, and whether you like it or not, you are going to be transfigured by my love"—that's coercion, violence, tyranny. That's what so-called benevolent dictators do. That's the imposition of the good on somebody who doesn't want it. Sadism in the name of God. How many times has religion done that? The Taliban were doing it. The Inquisition was doing it. The New England Puritans were doing it to the so-called "witches" down in Salem. "For your good, we are going to impose the good!" "But thank you very much, I don't want your good." That's why God loves rebels: God loves the Steven Daedeluses of this world who say: "I will not serve that in which I no longer believe," whether it call itself religion, language, or homeland. (It's at the beginning of Joyce's *Portrait of the Artist*.) I suspect that God would prefer people not to serve that in which they do not believe. God prefers honest people who rebel rather than the lackeys, the "creeping Jesuses who would do anything to please us." I don't want to get into a cult of the rebel here. But God admires people like Job and David—who argue with God. God admires Jesus on the cross, who says: "Why have you forsaken me? Come on, give me an answer to this." God likes that.

Q: *In "Desire of God" you mention, quite prophetically: "there is a growing problem of closure to the other. I am sure, if it has not already become a problem here in the United States, it will become one—the problem of how one can relate openly and hospitably and justly to the other, without demonization."[18] These words obviously resonate in light of the current wave of terrorism. However, let's ask this question from an ecocentric perspective: do you have any thoughts on how one can or should relate openly and hospitably and justly to the nonhuman other—animate and inanimate? We demonize the nonhuman—*

RK   We demonize all the time. When people want to show what the devil is they usually take an animal. Just look at medieval and Renaissance portraits of demons. The iconography of *The Last Judgment* is full of this: goats, bats, snakes, dragons, griffins, dogs, gargoyles.[19] I believe that's a real question. I think it's something we in Western philosophy and in our excessive anthropocentrism have sometimes ignored, that is, the *alterity* of nature: of trees and of animals, and so on. One thing I've taken great courage and guidance from is my own children's

18. "Desire of God" (with Discussion) in *God, the Gift, and Postmodernism*, edited by John D. Caputo and Michael J. Scanlon (Bloomington and Indianapolis: Indiana University Press, 1999), pp. 112–145, 135.

19. See the first two chapters of my *Strangers, Gods, and Monsters* (London & New York: Routledge, 2002).

sensitivity in this regard. They are vegetarians and very opposed to wearing fur coats or buying factory-produced food. I think there's a growing awareness in the new generation, which is very important as long as it's kept in balance with being good to your neighbor who's starving down the street (and perhaps can only afford factory food). I find there are many young people in Boston or New York who go down to protest against Bush or the death penalty as much as they will concern themselves with cruelty to animals and the pollution of nature. That's good. The balance is important. There's no point ignoring social and human issues out of some kind of obsession with eating "natural" food. That's just taking food as a surrogate symbol that can be "purified" as the world disintegrates before the ravages of global poverty and late capitalism. There can sometimes be, for example, a certain New England obsession with health and the natural—a demonization of smoke, a demonization of alcohol, a demonization of sex (although it often goes hand in hand with fantasy sex or underworld sex in Las Vegas and Hollywood, so it can be very ambiguous). There is a residual *puritanism* in American culture, I think, and a certain demonization of the pagan earthiness of things. That may include food prohibitions against eating fish or "killing" tomatoes, etc., as well as the stringent laws against smoking, drinking, or sexual language. But that's only *half* the story—the *official* version as it were. The other half is very different, and leads to all kinds of perversions, doublethink, and doubletalk. It's a messy world, full of double messages. I'm not saying, therefore, that you should tolerate cruelty to animals and indiscriminately chop down trees. I'm saying you do your best, wherever possible and within the limits of the possible, to remain human while doing the *least* amount of harm to nature or to animals or to your fellow human beings. Somewhere along the line, the refusal of smoke, sex, alcohol, and meat in an *absolutist* fashion can, to my mind, smack of the old moralism. It can slip into dualism even with the very best of intentions—and I'm always wary of that. So I would say: "Be vegetarian. Fine. But when you find yourself in a situation where you go to another country and there's only meat on the table, have some meat." If I go to a tribe in Africa and they give me goats' eyeballs, I may not particularly like it, but I'm not going to offend my host by saying: "I don't eat goats' eyeballs!" I'll eat it—raw or cooked. That's the kind thing to do. That's accepting the hospitality of the other as other. Or as the Dalai Lama advised his monks, "Eat whatever is dropped into your begging bowl."

Q: *In* The God Who May Be *you open up the question of discernment, whether we're facing saturation or the desert. You claim that: "For the theist Marion, no less than for the atheist Derrida, we are left with the dilemma of 'holy madness,' how to judge between true and false prophets, between good and evil ghosts, between holy and unholy messiahs.*"[20] *Even though Caputo and Derrida are suspicious of criteria—I guess we all are a little suspicious—how should we nevertheless judge between the true and the false, between good and evil? After Derrida, how do you treat criteria?*

RK: You do so by trying to discern and judge more carefully, more cautiously, more critically. And I would say more hermeneutically. You don't have to get rid of criteria altogether. Derrida would say: "Well, of course we have to make decisions all the time. We judge and we use criteria. We have to do that: we couldn't not do it." Strictly speaking, that's already a compromise. That's already entering into the economy of things. And I just find the gap in Derrida between our decisions and undecidability too polar. That's my problem: it's too antithetical, too aporetical, too impossible. Decisions are "too difficult" in the deconstructive scencario. They are all made in "fear and trembling" because we're "in the dark"! At the 1999 Villanova exchange I asked Derrida: "How can you read in the dark?" He said: "We can *only* read in the dark." But I want to turn the light on! Even if it's only a flashlight—that will remove a little of the darkness and confusion. I don't believe in *absolute* light or total enlightenment for us ordinary mortals. It doesn't have to be either absolute light or total darkness. It doesn't have to be that hard. We're not all desperate desert fathers waiting for Godot as the apocalyptic dusk descends! It doesn't have to be that angst-ridden or melodramatic. The world is a place of light and dark: we always have a bit of both.

Q: *Derrida might say that the world is in such a mess because we assume we can read in the light and that all decisions are easy.*

RK: I can understand what he's saying in terms of an excessive hubris and arrogance on behalf of a certain Enlightenment, on behalf of rationalism, on behalf of science and technology. There I agree with him. But I'm not sure that's the way most people in the world today actually think or live. Most people are confused and bewildered. They're not cocksure *cogito*s in need of deconstruction but wounded, insecure, fragile subjects in search of meaning.

Q: *What about religious dogmatism?*

RK: Oh, before the Enlightenment it was worse. What I'm saying is: to think you possess the light and everybody else is in darkness is a recipe for imperialism, colonization, injustice, holy war, Jihad, "Good versus Evil." We're witnessing it again today. Nobody has a prerogative on

20. "Desiring God," in *The God Who May Be*, p. 80f.

light or the good. But that doesn't mean we're all condemned to a kind of total darkness, *khôra,* undecidability. I think everything should be deconstructed; but the question for me is: what's it like *after* deconstruction? That's why I still believe in hermeneutics. Derrida doesn't. I believe in reminiscences, resurrections, reconciliations. They're all temporary, they're all provisional, they're all muddling through. Granted—but they do happen. I believe in paths. Not massive metaphysical viaducts or Golden Gate Bridges between the contingent and the absolute, but I do believe in little footbridges—the kind you get in Harrison Ford movies. Hermeneutic ladders. I find that deconstruction fo!'ows the template of the Lazarus parable: the implacable metaphor of the gulf that separates (a) paradise, the Absolute, the impossible from (b) the land of the living—our finite, everyday, contingent, mortal world. The deconstructive gulf radically segregates the two. There's an unbridgeable gap between the divine and the human, the impossible and the possible. The deconstructionist Abraham won't allow Lazarus to send a message back to his brothers to warn and instruct them. It is too late. The kind of hermeneutics of religion that I'm talking about, by contrast, would be much more guided by the paradigm of Jacob's ladder, where there's *to-ing* and *fro-ing,* lots of people going up and down, in both directions. No *absolute* descent or *absolute* ascent. It's little people going up and down ladders. And that, to me, is how you work toward the kingdom. Each step counts. Messianic incursion, incarnation, epiphany is a possibility for every moment of our lives. But because we are finite and temporal, the infinite can pass through time, but it can never remain or take up residence in some absolute or permanent present. That's the difference between the eternal and time. They can crisscross back and forth, up and down, like the angels on Jacob's ladder. But they are never identical, never the same. That's what a hermeneutic affirmation of "difference" is all about. As opposed to deconstructive *différence,* which in my view, gives up hope in the *real possibility* of mediation and transition.

Q: *One more question generated by "Desire of God." Whereas someone like Marion may turn to mystical theology and a phenomenology of saturation, I concur with you in your affirmation of "hermeneutical retrievals and re-imaginings of biblical narratives and stories."* [21] *Could you briefly comment on the possible nature or direction of these retrievals and re-imaginings? And could you perhaps suggest how such retrievals could inform—and be informed by—a philosophical theology of gift/ing? For Kevin Hart and Jean-Luc Marion and others, they draw from mystical theology, but they seem to be turning away from biblical resources.*

21. Kearney, "Desiring God," op. cit. pp. 80f.

RK: That's why I'm into the hermeneutics of narrative imagination, where-
        as they're into a more deconstructionist position (yes, even Marion in
        my view). There *is* a difference in that regard. So while I learn from
        deconstruction, I really am closer to hermeneutics. I try to negotiate
        between the two, but I'm closer to hermeneutics—what I call a "dia-
        critical hermeneutics." It's not the romantic hermeneutics of Gadamer
        and Heidegger and Schleiermacher: getting back to the original event
        and reappropriating the inaugural moment. I don't endorse that kind
        of hermeneutic retrieval of the originary—some primal unity. Nor
        would I uncritically endorse what Jack Caputo calls "radical herme-
        neutics"—which is really another word for deconstruction—because
        it doesn't sufficiently allow, in my view, for valid retrievals, recogni-
        tions, or reconciliations. In *Strangers, Gods, and Monsters* I propose a
        diacritical hermeneutics that is a third way.[22] This approach is close
        to that of thinkers like Paul Ricoeur, David Tracy, and Jim Olthuis. I
        propose mediations, connections, inter-links, and passages back and
        forth. So it's neither (a) a reappropriation and fusion of horizons à
        la Gadamer, nor is it (b) a complete gulf, separation, or rupture à la
        Caputo, Lyotard, and Derrida. Diacritical hermeneutics holds that
        faith is helped by narratives. Now I don't privilege in any exclusivist
        sense the Christian narratives over the Jewish or the Islamic or indeed
        the nonmonotheistic. I just say: "They're the ones I know best." If I
        were a Muslim, I'd work with Muslim narratives. If I were Jewish, I'd
        work with Jewish texts. (Indeed, as a Christian, I generally work with
        both Christian *and* Jewish narratives.) My niece, Emma, has become
        a Buddhist: I learn from Buddhist stories and I try to include them
        in my work. I still do it from a Christian perspective because that's
        what I'm most familiar with. But if I'd grown up in Kyoto, I would
        invoke the Buddhist texts first. I don't believe that any religion has an
        absolute right to the Absolute. There is no one Royal Route. There
        should be no proprietal prerogatives here. They're all narrative paths
        toward the Absolute. And if you happen to be born on this particular
        road or route rather than another one, and you've walked it for twenty
        or thirty years, then you know it better than another one, and you can
        help other people walk it. And from your knowledge of it, when you
        come to a crossroads, you may have more interesting and intelligent
        dialogue with the person who has come along the other highway. You
        know where you've come from and you can talk to them about it. They
        can learn from you and you can learn from them. Whereas if you say
        immediately: "Oh well, to hell with my highway! I'm only interested
        in yours," they might well respond: "Well, I'll tell you about mine,
        but do you have anything to add to the conversation?" And you'll

22. Richard Kearney, introduction to *Strangers, Gods, and Monsters.*

say: "No, no! I hate everything about my road! I've learnt nothing." I'm always a bit suspicious of overzealous converts who repudiate everything in their own traditions and look to some New Age trendy alternative for a solution—and that can be a Buddhist becoming a Christian as much as a Christian becoming a Buddhist. I'm all for dialogue between the two. Some people have to change their religions to shake off the tyranny of their tradition. Their experience may be *so* negative that they *need* to do that. And here you can have a kind of religious or cultural transvestism that is very helpful: you wear the clothes of another religion and through it you can see the spiritual in a way that you couldn't have done previously. I'm not against conversion as such, unless it's from one absolutist disposition to another absolutist disposition. I don't think any religion should be absolutist. I think it should be *searching for* the Absolute but the *search itself* should not be absolutist because that's to presume we can own the Absolute.

Where I am wary of a certain mystical New Ageism or deconstructionism is their tendency to repudiate historical narratives and memories as invariably compromising and totalizing. I see narratives and memories as necessary mediations. If you don't go down the route of hermeneutic reinterpretation, which is a "long route," as Ricoeur says, an arduous labor of reading and rereading,[23] then you must go toward the desert like Derrida and Caputo and their an-khorites. Which is hard. Or else you go toward the opposite, mystical extreme—not toward *khôra* this time (with Derrida and Caputo) but toward the "saturated phenomenon" or hyperessential divinity (with Marion or Michel Henry). But then it's another kind of "holy terror," because you're completely *blinded* by it. You embrace another kind of "dark" (from overexposure to the Absolute in the dark night of the soul). Here too it seems to me there is no interpretation possible. It's immediate, nonmediated presence. In both cases—whether you're going into the emptiness and undecidability of the *khôra* or whether you're going into the blinding overexposed splendor of divine saturation—you are subjected to an experience of "holy madness." Now, I'm not against that *as a moment.* But you can't live with the moment forever: you've got to interpret it after the event. Otherwise, what's the difference between Moses and the burning bush and Peter Sutcliffe in his pickup truck claiming he's hearing a so-called divine voice that says: "Go and kill prostitutes, do my will, clear the world of this evil scourge"?[24] What's the difference? There *must* be a difference. And we must try to discern as best we can between (a) psychopaths like Charlie Manson or Peter

23. See Paul Ricoeur, *Hermeneutics and the Human Sciences* (Cambridge: Cambridge University Press, 1981).

24. Peter Sutcliffe is the serial killer known as the "Yorkshire Ripper." He claimed that his killing spree was a divine mission.

Sutcliffe, who think they're on a divine mission to kill in the name of God, and (b) prophets like Moses or Isaiah, who go out to liberate and comfort their enslaved people. You have to be able to even *vaguely* and *approximately* tell the difference. No?

Q: *So we return to the problem of Abraham sacrificing his son?*

RK: Yes, but my reading of this episode is very different from Kierkegaard's and closer to Levinas's. The way to read that, I suggest, involves a critical hermeneutic retrieval. The story illustrates how monotheistic revelation is antisacrifice; it marks a move away from human sacrifice. This may be read, accordingly, as a story about the transition from a prerevelation to a revelation of monotheism. The first voice that Abraham hears—"Kill your son"—is, by this account, his *own voice*. It's the voice of his ancestral, tribal, sacrificial religion. But the second voice that says, "Do *not* kill your son," is the voice of the kingdom. That's how I read it. I think we should read every story in the Gospels according to the principle "Where is justice being preached here and where is injustice?" Where there's evil, you have to say "No" to it. You can find other passages in the Bible that say: "Go out and kill all Gentiles or Canaanites." If you take that literally you're into the Palestinian/Israeli situation or the war in Bosnia or Northern Ireland or Al Qaeda and the Taliban. You are into holy war. We should read such texts hermeneutically, critically, and say: "No! That was an interpolation by certain zealous scribes during a certain century." We need historical research on this. We need to demythologize it and say: They were trying to justify the occupation of their neighbors' lands. So ignore that mispresentation of divine revelation and look rather to the Psalms, where God calls for the protection of the widow, the stranger, and the orphan. The stranger is your neighbor—*that's* God speaking. "Go out and kill Canaanites" is *not* God speaking—that's *us* speaking. Knowing the difference is a matter of hermeneutic discernment. And it's a matter that concerns every believer, every reader of Scripture.

Q: *Nietzsche asks, "Can there be a God beyond good and evil?"*[25] *Maybe we're just projecting our idea that God is "simply good"; that God can only do "purely good things"?*

RK: Everyone makes their choice, but the God of love and justice is the only God I'm interested in. I'm not interested in the God of evil, torture, and sadism. I'm just not interested in those Gnostic (or neo-Gnostic) notions that see the dark side of God—destruction and holocaust—as an indispensable counterpart to the good side. Such theories or theodicies can justify *anything*.

---

25. Nietzsche asks in sec. 55 of *The Will to Power,* ed. Walter Kaufmann, trans. Walter Kaufmann and R. J. Hollingdale (New York: Vintage, 1968): "Does it make sense to conceive a god 'beyond good and evil'?"

Q: *But there is that possibility?*

RK: There *isn't* that possibility—for me, or at least it is one I refuse. It's
      how you interpret it. You can, of course, interpret divinity in terms
      of a moralizing God, where you say: "Oh, homosexuality, masturba-
      tion, divorce, sex outside of marriage, etc. is evil." That's the Christian
      Coalition, Jerry Falwell, Ian Paisley—they seem to know what's good
      for all of us! I'm against such a *moralizing* God but I'm not against an
      ethical God. There's a big difference. I *don't know* what the absolutely
      good is. How could anyone know? But I do *believe*—precisely because
      I can't know—the good exists and I will do everything to try to differ-
      entiate and discern (according to what Ignatius calls "the discernment
      of spirits") as best I can between the God of love and the pseudo-God
      of hate. I do believe that the divine is the good. In fact for me "God"
      is another name for "the good" rather than "the good" being another
      name for God. We don't know what the good is. We don't know what
      God is either. But they *must* be the same because if not, there's no way
      to avoid theodicy and its ruinous logic: "This war is necessary. It's all
      part of the will of God. It's the necessary dark side to God." Jung's
      answer to Job. Pangloss's answer to the Lisbon earthquake. Hegel's
      answer to the Terror. The rise of Divine Reason run amok. As humans,
      I agree, we have to confront the *thanatos,* the shadow in ourselves, the
      sadistic instincts, the perversions, the hate, the evil, the aggression. *We*
      have to confront the shadow in ourselves. But divinity doesn't have
      to confront the shadow in itself—because if it has evil in itself it is
      not God. If you say, "The shadow in God—the sacrifice of innocent
      children, the torture of victims—is part of God's will," well, frankly
      I'd prefer to burn in hell rather than believe in a God who justifies
      the torture of innocent children. And I'm not ambiguous about that.
      That said, I take a very dramatic example here that very few people
      would say is good because on many occasions it's very hard to tell
      what's absolutely good or evil. It is very hard for people to justify the
      torture of an innocent child. Should the Americans have dropped the
      atomic bomb in Hiroshima? I would say "No," but I'm not going to
      be too moralistic about that because I know there's an argument. You
      can negotiate that. Should a woman have an abortion? I would say:
      "Ideally not, but it's her right, and if she believes she is doing what is
      right, on balance, it may be the right thing for her to do." So I think
      a law that says "You can never have an abortion" is wrong. Abortion
      is very complex. It can be right in some respects, and wrong in oth-
      ers—*at the same time.* It may be right *and* wrong. Morality is often
      grey on grey; it's not black and white. Let's just say it is morally dif-
      ficult. And everyone—for or against—has a right to discuss it. That's
      what human morality is. It's not about absolutes. But when it comes

to God, who is absolute, either God is good or I'm not interested in God. This mixing evil with God is Gnosticism. I wrote my second novel, *Walking at Sea Level,* as an argument against that.[26]

Q: *There are all these other metaphysical characteristics ascribed to God: God is one, God is pure, and so on, and to say, "God is purely good"—*

RK: Well, I'm not sure I would use the word "purely" here because then you're back into puritanism. But I do insist on the claim that God is unconditionally and absolutely good or God is not God. I would not claim that I know what the good is. I would simply *try* to discern better between what is good and what is evil, or what is better and what is worse, what is more or less just in a *given* situation. I can recognize many instances of good acts where people put others before themselves and give up their lives or give up their wealth—that, to me, is a good thing to do. I want to reserve the right to say that. Whereas when somebody chops a child's head off, I want to be able to say: "That's *not* a good thing." I think most people would agree. That's not an absolutist disposition: it is common sense, practical wisdom, what the Greeks called *phronesis,* the Latins *prudentia.* Whenever someone does a good act—gives a cup of cold water to a parched neighbor—he or she is making God that little bit *more* real and actual and incarnate in the world. When someone does evil—torturing innocent children or simply stealing the cup of cold water from the parched neighbor who needs it more—he or she is refusing the possibilizing-desiring-transfiguring promise of God. In that sense evil is the refusal to let God exist.

Q: *In your legendary 1984 interview with Derrida, he explains that there have always been "heterogeneous elements" in Christianity.[27] Was he referring to scriptural motifs or mystical theology? Or both?*

RK: I don't know. You'd have to ask him. But I suspect that what he means by that is probably similar to what I've just been saying. There's no one pure religion. Christianity is heterogeneous. It draws from pagan elements, Jewish elements, Greek elements, etc.

Q: *The context was Greek philosophy or metaphysics, mainstream Christianity, and you referred to the official dogmas of the dominant churches, and then*

26. See my *Wlaking at Sea Level* (London: Hodder and Stoughton, 1998).

27. Richard Kearney asks Derrida the following question in his interview with him in *Dialogues with Contemporary Continental Thinkers: The Phenomenological Heritage: Paul Ricoeur, Emmanuel Levinas, Herbert Marcuse, Stanislas Breton, Jacques Derrida* (Manchester, U.K.: Manchester University Press, 1984), pp. 116–17: "But did not Judaism and Christianity represent a heterogeneity, an 'otherness' before they were assimilated into Greek culture?" To which Derrida replied: "Of course. And one can argue that these original, heterogeneous elements of Judaism and Christianity were never completely eradicated by Western metaphysics. They perdure throughout the centuries, threatening and unsettling the assured 'identities' of Western philosophy."

Derrida said: "Oh, no, I can see that there are heterogeneous elements."
But I didn't know if he meant biblical theology and some of the mystical
texts.

RK: Generally speaking, when Derrida says "There are heterogeneous
        elements" that's good news from his point of view. So I think he just
        wants to say: "Look, as I would interpret it, Christianity isn't just
        this triumphalist, totalizing, dogmatic, absolutist, intolerant body of
        beliefs. It's actually quite porous and permeable to dialogue with its
        other." And I would agree wholeheartedly with him here.

Q: *And there are marginal voices.*

RK: Exactly.

Q: *Having cited that line, do you think Derrida prefers the biblical over the*
        mystical?

RK: It depends how you define "the biblical" and "the mystical." There are
        elements of the mystical in Derrida. He is very taken, for example,
        by Pseudo-Dionysius, Eckhart, Silesius, Cusanus. But I think there
        are other forms of mysticism that Derrida would not have much time
        for: particularly the fusional and somewhat hysterical claim to be "one
        with God."

Q: *I haven't read many mystical theologians, but most of them say we can't*
        speak about God and then—

RK: They go and speak about God.

Q: *Yes, and affirm all the dogmas and say, "God is definitely Trinitarian,"*
        "God is this," and "God is that," and they just seem to slide back into this
        totalizing discourse.

RK: Then they're not really good mystics, I would say.

Q: *Wouldn't mystical theology—taken to its logical or alogical conclusion—*
        have to say: "I'm going to suspend my beliefs on, say, the creeds of the
        churches, because the creeds are as positive as you can get"? I was just
        wondering how the mystics can balance their mysticism with their
        denominational affirmations. Dionysius wasn't considered a heretic.

RK: Most of them were. Eckhart was. John Scotus Erigena was. Bruno
        and Vico were. They were in favor one moment, out the next. These
        thinkers were trying to make sense to their fellow believers. They had
        had these deep, spiritual experiences and were profoundly touched
        and were trying to reconcile these experiences with the doctrine of the
        virgin birth or the Filioque or something like that. They were mucking
        along. They were trying to be loved and accepted by their brethren in
        the monastery. Otherwise they were out in the rain with no food. We
        compromise and we muddle through. I would say here, again, that

Derrida often discriminates: he picks and chooses—and rightly so. He's an à la carte rabbinical interpreter. Just think of his reflections on biblical passages in *Schibboleth* or "Circumfession," for example.[28] Or again in "Donner la mort" (*The Gift of Death*), where Derrida goes back to the Abraham story.[29] He takes what inspires him and rejects the kind of Zionist triumphalism that says: "Death to all Arabs." So he discriminates. You might say: "Well, *how* do you discriminate, Mr. Derrida, since there are no criteria and we can only read in the dark?" But that's another day's work. Maybe it's a performative contradiction but, happily, he does exercise it. He discriminates. He differentiates. He discerns. He's on the side of the good. Deconstruction is not a justification for evil. It's not an apologia for an "anything goes" relativism—as some of its critics unconditionally suggest.

Q: *In the end, deconstruction is just trying to affirm that whatever is going on in the world—*

RK: No, that's Heidegger. Derrida, as I understand him, is saying: "I'm for justice. I'm for the gift. I'm for the good. I'm for the democracy to come." He's not saying: "It doesn't matter whether it's democracy or totalitarianism. It doesn't matter whether it's justice or injustice. It doesn't matter whether it's gift or selfishness." He's not saying that at all. Derrida is on the side of liberty. All his thinking, politically and ethically, is emancipatory. The differences I have with Derrida are not in terms of his values and his politics—but how one gets there. That's a practical question. I think hermeneutics, *informed by* a certain deconstructive caution, vigilance, and scrupulosity, is a better way of getting there than deconstruction on its own (without hermeneutics). That's where I part company with Caputo, Derrida, and Lyotard. But they're all on the side of the good as I see it. I'm not saying: "We're morally pure." I'm saying that the good is something we aspire to, something that is "impossible" in its *absolute* sense but possible in all kinds of different tiny practical ways. The messianic is potentially present in every moment, even though we can never be sure whether it comes or goes.

28. Jacques Derrida's *Schibboleth—pour Paul Celan* (Paris: Galilée, 1986) and "Circumfession: Fifty-nine Periods and Periphrases" in *Jacques Derrida*, with Geoffrey Bennington (Chicago: University of Chicago Press, 1993).

29. Derrida's essay "Donner la mort" appears in the book *L'Ethique du don: Jacques Derrida et la pensée du don*, ed. Jean-Michel Rabaté and Michael Wetzel (Paris: Métailié-Transition, 1992). The English version of the essay is titled *The Gift of Death*, trans. David Wills (Chicago: University of Chicago Press, 1995).

4

If I Had a Hammer

Truth in Heidegger's Being and Time[1]

Lambert Zuidervaart

> "Love as gift . . . suggests a new thematization of meaning and truth as
> good connections, in contrast to both modernity's power, control,
> judgment, and postmodernism's disruption and dissemination of
> any claim of entitlement to meaning and truth."
>
> James H. Olthuis[2]

Central themes in the recent work of James Olthuis echo the concerns of Martin Heidegger's pathbreaking *Sein und Zeit* (*Being and Time*): love (Heidegger: *Sorge*),[3] human existence as gift and call (Dasein),[4] and the hermeneutics of connection (*Erschlossenheit*).[5] In retrospect, even Olthuis's earlier writings on

1. A very early draft of this essay was presented in December 1994 to the "Philosophischer Kreis" at the Institut für Philosophie, Freie Universiteit Berlin, under the title "Truth as Disclosure: In Critique of Heidegger." Some of the essay's ideas were tested in a seminar on "Language, Truth, and Postmodern Culture: Heidegger, Rorty, and Derrida" that I led with James Olthuis and Hendrik Hart in the summer of 2000. I thank the participants at both occasions for their helpful comments. I especially want to thank Henk Hart for his detailed criticisms of a more recent version.

2. James H. Olthuis, "Crossing the Threshold: Sojourning Together in the Wild Spaces of Love," in *Knowing Otherwise: Philosophy at the Threshold of Spirituality,* ed. James H. Olthuis (New York: Fordham University Press, 1997), pp. 235–57; quote from pp. 247–48.

3. See, for example, James Olthuis's essay "Crossing the Threshold," cited in n. 2 above.

4. James H. Olthuis, "Be(com)ing: Humankind as Gift and Call," *Philosophia Reformata* 58 (1993): 153–72.

5. James H. Olthuis, "Otherwise than Violence: Toward a Hermeneutics of Connection," in *The Arts, Community, and Cultural Democracy,* ed. Lambert Zuidervaart and Henry Luttikhuizen (London: Macmillan; New York: St. Martin's, 2000), pp. 137–64.

fidelity in ethical relationships[6] remind one of lectures given prior to *Sein und Zeit,* in which biblical and Christian sources helped Heidegger reconceptualize "truth" as a process of keeping troth.[7] Thanks in part to the philosophy of Herman Dooyeweerd and D. H. T. Vollenhoven, who shared Heidegger's concerns but took them in a different direction, Olthuis has brought the reformational tradition into fruitful dialogue with post-Heideggerian thinking. He has contributed a creation-affirming voice to what is often a "hermeneutics of fallenness,"[8] maintaining, amid the complexities of this dialogue, an admirable passion for social justice in solidarity with the marginalized and oppressed. So Jim's retirement is an excellent occasion for a former student and grateful colleague to revisit the idea of truth (*Wahrheit*) in Heidegger's magnum opus. Many shared concerns surface in this idea, along with issues that continue to vex post-Heideggerian thinkers.

The conception of truth proposed by *Being and Time* is both provocative and problematic. On the one hand, Heidegger provides a way to reconnect technical accounts of truth within logic, epistemology, and philosophy of language with the cultural practices and social institutions from which such accounts take distance. He does so by developing an ontological alternative to a pervasive "logical prejudice" in Western philosophy.[9] On the other hand, Heidegger takes such a dim view of "everydayness" and public communication that attaining truth becomes the inexplicable privilege of "authentic" existence. This privileging of authentic existence ensnares his counterontology in the self-referential incoherence of theorizing what, according to his own theory, cannot be theorized.[10] The promise and the problems of Heidegger's proposal are meshed. To redeem its potential, one must criticize its inherent flaws and ideological functions.

I hope to show that *Being and Time* has much to offer for a critical hermeneutic theory of truth, more than could be acknowledged by Theodor W.

6. James H. Olthuis, *I Pledge You My Troth: A Christian View of Marriage, Family, Friendship* (New York: Harper & Row, 1975); *Keeping Our Troth: Staying in Love through the Five Stages of Marriage* (San Francisco: Harper, 1986).

7. See n. 42 below.

8. See James K. A. Smith, *The Fall of Interpretation: Philosophical Foundations for a Creational Hermeneutic* (Downers Grove, Ill.: InterVarsity, 2000), especially part two (pp. 85–129).

9. See Daniel O. Dahlstrom, *Heidegger's Concept of Truth* (Cambridge, U.K., and New York: Cambridge University Press, 2001). By "logical prejudice" Dahlstrom means a widespread assumption that assertions, propositions, sentences, and the like are the site of truth on which the truth of anything else depends. It is "the tendency to conceive truth in terms of a specific sort of discourse, namely, in terms of claims, assertions, and judgments, that are formed as indicative, declarative sentences. . . . For those who cling to this 'model of propositional truth,' 'the predicates "true," "false," are paradigmatically attributes of sentences, statements, claims, judgments, assertions, propositions, and the like'" (Dahlstrom, p. 17, citing an article by Carl Friedrich Gethmann). I should add that the logical prejudice need not be peculiar to correspondence theories of truth, although Heidegger's own conception is intended as an alternative to correspondence theories. It can also be found in coherence, consensus, and pragmatic theories of truth.

10. "Self-referential incoherence" is my cryptic formulation for the "paradox of thematization" so carefully described by Dahlstrom, pp. 202–10, 236–42, 252–55, 264–68, 433–56.

Adorno, whose critique of Heidegger shapes my own interpretation.[11] My aim is to fashion an alternative conception of truth that frees Heidegger's insights from what I consider to be a reactionary construction. As will become apparent, my alternative is to conceive truth as a process of life-giving disclosure to which a differentiated array of cultural practices and products contribute in distinct and indispensable ways. Linguistic claims and logical propositions belong to such an array, but so do, say, the practices and products of art. Let me first summarize Heidegger's argument for conceiving truth as disclosedness (sec. 1). Then I shall consider his claims that assertion or statement (*Aussage*) is a derivative mode of interpretation (sec. 2 below) and that Dasein's disclosedness is the primary locus of truth (sec. 3).[12]

1. Heidegger's Hammer

Section 44, titled "Dasein, Disclosedness, and Truth" (SZ 212–30), gives the central presentation of Heidegger's conception of truth in *Being and Time*. This section simultaneously concludes the book's first division, titled "The Preparatory Fundamental Analysis of Dasein," and the sixth chapter in this division, titled "Care as the Being of Dasein." It not only summarizes and deepens Heidegger's analysis of "being-in-the-world" as the "basic state of Dasein" but also marks a transition to interpreting this state as thoroughly temporal in division two (titled "Dasein and Temporality"). In this doubly laden context, Heidegger argues that the primary locus of truth is not propositions or assertions or discursive claims. Rather, the primary locus is the disclosedness of that being (Dasein) which, among other activities, understands and formulates and discusses assertions. While making this argument, Heidegger hammers the correspondence theory of truth, traditionally formulated as the *adaequatio intellectus et rei*, into a conception of "disclosedness" (*Erschlossenheit*) and "discoveredness" (*Entdecktheit*).

Heidegger aims to ask about the meaning of Being. He approaches this question by analyzing and interpreting Dasein (i.e., human being) as that entity for whom Being is a question. While distinguishing Dasein from entities such as tools that are "at hand" or "handy" (*zuhanden*) as well as from entities such as

11. Passages in translation are taken from Martin Heidegger, *Being and Time*, trans. Joan Stambaugh (Albany: State University of New York Press, 1996). Page numbers refer to the pagination in *Sein und Zeit* (abbreviated "SZ"), as found in the margins of English translations. The German edition I have used is *Sein und Zeit*, 15th ed. (Tübingen, Germany: Max Niemeyer, 1979). I have also consulted *Being and Time*, trans. John Macquarrie and Edward Robinson (New York: Harper & Row, 1962). I give preference to the Macquarrie/Robinson translation in retaining "Being" (capital "B") for "Sein" and in not hyphenating Dasein (which, for the most part, is not hyphenated in *Sein und Zeit* but is always hyphenated in Joan Stambaugh's translation). These modifications are made without comment in the citations and in my own text. Other relevant modifications to citations from the Stambaugh translation are marked by square brackets.

12. A more complete treatment, which I have provided elsewhere, would also examine the role that "authenticity" plays in Heidegger's emphasis on disclosedness.

scientifically defined physical things that are "objectively present" (*vorhanden*), Heidegger analyzes the three directions taken by Dasein's "being-in-the-world" (*In-der-Welt-sein*): "being together with the world," "being-with" others, and "being-one's-self." In more traditional language, which Heidegger carefully avoids, he distinguishes three types of relations—subject/object, subject/subject, and subject/self—only to argue that they form a unitary structure founded in Dasein's "being-in." Their unity becomes apparent from the terms he uses to summarize Dasein's orientation in the first two directions: taking care (*Besorgen*) of that which is handy, and concern (*Fürsorge*) toward fellow human beings. Both orientations rest in a more fundamental care (*Sorge*). Moreover, Dasein's dealings are guided by circumspection (*Umsicht*) toward the handy and by considerateness (*Rücksicht*) and tolerance (*Nachsicht*) toward others. These guides are made possible by the sight (*Sicht*) that characterizes Dasein's being-in as such. Such sight is what Heidegger calls understanding (*Verstehen*). Together with attunement (*Befindlichkeit*) and talk (*Rede*), understanding is one of three "equiprimordial" modes or structures (*existentialia*) of Dasein's being-in.[13]

Two fundamental points affect everything Heidegger writes about understanding and talk. First, both understanding and talk are modes of Dasein's disclosedness. Second, since Dasein's disclosedness follows the orientation of care, and since temporality (*Zeitlichkeit*) is "the ontological meaning of care" (sec. 65), temporality characterizes both understanding and talk (sec. 68). Let me briefly elaborate each point.

The first point pertains to the essential openness that characterizes Dasein. Unlike other entities, Dasein not only occupies a field of relationships but also holds itself open in these relationships. For Dasein, that which is at hand resides in a significant totality of relevance (*Bewandtnis*), even when Dasein experiences or analyzes what is at hand, in abstraction from its relevance, as something merely objectively present. So too, Dasein's selfhood is always constituted by coexistence with others for whom what is at hand has significance, even when we regularly experience ourselves as indifferent members of a mass public (as *das Man* or "the they"). In other words, Dasein is essentially open to its world and its fellows. It is because of this openness that the world lies open to human dealings and that, despite inauthenticity and indifference, human

13. Heidegger first identifies understanding and attunement as the constitutive and equiprimordial ways of Dasein's disclosedness and says they in turn "are equiprimordially determined by [*talk*]" (SZ 133). (To avoid confusion with Habermas's notion of discourse [*Diskurs*], I shall use other terms than "discourse" to render Heidegger's *Rede*—usually "talk" or "conversation.") Later he says that talk is "*existentially equiprimordial with attunement and understanding*" (SZ 161), thereby suggesting that talk is a third equiprimordial mode of disclosedness. Elsewhere, "falling prey" or "entanglement" (*Verfallen*) is added to the list of "the structures in which disclosedness constitutes itself" (SZ 334–35). At this point, not much hangs on whether only two or more of these are equiprimordial modes of disclosedness. Despite the originality and significance of Heidegger's discussion of attunement, especially with regard to fear (*Furcht*) and anxiety (*Angst*) (see secs. 30 and 40), I restrict my summary to understanding and talk, since these have a more direct bearing on Heidegger's critique of traditional theories of truth.

beings remain open to themselves and one another. In Heidegger's own words, Dasein (literally "there-being") "bears in its ownmost being the character of not being closed. The expression 'there' means this essential disclosedness. Through disclosedness, this being (Dasein) is 'there' for itself together with the Dasein of the world. . . . By its very nature, Dasein brings its there along with it. . . . *Dasein is its [disclosedness]*" (SZ 132–33).

The second point pertains to the kind of temporality that underlies understanding and talk, respectively, and unites them in the structure of care.[14] Heidegger arrives at the theme of temporality by examining "anticipatory resoluteness" as the authentic and most primordial truth of Dasein (SZ 297), as Dasein's "*authentic* potentiality-for-being-a-whole" (SZ 301). His interpretation of the temporality of understanding aims to uncover the "temporality of disclosedness in general" (sec. 68) and thereby to show how "the inauthenticity of Dasein is ontologically grounded" (SZ 335). Heidegger claims that understanding, which always projects Dasein's potentiality-of-being (*Seinkönnen*), is essentially futural, even when understanding is inauthentic.[15] In contrast to understanding, talk, which articulates the disclosedness constituted by understanding and attunement, does not have an essential temporalization, whether future, past, or present. "Factically," however, the "making-present" that characterizes inauthentic understanding has "a *privileged* constitutive function" in ordinary talk (SZ 349). Crucial in this context is the claim that both Dasein's disclosedness and its "basic existential possibilities" of "authenticity and inauthenticity" are "founded in temporality" in the manner described (SZ 350). By extension, the futural character of understanding, and the anticipatory resoluteness of authentic understanding, provide preconditions for the disclosure of other entities.

Reconstructed, and reduced to bare outline, Heidegger's argument against the traditional correspondence theory of truth, and for his own conception of truth as disclosedness, runs as follows:[16]

1. Dasein understands itself, others, and its world by projecting Dasein's own potentials and possibilities from within its own factual context. Understanding is characterized by projective thrownness or thrown projection.

---

14. Here and elsewhere I ignore the distinction between *Zeitlichkeit* (temporality) and *Temporalität* (Temporality) in *Sein und Zeit*. Karin de Boer gives a detailed account of this distinction in *Thinking in the Light of Time: Heidegger's Encounter with Hegel* (Albany: State University of New York Press, 2000).

15. Whereas authentic understanding throws itself into the future as a possibility, inauthentic understanding simply awaits the object of its concern. The related contrasts with regard to present and past are the authentic moment of vision (*Augenblick*) versus an inauthentic making present (*Gegenwärtigen*), and authentic repetition or retrieval (*Wiederholung*) versus inauthentic forgetting (*Vergessen*). Heidegger summarizes as follows: "*Awaiting that forgets and makes present* is an ecstatic unity in its own right, in accordance with which inauthentic understanding temporalizes itself. . . . The unity of these ecstasies closes off one's authentic potentiality-of-being, and is thus the existential condition of the possibility of irresoluteness" (SZ 339).

16. See especially SZ, secs. 31–34 and 44.

2. Through such projection, understanding (*Verstehen*) lets entities be encountered in their discoveredness (*Entdecktheit*) by Dasein in its disclosedness (*Erschlossenheit*).

3. Such an encounter is developed in interpretation (*Auslegung*) as a working out (*Ausarbeitung*) of projected possibilities.

4. When directed at understanding the world, interpretation works out the purposes for which something exists by elaborating its embeddedness in a purposive whole, on the basis of a prior understanding.[17] Often such circumspect interpretation is prepredicative.

5. Assertion or statement (*Aussage*) is a derivative mode of interpretation (*Auslegung*), which itself is an outworking (*Ausbildung*) of understanding.[18]

6. By "pointing out" or indicating (*Aufzeigen*) an entity in abstraction from its purposive involvements, assertion "determines" (*bestimmt*) something (predication—*Prädikation*) and communicates this indication and predication to others (communication—*Mitteilung*).

7. At the same time, unlike ordinary circumspect interpretation, which approaches a hammer, for example, as something serviceable within a totality of relevance, assertion forces the hermeneutical "as" back to "the uniform level of what is merely objectively present. . . . This levelling down of the primordial 'as' of circumspect interpretation to the as of the determination of objective presence is the specialty of the [assertion]" (SZ 158).

8. The communication of shared attunements and common understandings is made possible by talk (*Rede*), which gets expressed in language (*Sprache*) and which articulates meaning.[19]

17. More specifically, Heidegger argues that "circumspect interpretation" rests on the three projective involvements that understanding has with the world: fore-having, fore-sight, and fore-conception (*Vorhabe, Vorsicht,* and *Vorgriff*), which could also be translated as pre-possession, pre-view, and pre-conception. An interpretation is never a neutral gathering of bare facts. According to Heidegger, there is a circle in all interpretation, even in so simple an act as finding the right hammer for a particular task. "Every interpretation which is to contribute some understanding must already have understood what is to be interpreted" (SZ 152). This is the ontological basis for the familiar hermeneutical circle in the interpretation of texts.

18. Stambaugh translates *die Aussage* as "statement." I follow Macquarrie and Robinson in translating it as "assertion."

19. My formulation here ignores Heidegger's careful distinctions among intelligibility (*Verständlichkeit*), meaning (*Sinn*), the totality of significations (*Bedeutungsganze*), and significations (*Bedeutungen*). "Meaning" refers to that which can be articulated (*das Artikulierbare*) in talk, just as "intelligibility" refers to that which can be understood and interpreted. A crucial point for Heidegger's analysis of talk is that whatever is intelligible has already been articulated (*gegliedert*), even prior to being interpreted and asserted: "[Talk] is the articulation [*Artikulation*] of intelligibility. Thus it already lies at the basis of interpretation and statement [*Aussage*]" (SZ 161). The "totality of significations" refers to the entirety of what is articulated in talk. With this term, Heidegger draws attention to the claim that discrete articulations or "significations" belong to a larger totality. Similarly, although words accrue to discrete significations, this occurrence belongs to a larger process: "The totality of significations . . . *is put into* words" (SZ 161), and the totality of those words is language, in which talk gets expressed. (For more on the concept of "meaning," see SZ 150–53, 156, and 323–25.)

9. The making of assertions is only one of the many ways in which we communicate in talk. Assertoric communication is a special case of a more comprehensive "articulation of being-with-one-another understandingly" (SZ 162).

10. In a mass society, where Dasein is thrown "into the publicness [*Öffentlichkeit*] of the they" (SZ 167), talk ordinarily occurs as idle talk (*Gerede*) that closes off our being-in-the-world and covers over "innerworldly beings" (SZ 169). So too understanding ordinarily occurs as a restless, distracted, and uprooted curiosity (*Neugier*) that makes it impossible to decide "what is disclosed in a genuine understanding, and what is not" (SZ 173). Such idle talk, curiosity, and ambiguity manifest the "falling prey" (*Verfallen*) to public existence that characterizes Dasein in its inauthentic mode of being-in-the-world.[20]

11. The modern conception of truth treats assertion (*die Aussage*) or judgment (*das Urteil*) as the locus of truth. It defines truth as the judgment's agreement (*Übereinstimmung*) with its object (*Gegenstand*).

12. Contrary to common views, such agreement does not mean that mental representations (*Vorstellungen*) get compared among themselves or in relation to the so-called "real thing," but rather that the asserted entity "shows itself *as* [*that*] *very same thing*." The truth of an assertion is a being-true (*Wahrsein*), in the sense of discovering the asserted entity as it is in itself (SZ 218).[21]

13. Such being-true as to-be-discovering (*Entdeckend-sein*) is made possible ontologically by Dasein's basic state of being-in-the-world (SZ 219).[22]

20. Contrary to my formulation, Heidegger would not say that falling prey is restricted to a mass society. Idle talk, for example, "does not first originate through certain conditions which influence Dasein 'from the outside'" (SZ 177). Rather, falling prey "reveals an *essential*, ontological structure of Dasein itself" (SZ 179). Nevertheless, his characterization of falling prey is clearly indebted to and descriptive of a social condition in which the structure and principle of publicity (*Öffentlichkeit*) hold sway. In that sense, despite his disclaimer that the term "does not express any negative value judgment" (SZ 175), it is hard to read his account of "falling prey" or "entanglement" as anything other than a critique of mass society and of democratic tendencies within it.

21. My paraphrase from SZ 218 is closer to the Macquarrie and Robinson translation than to the Stambaugh translation. Heidegger writes that the discoveredness (*Entdecktheit*) of an entity "bewährt sich darin, dass sich das Ausgesagte, das ist das Seiende selbst, *als dasselbe* zeigt." Macquarrie and Robinson translate: "This uncoveredness is confirmed when that which is put forward in the assertion (namely the entity itself) shows itself *as that very same thing*" (p. 261). Stambaugh translates: "This [the referent is unspecified] is confirmed by the fact that what is stated (that is, the being itself) shows itself *as the very same thing*" (p. 201). A few lines later Heidegger writes: "Die Aussage *ist wahr*, bedeutet: sie entdeckt das Seiende an ihm selbst." Macquarrie and Robinson translate: "To say that an assertion '*is true*' signifies that it uncovers the entity as it is in itself." Stambaugh translates: "To say that a statement is *true* means that it discovers the beings in themselves." By rendering the singular "das Seiende" with the plural "beings," Stambaugh weakens the force of the sentence. Macquarrie and Robinson take a liberty by rendering "an ihm selbst" with "as it is in itself," but that phrase is prominent in the previous paragraph, where Heidegger writes "Das gemeinte Seiende selbst zeigt sich *so, wie* es an ihm selbst ist." (SZ 218).

22. In this context Heidegger says that his definition of truth provides "the *necessary* interpretation of what the oldest tradition of ancient philosophy primordially surmised and even understood in a pre-

The truth of assertion reaches back via interpretation "to the disclosed-ness of understanding" (SZ 223).

14. More specifically, just as discovering (*Entdecken*) and the discovered-ness (*Entdecktheit*) of entities are grounded in the world's disclosedness (*Erschlossenheit*), so the assertion's to-be-discovering (*Entdeckend-sein*) is grounded in Dasein's disclosedness (*Erschlossenheit*), without which the world would not be disclosed.

15. Hence, "only with the disclosedness of Dasein is the *most primordial* phenomenon of truth attained. . . . In that Dasein essentially *is* its disclosedness, and, as disclosed, discloses and discovers, it is essentially 'true.' Dasein *is 'in the truth'*" (SZ 220–21).

16. Dasein's disclosedness is both authentic (i.e., governed by Dasein's "own-most potentiality-of-being," SZ 221) and inauthentic (i.e., governed by "public interpretedness," SZ 222). Hence Dasein is equiprimordially not only in the truth but also in untruth. Yet inauthenticity and being in untruth are made possible by disclosedness and discoveredness; truth must be wrested from the inauthenticity of Dasein and the concealment (*Verborgenheit*) of entities.

17. The traditional conception of truth as the agreement of assertion and object covers up the ontological foundations from which such agreement derives (SZ 223–26). Contrary to this traditional conception, "[Assertion] is not the primary 'locus' of truth," but is itself grounded in the primary locus of truth, namely, in Dasein's disclosedness. Dasein's disclosedness is "the ontological condition of the possibility that [assertions] can be true or false (discovering or covering over)" (SZ 226).

18. Since disclosedness is essential to Dasein's being, "*all truth is relative to the being of Dasein*" (SZ 227), not in the sense that truth is left to subjective discretion or constituted by a transcendental subject, but in the sense that without Dasein's disclosedness there would be neither authenticity nor inauthenticity, neither discovering nor covering over, neither discoveredness nor concealment, and neither true assertions nor false assertions.[23] Truth is relative to Dasein's *being,* not to Dasein's will or to its consciousness.

19. Neither the dogmatic claim that there are eternal truths nor general skepticism about truth has an adequate ontological basis. Both posi-tions overlook the reciprocal and foundational relationship between truth and Dasein: just as truth belongs to the core of Dasein's being, so Dasein exists for the sake of truth. Moreover, such reciprocity extends to Being, toward whose understanding Dasein, in its disclosedness, is

---

phenomenological way." That is to say, his definition recaptures the alethic sense in which apophantic reason and discourse (*logos*) can be true, namely, "to let beings be seen in their unconcealment [*Unverborgenheit*] (discoveredness [*Entdecktheit*]), taking them out of their concealment [*Verborgenheit*]" (SZ 219). (See also the discussion of the concepts of *logos* and *aletheia* in Heidegger's Introduction, SZ 32–34.)

23. Note the three characterizations of truth in SZ 226: "disclosedness, discovering, and discoveredness."

predisposed. "'There is' [*Es gibt*] Being—not beings—only insofar as truth is. And truth *is* only because and as long as Dasein is. Being and truth 'are' equiprimordially" (SZ 230).

Some readers are tempted to accuse Heidegger of "subjectivizing" truth, in the sense of reducing it to a condition or quality of human existence: after all, he does claim that all truth is relative to Dasein's being. Yet such an accusation ignores his explicit opposition to subjectivism and his marked preference for substantives such as disclosedness and discoveredness over verbs such as disclose and discover. This leads other readers to claim that Heidegger turns truth into a state of Being, one for which Dasein's being-in-the-world is crucial but perhaps not decisive. Accordingly, the fatal flaw in Heidegger's conception, one that deepens in his later writings, might lie in his both dehumanizing and structuralizing a dynamic process of disclosure. It seems to me, however, that neither the first nor the second reading does justice to the scope of Heidegger's project and to fundamental tensions in his own conception of truth. There is a sense in which Heidegger both subjectivizes and dehumanizes truth. To derive an adequate alternative, one must wrestle with both tendencies in their dialectical tension.[24] Let me develop this "fore-conception" by investigating Heidegger's accounts of assertion (sec. 2 below) and disclosedness (sec. 3).

2. Assertion and Interpretation

Heidegger lays out the derivative character of assertion in order to deconstruct the ontological foundations of correspondence theories of truth. In the process, he makes a number of claims that, when taken together, diminish the role of assertions in the pursuit of truth and belittle their significance. Although such may not have been the clear intent of his formulations, arguably it has been their dominant effect, and it has led to readings that exaggerate antilogical tendencies in Heidegger's conception of truth. Let me first sketch two examples of how Heidegger can be read to this effect, and how alternative

24. I take the clue for this dialectical line of critical interpretation from Adorno's discussion of Heidegger in *Negative Dialectics*, even though I think Adorno misinterprets Heidegger's attempt to interrelate Dasein, truth, and Being. See Theodor W. Adorno, *Negative Dialectics*, trans. E. B. Ashton (New York: Seabury, 1973), pp. 59–131 (I will abbreviate this source as "ND"); *Negative Dialektik*, Gesammelte Schriften 6 (Frankfurt am Main: Suhrkamp, 1973), pp. 67–136 (I will abbreviate this source as "GS6"). Here are some representative passages from Adorno: "The concept of 'existential' things [*des Existentiellen*] . . . is governed by the idea that the measure of truth is not its objectivity, of whichever kind, but the pure being-that-way and acting-that-way of the thinker. . . . But truth, the constellation of subject and object in which both penetrate each other, can no more be reduced to subjectivity than to that Being whose dialectical relation to subjectivity Heidegger tends to blur" [*zu verwischen trachtet*] (ND 127; GS6: 133). "[Heidegger's notion of] historicality immobilizes history in the unhistorical realm, heedless of the historical conditions that govern the inner composition and constellation of subject and object" (ND 129; GS6: 135).

readings could counter what may not have been his clear intent. Then I shall analyze the claim that assertion is a derivative mode of interpretation.

Heidegger points out that the making of assertions [*Aussagen machen*] is only one of many practices within talk (alongside commanding, wishing, interceding, etc. [SZ 161–62]), and that self-expression, hearing, and keeping silent are constitutive for talk (SZ 162–65). Here he can be read as saying that the making of assertions is not nearly as important as traditional philosophy and linguistics have claimed, and that other practices and "existential possibilities" are more important to ordinary language than is the making of assertions. On a different and, I think, preferable interpretation, however, the main point about asserting would be that it normally occurs in connection with these other practices and as a way to actualize such existential possibilities. It is precisely because of such embeddedness, and because of the role of assertions in pursuing intersubjective understanding, that the making and discussing of assertions become crucial to public "talk" and deserve the special attention of philosophers and linguists, no matter how misguided previous accounts may have been. The task, then, would not simply be that of "*freeing* grammar from logic," as Heidegger puts it (SZ 165), but also liberating logic from its reification of the practice of making assertions.

Similarly, when Heidegger argues that the agreement of assertion and object derives from the disclosedness of Dasein and the discoveredness of entities, he embeds a thinner epistemological correspondence between subjective product and independent object in a thicker ontological harmony between the state of Dasein and the state of other entities. Described as a relation commonly understood as merely "objectively present" (SZ 224), the thinner correspondence comes to appear less important for truth than the thicker harmony. This despite the fact that Heidegger's account of the thicker harmony seems to remain within the modern correspondence theory's subject/object paradigm, to which he explicitly objects. On a different and more fruitful reading, however, the crucial "agreement" would not be between the assertion and the object but among those who make assertions about the object, as well as between the process of making assertions and recognized principles for intersubjective conversation. Such an alternative, with its emphasis on the search for intersubjective "agreement" in accordance with recognized principles, can be extracted from Heidegger's account of "being-in-the-world" as including "being-with" others. Yet his critique of correspondence theories and his locating of truth in Dasein's disclosedness make little of this intersubjective mode. In fact, his initial orientation to circumspect interpretation of the handy, combined with his disparaging view of the public sphere, makes it difficult to extract this alternative without violence.

What, more specifically, needs to be said about the purported derivativeness of assertion or statement (*die Aussage*)? To examine this topic, let me introduce a distinction and make a related comment. In the first place, the intelligibility of Heidegger's claims depends on a distinction between the making of assertions as a cultural *practice* and the availability of assertions as cultural *accomplishments.* Heidegger tends to elide or ignore this distinction. I shall mark it by using "asserting" and "assertion" as technical terms, respectively, for the practice and the accomplishment at issue. In the second place, the derivation of asserting and assertion from (the practices and accomplishments of) interpretation does not entail that the asserted (*das Ausgesagte*) simply acquires a definite character when asserted. Rather, the asserted can already array itself (or offer itself) in definable ways, and this array can impinge upon interpretation, even when interpretation is nonassertoric. Although such arraying and impinging do not by themselves give the asserted a definite character, neither does the asserted's becoming definable simply depend on its being asserted. The reasons for making this comment will emerge from my more detailed discussion of the purported derivation of *die Aussage* from interpretation (*Auslegung*). Let me turn first to Heidegger's account of what I have distinguished as asserting and assertion, before I examine his account of the asserted.

Asserting and Assertion

Heidegger distinguishes three significations of the term "assertion" (*die Aussage*): pointing out (*Aufzeigung*), predication (*Prädikation*), and communication (*Mitteilung*). Of these, pointing out, which lets an entity be seen from itself (SZ 154), is the primary signification. Heidegger considers predication to be founded in pointing out, which is broader, and he describes communication as an extension of pointing out and predication. The primacy he assigns to "pointing out" becomes apparent from his unifying definition of assertion as "*a pointing out which communicates and defines*" [*mitteilend bestimmende Aufzeigung*] (SZ 156). He does not define assertion as predication that points out and communicates or as communication that points out and predicates. So too, he does not describe assertion as a mode of talk but as a mode of interpretation.

Heidegger's account of interpretation has a prior orientation to the purposive conduct of craftspersons and the users of tools. This orientation shapes the contrast Heidegger draws between the categorical statement "the hammer is heavy," understood by logicians to mean "this thing, the hammer, has the property of heaviness," and related formulations common to ordinary talk:

"Initially" there are no such statements in heedful circumspection. But it does have its specific ways of interpretation which . . . may take some such form as "the hammer is too heavy" or, even better, "too heavy, the other hammer!" The primordial act of interpretation lies not in a theoretical sentence, but in circumspectly and heedfully putting away or changing the inappropriate tool "without wasting words." (SZ 157)

Given this prior orientation to purposive conduct, Heidegger analyzes assertion primarily as a practice rather than an accomplishment, and one that is originally purposive, although tending toward abstraction:

> The [assertion's] pointing out is accomplished on the basis of what is already disclosed in understanding, or what is circumspectly discovered. The [assertion] is not an unattached kind of behavior which could of itself primarily disclose beings in general, but always already maintains itself on the basis of being-in-the-world. (SZ 156)

By emphasizing the practice of *asserting* and its ontological roots in Dasein, Heidegger creates the impression that *assertions as such,* as accomplishments, are cut off from the totality of human involvements with the world, with theoretical assertions being the farthest removed.

Unfortunately Heidegger's approach presupposes a problematic hierarchy of originality according to which the accomplishment is derivative from the practice, and the more explicit and more definite practice is derivative from ones less explicit and less definite. Only such a hierarchy can explain why predication should be considered "narrower" than pointing out (rather than, for example, more precise and inclusive), or why asserting "x is y" should be thought to arise via modification from circumspect interpretation (rather than simply constituting one type of purposive conduct, perhaps, or shaping or even giving rise to circumspect interpretation). While I acknowledge, with Heidegger, that, once accomplished, an assertion can be discussed and analyzed in its own right and in abstraction from the occasion and circumstances for making the assertion, this fact in itself does not warrant the view that accomplished assertions are cut off from other human involvements with the world.

In addition, the force of "pointing out" depends on its connections with predication and communication. I see no reason to think that a prepredicative and noncommunicative pointing out would have any intrinsic connection with asserting and assertions. Consider, for example, Heidegger, in the privacy of his shop, simply pointing his finger at a hammer while thinking, "The hammer is too heavy." He might be pointing something out, but he would not be asserting anything, nor would any assertion become available as an accomplishment. Far from being founded in pointing out, predication is that which allows any pointing out to become assertoric. Insofar as asserting is an illocutionary act that requires an interpretable utterance in a public language, a private thought not communicated to anyone else, no matter how "pointed," would be neither predicative nor assertoric. What allows the entity to be "seen from itself" is not the pointing out as such, but rather the predication by way of which something can be taken as something distinct from something else.[25] Furthermore, predication as a practice cannot get

---

25. This predicative manner of taking something is to be contrasted with the manner of taking entities as something-as-which in prepredicative interpretation. Cf. SZ 148–49 and 157–58.

off the ground in the absence of predications as accomplishments: not only does the practice simply consist of formulating and discussing predications, but also such formulation and discussion necessarily refer to previously accomplished predications.

My criticisms have implications for two corollaries to Heidegger's position that assertion is a derivative mode of interpretation. The first corollary is that assertion has the same thrown projection that characterizes understanding as a mode of Dasein: "Like interpretation in general, the [assertion] necessarily has its existential foundations in fore-having, fore-sight, and fore-conception" (SZ 157). Looked at from one direction, this characterization of assertion is unobjectionable, but trivial: to the extent that it is an interpretative practice, the making of assertions draws on a hermeneutical fore-structure. Looked at from another direction, however, Heidegger's characterization detaches assertions as such from their conversational texture and demotes their predicative status. He does not emphasize sufficiently that the hermeneutical fore-structure on which asserting draws is itself shaped in part by the predications already available in conversation and language. Nor is such predicative preshaping of the hermeneutical fore-structure a mark of falling prey. Yet Heidegger is right to resist the tendency for accomplished assertions, when singled out for discussion in contexts of argument or theory, to float free from their hermeneutical matrix. He is also correct to counter any privileging of accomplished assertions in the formation of that matrix.

The second corollary is that, according to Heidegger, assertion characteristically turns the "existential-hermeneutical 'as'" of circumspect interpretation into an "apophantical 'as.'" Heidegger describes this transition as the "leveling down of the "primordial 'as'" (SZ 158). The term "leveling down" (*Nivellierung*) captures the gist of Heidegger's account. He does not call the transition from the hermeneutical to the apophantic a "heightening" or an "enriching" or a "making more precise." He says that under the impact of assertions the "as" of circumspect interpretation gets "cut off" (*abgeschnitten*) and "forced back" (*zurückgedrängt*), that it "dwindles" (*sinkt herab*) (SZ 158). Such strong language presupposes that the fullness of prepredicative interpretation is somehow paradigmatic for all interpretative practices, and that the apophantic "as" peculiar to assertion is primarily a modification of the hermeneutical "as." If instead, as I have suggested, one anchors the making of assertions in conversation and ordinary language, and if one ties the possibility of asserting to the availability of predications, then the transition from interpretation to assertion need not involve a leveling or dwindling. The transition would be not so much a *modification* as a *movement* from one level to another, not a leveling but a leap. Accordingly, the "leveling" would lie not in the transition from *hermeneuein* to *apophansis* but in Heidegger's account of the transition. In fact, this is where I think the leveling lies.

The Asserted

Heidegger's leveling undermines his account of what gets asserted (*das Ausgesagte*). Although his account promises to break with epistemic subjectivism and the representational theory of knowledge that has dominated modern philosophy, it also introduces ambiguities that take a toll on his conception of truth.

Heidegger rightly insists in various places that what is asserted is not a "representation" (*Vorstellung*), neither a mental object nor a state of consciousness (SZ 62, 154, 217–18). At the same time, the asserted is not the "content" or "meaning" of an accomplished assertion (SZ 155–56). Much less is the asserted a free-floating proposition that "exists" independently of assertoric practices and accomplishments (SZ 159–60). Rather, what is asserted, he argues, is the entity itself in a certain mode of its givenness. For example, when one says, "The hammer is too heavy," what is asserted—and in this is allowed to "be seen from itself" or "discovered for sight"—is the hammer itself, a "being in the mode of its being at hand" (SZ 154). The hammer is put forward (*ausgesagt*) and is explicitly determined as being "too heavy" for some purpose. And in uttering this assertion, one is sharing with others the hammer as so "seen" with such a definite character:

> As something communicated, what is spoken [*das Ausgesagte*] can be "shared" by the others with the speaker [*mit dem Aussagenden*] even when they themselves do not have the beings pointed out and defined in a palpable and visible range. What is spoken [*das Ausgesagte*] can be "passed along" in further retelling. . . . But at the same time what is pointed out can become veiled again in this further retelling, although the knowledge and cognition growing in such hearsay always means beings themselves and does not "affirm" a "valid meaning" passed around. (SZ 155)

In elaborating this analysis, Heidegger is of two minds. On the one hand, he wants to say that the asserter does not constitute or create the asserted in its specific character as asserted, but rather lets the entity stand out as it is in itself in a certain mode of its givenness. The hammer simply *is* too heavy or too light or too big for some purpose, and the asserter simply points the hammer out (or lets it be seen) in this regard. On the other hand, because he insists on the derivativeness of assertion, Heidegger also wants to claim that, as predication and communication, assertion does something to the asserted: predication "narrows" (*Verengung*) the asserted, "determines it" (*bestimmt*), and makes it "*explicitly* manifest" (ausdrücklich *offenbar zu machen*); and communication shares the asserted with others (*teilt . . . mit dem Anderen*) (SZ 154–55). In principle, assertion turns something at hand, such as the hammer, into something objectively present (or lets it turn into such) and veils its handiness (or lets this become veiled):

Something *at hand with which* we have to do or perform something, turns into something "about which" the [assertion] that points it out is made.... Within this discovering of objective presence which covers over handiness, what is encountered as objectively present is determined in its being objectively present in such and such a way. Now the access is first available for something like *qualities.* (SZ 158)[26]

Heidegger seems to claim both that the asserted entity simply presents itself and that asserting affects the asserted.[27]

Heidegger's account of the asserted argues correctly that the accomplished assertion is about an entity (or a range of entities) in a certain mode of its givenness. This "aboutness" is not a third thing in addition to the assertion and the entity; indeed, it is not a thing at all. Rather, "aboutness" simply indicates the mutual mediation of the assertoric practice and that toward which one can engage in this practice.[28] Moreover, Heidegger rightly suggests that the entity asserted allows itself to be asserted and even, in a sense, calls forth the assertion.

To indicate the entity's "givenness" for assertoric practice, let me introduce "predicative availability" as a technical term.[29] The term suggests that, among the many ways in which entities are available (Heidegger: at hand) for human

26. The translation of the first sentence in this quotation is somewhat misleading. The point of this particular sentence is not that some entity changes from being at hand into something else, but rather that a changeover (*Umschlag*) occurs in Dasein's fore-having, from a circumspect "with which" to an assertoric "about which": "Das *zuhandene Womit* des Zutunhabens, der Verrichtung, wird zum '*Worüber*' der aufzeigenden Aussage" (SZ 158). It is relative to this changeover in Dasein's fore-having that the entity also undergoes a change: its handiness becomes veiled, its objective presence gets discovered, and it gets defined (*bestimmt*) as a "what" rather than being interpreted as a "with which."

27. A similar ambiguity returns in Heidegger's subsequent account of the truth of assertion. On the one hand, confirming the truth of an assertion depends on whether the asserted entity "shows itself *as [that] very same thing.* Confirmation [of an assertion] means the *being's showing itself in its self-sameness.* Confirmation is accomplished on the basis of the being's showing itself" (SZ 218). On the other hand, the truth of an assertion simply is the assertion's capacity to *discover* the entity in its (specific) identity: "To say that [an assertion] is *true* means that it discovers the beings in themselves [*sie entdeckt das Seiende an ihm selbst*]. It asserts, it shows, it lets beings 'be seen' (*apophansis*) in their discoveredness. The *being true* (*truth*) of the [assertion] must be understood as *discovering* [*entdeckend-sein*]" (SZ 218). I take up this ambiguity concerning assertoric truth below.

28. In fact, Heidegger says that all talk, whether assertoric or not, is about something. "[Talk] is [talk] about.... That which [talk] is *about* does not necessarily have the character of the theme of a definite statement; in fact, mostly it does not have it. Even command is given about something; a wish is about something. And so is intercession.... In all [talk] there is *what is spoken* as such, what is said as such when one actually wishes, asks, talks things over about..." (SZ 161–62).

29. Readers familiar with the ontology developed by the Dutch philosophers Herman Dooyeweerd and D. H. T. Vollenhoven will recognize the term "predicative availability" as a modification of their notion of a "logical" (or "analytic") "object function." I avoid their particular terminology for two reasons: it presupposes a subject/object paradigm, which both Heidegger and I want to challenge, and the terms "logical" and "analytic" are less precise than "predicative." I recognize, however, that the account of subject/object relations given by Dooyeweerd and Vollenhoven breaks with the epistemological emphasis of the modern subject/object paradigm. For a concise and updated version of this account, see Hendrik Hart, *Understanding Our World: An Integral Ontology* (Lanham, Md.: University Press of America, 1984), pp. 221–42. See also Herman Dooyeweerd, *A New Critique of Theoretical Thought*, rpt. ed., vol. 2, trans. David H. Freeman and H. De Jongste (Philadelphia: Presbyterian and Reformed Publishing, 1969), pp. 386–91.

practices, they also offer themselves to us in a way that lets us make assertions about them. We do not impose such availability upon them, nor does our assertoric practice alone create their identity, even though asserting can help shape their identity, for better or worse. At the same time, the predicative availability of entities is only one of the many ways in which they can engage us. It is also one way in which many entities, lacking predicative capacities and practices of their own, cannot engage one another.

Heidegger's account of predicative availability goes astray when he tries to ground the asserted in the discovered. This attempt leads him to claim *both* that the asserted entity is predicatively and nonpredicatively available *and* that, when asserted, the entity's nonpredicative availability becomes veiled or, as it were, undiscovered. Two problems come to the fore. In the first place, predicative availability comes to be seen as a distorting or an opposing of nonpredicative availability, rather than simply another mode of availability that can support nonpredicative modes and can receive support from them. Rather than covering up the hammer's nonpredicative availability for hammering, for example, the hammer's availability for being predicated as "too heavy" makes its nonpredicative availability more broadly and precisely accessible. In the second place, Heidegger assigns assertoric practice a constitutive or constructive force that belies its limited "space" in the range of human practices. As we have seen, Heidegger sometimes suggests that asserting determines (*bestimmt*) the asserted, and that the true assertion discovers the entity. In contrast, it would be better to say that asserting discovers not the entity as such but the entity in its predicative availability. My alternative formulation has a direct bearing on Heidegger's conception of truth as disclosedness, the topic of the next section.

3. Correspondence and Disclosure

When he analyzes the derivative character of assertion in section 33, Heidegger has in view the position, advanced in section 44, that Dasein's disclosedness, not assertion, is the primary locus of truth. To establish this position, the three subsections of section 44 (a) explore the ontological foundations of traditional correspondence theories of truth as the agreement of assertion and object (SZ 214–19), (b) demonstrate the derivative character of such theories (SZ 219–26), and (c) analyze the kind of Being that truth as disclosedness possesses (SZ 226–30). Without rehearsing every step in Heidegger's extended argument, I shall follow his outline to discuss (1) the connection between truth and the correctness of accomplished assertions, and (2) the connection between assertoric agreement and Dasein's disclosedness. Several clues for my critical reading of section 44 come from the work of Ernst Tugendhat.[30]

30. Ernst Tugendhat, "Heideggers Idee von Wahrheit," in *Heidegger: Perspektiven zur Deutung seines Werks,* ed. Otto Pöggeler (Cologne and Berlin: Kiepenheuer & Witsch, 1970), pp. 286–97; translated by

Correctness and Truth

In harmony with my own criticisms of Heidegger's account of the asserted, Tugendhat argues that the first subsection of section 44 slides through three different formulations of the truth of an assertion, implicitly distancing itself from Husserl's theory of truth, to arrive, without sufficient argumentation, at Heidegger's own characteristic idea of truth.[31] In moving from Husserl's static conception of the assertoric act as a mode of intentionality to a more dynamic conception of assertion as a mode of disclosedness, Heidegger capitalizes on an unexamined ambiguity in the concept of "uncovering" or "discovering" (*Entdecken*):

> In the first instance, [discovering] stands for pointing out (*apophainesthai*) in general. In this sense every assertion—the false as well as the true—can be said to [discover]. Nevertheless, Heidegger [also] employs the word in a narrow and pregnant sense according to which a false assertion would be a covering up rather than an [discovering]. In this case . . . the truth lies in [being-discovered] [*Entdeckendsein*]; however, what does [discovering] now mean if it no longer signifies pointing out [*Aufzeigen*] in general? How is *aletheia* to be differentiated from *apophansis?*[32]

Tugendhat replies that Heidegger gives no answer, for he "fails to expressly differentiate . . . between the broad and the narrow meaning of [discovering]."[33]

Against Heidegger, Tugendhat insists that the truth or falsity of an assertion cannot lie merely in its discovering or covering up an entity, but must lie more specifically in how such discovering or covering up takes place. Just as the true

---

Richard Wolin as "Heidegger's Idea of Truth," in *The Heidegger Controversy: A Critical Reader,* ed. Richard Wolin (New York: Columbia University Press, 1991), pp. 245–63. My modifications to this translation (indicated by square brackets) are intended to maintain some consistency with the Stambaugh translation of *Being and Time.* A longer version of Tugendhat's critique occurs in a seminal study that has not been translated into English: Ernst Tugendhat, *Der Wahrheitsbegriff bei Husserl und Heidegger,* 2d ed. (Berlin: Walter de Gruyter, 1970).

31. Tugendhat, "Heidegger's Idea," pp. 250–52; "Heideggers Idee," pp. 288–89. The three formulations, all of them on SZ 218, are: (1) The assertion is true if it discovers the entity "*just* as it is in itself." (The word "just" appears in the Macquarrie and Robinson translation, p. 261, but not in the Stambaugh translation, p. 201. Heidegger's formulation in German reads "Das gemeinte Seiende selbst zeigt sich so, wie es an ihm selbst ist.") (2) The assertion is true if it discovers the entity "in itself." (3) The assertion is true if it discovers the entity. Whereas Tugendhat accuses Heidegger of sliding through these three formulations, Dahlstrom argues that formulations (2) and (3) can be understood as synonyms or metonyms for (1), and he gives textual evidence for this interpretation (pp. 405–7). I think that Tugendhat could easily concede this reading without giving up his main criticism, however. In this connection, see n. 21 above.

32. "Heidegger's Idea," p. 254; "Heideggers Idee," pp. 290–91. Although Tugendhat applauds Heidegger's "dynamic" conception of assertion as a mode of disclosedness, I wonder how dynamic this conception can be, given Heidegger's emphasis on disclosedness as a state of Being rather than on disclosure as a process of mediation.

33. "Heidegger's Idea," p. 254; "Heideggers Idee," p. 291.

assertion discovers the entity *as the entity is in itself,* so the false assertion "[covers up] [*verdeckt*] the entity as it is in itself, and it does this in that it [discovers] it in another way than the way it is in itself."[34] Although Heidegger is right to ground the truth of assertions as correctness (*Richtigkeit*) in the truth of entities as discoveredness or (in the term he later prefers) unconcealedness or unconcealment (*Unverborgenheit*), he simply bypasses Husserl's insight that the truth of entities is not their givenness as such but rather their self-givenness, a "superior mode of givenness."[35] As a pointing out that aims at truth, assertion tries to measure the entity's givenness against that entity's self-givenness. Hence, Tugendhat argues, assertion must be directed not simply by the entity as it shows itself but by the entity as it manifests itself *in itself:*

> Self-sameness is the critical measure of unconcealedness [*des Entbergens*]. Only if this second meaning of being-directed is recognized in its autonomy can it profitably be clarified with the help of the first; so that one can say that the false assertion covers up the entity and that only the true assertion genuinely unconceals [*entbirgt*] the entity—that is, as it is in itself.[36]

According to Tugendhat, it is only because Heidegger first ignores the distinction between givenness and self-givenness, and then equates truth with discovering as *apophansis,* that he can subsequently regard untruth as an aspect of truth, rather than as something opposed to truth.

To provide terminological markers for Tugendhat's criticisms, I shall distinguish between the "correctness" of an accomplished assertion and the "predicative self-disclosure" of the asserted entity in its predicative availability. By "predicative self-disclosure" I mean a process whereby an entity, in its predicative availability, offers or manifests itself in relevant accord with nonpredicative aspects of its availability.[37] I agree with Heidegger (using my own terminology) that both assertoric correctness and predicative self-disclosure are grounded in a more comprehensive mediation of disclosive practices and systatic availability.[38] But I also agree with Tugendhat that, to connect this mediation with

34. "Heidegger's Idea," p. 255; "Heideggers Idee," p. 291.

35. "Heidegger's Idea," p. 256; "Heideggers Idee," p. 292.

36. "Heidegger's Idea," p. 257; "Heideggers Idee," p. 293. The translation of Tugendhat's essay does not bring out the close terminological connection between the assertion's correctness (*Richtigkeit*) and the assertion's being directed (*gerichtet*) by the entity's self-givenness.

37. This is a general but not an exhaustive stipulation. Not included, for example, would be first-order statements about which one makes second-order statements (assuming for the sake of illustration that first-order statements can properly be called entities). In such cases, the relevant accord might be with other predicative aspects of the "entity's" availability.

38. The adjective "systatic" derives from Herman Dooyeweerd's discussion of the "intermodal systasis of meaning" that grounds any "theoretical synthesis." In Dooyeweerd's account, "systasis" refers to the wholeness or integrality with which the "modal aspects" of reality present themselves in ordinary or "pretheoretical" experience. See *A New Critique of Theoretical Thought,* vol. 2, pp. 427ff. My term systatic availability refers to the multidimensional "handiness," both predicative and nonpredicative, of the entities with which human beings have dealings.

the concept of truth, one must have a way to distinguish between true and untrue "discoverings," "unconcealments," and the like.

At the same time, I want to avoid Tugendhat's tendency to anchor the distinction between true and untrue in the "self-givenness" of the asserted entity. Although an accomplished assertion about an entity does aim to discover the entity as that entity manifests itself "in itself," not all accomplished assertions are about entities, nor is such discovering sufficient for the assertion to be correct, nor does an entity's manifesting itself occur in isolation from other entities. Accomplished assertions can be about processes or actions rather than about entities (e.g., "To err is human"); the correctness of accomplished assertions depends in part on how they are formulated and used, and not merely on how they "accord" with what is asserted; and the entity's manifesting itself occurs in relationship to other entities, including those entities (i.e., human beings) to whom the entity is manifesting itself. The Husserlian notions of self-givenness and "evidence" have a static quality that belies the dynamics uncovered, albeit only partially, by Heidegger's notion of discoveredness. To avoid the static connotations of "self-givenness," I have adopted the term "predicative self-disclosure."

All that having been said, an account is still required for the predicative self-disclosure of asserted entities and the correctness of accomplished assertions. Earlier I introduced the term "predicative availability" to refer to the fact that entities (and not only entities) offer themselves to us in ways that let us make assertions about them. I also said that asserting something discovers the entity in its predicative availability. Now it can be added that, when correct, an accomplished assertion discovers the entity in its predicative availability in a manner that accords with other relevant ways in which the asserted entity is available. Imagine, for example, that a carpenter says, "Too heavy, give me the other one," in a certain context. If correct, her (implicit) assertion "The hammer is too heavy" discovers the hammer as something of which relative heaviness can be predicated. It discovers this in a way that accords with the (un)suitability of the hammer for the task at hand.

Accordingly, asserting can go wrong in two ways: (1) by failing to discover the entity in its predicative availability and (2) by discovering this in a manner that fails to accord with other relevant ways in which the entity is available. The first way usually results in assertions that are "false" in the sense of being misleading or misplaced (e.g., claiming "The hammer is too heavy" when the tool in question offers itself for predication not as a hammer but as a pipe wrench). The second way usually results in assertions that are "false" in the sense of being inaccurate (e.g., claiming "The hammer is too heavy" when the hammer in question is very well suited for the task and for the carpenter in question).

Those are not the only ways in which asserting can go wrong. For example, the asserter can misspeak or can respond inappropriately to a question or can deliberately lie. In addition, the "fore-structure" of a speech community can be such that false assertions are routinely made about an entire range of entities. Hence, looked at from the side of assertoric practice, the measure of truth cannot be a single criterion such as the traditional "correspondence with the object" or the Heideggerian "discovering the entity [(just as it is) in itself]." Rather the measure must be a complex of considerations that may not be specifiable as necessary and sufficient conditions.

Satisfying this complex depends in part on the entity's predicative self-disclosure. In the usage proposed above, "predicative self-disclosure" refers specifically to the asserted entity in its predicative availability. This usage acknowledges that entities disclose themselves when they are neither asserted nor predicatively available. In fact, if entities did not disclose themselves in nonpredicative ways for nonassertoric practices, most of them would be incapable of predicative self-disclosure. This is an indispensable insight to be retained from Heidegger's account of handiness. But my usage of "predicative self-disclosure" also notes that entities disclose themselves when they are asserted and are predicatively available.

The predicative self-disclosure of an asserted entity lies in its offering itself for predicative practice reliably and in accordance with other ways in which the entity is available. The self-disclosing entity offers itself not simply "just as that entity is in itself," as Tugendhat claims, but rather just as that entity is available to us in some other respect. When the hammer discloses itself as something about which one can accurately claim "The hammer is too heavy," it offers itself just as that hammer is available for a particular task of carpentry, say, for setting nails. As is the case with asserting, an entity's predicative self-disclosure can misfire in a couple of ways: either (1) the entity can withdraw from the assertoric field, in which case it becomes or remains predicatively unintelligible (although most likely available in other ways), or (2) the entity can offer itself for predicative practice but not just as it is available in some relevant way, in which case the entity becomes predicatively confusing. In the first case, we might find ourselves "unable to say anything," in the sense of being unable to make an assertion about the entity. In the second instance, we might find ourselves "not knowing quite what to say," in the sense of finding our assertions about the entity repeatedly "off the mark." Although neither of these misfirings may be prevalent in our dealings with hammers and the like, they occur frequently in our dealings with one another.

My account of assertoric correctness and predicative self-disclosure has the advantage of differentiating *aletheia* from *apophansis* without either resorting to a static notion of self-givenness, à la Tugendhat, or turning incorrectness and predicative hiddenness into aspects of truth, à la Heidegger. At the same time, this account serves to strengthen the Heideggerian intuition that assertoric correctness, although an aspect of truth, is neither the sole or primary locus of truth nor the key to a comprehensive conception of truth. Now let's see what clues to a more comprehensive conception of truth occur when Heidegger grounds the "agreement of assertion and object" in Dasein's disclosedness.

Agreement and Disclosedness

To show how the purported agreement of assertion and object derives from Dasein's disclosedness, and thereby to transform the traditional conception of truth, Heidegger traces a path from ordinary language to what could be called theoretical metalanguage. His account goes roughly as follows (SZ 223–26):[39]

1. In talk Dasein expresses itself as a being toward entities that discovers entities.
2. In the practice of asserting, Dasein expresses itself about discovered entities and communicates how these are discovered.
3. The "aboutness" of the accomplished assertion [*in ihrem Worüber*] preserves the discoveredness of the entity asserted.
4. As something expressed by Dasein, the accomplished assertion becomes something at hand and further discussable, and the entity's discoveredness also becomes handy. At the same time, the accomplished assertion, which preserves discoveredness, has a relation to the asserted entity.
5. Subsequent discussion of the accomplished assertion exempts Dasein from discovering entities in an original way, even though in such discussion Dasein does enter a "being toward" those entities whose discoveredness the assertion preserves.
6. Because of such discussion at one remove, which is common in public talk, the assertion's handiness gets covered up, and the discoveredness of the asserted entity becomes an objectively present conformity between the accomplished assertion and the asserted entity.
7. Hence the original connections among Dasein, entities, and assertion get reduced to an objectively present conformity or agreement between an objectively present assertion and an objectively present object.
8. As a result, says Heidegger, "Truth as disclosedness and as a being toward discovered beings—a being that itself discovers—has become truth as the agreement between innerworldly things objectively present" (SZ 225). Moreover, this objectively present agreement *seems* primary and not derivative because Dasein ordinarily understands itself and Being in terms of what is encountered as objectively present. Traditional ontology simply strengthens such an understanding.

Earlier I questioned two corollaries to Heidegger's claim that assertion is a derivative mode of interpretation: that assertion has the same thrown projection as understanding has, and that assertion "levels" the existential-hermeneutical "as" into an apophantical "as." Heidegger's derivation of agreement from disclosedness brings to light a third and equally questionable corollary, namely,

39. My summary introduces the terms "practice of asserting" and "accomplished assertion" at points where these seem consistent with Heidegger's account.

that the sharing and discussing of accomplished assertions spares Dasein a direct encounter with entities themselves in "'original' experience" and thereby helps turn accomplished assertions into objectively present things (SZ 224). Deep in the "fore-structure" of Heidegger's phenomenology lies the image of authentic existence as having direct dealings with equipment and with that which equipment makes available—the image of *Homo faber* as the attentive craftsperson who can get on with his or her work "without wasting words." The image suggests that the more indirect and mediated our dealings become, the more we drift from authentic understanding, interpretation, and talk. Once one abandons this image, already ideologically loaded in the 1920s, one becomes dubious about the entire notion that public talk spares us a direct encounter. There are two reasons for this: first, no experience of entities is direct and original, and, second, public talk mediates even the most "original" experience. Heidegger's account of assertion remains caught in the dream of eidetic intuition, despite his shifting Husserlian phenomenology from the realm of theoretically perceived noemata to the realm of circumspectly interpreted entities.[40]

The dream of a direct encounter clouds Heidegger's account of the connection between agreement and disclosedness. His account begins with the assumption that Dasein's original self-expression and orientation and discovering are such that the entities discovered are truly discovered and that their discoveredness itself is true. Hence Dasein's disclosedness can itself be described as truth. Yet, as Tugendhat points out, to describe disclosedness as truth is to preclude asking how Dasein's disclosedness can be truly disclosive and how it can be false. Even if the agreement of assertion and object is derivative from a more primordial truth, that from which this agreement derives must be such that it can itself be distinguished from untruth. As it stands, Heidegger's account of the connection between agreement and disclosedness could just as readily be given for the lack of agreement between assertion and object.

One way out of the impasse would be to identify principles according to which human self-expression, orientation, and discovering can be more or less true. If "correctness" indicates such a principle for the practice of asserting, perhaps there are parallel principles for other ranges of human practice, such as resourcefulness in the production and use of goods and services or solidarity in the development of human communities or justice in the governance of social institutions. It would be nonsense, of course, to equate adherence to

40. Cf. Theodor W. Adorno, *Against Epistemology: A Metacritique, Studies in Husserl and the Phenomenological Antinomies,* trans. Willis Domingo (Cambridge, Mass.: MIT Press, 1982), pp. 186–234; *Zur Metakritik der Erkenntnistheorie: Studien Über Husserl und die phänomenologischen Antinomien,* Gesammelte Schriften 5 (Frankfurt am Main: Suhrkamp, 1970), pp. 190–235. In *The Philosophical Discourse of Modernity: Twelve Lectures,* trans. Frederick Lawrence (Cambridge, Mass.: MIT Press, 1987), Jürgen Habermas argues that, in both earlier and later articulations, Heidegger "remains caught in the problems that the philosophy of the subject in the form of Husserlian phenomenology had presented to him" (p. 136).

such principles with the achievement of assertoric "truth." Yet there may be a more comprehensive sense of truth according to which "being in the truth" amounts to fidelity to that which people hold in common and which holds them in common. That which holds them in common could be principles of the sort already mentioned. That which they hold in common may or may not be in line with such principles. Yet their holding something in common requires appeals or gestures toward such principles, even when the appeal is self-serving or the gesture is ideologically distorted. Moreover, for the principles to hold people in common, people must themselves hold something in common. Correlatively, infidelity to the commonly holding/held amounts to "being in untruth." From this description it appears that Dasein's "disclosedness" is itself a site of public struggle over principles for human existence. Whether the commonly holding/held sustains and promotes life is always implicitly at issue.[41]

My emphasis on fidelity to the commonly holding/held recalls an etymological link between "truth" and "troth" that Heidegger had discovered before he wrote *Sein und Zeit*. Although one does not want to make etymology do the work of philosophical argument, it is at least noteworthy that "true" derives from the Old English word "treowe," which means "faithful." "Truth" derives from the Old English word "treowth"—"fidelity"—which is also a source of the word "troth." Moreover, "true" is commonly used to mean steadfast, loyal, honest, or just, and one archaic meaning of "truth" is fidelity.[42] If one took the more comprehensive sense of truth to involve fidelity to the commonly holding and commonly held, then the pursuit of assertoric correctness could be seen as one important but limited way in which truth occurs. Similarly, the failure or refusal to pursue assertoric correctness could be regarded as contrary to truth, not only in the sense of leading to assertoric "falsehood" but also in the sense

41. I elaborate this notion of fidelity, and connect it with the idea of life-giving disclosure, in chapter 4 of *Artistic Truth: Aesthetics, Discourse, and Imaginative Disclosure* (New York: Cambridge University Press, 2004). There I develop an idea of truth as "a process of life-giving disclosure marked by fidelity to the commonly holding and commonly held."

42. In *The Genesis of Heidegger's "Being and Time"* (Berkeley: University of California Press, 1993), Theodore Kisiel introduces "troth" to translate Heidegger's use of *verwahren* (in the early 1920s) for a non-theoretical and practical or even religious sense of truth. The most prominent usages occur in Heidegger's courses on Aristotle's *Nicomachean Ethics* and in his October 1922 typescript titled "Phänomenologische Interpretationen zu Aristoteles (Anzeige der hermeneutischen Situation)." Kisiel suggests that Heidegger's concept of truth as "taking into troth and holding in troth" derives from his appropriation of Christian sources such as Paul, Augustine, and Luther, which "infiltrate Heidegger's understanding of the Aristotelian senses of practical truth" (p. 226). Heidegger, commenting on Aristotle, claims that holding being(s) in troth (*Seinsverwahrung*) is the fundamental experience of truth. Moreover, *nous, sophia, episteme, techne,* and *phronesis* are all modes of "true-ing." In a gloss to Heidegger's handwritten note to the October 1922 typescript, Kisiel connects troth to care as well: "To care is to take into troth and hold in troth, the kind of having . . . involved in the habits of truth" (pp. 537–38 n. 17). See further Kisiel, pp. 227–75, 302–6, 491–92. Michael Bauer, by contrast, translates "verwahren" as "truthful safe-keeping." See Martin Heidegger, "Phenomenological Interpretations with Respect to Aristotle: Indication of the Hermeneutical Situation," *Man and World* 25 (1992): 355–93.

of undermining other ways in which fidelity to the commonly holding/held is to be practiced.

Such an approach would have several advantages over the account given by Heidegger. In the first place, a more comprehensive conception of truth would not preclude distinguishing truth from untruth but would rather make available a number of respects in which such a distinction can be drawn. Second, there would be no need to see the discussion of accomplished assertions as more remote from primordial truth, since such discussion would simply be one of the many ways in which the pursuit of truth occurs. Third, truth would not be turned into a state of Dasein's being, but would rather be seen as a dynamic, multifaceted, and fragile calling in which everyone always has a stake and to which no one can avoid making a reply. Fourth, the agreement between assertion and object, which itself is only one component of assertoric "truth," would no longer direct our understanding of what truth is like, not even in the inverted Heideggerian sense that comes from trying to show how such agreement derives from disclosedness. The relation of epistemic subject to epistemic object that strongly colors Heidegger's account of disclosedness would no longer be the point of departure for understanding what truth is like.

At the same time, the proposed conception respects Heidegger's insistence on the temporal character of truth. The principles already mentioned are not timeless absolutes but rather historical horizons or orientations. They are historically learned, achieved, contested, reformulated, and ignored, and their pursuit occurs amid social struggle. Moreover, the description of these principles as "commonly held" does not mean that they are always and everywhere recognized, or that they provide the heavy artillery of common sense. Rather, it means that when people in modern societies find themselves pushed to the extremes of their self-understanding and their shared talk, they cannot avoid a struggle over these very principles.

To summarize: I have argued in sections 2 and 3 that Heidegger underestimates the role of predication in assertion, and that he incorrectly portrays predicative availability as a distorting of nonpredicative availability. Heidegger is right to try to ground the correctness of assertions in a more comprehensive mediation of disclosive practices and systatic availability. For this attempt to succeed, however, assertoric correctness must be seen as one of many principles in accordance with which the disclosure of culture, society, and human life can be more or less true.

In Olthuisian terms, assertoric correctness must be regarded as one of the good connections with which human beings in modern societies are gifted and to which they are called. Or, to adapt Pauline language from a text Olthuis frequently cites, pursuing assertoric correctness is an important way, but only one way, "to work out [our] salvation with fear and trembling" (Phil. 2:12). It is part of, but by no means all of, "speaking the truth in love" (Eph. 4:15). Olthuis's "hermeneutics of connection" highlights both the contexts of this pursuit and the need to align it with fidelity to other principles. When prophecy is required, our asserting may need to hammer; where celebration, to sing; where consolation, to caress—and sometimes, as in Isaiah, all three.[43] An alignment with responses to other callings is equally crucial. All the correct asserting in the world will not by itself repair the damage done by social injustice or ecological violence. Nor, of course, will incorrect asserting or sheer nonasserting let justice and peace embrace. Jim's wisdom to see such connections despite modern domination, and his courage to make them amid postmodern disruption, are blessings of generosity for which I am profoundly grateful.

43. See especially Isaiah 40:1–11, the prologue to Deutero-Isaiah, which Olthuis's "Biblical Foundations" course once encouraged me to study.

5

In God We Trust?

Biblical Interpretation and the Hermeneutics of Suspicion

Merold Westphal

There do indeed seem to be, as Derrida has suggested, two interpretations of interpretation, though my interpretation of that difference will be somewhat different from his. According to one account, interpretation is deciphering or decoding. I shall call it the D/D model. An-cay ou-yay eak-spay ig-pay atin-lay? Many of you can easily decode this strange sounding utterance as the question, Can you speak pig Latin? On the D/D model of interpretation (1) the meaning (proposition) to be grasped is for all practical purposes unambiguous, clear, and distinct; (2) our acquaintance with it is prior to and independent of the text (sentence, statement) that becomes its bearer; and (3) interpretation consists in deciphering the text so as to recognize (or perhaps recollect) a meaning to which we have extratextual access.

Generalized, this theory claims that meaning is prelinguistic or extralinguistic and that language or text is the series of coded messages that must be deciphered if the meaning intended by some author is to be rightly identified. We invoke such a theory when we speak in a familiar way about propositions (as distinct from sentences or statements). "Es regnet" and "It is raining" are two sentences, in German and English respectively, that "express the same proposition" and can be used in statements to assert that proposition. But while the sentences and statements are in a particular language, it is clear that the proposition they express is not. It is a prelinguistic or extralinguistic meaning whose coded transmitters are to be found in such texts as "Es regnet" and "It is raining." To interpret those texts is simply to decode them, to ascend from the cave of language, with all its particularity, contingency, and flux, to the Platonic heaven of fixed and transparent meanings.

I once heard a distinguished Reformed theologian give a lecture on the perspicuity of Scripture that presupposed, I believe, this interpretation of interpretation. Only in retrospect has it occurred to me that it was more Cartesian than biblical. To the troubling conflict of interpretations and traditions of interpretation he posed method as the solution. If the exegete employs the grammaticohistorical method with care and rigor, the result will be the single, fixed, transcultural meaning of the text. The method is the key to the code that enables the reader to decipher the text. Having gazed on that meaning, the interpreter can then communicate it by recoding it in the sentences of some language. St. Paul sends his message to the theologian in Greek; the theologian conveys it to the reader in English. But the goal is to have all three gazing at the same extralinguistic meaning, picked out in the first place by the Pauline intention. While the text is the bearer of the meaning in each instance, it is in no sense constitutive of the meaning. This is what Derrida calls the postal system of meaning. Whether I send my manuscript (proposition) to the publisher (listener, reader) by United Parcel Service (Greek sentence) or Federal Express (English sentence) makes utterly no difference to its meaning.

One might construe this line of thought as the refusal to take the hermeneutical turn. For the argument could be stated this way: when approached with the correct method, the Bible interprets itself. We do not have to interpret it. But, as already indicated, rather than interpret the D/D model of interpretation as a rejection of interpretation, I interpret it as the rejection of another interpretation of interpretation, the one most people would have in mind today when speaking of the hermeneutical turn in contemporary philosophy.

According to this second view, every act of interpretation is a translation, whether it moves from one language to another or stays within a single language and whether it happens more or less automatically in everyday life or is a deliberate act, as when a preacher sets out to interpret the text for next Sunday's sermon. The force of the translation model will be clear to anyone who has tried to translate a text from one language to another. It becomes quite quickly evident that the original language is not, like the pig Latin above, simply a coded version of the language into which it is to be translated. Translating is always more than decoding and, to put it in Gadamer's terms, is never merely reproductive but also productive. A translation is never a mirror image, a duplication of the original, and to interpret a text, whether it be a law, a Scripture, a poem, or whatever is in part to become an author. For, on this model, language is constitutive of meaning. To translate is to say the same thing differently, which means not quite to say the same thing.

Closely related to the translation model is the performance model, and I present them as complementary ways of expressing the second interpretation of interpretation. I shall call them, taken together, the T/P model of interpretation. Where this model is in play, the world is usually treated as a text, so that what is said about interpreting a text in the narrow, literal sense of the term also applies to construing the world, to the seeing as that we call perception or conception. The D/D model has a similar extension beyond interpreting texts in the literal sense.

On the performance model interpreting a text is like performing a play or a sonata. The text to be interpreted is to some degree determinate. I can tell whether that note is an F# or a G# and whether that word is "cat" or "hat." But the determinate text underdetermines the interpretation. In the case of coding there is an algorithm by means of which one can mechanically calculate (I have assiduously avoided speaking of translation in this context) the decoded text for which the coded text stands. But that is just what is missing according to the performance model (and the translation model—as anyone familiar with computer translation knows). This is why in each performance the interpreter becomes a coauthor with the playwright or composer. Nor can there be, in such circumstances, a single interpretation that, by being right, condemns all others to being wrong. There will be numerous interpretations (performances) of *Hamlet* or the *Waldstein Sonata* that will be recognized by the most discriminating judges to be of superior quality. The choice between Olivier's *Hamlet* and Branagh's is not between right and wrong, any more than the choice between Schnabel's Beethoven and Brendel's.

Of course, this does not mean that anything goes, and it would be seriously misleading to suggest that on the performance model matters of correctness and incorrectness are simply replaced by other values, perhaps aesthetic. There are many ways in any performance to get it wrong. One can play the wrong notes or say the wrong words, to mention only a couple. But it remains the case that when I've gotten everything right that the text dictates, there remains considerable leeway, indeterminacy, or, if you like, undecidability that I am compelled to decide before I will be able to offer anything that will count as my interpretation. The most recent film version of *Romeo and Juliet* and the Al Pacino take on *Richard III* give some idea of how considerable this leeway can be. Or one can compare Pope's translation of the *Iliad* with Fagles's. There is a gap between text and interpretation that neither the author nor any hermeneutical method can fill in, but only the performer.

It is variations on the T/P theme that constitute the hermeneutical turn in contemporary philosophy. I offer three negative theses about it. First, the hermeneutical turn is not inherently postmodern. It can be found, to be sure, in thinkers like Nietzsche, Derrida, and Rorty. But it is at the heart of the philosophical hermeneutics of Gadamer and Ricoeur, and Heidegger's development of the model is at least as close in spirit to these two as to the postmodern themes in his work. Its roots go back at least to Kant. One finds it in Kierkegaard, in Kuhnian philosophy of science, in American pragmatism, and in the later Wittgenstein. It transcends the boundaries of any single philosophical ideology.

Second, it is not inherently secular. It belongs to Kierkegaard as much as to Nietzsche, to Gadamer and Ricoeur, with their openness to the religious, as much as to Derrida and Rorty in their atheism. So it might deserve a place in our own attempts to think in a Christian way about matters of interpretation. What I have been calling the hermeneutical turn can also be called the hermeneutics of finitude. As such it can be placed in the context of Christian thinking about the epistemic meaning of our createdness, about what it means that we see "through a glass, darkly" or "in a mirror dimly" (1 Cor. 13:12).

On the T/P model, all seeing is *seeing-as*. It is construal rather than mirroring. For all seeing-as is *seeing from* some perspective (Nietzsche) or *seeing within* some paradigm (Kuhn) or language game (Wittgenstein) or horizon (Gadamer). We never attain the view from nowhere (Nagel). Our finitude consists in our embeddedness in some particular location in historical, cultural, linguistic, ideological space. Theologically construed, this means not only that our interpretations do not dwell in that heavenly world of propositions, but in some earthly site that is different not only from other human earthly sites (in the aftermath of Babel), but also from the divine point of view. The hermeneutics of finitude can be read as a commentary on Isaiah 55:8–9:

> For my thoughts are not your thoughts,
>   nor are your ways my ways, says the LORD.
> For as the heavens are higher than the earth,
>   so are my ways higher than your ways
>   and my thoughts than your thoughts.

Third, the T/P model does not stand in a simple either/or relation with the D/D model. We can't and in any case shouldn't simply abandon the latter for the former. For the task of the T/P model is not to abolish the D/D model but to interrupt it, to qualify it. The heart of the D/D model, insofar as it is not simply a device for maintaining a monopoly on truth and on the power that comes with it, is the reminder that to interpret is to construe the thought of another. I am not free the make up the meanings as I would like to find them. The cook may season to taste, but the interpreter may not simply translate to taste. It is essential to listen to the voice of the other and to preserve its otherness.

The T/P model is a reminder that there are limits to our ability to do this, that we kid ourselves if we think we have completely neutralized our own horizons, which include our tastes, and become a tabula rasa on which the text can simply rewrite itself. But it does not follow that we can do as we please or that the hard task of listening to the other has suddenly become easy or even disappeared. Nostalgic objectivism seeks to discredit the hermeneutical turn by interpreting it as an "anything goes" attitude. But the hermeneutical turn regularly gives the lie to this calumny by the seriousness with which it takes the otherness of the text.

According to the hermeneutics of finitude, the T/P model of text and world interpretation, interpretation is always underdetermined; there is a gap between text/world and interpretation that only the interpreter can fill in. The hermeneutics of suspicion notes that just where the work of interpretation is productive and not merely reproductive, the interests of the interpreter often play a decisive role; and these interests are not necessarily honorable. They may be morally problematic, even from the standpoint of the interpreter, in which case interpretation and self-deception will be inseparable.

Thus Marx, Nietzsche, and Freud, the three great masters of suspicion according to Ricoeur, point, respectively, to the ways our interpretations provide us with ideological legitimation of social oppression, expressions of an amoral will to power we would like not to acknowledge, and wish-fulfillments that gratify immoral desires while flattering our self-image. They provide sermons on Jeremiah 17:9, "The heart is devious above all else; it is perverse—who can understand it?" and on the Pauline reminder in Romans 1:18 that the wicked are those "who by their wickedness suppress the truth." These three are the great secular theologians of original sin, translating what Paul, Augustine, Luther, and Calvin have to say about the noetic effects of sin into their own theoretical discourse. They tell us that they can get along quite well without the concept of God, thank you, but not without the concept of sin, or at least its obvious correlate.

In other words, like the hermeneutics of finitude, the hermeneutics of suspicion is not inherently secular. No doubt it is Foucault's Marxian/Nietzschean reflections on the linkages between knowledge and power that are the most discussed form of suspicion today. But the secular versions always have an aura of plagiarism about them, through failure to acknowledge their biblical origins. Nor, in the absence of a full-fledged theology of sin, are they able to make as much sense of their findings as the Reformed theologian could, if s/he were less concerned with refuting the attacks upon Christendom that emerge from these secular thinkers and more concerned to recognize their authentically, if unintentionally, prophetic character.

So the first thing to notice about the hermeneutics of suspicion is that it ought to be an essential ingredient in any Reformed hermeneutic. There is an important corollary to the recognition that suspicion is directed toward the noetic or hermeneutic effects of sin. The Cartesian strategy for solving the problem is doubly mistaken. It is just this strategy that is embedded in the D/D model of interpretation, which is in large part motivated by the desire to eliminate what suspicion uncovers. First, once we see that sin is the root of the problem, we should be able to see that method is the wrong prescription. Spiritual disciplines play an important role in our sanctification, but we misunderstand that role badly if we think of them as methods of holiness. Second, the D/D model purports to eliminate the productive contribution of the interpreter entirely, whether it be innocent or not, freeing the text/world completely from outside contamination. We become perfect mirrors, not finite and sinful construers.

But, once we see that we are dealing with sin, we should be able to see this as a not too subtle form of perfectionism. There may be a place for it in some form of Wesleyan hermeneutics, but not, I should think, in any Reformed hermeneutics.

Three further observations may help to clarify the nature of the hermeneutics of suspicion. First, suspicion raises questions about motive and use, not truth. In this it differs from skepticism. The latter challenges the truth claims of our beliefs, suggesting either that there is sufficient evidence against a belief to discredit it or, at the very least, insufficient evidence for a belief to allow us rationally to hold it. Suspicion doesn't ask whether our beliefs are true or whether they have sufficient warrant. It asks what (possibly disreputable) motives lead us to hold them and what (possibly disreputable) uses we put them to. How do they function in the personal and corporate lives of believers?

The sad story is that Christianity that is impeccably orthodox by reference to the ecumenical creeds, and perhaps the Reformed creeds as well, has been used to legitimate anti-Semitism, other forms of racism (including slavery, apartheid, and white supremacy), various forms of cultural imperialism, the oppression of women, militaristic nationalisms, various forms of economic exploitation, and the kind of distinction between the sinners and the righteous that Jesus so sharply opposed. The list could easily be extended, but it should be sufficiently clear that we are in quite different territory from that of debates over the evidential status of faith vis-à-vis reason. And it should be clear that prophetic piety (e.g., Kierkegaard, liberation theology) has even better reason to be suspicious of these unholy alliances than does secular modernity (e.g., Marx, Freud) or postmodernity (e.g., Nietzsche, Foucault).

Second, when the Pauline hermeneutics of suspicion speaks of wickedness suppressing the truth, it is not an all or nothing affair. It is not necessary to obliterate biblical truth or repudiate Christian tradition wholesale in order to create God in my (our) own image and put God to work in my (our) service. Selective editing at key points will do the trick. This is why the theology that legitimizes racial violence or the moral superiority of those like me can be ultraorthodox in such questions as the Trinity or justification by grace through faith.

Finally, suspicion is not incompatible with trust. It is relatively easy for me to be suspicious of your theology. I can see the speck in your eye more easily than the log in my own (Matt. 7:1–5). If I stop at that point I show myself to be a Pharisee in the worst sense of the term. But I can make myself and my community the object of suspicion. If I do I may well come to the conclusion that just as I have probably never truly and fully loved my neighbor as myself, so I have never worshiped the true God and not an idol, a god produced in significant part by my own wish-fulfilling will to power. But this only means that I am a sinner—in my epistemic life as well as in my moral life. Not only is this awareness not incompatible with the trust that God nevertheless loves me, has justified me, and is at work in my sanctification, it is normally thought (surely in Reformed contexts) to be an essential ingredient in that trust. Nor is this awareness incompatible with the trust that my understanding of God, marred as it is by my own interested editing, reflects my real (but imperfect) contact with divine perfection, contact that can be purified in this life and will be perfected in the life to come.

It seems obvious to me that any Reformed hermeneutics needs to be a hermeneutics of suspicion, that we need to subject our theologies and our readings of the Bible to the kind of rigorous self-examination that we can learn from Marx, Nietzsche, and Freud and from rereading Amos, Jesus, Paul, and James in the light of what we learn from that unholy trio. But putting the point in that way makes it look as if I have overlooked another crucial question, or (if you're sufficiently suspicious) that I am avoiding it. That question, which can no longer be postponed, is not whether we should be suspicious of *our* theologies and *our* readings of the Bible. That they are human, all too human, goes without saying, I should think, for any Reformed thinking that has not sold its soul to Cartesian/Platonic strategies for transcending the human condition. The question is whether we should apply our hermeneutics of suspicion to Scripture itself.

I must confess that the idea makes me uncomfortable. Of course, the biblical writers are as finite and sinful as our favorite theologians and exegetes, including ourselves. But isn't the Bible more than their perspective on the matters they discuss? Isn't it the Word of God? Wasn't the Danish preacher invented by Kierkegaard at the end of *Either/Or* right to suggest that "as against God we are always in the wrong"?[1] If we approach the biblical narratives with suspicion, do we not lapse into the Gnostic heresy of making the God of the story into the villain and those who oppose him into the hero? Isn't it with good reason that whose who speak of the Bible as the Word of God are extremely reluctant to practice a hermeneutics of suspicion on the biblical text, while those who do engage in such a practice are extremely reluctant to speak of the Bible as the Word of God? You pays your money and you makes your choice. Either/Or!

My instincts tell me it is just that simple. But perhaps it is not. I want to describe a hermeneutics that both affirms that the Bible is the Word of God and allows us to approach the text with suspicion. Whether it is a genuinely Reformed hermeneutics will no doubt be a matter of theological debate, but it has its roots in a thinker with deep Reformed roots, Nick Wolterstorff. In *Divine Discourse,* he invokes speech act theory to develop a theory of double

---

1. Søren Kierkegaard, *Either/Or,* trans. Walter Lowrie (Garden City, NY: Doubleday, 1959), vol. 2, p. 343.

discourse.[2] The locutionary act (uttering, inscribing sentences in a given language) of one person may become the illocutionary act (promise, command, assertion) of another. Thus, for example, when Augustine heard the child saying, "Take and read," he understood it to be God speaking to him. The child uttered the sentence, but God gave the command.

In the case of deputized speech, the second person may supervise the production of the locutionary act by the first very closely. Thus the president or secretary of state may give an ambassador very explicit instructions about what to say to a foreign government, or a boss may dictate a letter to a secretary. If the boss dictates as I do, not only the very words will be given, but the paragraphing and punctuation as well. In other instances, however, this supervision is much weaker or even absent. Then we can speak of *appropriated* rather than *deputized* or dictated speech. The ambassador speaks on the basis of a general policy rather than explicit instructions. Or someone says what I was wanting to say, and I support her by saying, "She speaks for me, too." Or a secretary may receive a letter while the boss is gone and compose a letter that becomes the boss's reply when she signs it on her return. The words, composed by the secretary, become the word (commitment, instruction) of the boss. We can think of deputized speech as a special case of appropriated speech, the one in which the authorization by which the locutionary act of one becomes the illocutionary act of another comes prior to the locutionary act rather than after it.

We are familiar with such modes of double discourse in daily life. Wolterstorff suggests that we think of the Bible as the Word of God in these terms. The whole of the Bible is the Word of God because God has appropriated all the human inscriptions that make it up (and some of the utterances it records, e.g., Moses' "Let my people go" but not Pharaoh's reply), thereby making them divine speech acts.

Wolterstorff suggests two consequences of this model for biblical hermeneutics. First, it should be a hermeneutics of authorial discourse. It should not ask "What did the author intend?" but "What did the author say? What speech act did the author perform?" (NB: By eschewing authorial intent as the legitimate goal of hermeneutics, Wolterstorff distances himself from the most popular form of the D/D model of interpretation. But by repudiating the performance model as subjectivistic, he betrays a nostalgia for the objectivism the D/D model promises and the T/P model presents as suspiciously wishful thinking.)

Second, biblical hermeneutics will have to be a double hermeneutics. As an initial step we will have to determine as best we can what speech acts the human author performed by inscribing the text; then we shall have to determine as

---

2. Nicholas Wolterstorff, *Divine Discourse: Philosophical Reflections on the Claim That God Speaks* (New York: Cambridge University Press, 1995), ch. 3.

best we can what speech acts God performs by appropriating it and making it God's Word. The assumption is that the two aren't necessarily the same.

Wolterstorff's concern is not with the hermeneutics of suspicion, but his account leaves the door open for the following account. Although we cannot rightly be suspicious of God, we can approach the biblical text with suspicion while engaged in the first hermeneutic; for there we are asking what speech act the human author is performing and for that purpose questions of motive and function are relevant along with questions of propositional content. When we come to the second hermeneutic, however, things are different. When God becomes the author by appropriating human words, we suspend suspicion, remembering that "as against God we are always in the wrong." Still, our suspicion of the human authors may play a significant role in determining what speech acts we attribute to God.

This distinction, according to which we are willing to find fault with the human authors but not with the divine author, may seem artificial. But it may seem less so if we consider a case that involves truth rather than goodness. Biblical writers are often wedded to a geocentric cosmology that comes very close to what has been called the "three-story universe," according to which the dead are to be found quite literally below us, somewhere within the earth, and God quite literally above us, somewhere in the heavens. It can be said that they assert this worldview, or at least deeply presuppose it in what they do say. But even those who take the Bible to be the Word of God no longer hold that God asserts or deeply presupposes this view in speaking to us in and through the Bible. Cardinal Bellarmine thought it necessary to identify the speech acts of the human writers with the speech acts of God; but Galileo, when he said that the Bible tells us how to go to heaven rather than how the heavens go, did not. Reformed Christians have long since sided with Galileo.

Why would God appropriate a set of speech acts that at the very least deeply presuppose an erroneous worldview? (This analysis and thus the question can easily be extended to other kinds of "error" or "contradiction" in the biblical text.) Perhaps because God sees no obstacle to the divine purpose in doing so. Consider once again the boss who comes home and signs a letter she did not dictate. It may have stylistic features not entirely to her liking. It may even be factually erroneous. Explaining why the company need not accept an offer from a supplier, the secretary may have written that the company has three other suppliers who can provide the needed items. On her trip, the boss may have found a fourth, or discovered that a previous supplier is out of business. So the correct number is either four or two. She may still sign the secretary's draft, knowing that the point is made with sufficient precision for her purposes. The secretary asserts that the company has exactly three other suppliers. The boss asserts that the company has more than enough other suppliers. While we may attribute error to secretary, we do not attribute a lie to the boss.

In everyday life we do not insist on speech act identity between the two speakers in appropriated discourse. Nor, as the Galileo examples indicate, do we do so in morally neutral instances in the biblical context. So perhaps we need not do so in the morally charged contexts that invite the hermeneutics of suspicion. Do we find a patriarchalism or an anti-Semitism in biblical texts that we find (on biblical grounds) to be morally troubling? Perhaps we need to practice a double hermeneutics that is suspicious of the human authors of Scripture in the first instance and guided by that suspicion, but not suspicious of God, in the second instance.

Earlier on I said I wanted to describe a hermeneutics that arises within a Reformed context and that both affirms that the Bible is the Word of God and yet allows us to approach the text with suspicion. Some will find that it goes too far; others that it doesn't go far enough. I have not tried to provide a Goldilocks defense, showing that Wolterstorff's view, together with my extrapolations, gets it "just right." I have defended the view to the degree of trying to show a certain prima facie plausibility to it. Whether it can defeat the defeaters that will be offered from its left and its right I cannot say. So I do not offer it simply as the solution to the problem. I offer it as a possible solution that has the advantage of helping us to see with great clarity what is at stake.

Two closing suppositions bring us back to the question of suspicion and trust. Suppose we conclude that we must go at least this far in being suspicious of the biblical text. That does not preclude the possibility that we should trust that God is at work for our good in the scriptural texts in such a way that we should listen to them above all other texts.

Suppose, by contrast, we conclude that we cannot go this far. The Bible can be the Word of God only if it is sufficiently inspired (read: only if the production of its locutionary acts is sufficiently supervised) to render us "against God" whenever we approach the biblical text with suspicion. We will still not have a *theology* immune to suspicion, at least if the argument of the first part of this essay is correct. All our attempts at D/D interpretation will be interrupted and embarrassed by T/P insights; and into the space between text and interpretation opened up by those insights, assuming Reformed commitments about human sinfulness, interests are bound to creep that work toward suppressing (editing, revising) the truth. The biblical text may be as pure as the driven snow when it comes to embodying the word of God. It may be verbally inspired to the point where it is fully free of both factual error and moral fault. But we must work with our (mis)understanding of it; and it might be a bit too much to claim that our own understanding (individually or collectively) is verbally inspired to the point that it is immaculate and infallible.

But this is compatible with our trusting that God is at work for our good in and through our (mis)understanding of the Bible. In both cases we have suspicion and trust combined. In the one case we trust that God is working for our salvation through a Bible that is not as perfect as we might like it to be. In the other case we trust that God is working for our salvation through an understanding of the Bible that is not as perfect as God might like it to be.

The dialectic of suspicion and trust in hermeneutics is but a special case of the dialectic of sin and salvation.[3]

Bibliography

Derrida, Jacques. "Edmond Jabès and the Question of the Book" and "Structure, Sign, and Play in the Discourse of the Human Sciences." In *Writing and Difference*. Chicago: University of Chicago Press, 1978.

Foucault, Michel. *Power/Knowledge: Selected Interviews and Other Writings 1971–1977*. New York: Pantheon, 1980.

Gadamer, Hans-Georg. *Truth and Method*. 2d rev. ed. Trans. Joel Weinsheimer and Donald G. Marshall. New York: Crossroad, 1991.

Westphal, Merold. *Suspicion and Faith: The Religious Uses of Modern Atheism*. New York. Fordham University Press, 1998.

Wolterstorff, Nicholas. *Divine Discourse: Philosophical Reflections on the Claim That God Speaks*. Cambridge, U.K.: Cambridge University Press, 1995.

3. Support from the Pew Evangelical Scholars Program during the preparation of this essay is hereby gratefully acknowledged.

6

The Battle Belongs to the Word

The Role of Theological Discourse in David's Victory over Saul and Goliath in 1 Samuel 17

J. Richard Middleton

The story of David and Goliath has firmly imprinted itself on the mythic psyche of the Western world.[1] This story from 1 Samuel 17, which picks up on and amplifies ancient mythic themes of the youth who rises to the occasion to deliver a community from some monstrous challenge or danger and is amply rewarded for it, has become for us a paradigm through which we read all sorts of events.

This paradigm is so ingrained in our psyche that in the summer of 2000, during the U.S. Tennis Open, a sports commentator at the end of the men's singles final—which was won by Wimbledon champion Pete Sampras—noted that although David (the challenger) had tried valiantly, he had been unable to defeat Goliath (Sampras). A more appropriate example, perhaps, comes from the 2000 Sydney summer Olympic games. The greatest upset of those games occurred in Greco-Roman wrestling, where Alexandre Karelin, the six-foot, four-inch Russian undefeated champion—winner of three Olympic gold medals in the sport, undefeated in thirteen years of international competition—was defeated decisively by Rulon Gardner, a Wyoming farm boy who had never won a gold medal in any major wrestling competition. And, yes, said the commentator with great excitement, David has defeated Goliath![2]

---

1. An earlier version of this paper was presented in May 2001 at the annual meeting of the Canadian Theological Society at Université Laval, Québec City, QC. The paper was significantly revised with the aid of a Summer Professional Activities Grant from Roberts Wesleyan College and was presented in January 2003 as part of the Cultural Life Lecture Series at Roberts Weslyan College, Rochester, N.Y.

2. Bruce Birch discusses the power and attraction of the David and Goliath story in "The First and Second Books of Samuel," in *The New Interpreter's Bible*, vol. 2 (Nashville: Abingdon, 1998), 1113–15 ("Reflections").

In its explicitly religious use, Christians have often read the story typologically, as prefiguring Jesus' unlikely victory over the monstrous powers of evil, and, by extension, our own victory over evil, as we participate in what Christ has accomplished. One contemporary manifestation of this use of the story is the contemporary praise song "The Battle Belongs to the Lord," whose title is taken from 1 Samuel 17:47.[3] Utilizing militaristic language of armor and weapons, powers of darkness, enemies and courage, the song articulates Christian confidence in overcoming all the evil that confronts and opposes us, on analogy with David's victory over Goliath.

And, of course, these are all appropriate uses of this paradigmatic story, celebrating the victory of the young, unknown David over the towering, battle-seasoned Philistine, against all humanly calculated odds. But a careful reading of the story as found in 1 Samuel 17 discloses some other dimensions of the text that are not often noticed, and that I intend to pay attention to. Not only are these crucial dimensions of the story itself, but they raise important questions for us as contemporary readers of Scripture.

My approach to 1 Samuel 17 in this essay will be twofold. First, I will engage in a close reading of 1 Samuel 17, attending to the text's own foregrounding of speech as key to David's rise. This emphasis on the role of speech (especially theological speech—talk about God) is something not often mentioned in popular interpretations of the story. In highlighting David's verbal victory over Saul and Goliath, I will attempt to read the story *with* David, sympathetically.[4]

But, second, I will problematize this sympathetic reading by raising a fundamental ethical question about the legitimation of violence in this portrayal of David. This ethical question arises initially for me as a contemporary reader of the story, and is undoubtedly influenced by the profound ethical vision of my teacher and colleague, James Olthuis (in whose honor this collection of essays is published). Nevertheless, I will explore a number of ways in which the question is not extrinsic to the text, derived solely from contemporary ethical sensibilities, but is itself rooted in and suggested by a careful reading of various intra- and intertextual details.

In my ethical interrogation of the text, it is my goal to practice what Olthuis has articulated as a nonviolent "hermeneutics of connection."[5] Olthuis's hermeneutics is an extension of his basic Christian ethical stance of nonviolent love,

---

3. "The Battle Belongs to the Lord," words and music by Jamie Owens-Collins, copyright © 1984 by Fairhill Music, Inc.

4. Walter Brueggemann takes the David and Goliath story to be an upbeat, naïve celebration of David, in contrast to what he regards as other, more complicated accounts and portrayals of David in the Old Testament. See Brueggemann, *David's Truth in Israel's Imagination and Memory* (Philadelphia: Fortress, 1985), chap. 1: "The Trustful Truth of the Tribe" (for the David and Goliath story, see pp. 30–35), and also his commentary *First and Second Samuel*, Interpretation (Louisville: John Knox, 1990), pp. 127–134. The analysis in *David's Truth* also emphasizes the central place of David's speech in the story.

5. James H. Olthuis, "Otherwise than Violence: Towards a Hermeneutics of Connection," in *The Arts, Community, and Critical Democracy,* ed. Lambert Zuidevaart and Henry Luttikhuizen, Cross-Currents in Religion and Culture (London: Macmillan, 2000), pp. 137–64.

which involves honoring the alterity of the other without suppressing one's own subjectivity (for that would do violence to the self). Nonviolent love thus involves both attending to the other and being fully present to the other, in a manner that takes seriously both partners in the relationship. Thus, following my teacher, I intend to engage the story of 1 Samuel 17 in a critical dialogue, listening for and attending to the text's own distinctive voice (without subsuming it to my own), while bringing myself as a human subject fully to the interpretive conversation (eschewing the illusion of objectivity). As Olthuis has beautifully articulated, the affirmation of subjectivity is not an impediment to good interpretation. On the contrary, healthy interpretation begins when we subjectively open ourselves to listen attentively to the voice of another. Thus I start with a sympathetic reading of David's victory.

A Sympathetic Reading of David's Victory—The Priority of Speech

The Battle Scene (1 Samuel 17:48–54)

The first thing that strikes the reader as quite odd about this story is how little space in the 58 verses that make up the narrative is devoted to the actual battle between David and Goliath—only four verses.

> When the Philistine drew nearer to meet David, David ran quickly toward the battle line to meet the Philistine. David put his hand in his bag, took out a stone, slung it, and struck the Philistine on his forehead; the stone sank into his forehead, and he fell face down on the ground.
> So David prevailed over the Philistine with a sling and a stone, striking down the Philistine and killing him; there was no sword in David's hand. Then David ran and stood over the Philistine; he grasped his sword, drew it out of its sheath, and killed him; then he cut off his head with it.
> When the Philistines saw that their champion was dead, they fled. (1 Sam. 17:48–51)[6]

Then follow three almost perfunctory verses on the rout of the Philistine army.

> The troops of Israel and Judah rose up with a shout and pursued the Philistines as far as Gath and the gates of Ekron, so that the wounded Philistines fell on the way from Shaaraim as far as Gath and Ekron. The Israelites came back from chasing the Philistines, and they plundered their camp. David took the head of the Philistine and brought it to Jerusalem; but he put his armor in his tent. (1 Sam. 17:52–54)

6. All block, indented quotations of Scripture are from the NRSV. Occasional biblical quotations in the text of the essay that depart from the NRSV are my own translations.

But these short action scenes come late in the text and are continually delayed—by talk. Typically, dialogue fills the space, and delays the action. However, what sets up the story initially is a monologue, a speech with no response.

The Opening Scene—The Philistine Challenge (1 Samuel 17:1–11)

Now the Philistines gathered their armies for battle; they were gathered at Socoh, which belongs to Judah, and encamped between Socoh and Azekah, in Ephes-dammim. Saul and the Israelites gathered and encamped in the valley of Elah, and formed ranks against the Philistines. The Philistines stood on the mountain on the one side, and Israel stood on the mountain on the other side, with a valley between them. And there came out from the camp of the Philistines a champion named Goliath, of Gath, whose height was six cubits and a span. He had a helmet of bronze on his head, and he was armed with a coat of mail; the weight of the coat was five thousand shekels of bronze. He had greaves of bronze on his legs and a javelin of bronze slung between his shoulders. The shaft of his spear was like a weaver's beam, and his spear's head weighed six hundred shekels of iron; and his shield-bearer went before him. He stood and shouted to the ranks of Israel, "Why have you come out to draw up for battle? Am I not a Philistine, and are you not servants of Saul? Choose a man for yourselves, and let him come down to me. If he is able to fight with me and kill me, then we will be your servants; but if I prevail against him and kill him, then you shall be our servants and serve us." And the Philistine said, "Today I defy the ranks of Israel! Give me a man, that we may fight together." When Saul and all Israel heard these words of the Philistine, they were dismayed and greatly afraid. (1 Sam. 17:1–11)

This first scene, in which the Philistine champion appears (vv. 1–11), has two main foci. The first focus is a most uncharacteristically detailed description of Goliath's armor and weapons. It is uncharacteristic because Hebrew narrative rarely provides such detailed visual descriptions; stylistically, it is much more like Homer than the Bible.[7] But it does serve to present Goliath as a formidable

7. Erich Auerbach, in his famous study, *Mimesis: The Representation of Reality in Western Literature*, trans. Willard R. Trask (Princeton, N.J.: Princeton University Press, 1953), calls this characteristic of Homer "fully externalized description" (p. 22) and contrasts it with Old Testament narrative, which he suggests typically withholds such explicit description and is, instead, "fraught with background" (p. 12). For Auerbach's full analysis of the contrast between Homer and the Old Testament, which ranges from stylistic differences regarding visual description and depth of characterization to matters of the texts' substantive theological and ontological claims, see ch. 1: "Odysseus' Scar" (pp. 3–23). For his use of the binding of Isaac narrative in Genesis 22 as a test case for his analysis, see pp. 7–12. It is interesting that this similarity of the opening scene in 1 Samuel 17 with Homeric modes of description occurs in a text about Philistines, who are associated by a complex web of connections (via biblical and classical sources and archaeological evidence) with ancient Greece and the Aegean world. For an attempt to sort out these connections as to their historicity, see Israel Finkelstein, "The Philistines in the Bible: A Late-Monarchic Perspective," *Journal for the Study of the Old Testament* 27, 2 (2002): 131–67. Finkelstein (p. 147) also notes that the idea of a contest of champions (including speeches before battle) can be seen as "Homeric" (Hector versus Ajax, *Iliad* 7.206–304; Paris versus Menelaus, *Iliad* 3.355–94), and that the description of Goliath's armor evokes that of Achilles (*Iliad* 18.480, 606–12; 19.153, 369–85).

challenge to Israel. Both the size of this champion and the sheer weight of his military accoutrements are amazing. His armor weighs one hundred and twenty-five pounds and his spearhead alone weighs over fifteen pounds. And the man himself is gigantic. Even if we amend the six cubits and a span of the Masoretic text (which would make him nine feet six inches tall) to the more modest four cubits and a span found in both the Septuagint and a Hebrew manuscript of Samuel from Qumran, he would still be almost seven feet tall (taller than any known human remains from antiquity). In his great size and in his formidable armor and weaponry, Goliath is portrayed as the epitome of the powerful Philistines, who are regarded in the text as a primary threat to Israel. Indeed, in 1 Samuel 17, the name Goliath is used only twice (in vv. 4 and 23). He is typically called simply "the Philistine." He is *the* Philistine par excellence.

But the other focus of this first scene, over which the narrator lingers, is what Goliath says, his arrogant challenge to Israel (starting in v. 8). Come on, fight me! I'm a Philistine, he boasts. But you, bah! You're slaves of Saul. Choose a representative and let him come and face me alone. Now, what the NRSV renders twice as "kill" in verse 9 is the powerful Hebrew verb *hikâ* (the root *nikâ* in intensive/causative form), which the King James Version renders famously as "smite." If your champion prevails, says Goliath, and *smites* me . . . or if I *smite* him—well, that will decide the battle, one way or another.[8]

And to make it clear that this is a monologue, a speech with no reply, verse 10 continues with "And the Philistine said," which is strictly unnecessary, as he had just been speaking in verses 8–9. Its redundancy suggests that there was no response to his challenge in the previous two verses.[9] Perhaps there was just a communally indrawn breath from the Israelite troops. So, the Philistine speaks again, after a pregnant pause, in effect saying, What's the matter? I've just insulted you. Come on, send someone out to fight me!

And again, there is no reply. The text says that King Saul heard, as did "all Israel" with him (v. 11)—but their only response was terror. They were paralyzed with fear.

David's Visit to the Front (1 Samuel 17:12–24)

This first scene (vv. 1–11) is juxtaposed with the next (vv. 12–24), in which the young David is sent by his father to bring food to his three eldest brothers, who are part of Saul's army. Actually, this next scene has two parts. It begins with a description of a typical state of affairs, depicting a pattern in which

---

8. I have chosen not to use quotation marks for my own paraphrases of various speeches in the text. I will reserve quotation marks for direct quotation.

9. This is based on a suggestion of Robert Alter concerning another such speech resumption in v. 37. See Alter, *The David Story: A Translation and Commentary of 1 and 2 Samuel* (New York: Norton, 1999), p. 107.

David travels back and forth between his home and the battlefront and in which Goliath appears at the front twice daily to utter his challenge.

> Now David was the son of an Ephrathite of Bethlehem in Judah, named Jesse, who had eight sons. In the days of Saul the man was already old and advanced in years. The three eldest sons of Jesse had followed Saul to the battle; the names of his three sons who went to the battle were Eliab the firstborn, and next to him Abinadab, and the third Shammah. David was the youngest; the three eldest followed Saul, but David went back and forth from Saul to feed his father's sheep at Bethlehem. For forty days the Philistine came forward and took his stand, morning and evening. (1 Sam. 17:12–16)

Then this typical state of affairs is followed by an account of one particular visit of David to the front, which happens to coincide with one of Goliath's challenges.

> Jesse said to his son David, "Take for your brothers an ephah of this parched grain and these ten loaves, and carry them quickly to the camp to your brothers; also take these ten cheeses to the commander of their thousand. See how your brothers fare, and bring some token from them."
>
> Now Saul, and they, and all the men of Israel, were in the valley of Elah, fighting with the Philistines. David rose early in the morning, left the sheep with a keeper, took the provisions, and went as Jesse had commanded him. He came to the encampment as the army was going forth to the battle line, shouting the war cry. Israel and the Philistines drew up for battle, army against army. David left the things in charge of the keeper of the baggage, ran to the ranks, and went and greeted his brothers. As he talked with them, the champion, the Philistine of Gath, Goliath by name, came up out of the ranks of the Philistines, and spoke the same words as before. And David heard him.
>
> All the Israelites, when they saw the man, fled from him and were very much afraid. (1 Sam. 17:17–24)

When David arrives at the scene of battle, he finds the Israelite army camped on the other side of the valley from the Philistines and shouting the battle cry—whooping it up, hurling insults (v. 20). But that is the extent of the battle. Given the suggestion of "fighting" in verse 19, this revelation in verse 20 is a rhetorical letdown.

And as David arrives, Goliath comes forth from the Philistine ranks and gives his usual spiel (which isn't actually repeated in v. 23—perhaps if it were, that would delay the action a bit too long). This time, however, the Israelite army doesn't even wait for the monologue. The difference between their previous response in verse 11 and their response here in verse 24 is significant. They no longer wait for the speech. As soon as they see the Philistine, they run away in fear (v. 24). And David, who is present to hear the Philistine's speech (v. 23), undoubtedly witnesses this display of fear on the part of the Israelite troops. Then the multiple scenes of dialogue begin in earnest.

David's Conversations with the Troops (1 Samuel 17:25–30)

The Israelites said, "Have you seen this man who has come up? Surely he has come up to defy Israel. The king will greatly enrich the man who kills him, and will give him his daughter and make his family free in Israel." David said to the men who stood by him, "What shall be done for the man who kills this Philistine, and takes away the reproach from Israel? For who is this uncircumcised Philistine that he should defy the armies of the living God?" The people answered him in the same way, "So shall it be done for the man who kills him."

His eldest brother Eliab heard him talking to the men; and Eliab's anger was kindled against David. He said, "Why have you come down? With whom have you left those few sheep in the wilderness? I know your presumption and the evil of your heart; for you have come down just to see the battle." David said, "What have I done now? It was only a question." He turned away from him toward another and spoke in the same way; and the people answered him again as before. (1 Sam. 17:25–30)

First, in verse 25, David hears someone say, Have you seen this guy? He comes to insult us! And whoever *smites* him the king will reward greatly. Now David is standing right there and clearly hears this. Nevertheless, he says aloud, in verse 26 (rhetorically, for effect), to the group of men standing near him, Tell me again what will be done for the person who *smites* that Philistine and takes away the insult from Israel. Then David intensifies the rhetoric. For whereas the previous speaker had mentioned the Philistine insulting the Israelite troops, David asks, Who is this Philistine that he dares insult the army *of the living God?* The troops then answer David, Thus and so (as the narrator puts it) will be done for the one who *smites* him (v. 27).

Notice what David has done. He has put himself forward by his rhetoric (his words) to be noticed as someone interested in the defeat of this threat to Israel. And the reader might think that he is entirely too forward, even calculating and prideful. But that objection might simply suggest that we've never been in a situation of marginality, where we had to force others to notice the contribution we might make if given half a chance.

However we evaluate that forwardness or self-promotion (which is clearly in the text), it is important to note that David reframes the insult from something done to Israel, to something done to God. This is the first time in the story that someone has spoken of God.

But Eliab, David's oldest brother, overhears the conversation and is incensed (v. 28). What might be the basis of his anger and indignation? Could it be that he had been passed over by Samuel in chapter 16 and saw the prophet anoint this, his youngest brother, to be the future king of Israel? Is he motivated here by jealousy? Or, alternately, does he feel some guilt or shame about his own paralysis in the face of this Philistine threat? Or could it be some combination of jealousy and shame? It is certainly a fact that a great deal of anger is rooted in insecurity and a sense of inadequacy. Lashing out is a typical form of avoidance of our own problems. So, Eliab criticizes David and questions his motives, and claims to know the evil in his (David's) heart. You're getting too big for your britches, he in effect says. Just who do you think you are?

And David's response (in verse 29) is perhaps the most telling line in the entire story: "What have I done now? It was only a question" (NRSV). Or, "it was only talk" (Robert Alter). Actually, the Hebrew has David ask Eliab a question: *hălô' dābār hû'*. Literally, "Wasn't it [just] a word?"

An intriguing comment about the importance of David's talk or words occurs in the previous chapter of 1 Samuel. There, in chapter 16, Saul had sent his servants to find a skilled musician for him, to soothe his moods. One servant reports that he has found David, and in verse 18 describes him in a fivefold characterization. Besides being (1) a good musician, he is described as (2) a strong or valiant warrior (something Saul will explicitly deny later, in ch. 17), (3) good-looking (something Goliath will later notice); and (4) Yahweh is with him, adds the servant. But tucked away in this list of characteristics (right in the middle), the servant observes that David is (5) "skilled of speaking" (*nĕbôn dābār*). Since David never actually speaks in chapter 16, this may well be a comment on chapter 17. We are, at the very least, put on notice about David's skill with words.

So, yes, it was only talk. But then David turns to another person nearby and talks some more (v. 30). He proceeds to ask the same question about what will be done for the man who defeats the Philistine. And he is answered by multiple people, to the same effect as before.

Then the word (the talk) begins to spread about David, this nobody, just a shepherd (probably a teenager). And this talk (just words) gets repeated to Saul, the king of Israel, living in fear of Goliath and the Philistines (v. 31). And Saul calls for David. (You see, first you have to get the interview.)

David's Conversation with Saul (1 Samuel 17:31–37)

When the words that David spoke were heard, they repeated them before Saul; and he sent for him. David said to Saul, "Let no one's heart fail because of him; your servant will go and fight with this Philistine." Saul said to David, "You are not able to go against this Philistine to fight with him; for you are just a boy, and he has been a warrior from his youth." But David said to Saul, "Your servant used to keep sheep for his father; and whenever a lion or a bear came, and took a lamb from the flock, I went after it and struck it down, rescuing the lamb from its mouth; and if it turned against me, I would catch it by the jaw, strike it down, and kill it. Your servant has killed both lions and bears; and this uncircumcised Philistine shall be like one of them, since he has defied the armies of the living God." David said, "The LORD, who saved me from the paw of the lion and from the paw of the bear, will save me from the hand of this Philistine." So Saul said to David, "Go, and may the LORD be with you!" (1 Sam. 17:31–37)

The first thing David says to Saul (in v. 32) is, Don't let anyone be afraid! This young boy not only manages to get a hearing, he accurately discerns the root issue here—as those on the outside of power are often able to. The root issue is fear, outright paralysis in the face of what seems to be an overwhelming threat. And he immediately has a proposal for addressing that threat. "Your servant," he says (deferentially referring to himself), will do battle with this Philistine. That's quite a combination of self-deprecation and outrageous forwardness!

And I'd imagine that Saul's jaw drops open. You can almost hear him sputter, But you can't do that! You're just a youth and he's a seasoned warrior!

Whereas the prophet Jeremiah will later object, at his call, that he is just a youth, and both Moses and Jeremiah tell Yahweh that they have no skill in speaking (Exodus 3; Jeremiah 1), here David is ready for the job. It is Saul who believes that David is unqualified due to his chronological age and his lack of experience and formal credentials. So Saul discounts David. He is not part of the established institution (the army) and has no battle experience.

But David has transferable skills and he explains this in his speech to Saul (in vv. 34–37), which is a masterful presentation of his résumé, his curriculum vitae.

Using deferential language, referring to himself as "your servant" (in vv. 34 and 36), David nevertheless deftly and skillfully articulates his own accomplishments as a shepherd. When a lion or a bear would attack the flock, explains David, I would go out after it, *smite* it, and deliver or rescue the sheep. And then, if the beast attacked me, I would seize it, *smite* it, and kill it. The deferential "your servant" thus belies David's forceful assertion of agency, his ability to act decisively. Indeed, he uses six verbs in the first person singular, five of which are in the Hebrew *hiphil* or causative stem. This choice of language has the cumulative effect of rhetorically presenting David as an active, powerful, dynamic agent or subject (he is no passive doormat, but someone to be reckoned with).

Having recounted this life experience, David then comes to the punch line of his argument in verse 36, namely, that this experience is transferable to the task at hand. Both lion and bear, he says, "your servant" *smote*. And this Philistine will be like one of them, since he has insulted the armies of the living God. Again, we find David's powerful reframing, his use of theological language to depict the Philistine threat. The threat isn't, as David articulates it, simply a military matter—this has to do with *God*.

And just as the Philistine earlier (at the end of v. 9) received no reply (from Saul or Israel) after his challenge, and so had to resume the challenge (in v. 10), so David at the end of verse 36 receives no reply from Saul, who still seems to be dazed by David's bold, improbable offer. He's in shock. So, David resumes his speech in verse 37, and takes the opportunity to put an even more explicit theological spin on matters.[10]

10. This is the point at which Alter (p. 107) makes his suggestion about speech resumption and lack of response, which I have applied also to Goliath's earlier speech.

It is not just that the Philistine has insulted God (which David has previously mentioned in his question to the troops and now in his words to Saul), and it is not just that David is a powerful agent, who is able to defeat Goliath (as he has just articulated in his job interview). David goes on to appeal directly to God's own agency (to God as actor), both in his past shepherd experience and in the battle to come. Yahweh, who delivered/rescued me from the lion and bear, will deliver/rescue me also from this Philistine (v. 37). That David here uses the divine name Yahweh and the verb "deliver"/"rescue" (*nāṣal*), both of which are associated with God's powerful intervention on behalf of Israel at the exodus, makes this a particularly bold claim.[11]

And Saul gives him the job. "Go, and may [Yahweh] be with you!" It is possible that Saul responds with genuine piety. It is more likely, however, that he articulates a piety he thinks would be appropriate, without really believing it. He may well be simply out of options and figures that he might as well send David out, before full battle is joined. I can even entertain the possibility that his answer is ironic, like wishing someone to live in interesting times. Go and may Yahweh be with you—you'll need it!

David and Saul's Armor (1 Samuel 17:38–41)

Saul clothed David with his armor; he put a bronze helmet on his head and clothed him with a coat of mail. David strapped Saul's sword over the armor, and he tried in vain to walk, for he was not used to them. Then David said to Saul, "I cannot walk with these; for I am not used to them." So David removed them. Then he took his staff in his hand, and chose five smooth stones from the wadi, and put them in his shepherd's bag, in the pouch; his sling was in his hand, and he drew near to the Philistine.

The Philistine came on and drew near to David, with his shield-bearer in front of him. (1 Sam. 17:38–41)

This famous scene, in which Saul attempts to foist his own armor and sword on David, is significant for a number of reasons. First, it reminds us of the earlier description in which Goliath's armor and weapons are described (vv. 5–7), and by comparison Saul's seems paltry. It's like producing a World War I single-propeller biplane with a Gattling gun to go up against an F-18 fighter jet that can do Mach 2, equipped with Sidewinder missiles. There would be no contest. The point here is that David cannot hope to fight Goliath on his own terms and win.

There is also the further possibility that the scene with Saul's armor and sword indicates that David's willingness to fight the giant is predicated on the knowledge that he can use his mobility to his advantage. He did, after all,

11. The divine name Yahweh is revealed to Moses in Exod. 3:14–15 in connection with God delivering (*nāṣal*) the Israelites from Egyptian bondage (Exod. 3:8). *Nāṣal* is also used of this deliverance in Exod. 5:23; 6:6; and 18:9.

pursue the lion and the bear, and did not need either sword or armor to defeat them. It is thus possible that the earlier description of Goliath's weighty armor might serve the narrative purpose of alerting the reader to David's awareness of what is, from his perspective, a limitation on Goliath's part. The giant's armor, formidable as it is, weighs him down—and suggests to David a way to defeat him.[12]

Saul, however, does not grasp any of this. In fact, Saul is portrayed here quite badly. First of all, the king of Israel, who stands head and shoulders above other men (according to 1 Sam. 9:2), seems oblivious to the fact that his armor would simply be too big and heavy for the smaller David. But the episode with the armor also shows that Saul gives no credence either to David's past experience with the lion and bear (which required mobility but no sword or armor) or to his theological framing—certainly the more important point. God simply does not enter into Saul's equations.

The episode with Saul's armor thus suggests a subtle comparison between Goliath and Saul—both of whom are armored (though one better than the other), both of whom are tall (though one taller than the other), both of whom despise David and look down on him (Goliath will do this in a moment). But, more important, neither the Philistine champion nor the Israelite king has any regard for the God of Israel as a significant factor in history. In the end, both Goliath and Saul stand—in different ways—in opposition to David. And it is appropriate to think that in this narrative David does battle with them both.

It is even possible that David's agonistic or oppositional relation to Saul is evident in the straightforward, almost brusque, comment he makes in verse 39, which is characterized by a definite lack of deferential language, in contrast to his earlier language of "your servant." After trying on the armor, he says simply, "I cannot walk with these; for I am not used to them."

David, then, without the armor, approaches the Philistine with shepherd's stick, sling, and stones. At last we're getting down to the action! But no, it is delayed once again, by dialogue.

David and Goliath Exchange Words (1 Samuel 17:42–47)

When the Philistine looked and saw David, he disdained him, for he was only a youth, ruddy and handsome in appearance. The Philistine said to David, "Am I a dog, that you come to me with sticks?" And the Philistine cursed David by his gods. The Philistine said to David, "Come to me, and I will give your flesh to the birds of the air and to the wild animals of the field." But David said to the Philistine, "You come to me with sword and spear and javelin; but I come to you in the name of the LORD of hosts, the God of the armies of Israel, whom you have defied. This very day the LORD will deliver you into my hand, and I

12. This possibility is suggested by Peter D. Miscall, *The Workings of Old Testament Narrative*, SBL Semeia Studies (Philadelphia: Fortress; Chico, Calif.: Scholars, 1983), p. 60; and Anthony F. Campbell, "Structure Analysis and the Art of Exegesis (1 Samuel 16:14–18:30)," in *Problems in Biblical Theology: Essays in Honor of Rolf Knierim*, ed. Henry T. C. Sun and Keith L. Eaders (Grand Rapids: Eerdmans, 1997), p. 89.

will strike you down and cut off your head; and I will give the dead bodies of the Philistine army this very day to the birds of the air and to the wild animals of the earth, so that all the earth may know that there is a God in Israel, and that all this assembly may know that the Lord does not save by sword and spear; for the battle is the Lord's and he will give you into our hand." (1 Sam. 17:42–47)

When Goliath sees who has come out to fight him, he reacts—like Saul—to David's youth and despises him. Then follows more dialogue, in which the Philistine mocks David's weapons, curses him by his gods, and tells him to prepare to die and to have his body desecrated by exposure to wild animals (in vv. 43–44). David's response, which is the longest speech in the entire narrative (vv. 45–47), contains a concentration and accumulation of God language. Whereas previously David has mentioned God twice (vv. 26 and 36) and Yahweh once (v. 37), in this single speech (vv. 45–47) we find two references to God and four to Yahweh, one of these in the compound name Yahweh of Hosts. This proliferation of references to God accrues around three theological statements that David makes. It is perhaps important to note that David fearlessly addresses these statements not only to the Philistine, but probably to the listening Israelite troops as well.

First of all (in v. 45), David contrasts *the weapons or source of power* of the Philistine with his own source of power: You come to me with sword, spear, and javelin (powerful conventional weapons). I come to you in the name of Yahweh of Hosts, God of the armies of Israel, whom you have insulted. David is not afraid to claim that he comes in God's name and that this, by implication, more than compensates for his lack of traditional "firepower."

David's second theological statement (in v. 46) is an assertion of what we might call *divine-human synergy*, and it involves a twofold claim. This twofold claim serves to interpret the anticipated victory over Goliath. On the one hand, *Yahweh* will deliver the Philistine over to David (God's agency is primary). Yet, on the other hand, this divine agency will be manifested precisely *through David's agency*, which is articulated using and heightening the language of Goliath's challenge, but this time with David as subject: I will *smite* you, and cut off your head, and give the corpses of the entire Philistine army to the wild animals to desecrate.

The third theological claim David makes in his speech to Goliath concerns the *purpose* or *outcome* of this Philistine defeat through David's agency. That purpose or outcome is twofold. First, as a result of his victory all the earth will know that there is a God in Israel (v. 46). The recognition of the reality of Israel's God seems to be David's foremost concern. But a second purpose or outcome is stated in verse 47, namely, that all this assembly (the assembly of Israel) will know—because in David's opinion they *don't* know, or they wouldn't be paralyzed—that Yahweh doesn't save or deliver by means of conventional weapons of power. The battle, says David, belongs to the Lord. God controls the outcome, not human actors. And so David tells Goliath, Yahweh is the one who will deliver you over to us.

Now, it is important to note that neither the character of David nor the narrator understands human action or human agency to be insignificant. Indeed, among the important human contributions David brings to the battle are (1) his life experience defending the flock, (2) perhaps his perceptive discernment that his mobility and skill with a sling would count for something against the heavily armored Philistine, and (3) certainly the shrewd tactical move in verse 48 of suddenly running forward to get in range for his shot—aiming for probably the only vulnerable spot on Goliath's anatomy, the forehead (where neurologists now know is the highest concentration of nerve endings in the body, and where the brain is closest to the skull itself).[13] Without all this human experience, discernment, and skill, it is likely that Yahweh's power in this story would be stymied. So the text is not contrasting the human and the divine per se. Rather, it is David's claim that Yahweh is at work precisely *through* human agency and experience—but agency and experience that seem by official or institutional standards to be marginal and insignificant.

And even though Yahweh is at work through the skillful actions of David, the way the story unfolds suggests that even more important than actions are *words*. Indeed, it is words that articulate the *claim* of both human and divine agency, human words that people speak—especially that David speaks. The battle, indeed, belongs to the Lord, as verse 47 claims. But I want to suggest that in 1 Samuel 17 the battle belongs to the *word* as much as to the Lord.

And by the time David has finished his speech to Goliath (at the end of v. 47), a speech overheard by Israel, and by Saul—a speech that brings to a climax David's explicit theological framing of the conflict—at least one battle has already been won: the contest with Saul for the leadership of Israel. Yes, David will defeat the Philistine and that will require both word and sling. But his defeat of the paralyzed, fearful Saul is already accomplished. And wasn't it just a word?

But words are crucial in this text, and speech is revelatory of character. In particular, speech reveals who is the more qualified leader. David's earlier questioning of bystanders (in v. 26) characterizes him as a go-getter, who is willing to take the initiative to get a hearing with Saul. And David's explicit theological speech—not only during that questioning, but also in his interview with Saul (vv. 36–37) and finally in his confrontation with Goliath (vv. 45–47)—characterizes him as one who takes the God of Israel seriously and who expects this God to act in concrete ways, on behalf of his people.

This is a significant contrast with Saul. Both his initial *lack* of speech—his failure to respond to Goliath's threat (v. 11)—and his later incredulous words

13. On the question of what sort of helmet would leave Goliath's forehead exposed, see Finkelstein, "The Philistines in the Bible," p. 146, n. 25. Finkelstein explores how the description of Goliath's armor and weapons in 1 Samuel 17 corresponds to what is known of military accoutrements from the Levant and the Aegean throughout various time periods (pp. 142–48).

in response to David's offer to fight the Philistine (v. 33) serve to portray Saul as a weak, paralyzed leader, who does not take the God of Israel seriously as a significant factor in human affairs. But more than that, the final scene of the narrative portrays Saul as an anxious, dithering, even senile leader, who doesn't know who David is.

The Final Scene—Saul's Inquiry into David's Identity (1 Samuel 17:55–58)

When Saul saw David go out against the Philistine, he said to Abner, the commander of the army, "Abner, whose son is this young man?" Abner said, "As your soul lives, O king, I do not know." The king said, "Inquire whose son the stripling is." On David's return from killing the Philistine, Abner took him and brought him before Saul, with the head of the Philistine in his hand.⁸Saul said to him, "Whose son are you, young man?" And David answered, "I am the son of your servant Jesse the Bethlehemite." (1 Sam. 17:55–58)

Having just interviewed him, so to speak, in verses 31–37 and having previously brought the young David to his court in 1 Samuel 16, Saul is here in this final scene perplexed about David's identity. Yes, I know that chapters 16 and 17 are probably two independent traditions about David's introduction to Saul. But some editor saw fit to put them together and thus to highlight Saul's lack of perceptiveness by his perplexed query to Abner, his commander. Indeed, the question (Whose son is that youth/lad?) shows Saul's preoccupation with institutional legitimacy. David's is defined as being young and his identity must be located in terms of family and connections, patriarchally conceived. When Abner swears he doesn't know the answer to Saul's question, Saul presses him to inquire into the matter, repeating both elements of the inquiry (David's youth and parentage). And finally when Abner brings David to Saul, Saul asks David face to face, again noting his youth and inquiring into his parentage: "Whose son are you, young man?" That this final repetition of the question is addressed directly to the one who has just defeated the Philistine giant and initiated a rout of the entire Philistine army (and is portrayed as standing before Saul with Goliath's head in his hand) serves to portray Saul as utterly clueless. And David answers, almost incredulously: I'm Jesse's son, from Bethlehem. Duh!?!

Of course, I may be reading too much into Saul's questioning and into David's answer. Even if the text does not intend to portray Saul as a dithering idiot, this seems to be a rhetorical *effect* of the text—at least on this reader. However one decides this particular matter, it is quite clear that David's contest is not just with Goliath, but also with Saul. Underneath and around the explicit, overt battle (involving both words and deeds) between David the shepherd boy and the giant Philistine is the implicit, more subtle—but nevertheless real—contest between the uncredentialed but courageous David, and the official but impotent and paralyzed leader of Israel, King Saul. Whereas the former contest was said (early in the story) to have as an outcome that David will receive the king's daughter in marriage and freedom (from taxation?) for his family (v. 25), the latter purely verbal contest will have as its (unsaid) outcome the right to the leadership of Israel, as becomes clear by the placement of the David and Goliath story at the start of David's meteoric rise in power and popularity—a rise that begins in the next chapter and that culminates with David's ascent to the throne in 2 Samuel 5.

Most crucially, David's defeat of both Saul and the Philistine depends on his mode of speech. It is thus clear that in 1 Samuel 17 words matter.[14] The story is not simply a naïve celebration of the rise of the inexperienced underdog who risks everything against insurmountable odds in a bold and daring action against a powerful opponent. It also involves a contest of words.

And this contest is won by David because of his explicit theological framing of a real situation of public (even military) conflict in terms of an affront to God and the victory of God over the enemy of his people—a victory explicitly linked with human action (David's action). While David's assertion to Saul that he is able to defeat Goliath is certainly a bold claim, even bolder is his further claim that his victory is God's victory—Yahweh is the one who will deliver him (and, by implication, all Israel) from the Philistine champion (and thus from the Philistine army).

Problematizing David's Speech—The Ethical Question

So far, I have been reading the text *with* David, sympathetically, on his behalf. In this respect, I have followed the basic approach of most commentaries on 1 Samuel 17, which interpret the outlines of the David and Goliath story as a relatively uncomplicated, unambiguous celebration of David's rise to power, either as a genuine memory of David (a story in its own right) or as a cipher for later Judaean ascendancy over its enemies.[15] My only complication of this simple reading has been to emphasize the importance of David's *speech* in the narrative and to note that his contest has been with *both* Saul and Goliath—but these are also gains of recent studies of the text.

It is now time, however, to problematize even this more nuanced reading of the narrative, to challenge either version of a naïve, uncomplicated affirmation of David's rise. The basic question I want to raise is whether David's theological framing of a situation of marginality and conflict is ethically appropriate. Is it right, for either David or us today, to draw God into human affairs, especially into historically conditioned situations of threat or conflict, such that an insult to us is interpreted as an insult to God (vv. 26 and 36) and that God is portrayed

14. This could be seen as a pun on *dabar*, which can mean either "word" or "matter/issue." Words, indeed, are the central matter/issue in 1 Samuel 17.

15. For the latter approach, see P. Kyle McCarter Jr., *1 Samuel*, Anchor Bible, vol. 8 (New York: Doubleday, 1980), pp. 294, 297; and Finkelstein, "The Philistines in the Bible," pp. 147–48.

as acting through us against our enemies (vv. 45–57), who are taken simply to be God's enemies? Even when we are in a situation of relative powerlessness vis-à-vis our opponents (as David was), is it appropriate to claim that God is on our side of the conflict? This is a very difficult question, not subject to any simple answer. There are, in my opinion, two important considerations here.

On the one hand, we need to be open to the genuine possibility of discerning God at work in situations of conflict and threat in the real world. The denial that such a discernment would ever be possible leaves us trapped in the straitjacket of autonomous secularism or possibly in some form of hyper-transcendent spirituality. In either case, we would be in danger of denying the reality and relevance of God for ordinary human life (which is inextricably messy and permeated by conflict). If we are to take seriously the reality of the biblical God (who is not a human construct), we cannot exclude, in principle, the sort of theological framing that David engages in.

On the other hand, however, we need to take with utmost seriousness the danger of fanaticism, where we are unable to distinguish our agendas and perspectives from God's. The inability to make such a distinction puts us in danger of denying the transcendence of God, and thus exempting ourselves from the possibility of judgment. If God simply acts through us, and our enemies are God's enemies, how could God ever call us, and our actions, into question? To put the issue another way, what formal or structural difference is there between David's theological framing of his victory over Goliath and the theological framing of conflict that we find in Osama bin Laden and the al-Qaeda movement? Both sets of actors (ancient and contemporary) perceive themselves as in the minority, facing monstrous opposition, and claim that God works through them in explicitly violent ways.[16]

The David and Goliath story thus raises for me, as a reader of Scripture, a central ethical question about the appropriate use of theological language in situations of conflict. On the face of it, I find such language, especially when used to legitimate a military victory, highly problematic. Nevertheless, simply rejecting this use of theological language out of hand is not a viable option—not if I want to remain in significant connection with Scripture, which certainly contains such uses. Nor may I reinterpret the text of 1 Samuel 17 to make it say what I want it to, which would be an act of interpretive violence, subsuming the otherness of the text under my own voice.

As an alternative to both forms of interpretive violence, I propose that we pay attention to some important features of the text itself. Some of these are *intra*textual features, found *within* the text of 1 Samuel 17, and some are *inter*textual features, which arise from arise from reading 1 Samuel 17 in conversation with

---

16. I have explored this ethical issue in "Created in the Image of a Violent God? The Ethical Problem of the Conquest of Chaos in Biblical Creation Texts," *Interpretation* 59/4 (2004), and in "Identity and Subversion in Babylon: Strategies for 'Resisting Against the System' in the Music of Bob Marley and the Wailers," ch. 9 in *Religion, Culture, and Tradition in the Caribbean*, ed. Hemchand Gossai and N. Samuel Murrell (New York: St. Martin's, 2000), 181–204.

other parts of 1 and 2 Samuel (which was originally, after all, one continuous book). In particular, I want to examine five interlocking questions or issues that arise from such intra- and intertextual reading, each of which serves, in different ways, to problematize my prior uncomplicated reading of 1 Samuel 17.

Who Killed Goliath?

First of all, there is the famous question of who really killed Goliath. Careful biblical readers have long noted that 2 Samuel 21:19 (near the end of 1 and 2 Samuel) credits the victory over Goliath to Elhanan, one of David's warriors. This claim occurs in a brief note concerning the victories of four of David's warriors over four Philistine giants (2 Sam. 21:15–22). This brief note itself occurs in the final four chapters of Samuel, which are often thought to contrast sharply in style with that of the rest of the book and which most scholars have concluded constitute a sort of appendix of disparate material that was added to Samuel at some later date.[17]

A now famous explanation, which tries to reconcile the two seemingly contradictory accounts—going back to the nineteenth century—has been to claim that Elhanan and David are the same person and that Elhanan is David's personal name, while David is his throne name.[18] This claim, however, besides having no support from anywhere else in Scripture, makes no sense of the context of 21:19, since David is clearly differentiated from Elhanan in 21:15–22.[19] Certainly, the book of Chronicles, which is a later rewriting of Israel's history, after the exile, understood Elhanan to be different from David, and found it problematic. Thus the parallel text in 1 Chronicles 20:5 changes Goliath to "the brother of Goliath" in order to remove this difficulty.[20] Chronicles actually removes a number of "difficulties" from the story of David so as to sanitize his reign (thus the Bathsheba and Uriah incident is entirely missing from Chronicles). In the case of the note about Elhanan, it is significant that whereas 2 Samuel 21:15–22 lists Goliath as the third of four Philistines said to be defeated by David's warriors, 1 Chronicles 20:4–5 conveniently omits the first of these four, since that section of the text portrays David as too weak to fight and hence prevented by his warriors from going out to battle anymore.

---

17. These four chapters have a chiastic structure (though the units are of quite varied length), consisting of a narrative (21:1–14), a list (21:15–22), a poem (ch. 22); then a poem (23:1–7), a list (23:8–39), and a narrative (ch. 24).

18. This interpretation was first suggested by J. F. Böttcher, *Neue exegetische-kritische Ährenlese sum Alten Testament*, vol. 1 (Leipzig: Barth, 1863), pp. 233–35, and popularized by A. M. Honeyman, "The Evidence for Regnal Names among the Hebrews," *Journal of Biblical Literature* 67 (1948), pp. 23–24. Cited in P. Kyle McCarter, Jr., *2 Samuel*, Anchor Bible, vol. 9 (New York: Doubleday, 1984), p. 450.

19. Neither is it likely these are two different Philistines with the same name or title (as has sometimes been suggested), since both texts—in a rather distinctive phrase—compare the shaft of Goliath's spear to a weaver's beam (1 Sam. 17:7; 2 Sam. 21:19).

20. 1 Chron. 20:5 supplies the name Lahmi for Goliath's brother, which is taken from *bêt hallaḥmî* (Bethlehemite), a phrase that designated Elhanan's tribal affiliation in 2 Sam. 21:19.

What, then, might be the relationship between the two accounts of the killing of Goliath? Is it, as most scholars have concluded, that a victory by one of David's warriors was later transferred to David himself? And, if so, was there at one time an independent story of David's victory over a Philistine, whose true name has now been forgotten? However one decides that matter, we are still left with the fact that some editor appended 2 Samuel 21:15–22 to the narrative of 1 and 2 Samuel and that this appendix portrays Elhanan's victory over Goliath as occurring while David is so weak that his men prevent him from going out into battle. Whatever the editorial intent, which is no longer recoverable with any certainty, one powerful *effect* of the placement of this text at the conclusion of the extended narrative of David's reign is that it subverts or destabilizes any naïve affirmation of the claims of 1 Samuel 17.[21] This is something that canonical readers of Scripture cannot afford to ignore.

The Difference between Hebrew (MT) and Greek (LXX) Texts of 1 Samuel 17

Another important issue that readers of Scripture need to grapple with is that the version of the David and Goliath story found in one important edition of the Septuagint (LXX) differs significantly from the version found in the Masoretic Text (MT). It is now well known that the Septuagint is not a single entity, but that there are various textual traditions of Old Greek renderings of the Hebrew Bible. The final phase of one important textual tradition is represented by Codex Vaticanus (LXX^B), a fourth-century codex or book that includes both Old and New Testaments in Greek. This particular Greek Bible contains significant omissions in 1 Samuel 17–18, when compared to the Hebrew MT. Those sections of the David and Goliath story that are missing include David's visit to the front and conversation with the troops, followed by the report of this conversation to king Saul (17:12–31) and the final scene in which Saul inquires of David's identity (17:55–58), as well as a few other lines concerning the battle itself (17:41, 48b, and 50).[22] In other words, quite a bit—though not all—of the dialogue scenes that present David's self-promotion and that signal the beginning of his verbal victory over Saul is missing from Codex Vaticanus.

Prior to the discovery of the Dead Sea Scrolls it was typical to explain discrepancies between the LXX and the MT by assuming that the LXX was at fault. Perhaps the translators mistranslated the MT or even added to the text

---

21. Birch (*New Interpreter's Bible,* 2:964) gives further insightful analysis of the canonical function of the appendices of 2 Samuel 21–24 in calling into question absolutist tendencies of the Davidic monarchy.

22. The sections from ch. 18 that are missing in LXX^B include verses 1–5, 10–11, 17–19, and 29b–30. In all, LXX^B is missing thirty-nine of the eighty-eight verses of 1 Samuel 17–18 found in the Hebrew MT. For analysis of the differences in the text of 1 Samuel 17–18 between the MT and LXX, see McCarter, *1 Samuel,* pp. 284–309; Ralph W. Klein, *1 Samuel,* Word Biblical Commentary, vol. 10 (Waco: Word, 1983); and Dominique Barthélemy, David W. Gooding, Johan Lust, and Emanuel Tov, *The Story of David and Goliath: Textual and Literary Criticism,* Orbis Biblicus et Orientalis, vol 73 (Göttingen, Germany: Vandenhoeck & Ruprecht, 1986).

(though in 1 Samuel 17 it looked like they had omitted sections of the text). However, the fact that portions of the Hebrew Bible found at Qumran are closer to various versions of the LXX suggests that matters are not that simple. Indeed, there is a Qumran Samuel text (4QSam[a]) that is closer to Codex Vaticanus than to the MT when it comes to 1 Samuel 17.

There is at present no unanimity about the textual history of 1 Samuel 17 in the MT. Although it is possible that originally two independent versions of the David and Goliath story were woven together, the sections of the story unique to the MT do not seem to constitute an independent narrative. Thus it is more likely that either an originally longer story was shortened at some point or that an originally shorter story was later lengthened by additions (all these positions have been argued).[23] However one decides this issue, the question still remains as to which version of the story is to be preferred. To put it differently, which version ought we to read today? Apart from the question of whether David or Elhanan "originally" killed Goliath, is it possible to say which extant version of the David and Goliath story in 1 Samuel 17 is scriptural, or canonical? Indeed, as a matter of historical fact, *both* have been canonical, since Codex Vaticanus functioned as Scripture for a significant portion of the Christian church (who had no practical access to the MT) over the course of a number of centuries. What is the theological significance of this textual (even canonical) diversity? And how does it bear on our reading of the David and Goliath story today? Those are difficult questions to answer. Minimally, the fact that we have to choose which version of the story to read complicates our reading and disabuses us of any simplistic attempt at providing a definitive interpretation.

Does the Narrator or God Ever Validate David's Theological Interpretation?

A further problem for any naïve, uncomplicated reading of 1 Samuel 17 is that David's theological framing of his victory over Goliath is never validated by either God or the narrator. Although it is characteristic of 1 and 2 Samuel that both the character of God and the narrator typically refrain from evaluative judgments about characters in the story,[24] there are exceptions. Some of the most explicit (negative) judgments in the book include (1) God's statement to Samuel that the people's desire for a king is simply a new form of their age-old rejection of divine rule (1 Samuel 8); (2) God's clear condemnation of David's sin concerning Bathsheba and Uriah, conveyed through the prophet Nathan (1 Samuel 12); and (3) God's censure of David's census of the people (2 Samuel 24). In the case of

23. For a discussion of the various arguments by both biblical scholars and textual critics, see Barthélemy et al., *Story of David and Goliath.*

24. Lyle Eslinger notes that "The narrator of the Dtr narratives is far less concerned with approbation or disapproval, whether of divine or human character, than he is generally thought to be." Eslinger, "A Change of Heart: 1 Samuel 16" (pp. 341–61), in L. Eslinger and G. Taylor, eds., *Ascribe to the Lord: Biblical and Other Studies in Memory of Peter C. Craigie,* JSOTSupp 67 (Sheffield, U.K.: JSOT Press, 1988), p. 355, n. 19.

David's victory over Goliath, however, it is significant that there is no statement from either God or the narrator to corroborate David's theological interpretation of that event. Given the fact that the narrator sometimes notes that Yahweh was with David (1 Sam. 18:14; 2 Sam. 5:10), it is telling that he refrains from any such comment in connection with the Goliath episode.[25] Only Jonathan explicitly agrees with David's interpretation, something that comes to light when he pleads with Saul to save David's life and gives as a reason that "He took his life in his hand when he attacked the Philistine, and the LORD brought about a great victory for all Israel. You saw it and rejoiced" (1 Sam. 19:5). But not only is Jonathan predisposed to such an interpretation since he himself engaged in a similar theological framing of his own daring battle with the Philistines on a previous occasion (1 Sam. 14:6, 10, 12), he is David's closest friend and thus presumably biased in his favor.[26] The lack of corroboration, however, by either the narrator or God constitutes an important lacuna in the text. It thus remains an open question from the point of view of the text itself whether David's explicit theological framing of his victory was appropriate.[27]

David's Good Looks and His Status as a Warrior

The portrayal of David in 1 Samuel 17 as one who is significantly different from Saul, and thus who wins over Goliath on different grounds from Saul, is complicated by the fact that chapter 16 previously attributed to David two characteristics that are also true of Saul. First Samuel 16:18 describes David as a powerful warrior (something Saul explicitly denies in his interview with

25. Various characters in the narrative also recognize that Yahweh is with David (Saul's servant: 1 Sam. 16:18; Saul: 1 Sam. 18:12, 28).

26. One other person who may also agree with David's interpretation is Abigail (who later becomes his wife), although her agreement is less explicit than that of Jonathan. In 1 Samuel 25 Abigail not only affirms that David fights Yahweh's battles and that Yahweh is against David's enemies, but (depending on the intended nuance of her language) she may even allude to the victory over Goliath. Like Jonathan's agreement with David, however, Abigail's opinion on the matter is decisively conditioned by her relation to David, in this case by her attempt to get on his good side.

27. On the issue of the text's evaluation of David, it may be relevant to note Robert Alter's point that a person's first words in Hebrew narrative are often revelatory of his or her character. It is thus telling that David's first recorded speech is his inquiry into the reward that comes from defeating Goliath (1 Sam. 17:26). Thus, beyond the function of putting himself forward as a candidate for fighting Goliath (which I previously suggested), it is possible that David's first speech reveals his baser instincts, which must be taken into account along with his more noble claim to be concerned with the insult to Israel's God. In this light, perhaps we need to reconsider Eliab's upbraiding of David and his claim to know the evil of his heart (v. 28). Perhaps, as Keith Bodner has suggested, Eliab's critique of David is "double-voiced," expressing not just his own sense of outrage at his young, upstart brother, but also the narrator's hint that all is not right in David's "heart." Indeed, David's defensive response to Eliab, "What have I done?" recurs in other contexts in 1 Samuel, where David tries to deflect various accusations (20:1, with Jonathan; 26:18, with Saul; 29:8, with Achish, king of Gath). See Keith Bodner's perceptive essay, "Eliab and the Deuteronomist" (*Journal for the Study of the Old Testament* 28/1 [2003]: 55–71), in which he addresses the narrative function of Eliab's earlier appearance (in 1 Sam. 16:6–7) and the reappearance of much of Eliab's phraseology in the prophet Nathan's parable directed in critique of David and in David's initial response to the parable (2 Samuel 12).

David), and both 1 Samuel 16:12 and 18 describe him as good-looking (something Goliath notices when David approaches him).

While I would not want to claim that good looks are an impediment to godly character or to heroic action on behalf of God, it is interesting that when Saul is first introduced back in 1 Samuel 9:2, he is described as "a handsome young man. There was not a man among the people of Israel more handsome than he; he stood head and shoulders above everyone else." This characterization has led many commentators to suggest that we have here an indication of Saul's superficiality, as if external appearance (both good looks and height) were a legitimate qualification for leadership of Israel. The question, then, is why Saul's servant mentions this particular characteristic of David (16:18), especially when God tells Samuel earlier in the same chapter, at David's anointing, that he does not value external appearance, but looks at the heart (16:7). Even more pointedly, why does the narrator himself mention David's good looks in a threefold description, just verses after God's disavowal of the importance of external appearance? When David is described as (literally) "ruddy, with handsome eyes, and good *looking*" (16:12), the phrase that God *looks* not at appearance but at the heart (16:7) is still ringing in our ears.

Similarly, why is David described as a warrior in chapter 16, but as inexperienced in battle in chapter 17? Although David is probably not a child (as he is sometimes popularly depicted), it is clear that he is portrayed in 17:12–15 as too young for the Israelite army (only his three eldest brothers have joined), and that his lack of military experience distinguishes him from both Goliath and Saul. Indeed, that David is not a member of the army and does not fight with traditional weapons is integral to his claim in 1 Samuel 17 that Yahweh is the source of his power. Yet 1 Samuel 16:18 describes him emphatically, in two powerful Hebrew phrases, as "a valiant warrior/mighty man" and "a man of battle/war."

The question, then, is why some editor juxtaposed these two quite different introductory characterizations of David? Or, since questions about editorial intent are ultimately unanswerable with any certainty, we may ask what the rhetorical effect is of reading the David and Goliath story in the context of the prior portrayal of David as a good-looking warrior in chapter 16. To say the least, this introduces a further complication into what initially seemed to be a relatively uncomplicated affirmation of David's victory over Goliath. In particular, it introduces an ambiguity concerning the *basis* of David's victory and of his later rise to power, which seems tied to this victory. This ambiguity is heightened in the next chapter of 1 Samuel when David skyrockets in popularity as a great warrior: "Saul has killed his thousands, and David his ten thousands" (18:7). Besides his ability to outdo Saul in killing Philistines, one wonders whether David's popularity with the women of Israel, who come out to sing his praises, is not at least partially dependent on his good looks.

Divine-Human Synergy or Effacing of the Subject?

A careful reading of the rhetoric of David's speeches, however, already suggests a fundamental ambiguity about the basis of his victory over Goliath. Earlier I noted what I called a divine-human synergy or cooperation in David's theological speech, in that he claimed that God was working through his (David's) action. However, careful attention to his lengthy speech with Goliath directly before the battle discloses a perceptible shift between an articulation of divine-human synergy and what I would call an "effacing of the subject." That is, David's claim that God is working through his actions comes to be made in a manner that rhetorically obscures or effaces his own part in the battle. In 1 Samuel 17:46, the cooperation or synergy is emphasized. *Yahweh* will deliver you into my hand and *I* will smite you and cut off your head and desecrate the corpses of the Philistine army. Indeed, in this statement of synergism, *David's* action is foregrounded—God gets one verb, David gets three. Yet in the two verses that frame this claim to synergy or cooperation (vv. 45 and 47), *God's* action is emphasized and David's is completely obscured. Thus, in verse 45, David contrasts Goliath's powerful weapons (sword, spear, and javelin) not with his own more modest weapons (staff and sling), but with the name of the Lord of Hosts, the God of the armies of Israel—which is the source of his power. And in verse 47, David contrasts two ways in which the victory over Goliath and the Philistine army may be attempted. He juxtaposes deliverance by weapons—sword and spear (presumably Saul's modus operandi)—with deliverance more directly by God (with no weapons mentioned at all)—the battle belongs to Yahweh.

The question may be asked as to which is the preferable mode of speech. Is it better to claim outright that God works through our actions, while foregrounding our actions (which could lead to hubris, to pride, to self-exaltation), or to obscure our actions and attribute the outcome to God alone? The second alternative may seem initially to be more pious. However, I have a vivid memory from one of my first experiences of preaching as a teenager. When one of my college professors took me aside after to thank me for the message, I piously said something like, "It wasn't me, it was the Lord." To which he wisely replied, "Never say that; if you hadn't taken the time to prepare the sermon, God couldn't have spoken through you in the way that he did." This wise advice, that genuine piety isn't served by suppressing our subjectivity or by denying responsibility for our own actions, can provide an important perspective for critical reflection on the slippage in David's speech. Whereas explicit claims to divine-human synergy are, of course, dangerous, the alternative form of discourse, in which we efface our own subjectivity or agency, may be equally—if not more—dangerous. The danger lies in the fact that it becomes easier to attribute all sorts of subethical, inappropriate human action to God's will if we're not explicit about our responsibility for such action. "It's not me, it's God" may sound pious, but it represents a supremely dangerous form of discourse. It is much better to simply own up to our own role and to our own perspective.

But either mode of theological discourse can be dangerous, especially when we apply such discourse to a situation of conflict, when our opponents are identified with God's enemies—particularly when violence is involved. Whatever our pious intentions, such theological discourse may function to legitimate our own aspirations and ambitions by identifying them, without remainder, with the will of God.

It is interesting that in the later story of David's adultery with Bathsheba and his subsequent attempt to cover it up by killing her husband Uriah (2 Samuel 11), this moral failure turns on the matter of whose perspective is right, David's or God's. This theme is expressed by the use of the phrase "evil in [someone's] eyes" at two crucial points. Whereas David assures Joab, his general, not to regard the death of Uriah (which he had participated in) as evil in his eyes (11:25), the text goes on two verses later to say that the matter was, however, evil in Yahweh's eyes (11:27).[28] The contrast is explicit and suggests the need to distinguish clearly our (fallible) perspectives from God's perspective and not to imagine that our perspective is absolute. Identifying the two is tantamount to idolatry, putting ourselves in God's place, and is precisely what allows us to commit violence with impunity. I have thus come to wonder whether David's theological discourse in 1 Samuel 17 (especially when combined with his evident self-promotion in the text) signals the beginning of the very trajectory that culminates in his acts of adultery and murder in 2 Samuel 11. Could David's mode of speech in 1 Samuel 17 signal the beginning of an attitude on David's part—an attitude that does not sufficiently distinguish his own agenda from God's—that leads to his later overstepping of bounds with Bathsheba and Uriah?[29]

The question is, of course, unanswerable in any definitive way, as is the broader ethical question I have raised in the second half of this essay. Such questions are technically un/decidable, in that there is simply no incontrovertible ground or basis for a decision. Yet neutrality is impossible. Decisions must—and will—be made. Life must be lived. And Scripture will be interpreted. Serious wrestling with such ethical questions in the very process of interpreting Scripture, however, constitutes a faithful mode of engagement with the text and, indeed, with the God to whom the text testifies. The struggle of biblical interpretation may thus be understood as an aspect of moral formation, as communities of readers seek to attend to—and embrace—God's claim on the complexity of human life. It is this ethical understanding of the interpretive process that James Olthuis so well exemplifies in his life, his teaching, and his writing—for which I (along with many of his students) remain immensely grateful.

---

28. This is often obscured in contemporary translations. A more literal rendering clearly links the David story with the time of the Judges, when everyone "did what was right in their own eyes" (Judges 17:6; 21:25), and with the typical negative judgment on the later kings of Israel and Judah, who did evil in the eyes of Yahweh.

29. I have addressed this possibility more systematically in "Is Violence the Primal Sin? The Socio-Ethical Significance of Boundary Transgression in Genesis 3," a paper presented in May 2003 at the annual meeting of the Canadian Society of Biblical Studies, at Dalhousie University, Halifax, Nova Scotia.

Part Two

LOVE,
SELFHOOD,
AND THE GIFT
OF COMMUNITY

7

Face-to-Face

Ethical Asymmetry or the Symmetry of Mutuality?
[1996]

James H. Olthuis

I n its heart, postmodernism is a spiritual movement that resists the total-izing power of reason. It is that resistance, and the concomitant celebration of difference and diversity, that marks a wide array of disparate discourses as postmodern. Ethically, postmodern discourses share an alertness to plurality and a vigilance on behalf of the other. Modernist rational ethics, in its Enlighten-ment dream of a world increasingly controlled by a pure rationality, has shown itself not only blind and indifferent to those who are other and different, those who fall outside the dominant discourse, but violent and oppressive to them. For many, the marginalized and voiceless, the dream has been an unrelenting nightmare. And it continues unabated. In the words of Jacques Derrida, "never before, in absolute figures, never have so many men, women, and children been subjugated, starved, or exterminated on the earth."[1] Not only is our time "out of joint," he exclaims, conjuring up the ghost of Hamlet, "but space, space in time, spacing."[2] What now? The foundations are trembling; there is an incommensurability of voices, a pluralism of discourses, communities of the groundless, enclaves of the homeless.

As Emmanuel Levinas says, "The essential problem is: can we speak of an absolute command after Auschwitz? Can we speak of morality after the failure of morality?"[3] What now after the reign of reason? What if we don't

1. Jacques Derrida, *Specters of Marx,* trans. Peggy Kamuf (New York: Routledge, 1994), p. 85.
2. Ibid., p. 83.
3. Tamara Wright, Peter Hughes, and Alison Ainsley, "The Paradox of Morality: An Interview with Emmanuel Levinas," in *The Provocation of Levinas: Rethinking the Other,* ed. R. Bernasconi and D. Wood (London: Routledge, 1988), p. 176.

have a morality or a religion within the bounds of reason? How do we negotiate civic covenants sensitive to differences of gender, race, creed, age, sexual orientation, and socioeconomic class? How are we to envision and give shape to a postmodern ethics of justice and compassion that includes the other, the disadvantaged, the marginalized, "the widow, orphan, and stranger"?[4]

After noting the impasse of modernist ethics, I want, in this essay, to pay particular attention to Emmanuel Levinas's plea for a different ethics, an ethics as "first philosophy"[5] that begins with responsibility rather than freedom, which finds moral focus in corporeality rather than in arguments, in pain rather than in concepts.[6] Of special concern will be the asymmetrical ethical relation in Levinas in which the other has priority over myself, a view that parallels closely the tendency in much Christian ethics to champion selfless *agape* over so-called selfish *eros*. The question will be raised whether in (rightly) challenging narcissistic self-interest, Levinas doesn't (inadvisedly) bring into ethical disrepute all concern for self-interest because, in his view, an individual subjective agent is not only a locus of enjoyment and self-interest, but also, inevitably, unavoidably, and irrevocably, an agent pitted against other agents. This seems to valorize the often adversarial quality of interpersonal relations as the inexorable human condition (which we then need to transcend to be ethical), rather than to envision such opposition itself as the breakdown of relations of mutuality in which my self-interest and the self-interest of the other may interface with each other to the harmonious enjoyment and enrichment of both parties. That is, I want to suggest an ethics of mutuality[7] in which self-sacrifice is seen not as the heart of ethics, but as an emergency compromise[8] ethic because of the breakdown of mutuality.

4. Derrida has an important discussion of justice in relation to law in "Force of Law: The Mystical Foundation of Authority," trans. M. Quaintance, in *Deconstruction and the Possibility of Justice,* ed. Drucilla Cornell et al. (New York: Routledge, 1992), pp. 3–67. For an earlier effort, on my part, to give embryonic shape to a postmodern ethic in terms of a Gadamerian narrative approach cross-pollinated by a deconstructionist ethics of dissemination, see "An Ethics of Compassion: Ethics in a Post-Modernist Age," in *What Right Does Ethics Have?* ed. Sander Griffioen (Amsterdam: VU Uitgeverij, 1990), pp. 125–46.

5. Emmanuel Levinas, "Morality Is Not a Branch of Philosophy, but First Philosophy," in *Totality and Infinity,* trans. A. Lingus (Pittsburgh: Duquesne University Press, 1969), p. 304, henceforth in text as TI. See also his "Ethics as First Philosophy" in *The Levinas Reader,* ed. Sean Hand (Oxford, U.K.: Blackwell, 1989), pp. 75–87. See also *Ethics as First Philosophy,* ed. A. Peperzak (New York: Routledge, 1995).

6. As one of the first Levinas-inspired North American studies, Edith Wyschogrod's *Saints and Postmodernism* (Chicago: University of Chicago Press, 1990), appealing for a saintly ethics of self-sacrifice, also calls for attention. Today there is a growing spate of books taking up the issue of deconstruction and ethics. Three of special note are Simon Critchley, *The Ethics of Deconstruction* (Oxford, U.K.: Blackwell, 1992); Zygmunt Bauman, *Postmodern Ethics* (Oxford, U.K.: Blackwell, 1993); and John D. Caputo, *Against Ethics* (Bloomington: Indiana University Press, 1993).

7. Such an ethics, I submit, adds a fourth approach to Alasdair MacIntyre's three broad versions of ethical enquiry: the Enlightenment encyclopedia, the deconstructivist genealogical, and the Thomistic traditional. See his *Three Rival Versions of Moral Enquiry* (Notre Dame, Ind.: University of Notre Dame Press, 1990).

8. Looked at from my perspective, Levinas could be said to have his own "compromise ethic" when, following recognition of the priority of the other, justice enters with the arrival of "the third"—another

In other words, the question is whether self-sacrifice is a compromise ethic due to the breakdown of mutuality (my position), or whether self-sacrifice is the only avenue to mutuality (Levinas's position). The discussion is complicated because the self-sacrifice Levinas calls for is not the sacrifice of the deepest self (*le soi*), for that self is *always already* sacrificed before it has itself to sacrifice—and has itself to sacrifice or not to sacrifice only on that basis. At bottom, the heart of the discussion is whether our common ethical concern is better served by describing the self as "substitution," "hostage," or "dis-interestedness," or by portraying the ethical self as "power-with," "responsibility-with," "suffering-with." Instead of conceiving the I (*le moi*) as necessarily, ontologically, and exclusively only a self-interested agent over against other agents, which then needs to be transcended in an ethical awakening to my true self (*le soi*) as substitution for the other, I want to suggest the ethico-ontological possibility of an agent self as power-with, responsibility-with, all the while retaining a realistic awareness of the propensity to power-over violence that constantly lurks within us, to which we so often capitulate, and in which we are so frequently implicated. Instead of an "other-wise than being,"[9] as substitution, as responsibility for, I'm suggesting a being-otherwise, not as mastering, but as connecting-with.

Modern Ethical Theory

Modern ethical theory in the spirit of the Enlightenment has striven to construct a rational foundation for morality. The benchmark of such theory, whether in utilitarian or Kantian dress, has been the effort to move ethical judgments beyond the contingency and time-bound contexts of moral actors. Inspired by the scientific ideal of objectivity, ethical theory attempted to secure so-called objective moral judgments free from the subjective desires, beliefs, and narratives of the agents who make them. A justified moral judgment needs to take a form that can and must be made from anyone's point of view, independent of time, place, and historical circumstance. Problems emerge and are solved only within the comprehensive framework of a unified "encyclopaedic rationality," as MacIntyre names it. Along these lines, for example, there are Kant's categorical imperative, Hare's universalizability, Baier's God's-eye point

---

"other"—and I am permitted to see myself as the other of the other. Whereas for me, mutuality is the normative and self-sacrifice the compromise, for Levinas something like the opposite seems true. Normative is the priority of the other (with the sacrifice of the agentic self) and the political compromise is the reciprocity involving a third. On the other hand, the difference is somewhat muted when it is recognized that for Levinas equality is the goal of the priority of the other. That is, from his viewpoint, the priority of the other is not seen as a compromise, but the asymmetry of priority is considered the condition for the symmetry of equality.

9. Emmanuel Levinas, *Otherwise than Being or Beyond Essence*, trans. A. Lingus (The Hague, Netherlands: Martinus Nijhoff, 1981). Henceforth in text as OB.

of view, and Rawls's original position. As Stanley Hauerwas and David Burrell put it: "What I am morally obligated to do is not what derives from being a father, or a son, or an American, or a teacher, or a doctor, or a Christian, but what follows from my being a person constituted by reason."[10] Moreover, the transcendental turn to the subject, especially in Descartes, Kant, and Husserl, led to an emphasis on a timeless, omniscient, disinterested observer and the loss of attention to the pain and suffering of bodies.

Modernist ethics assumed that reasonable debate should be able to settle our basic life questions. The intent was to arrive at rational agreement without having to resort to violence.[11] But the result has often been a tangle of conflicting positions, a quagmire of unresolved issues. There has been no easy line from moral theories to moral actions. Indeed, the increasing complexity of life has made the arguments even more complex and the disputes even more intractable. The transformation of moral life through rigorous application of moral theory has failed.

Ironically, not only has rational agreement remained out of reach, but the result has been indifference to the real life situations of many people, particularly women, children, and the otherwise marginalized. In general, the abstraction of the full flesh-and-blood person from an ethical case, and the case from its full historical and developmental context, has made the whole exercise of Enlightenment ethics artificial, futile, and alienating. When moral decisions are to be based on rationally grounded principles that are not relative to the character, motives, history, context, interests, gender, body, and worldview of the agents, moral agents are separated not only from all that makes them unique, but from the very corporeality and embeddedness that makes them human persons. There is no other word for such depersonalization than violence. In effect, the "personal" is considered morally significant *only* to the extent that it can be bracketed and translated into the "impersonal." Indeed, complete disembodiment and complete disinterest is regarded as the only appropriate starting point for moral reasoning in the modernist schema.

Anthropologically, in these modernist constructions, the human self is generally understood as some combination of mind and body in which mind has the primary role of controlling corporeal desire. Feelings and emotions are typically considered morally negligible because they merely happen to pre-existing, true, rational selves and are thus held to be transitory and capricious. Universal rules of conduct as our moral duties are contrasted with contingent pleasures of our individual passions. Thus, in the Kantian tradition, sympathy, compassion, and concern—the altruistic emotions—cannot play a substantial

---

10. Stanley Hauerwas and David Burrell, "From System to Story," in S. Hauerwas and L. Jones, eds., *Why Narrative?* (Grand Rapids: Eerdmans, 1989), p. 163.

11. Perhaps the most influential contemporary effort to defend modern rationality (as it attempts to avoid modernity's pathologies) is Jürgen Habermas's "discourse ethics" with its goal of "communicative rationality." See his *Moral Consciousness and Communicative Action* (Cambridge, Mass.: MIT Press, 1990).

role in morality and moral motivation because they are not products of human agency, but in fact easily divert us from the autonomy and freedom needed for moral judgment.[12]

Today, by virtually every account, this approach to persons has failed. And the failure of reason is especially obvious in the area of moral philosophy. It has become increasingly clearer that the scientific model of rationality and neutrality, with its pretense to universality and necessity, has, in fact, been unaware of its own particularity and contingency. Modernism's conviction that we can isolate impartial moral principles from our particular worldviews, loyalties, identities, histories, and communities has been revealed as its own particular faith. "There is no theoretically neutral, pretheoretical ground from which the adjudication of competing claims can proceed."[13] In effect, the culturally and morally particular was elevated to the status of the rationally universal, to the detriment and oppression of anyone and anything that is different, that is, who did not find her/himself within the discourse of universal reason. Thus, to take a classic example, Carol Gilligan has demonstrated that Lawrence Kohlberg's stages of moral reasoning champion a typical "masculine" ethics of duty and abstraction as the most highly developed, in contrast to an ethics of connection and responsibility more typical of women.[14] No wonder that women tended to rate much lower than men in "maturity" of moral reasoning!

We have now discovered, under the impetus of the masters of suspicion—Freud, Marx, and Nietzsche—that what was touted as the autonomous human self was in fact an illusion. The encyclopedist's appeal to timeless rational principles does not discard the burden of the past as they intended. Rather their appeal to a unitary conception of reason provides unwarranted privileged status to those who identify their own assertions and arguments with the deliverances of reason. Encyclopedic, impartial reason is exposed by the postmodern genealogist as the unwitting pawn of particular interests that mask their drive for power by false pretensions to neutrality, universality, and disinterestedness.[15]

Critics of modern ethics are unanimous that all our ideas and views are narrative-dependent, including, they emphasize, our view of rationality. There is no narrative-free judgment, and pretending that there is does violence to all, particularly to those who do not hold to the accepted view. While MacIntyre believes, in Gadamerian fashion, that commitment to some or other theoretical or doctrinal standpoint may be the requisite for—rather than the barrier to—genuine moral inquiry, he continues to believe that reason can move toward being authentically universal and impersonal. Such an alternative, which MacIntyre traces back to Plato and, for him, is best represented by

12. See Lawrence Blum, *Friendship, Altruism, and Morality* (London: Routledge & Kegan Paul, 1980), for an incisive critique of the Kantian tradition.

13. MacIntyre, *Three Rival Versions*, p. 173.

14. Carol Gilligan, *In a Different Voice* (Cambridge: Harvard University Press, 1982).

15. Michel Foucault, *Power/Knowledge: Selected Interviews and Other Writings*, ed. C. Gordon, trans. C. Gordon et al. (New York: Pantheon, 1980).

Thomism, remains, from a postmodern perspective, unacceptable and even naïve. Postmoderns insist that theory itself has failed. Picking up on Heidegger's critique of the institutionalization of reason whereby everything, in nature as well as in culture, is to be put under the sway of the desire to master and control, postmodernist thinkers such as Derrida, Foucault, and Levinas assail the logocentrism of Western thought.

Ethics before Ontology: The Priority of the Other

For Levinas, reason is the instrument by which an ego or society of egos makes same that which is different, possessing and domesticating it. Reason reduces the other, appropriates, disempowers, totalizes. The particular is placed under the general category. What is foreign, what is different, is subsumed within my system. It is made the same to remove its threat. All surprises prove to be just parts of the process, that is, not surprises at all. This is ontology.

Before ontology, however, exclaims Levinas, there is ethics, the relationship of responsibility to the other.[16] The other can never be present within my discourse, my theory, my thought, my ontology. Unless I allow myself to be instructed by the face of the other, I do not "relate" at all, but only dominate in terms of my paradigms and ontologies. The face of the other commands me: Thou shalt not kill. For Levinas the face is not a presence, but a trace, a trace that marks the escape of the other who cannot be contained, who has escaped the reduction to Being.

The face is the epiphany of the nakedness of the other, a visitation, a coming, a saying that comes in the passivity of the face, not threatening, but obligating. I encounter a face, my world is ruptured, my contentment interrupted; I am already obligated. Here is an appeal from which there is no escape, a responsibility, a state of being hostage. It is looking into the face of the other that reveals the call to responsibility as an-archic, that is, before any beginning, decision, or initiative on my part.

For Levinas the other is not another me, awaiting dialogue and reciprocity, as in Buber and Ricoeur. For Levinas my relation to the other is always asymmetrical. The other has ethical priority over the sameness of the I.

> I must always demand more of myself than of the other; and this is why I dis-agree with Buber's description of the I-Thou ethical relation as a symmetrical copresence. . . . This essential asymmetry is the very basis of ethics: not only am I more responsible than the other but I am even responsible for everyone else's responsibility.[17]

16. "'Religion' [is] the bond that is established between the same and the other without constituting a totality" (TI, p. 40).

17. Emmanuel Levinas and Richard Kearney, "Dialogue with Emmanuel Levinas," in *Face to Face with Levinas,* ed. Richard A. Cohen (Albany: State University of New York Press, 1986), p. 31.

The existence of the other, rather than a conception of the good, is the touchstone of moral existence. The face-to-face relation fissures being. Flesh-and-blood bodies, rather than arguments and concepts, give moral bearings.

The implications of this shift are only now beginning to surface and take shape. In the Cartesian view of the body as external object in space over against the subject as inner consciousness, the body as subject of experience was lost. Similarly, in the Kantian view, in which the having of feelings is morally indifferent, non-rational ways of knowing are devalued. Generally speaking, in the rationality tradition, sensory knowledge is useful, but it is never in itself knowledge of the human as human.[18] Since reason is that part of being human that is most human, only reason can know the properties of being, goodness, beauty, and unity. Thus, for Thomas Aquinas, touch is the lowest and least worthy of all senses because it is most unlike reason. Since the pleasures of eating, drinking, and having sex are pleasures of touch, it is a sin to engage in them solely for the pleasure of eating, drinking, and having sex.

In the rationality tradition there has been a conceptual neutralization of sensation. Spinoza gives voice to the dominant tradition: "Pain is the transition of a man from a greater to a lesser perfection."[19] Both pain and enjoyment have been rationalized and their sensory truth decimated. Even Heidegger, the archcritic of the metaphysics of subjectivity that he traces back to Plato and Aristotle, in the end still remains captive to this feature of the tradition. He takes the suffering out of pain by insisting that the essence of pain cannot be pain in a feeling sense.[20]

In contrast, in the postmodern picture I myself am my body. The body as a whole functions as a sensorium, a senser, a knower, a perceiver, a digester. Human knowledge is multidimensional. Sensing and feeling are as human as thinking. The human self includes perceptions, feelings, emotions, dispositions, attitudes, as well as thoughts. Others present themselves not simply as subjects of discourse, but, on a more fundamental level, as persons who eat, enjoy, lack, and so forth. For Levinas, alterity must communicate itself fundamentally otherwise than predicatively. In *Otherwise than Being* Levinas describes ethical obligation in terms of the subject's corporeal sensibility and proximity, vulnerability, and passivity toward the other. The ethical subject is subject to the other as "sensibility on the surface of the skin, at the edge of the nerves" (OB 15). Since the human person is susceptible to wounding and pain, ethics is a lived, bodily relation to the other. "Only a subject that eats can be-for-the-other" (OB 74).[21]

18. In "A Medieval Lesson on Bodily Knowing: Women's Experience and Men's Thought," in *Journal of the American Academy of Religion*, 57, 2 (1989): 341–72, J. Giles Milhaven has traced the impact of our limitation of knowledge to the rational.

19. Spinoza, *Ethics*, in *The Chief Works of Benedict de Spinoza*, trans. R. Elwes (New York: Dover, 1955), part 3, definition 3, p. 174.

20. See John D. Caputo, *Demythologizing Heidegger* (Bloomington: Indiana University Press, 1993), ch. 8, pp. 148–68.

21. Thus, Levinas worries that "Dasein in Heidegger is never hungry" (*Totality and Infinity*, p. 134).

"Ethics is the spiritual optics" (TI 78). "To recognize the Other is to recognize a hunger. To recognize the Other is to give" (TI 75).[22] The ethical "[f]ace to face remains an ultimate situation" (TI 81) and "in it things figure not as what one builds but as what one gives" (TI 77). This allows human sensitivity to pain, wounding, and suffering to be immediately ethically relevant. Ethics in this view is grounded in corporeality, in creatureliness, with a special marking because of pain, suffering, lapse, delay, and fissure. It is sensitive bodies in proximity that are the space of ethics, the fields of meeting.[23] In my very hearing of the child's cries I am ethically claimed.[24] Face-to-face, flesh-to-flesh, I am wounded by the other's wounding—and responsible for it. Responsibility is prior to freedom. "This responsibility appears as a plot without a beginning, anarchic . . . outside of all finality and every system" (OB 135). There is no need for a reasoning process to discover or erect a rational reason to provide the moral force.

The other is experienced as an appeal, an absence, in that it creates in me a restlessness for contact that I don't have.[25] And the other is experienced as an excess in that the trace of transcendence is inscribed in the face. "The Other is not the incarnation of God, but precisely by his face, in which he is disincarnate, is the manifestation of the height in which God is revealed" (TI 79). "Strictly speaking, the other is the end; I am a hostage, a responsibility and a substitution supporting the world in the passivity of assignation, even in an accusing persecution, which is undeclinable" (OB 128).

In *Against Ethics* John Caputo describes such views as "responsible" postmodernism because they answer a call from beyond our laws and principles, so that we can attend to the particulars, the lost, the different, the exceptions. This kind of ethic is not against laws, but is aware that laws and rules do not have authority in themselves. As Caputo puts it, with an allusion to Christ healing on the sabbath, we need "to keep the law honest, to keep the eye of the law on the withered hand."[26] Indeed, to simply do what the law dictates is to fall short of doing justice. The law needs to be under justice, not justice under law. Such responsibility demands an exceeding of the demands of the law, incarnating a response to which laws intend to point the direction, but sometimes, in fact, obscure. Likewise, Wyschogrod makes a plea for "excessive desire, a desire on behalf of the other that seeks the cessation of another's

22. "The-one-for-the-other is the foundation of theory" (Levinas, *Otherwise*, p. 136).

23. Elsewhere I have called these fields of meeting the "wild spaces of love" to emphasize they are as free for love as they are for control and violence. See my "Crossing the Threshold: Sojourning Together in the Wild Spaces of Love," *Toronto Journal of Theology* 11, 1 (1995): 39–57 (included as chapter 1 above).

24. Despite the considerable debt owed to Merleau-Ponty for his recovery of the agent body, John Caputo points out that his analysis, by overlooking improper and unbecoming, vulnerable and suffering bodies, "is still a form of idealism against which he always fought" (*Against Ethics*, p. 202). Whereas for Merleau-Ponty it is the resemblance between self and other, for Levinas it is the asymmetrical, unsurpassable difference that opens up ethics and discourse.

25. Not to forget or minimize the restlessness or unrest awakened on contact.

26. Caputo, *Against Ethics*, p. 149.

suffering and the birth of another's joy."[27] Similarly, although in his typically more dialectical fashion, Paul Ricoeur attempts to establish the primacy of the ethical aim (goodness) over morality by "granting rightful place to moral rules, without letting them have the last word."[28]

Asymmetry and Self-Sacrifice

All of this—the morality of corporeality, the spirituality of morality—finds deep resonance in my soul. Along with Levinas I see ethics not as something later, to be fitted in, but as the nature of life itself. Indeed, for me it is of the highest import that life be seen as *conatus amandi* (evocation to love) rather than as *conatus essendi*. In this way, ethics—in the sense of responsibility to love—is as old as creation itself. Love is the quickening, the quivering[29] that evokes life and permeates life. The call to justice and love belongs to the very fabric of everyday life, giving it shape and texture. In a world of violence, this call often arises most poignantly in the need of the neighbor and likewise is often discovered most acutely in the cry of suffering. Then the call comes as a summons: heal the wounds, bind up the brokenhearted. Being ethical is a primordial movement in the beckoning force of life itself. As gift and call, love is both the description of life and the prescription for life.

At the same time, I admit to a fluttering, sometimes throbbing, but always bothersome disquiet. For as much as I join with Levinas in his call to responsibility for the other, I am concerned that his emphasis on the priority of the other not give birth—albeit contrary to intention—to a guilting moralism calling for self-forgetfulness and self-forfeiture. For all its importance as a countermove to narcissism, calling for the ethical priority of the other not only has the feel of Utopian impossibility about it,[30] but, more ominously, may inadvertently proliferate the very violence it sets out to counteract.[31]

And even though for Levinas the feminine is the other par excellence,[32] what are we, in a time when women are emerging from patriarchy with agency and

27. Wyschogrod, *Saints,* p. xxiv.

28. Paul Ricoeur, *Oneself as Another,* p. 171. Chs. 7, 8, and 9 describe how for Ricoeur the ethical aim needs to pass through the sieve of the norm, even as, when the norm leads to situations of impasse, we go back to the aim.

29. In contrast to the "anonymous rustling" of Levinas (*Otherwise,* p. 3), the "incessant bustling" of the "there is [*il y a*], the horrible eternity at the bottom of essence" (*Otherwise,* p. 176).

30. Levinas does admit that "[t]here is a Utopian moment in what I say: it is the recognition of something which cannot be realised but, which, ultimately, guides all moral action" ("The Paradox of Morality," p. 72).

31. In *Against Ethics,* by referring to a sentence of Derrida's in *Truth in Painting,* Caputo calls it "an impossible dream, even a dangerous dream, inasmuch as promises of what is absolutely unmediated are usually followed by the most massive mediations" (p. 82). When legitimate self-needs are denied, they have a way of coming back with a vengeance, often in disguised, underhanded, and dangerous ways.

32. In *Totality and Infinity* Levinas describes the importance of the "gentleness of the feminine face" (p. 150) in establishing the intimacy of home, making space for hospitality to strangers, and thus establish-

voice, to make of a view that sees subjectivity as dispossession and subjection? What, indeed, are we to make of Levinas's subsequent depiction of maternity as the paradigm of the behavior of a human subject toward the other?[33]

In his claim that being-responsible-for-the-other is the constitution of true selfhood, Levinas is calling—certainly first and last[34]—for disinterest in, if not repudiation of, all self-interest. For Levinas, I am expiation for the other, held hostage by the other, to whom I must give preference over myself. "The self, the persecuted one" is, in fact, says Levinas, not "in the state of original sin; it is, on the contrary, the original goodness of creation" (OB 121).[35]

For Levinas an ethical relation is non-symmetrical because "I am responsible for the other without waiting for reciprocity, were I to die for it. Reciprocity is his affair."[36] "The face of a neighbor signifies for me an unexceptional responsibility, preceding every free consent, every pact, every contract" (OB 88). The face is both my superior that demands my attention and my subordinate, because in his/her vulnerablity s/he cannot compel me to give it.

In recognizing the dance of intersubjectivity as the crucial process in which the moral self is constituted, Levinas is, I believe, rightly claiming that my responsibility for my neighbor is not a function of or derivable from anything else other than that s/he is my neighbor. But does this necessarily mean, on an ethical level,

---

ing a subjectivity capable of ethical relationships. The feminine other is also "the Beloved . . . an extreme fragility, a vulnerability" (p. 256). Since traditionally the woman too often has been considered the other who needs to be put down by the man as same, Levinas's acknowledgment of the significant place of women contributes to a new ethics of respect for women. However, at the same time, in *Totality and Infinity*, his ambiguity in regard to the feminine emerges when, in relating the erotic to the feminine, he sees the erotic with its "return to the self" (p. 266) as less than ethical, and when he talks of the "beloved," the feminine, as "without responsibility," fading into "ambiguity, into animality" (p. 263). Moreover, it is not clear whether, for Levinas, a woman can also be agent, the lover as well as the beloved. See Luce Irigaray's two essays on Levinas, "The Fecundity of the Caress," in Iragaray, *An Ethics of Sexual Difference,* trans. C. Burke and G. Gill (Ithaca, N.Y.: Cornell University Press, 1993), pp. 185–217, and "Questions to Emmanuel Levinas," in *Re-Reading Levinas,* ed. R. Bernasconi and S. Critchley (Bloomington: Indiana University Press, 1991), pp. 109–29. For a careful and nuanced discussion and critique of Levinas's portrayal of the feminine, see Atie T. Brüggemann-Kruijff, *Bij de gratie van de transcendentie: En gesprek met Levinas over het vrouwelijke* (Amsterdam: VU Uitgeverij, 1993). Tina Chanter's recent *Ethics of Eros* (New York: Routledge, 1995) is also an excellent discussion of Levinas's views of the feminine and Irigaray's critique.

33. *Otherwise,* pp. 75–81. "Maternity, which is bearing par excellence, bears even responsibility for the persecuting by the persecutor" (p. 75). Although it is clear that the feminine, as the trope for subjectivity, is at the heart of the ethical, I am deeply concerned about the felicity of employing feminine imagery for human subjectivity, which could, particularly by women, be heard not only as conflating being a woman with motherhood but also once more and once again glorifying their submission. Much better, it would seem, if one wants to emphasize the importance of committed caring for the other, the bearing of each other's burdens, to talk of paternity as well as maternity as ethical figures par excellence. See Morny Joy, "Levinas: Alterity, the Feminine and Women—A Meditation," in *Studies in Religion,* 22, 4 (1993): 463–85.

34. "But egoism is neither first nor last" (*Otherwise,* p. 128).

35. For Wyschogrod, "a saintly life is defined as one in which compassion for the other, irrespective of cost to the saint, is the primary trait," and "whatever the cost to the saint in pain and sorrow" (*Saints,* pp. xxiii, 34).

36. Levinas, *Ethics and Infinity: Conversations with Philippe Nemo,* trans. R. Cohen (Pittsburgh: Duquesne University Press, 1985), p. 98.

the indiscriminate acceptance of others regardless of their motives, an ethical "disinterestedness" (OB 126) in my own welfare even "were I to die for it"?[37]

There can be no question about the need to avoid reducing the other to another self similar to me. The mystery of each unique identity means that there can be no question of having another person's experience. To the extent that I am a unique self no one else can replace me in my responsibility. In that sense human experience is always asymmetrical.

Human uniqueness—and asymmetry—comes to the fore especially in the intimate ethical relationships of friendship, marriage, and family. In an economy of reciprocity and exchange, things and people have instrumental value in promoting one's interests and are thus replaceable or may be substituted by things or people who meet the need(s) equally well. However, in ethical relations of mutuality persons are unique particulars and the beloved is different, incomparable, and irreplaceable (never a mere instrument). Each relation of mutual love is its own non-interchangeable relation. As opposed to a quantitative hierarchical scale of loves, we have a qualitative array of incommensurate loves in which "we love them all differently because they are incomparably different."[38] Thus, I express the "same" love to my children by loving them all "differently" because they are all unique individuals. You are my friend because you are you. That relation is incomparable with my relationship with anyone else, because nobody else is you.

The question is whether this asymmetry of experience calls for an ethical asymmetry in which the other normatively always has priority over me. Indeed, it seems to me that Derrida makes a good point when he asserts that "dissymmetry itself would be impossible without this symmetry" in which "I know myself to be other for the other. Without this, 'I' (in general: egoity), unable to be the other's other, would never be a victim of violence."[39] That is to say, human intersubjectivity as mutual responsibility is an ethical symmetry of empirical asymmetries. From his side, Levinas is afraid of ethical symmetry-talk, not because he does not accept intersubjectivity, but because he is convinced that such talk willy nilly involves a generalizing (i.e., totalizing) insistence that the other be responsible in the same way that I am. That is—and remains, no doubt—a clear and present danger. But is it inevitably the case? Is the only alternative to egoism altruism? Is my ethical insistence on human co-responsibility for justice, for example, necessarily an imposition of my views on others? If I (we) take seriously the situatedness of our freedom

37. It is clear that in actual life, due to the third party, Levinas is able to justify pragmatically self-defense in the face of aggression. The point is that he seems on the highest ethical level to disallow any and all self-interest.

38. Vincent Brummer, *The Model of Love* (Cambridge, U.K.: Cambridge University Press, 1993), p. 210.

39. Jacques Derrida, "Violence and Metaphysics: An Essay on the Thought of Emmanuel Levinas," in *Writing and Difference,* trans. A. Bass (Chicago: University of Chicago Press, 1978), p. 126. "That I am also essentially the other's other, and that I know I am, is evidence of a strange symmetry whose trace appears nowhere in Levinas's descriptions" (p. 128).

and fallibility, my (our) insistence on justice will recognize that there will be differences of response to the common call. More importantly—as I will consider in more detail below—if we begin with ethical symmetry, another possibility opens up in which self and other are not irrevocably and inevitably locked in an economy of war, but in a nonviolent economy of mutuality and love in which justice and care for the neighboring other is of one piece with justice and care of and for myself.

For his part, in insisting on ethical asymmetry, Levinas emphasizes the movement of the other to self (no responding self without an other summoning) at the cost of minimizing the corresponding movement of self to the other (no summoning other without responding self).[40] The result is that, ethically, instead of a two-directional interplay of mutuality, there is uni-directionality. For Levinas, prior to the ethical interruption of the other, the I (*le moi*) is fundamentally ignorant of, separate from, and closed off to the other. The other must storm the defenses of the self. There seems to be no room, ontologically, for the possibility of a self, of its own initiative, to reach out, attentive and open to the other. And when the ethical self is born ("awakened"), and is "hospitable," the self is, first and foremost, hostage to, and expiation for, the other. In Levinas's ethical asymmetry there is a necessary disinterest in self-concern and a corresponding complete non-indifference to others. "Subjectivity is not for itself; it is, once again, initially for another. . . . the other . . . approaches me essentially insofar as I myself—insofar as I am—responsible for him."[41]

It is true that in recognizing the other as higher (and lower) than myself, as an other for whom I am infinitely responsible, I avoid approaching the other as a rival whose power needs to be nullified. Granted, that is an enormous ethical advance over the modernist power-over mentality. However, one gets the idea that the only alternative to such imperialism is to recognize the other as higher than myself, one to whom I am hostage. Love of self seems to come down to forgetfulness of self and divestiture of all rights and interests. Aside from the impossibility of such divesting (which Levinas understands and accepts as the reality on the non-ethical level of ontology), that seems to be a dangerous message to pass on as the voice from on high. For the many who already struggle to believe that they have any right to have their own needs met and have little sense of their own power, this may encourage a further discounting of self and even self-effacement. On the other hand, for the many dedicated to the service of others who find such self-divestiture an impossibility, this may easily feed self-guilt or occasion escape into numbing diversions.

When we hear the paradoxical language ("obsession," "hostage," "substitution," even "occupation") that is descriptive of self for Levinas,[42] the questions

40. In *Oneself as Another*, Paul Ricoeur also voices his concern that Levinas one-sidedly emphasizes the relation of the other to self (p. 335ff.).

41. Levinas, *Ethics and Infinity*, p. 96.

42. In a context of narcissistic male domination, the hortatory use of such phrases would strikingly make the necessary point.

multiply. What can it possibly mean that I *am* substitution for her/him? Does it mean that in being concerned with myself I am violently denying my true self? Doesn't being hostage to the other suggest a wholesale capitulation to the other? If so, is this not another version of the call to self-less agapeic love in contrast to the self-interested love of *eros*? Moreover, what, on a practical level, does it mean to be totally responsible-for-the-other? How does one practice "substitution" for someone who has AIDS, or is unemployed, or is in an unhealthy relation? Suffering-with is one thing, but suffering-for? In general, it seems that the championing of the ethical priority of the other may in everyday life boomerang into a virtuous way of endorsing a demeaning submissiveness with the self-injury that inflicts and the potential backlash against others that it often invites. Don't such descriptions of self-extolling passivity, particularly from the viewpoint of women, risk being understood as the glorification of victimization?[43]

Now, this is clearly not what Levinas intends or envisions. He wants to move beyond a self-as-power-over to a self-as-service. With Levinas I agree (in distinction from any modernist, rationally based ethic) that "it is not a matter of thinking the ego and the other together, but to be facing. The true union or true togetherness is not the togetherness of synthesis, but a togetherness of face to face."[44] Consequently, Levinas wants to move beyond the confining and totalizing categories of being as power-against by a discourse of a morality "otherwise than being," which comes "before" ontology.[45]

Insofar as Levinas wants us to face up to the unconditionality of moral responsibility for love of neighbor, his call can scarcely be gainsaid. He would then be describing the metaphysical or normative conditions for ethical activity, without describing a concrete ethical agenda. The difficulty is that, for Levinas, proximity, the ethical site, is "before," "beyond," "otherwise" than a place of power: the true self (*le soi*) is called prior to power relationships. The implication is that an activity is not ethical unless there is a complete lack of self-interest and self-concern, a complete passivity without power. Indeed, such concern for self is, in his view, the non-ethical ontological self inevitably closed in on its own self-interest. Disinterest, expiation, total subjection to the other regardless of his/her motivations is what it means to be ethical.

Power-Over or Power-With

Here is where the rumblings become louder. Is the exercise of agentic power always power-against neighbor, and thus unethical? Does nonindifference to the other need to mean disinterest in self? In contrast, I want to suggest the possibility of an ethical exercise of power as power-with.

43. Cf. Joy, "Levinas," p. 484.
44. Levinas, *Ethics and Infinity*, p. 77.
45. Zygmunt Bauman reads this moral "before" as "better" (*Postmodern Ethics*, p. 72).

Levinas insists that one cannot escape the perspective of one's own self. I could not agree more. What I disagree with is his contention that one's perspective inevitably and irrevocably can only totalize the other because that is what it means to have power. Power *qua* power is power-over, and that means war. For Levinas the "invincible persistence," the *conatus essendi*, is interest.[46] "Being's interest takes dramatic form . . . in the multiplicity of allergic egoisms which are at war with one another." Through "calculation, mediation and politics" a "rational peace" of "reciprocal limitation and determination" is established (OB 4). Nevertheless, "interest remains" and "nothing is gratuitous" (OB 5). Interest, enjoyment, calculation, and possessions make up an economy of reciprocal exchange in the domain of being that is ontologically nonethical. Symmetry, interest, and reciprocity cannot avoid being egoistic, imperialistic, selfish. Consequently, to move beyond this means that for Levinas ethics must be "otherwise than being," a "total gratuity, breaking with interest" (OB 96). Indeed, the breakup of essence is ethics.

It is Levinas's view of power as inherently power-over that I see as highly problematic. Accepting that domination is indigenous to power and at the same time decrying such power-egoism leaves Levinas only one alternative: the ethical priority of the other.

Levinas is, in fact, accepting the long tradition[47] of envisioning power as fundamentally power-over.[48] He outlines his project in *Totality and Infinity* as developing discourse as a "non-allergic relation with alterity . . . where *power, by essence murderous of the other*, becomes, faced with the other and 'against all good sense,' the impossibility of murder, the consideration of the other, or justice" (TI 47; italics added). Again, in *Otherwise than Being*, Levinas asks, "[w]hy should the other concern me? . . . Am I my brother's keeper? These questions have meaning only if one has already supposed that the ego is concerned only with itself, is only a concern for itself" (OB 117). Thus, although Levinas is very critical of this ontology of power, calling it in fact "a philosophy of injustice" (TI 46), his move beyond into an ethical metaphysics of alterity consciously builds on and is dependent on a recognition of an ontology of being-as-power-over. His insistence on the necessity of an ethics of deference

46. "[*E*]*sse* is *interesse*; essence is interest" (*Otherwise*, p. 4).

47. For Levinas, "'I think' comes down to 'I can.' . . . Ontology as first philosophy is a philosophy of power" (*Totality and Infinity*, p. 46).

48. Paul Tillich, for example, defines power as "the possibility a being has to actualize itself against the resistance of other beings" (*The Courage to Be* [New Haven, Conn.: Yale University Press, 1952], p. 179). Paul Ricoeur claims that "[i]t is difficult to imagine situations of interaction in which one individual does not exert power over another *by the very fact of acting*" (*Oneself*, p. 220, italics added). Derrida concurs: "If it is true, as I in fact believe, that writing cannot be thought outside of the horizon of intersubjective violence, is there anything, even science, that radically escapes it?" (*Of Grammatology*, trans. G. Spivak [Baltimore: John Hopkins University Press, 1976], p. 127). He asserts that "[s]uch violence may be considered the very condition of the gift. . . . *The violence appears irreducible, within the circle or outside it, whether it repeats the circle or interrupts it*" (*Given Time: 1. Counterfeit Money*, trans. P. Kamuf [Chicago: Chicago University Press, 1992], p. 147).

to the other (because egoism is wrong) is concomitant with the recognition that it is ontologically impossible (because egoism is unavoidable).

Such thinking seems to take the basic opposition between closed selves with all the ambiguity this involves for personal interaction as a fundamental characteristic of human nature.[49] In this paradigm, in modern times given classic formulation in the work of Freud, Hegel, and Sartre, there are only two possibilities: dominate or be dominated. In this paradigm of violence, one either exercises power and becomes dominant and independent—that is, selfish—or one surrenders and becomes submissive and dependent—that is, other-directed.

In this model we have a world of ceaseless conflict and endless competition until one proves him/herself superior. But in such a world, when neither is able to surrender voluntarily, striving eventually becomes empty and meaningless because each person remains alone, disconnected, incapable of change and development. On the other hand, if we choose not to exercise our desire for power and subordinate our needs and interests, we have a relation with another person but at the cost of stifling our own needs and interests.

Within the confines of this paradigm, the route of self-sacrificial *agape* clearly has it all over the wiles of self-interested *eros*. *Agape*, as Nygren classically distinguished it in the Christian tradition, is supposed to be pure and disinterested love over against the egotistical and interested love of *eros*.[50] There is power without surrender (*eros*) or surrender without power (*agape*). Thus, for Reinhold Niebuhr, to take a modern Christian example, self-sacrifice is the end, goal, or ideal of history, and mutuality is a compromise ethic to accommodate fallen existence. "Sacrifical love (*agape*) completes the incompleteness of mutual love (*eros*)."[51]

My fundamental query is: how different, despite the details and complexities, is the position of Levinas? Levinas, it is true, does not ask us to deny or stifle our needs. Rather, acknowledging the needs and interests of the ego, we are then to interrupt them and put them out of play in accord with our higher ethical self. The questions return: Is there no legitimate ethical call to care of self and the needs of self? Is power of agency always self-interested, and therefore below the ethical plane?

Levinas is not unaware of the dangers. He exclaims, "But it is I, I and no one else, who am hostage for others." The "no one else" is important, for "to say that the other has to sacrifice himself to the others would be to preach human sacrifice!" (OB 126–27). Indeed, he admits that the responsibility for the other "is troubled and becomes a problem when a third party enters" (OB

49. "But the moral priority of the other over myself could not come to be if it were not motivated by something beyond nature. The ethical situation is a human situation, *beyond human nature,* in which the idea of God comes to mind (Levinas and Kearney, "Dialogue," p. 25, italics added).

50. Anders Nygren, *Agape and Eros,* trans. P. Watson (Philadephia: Westminster, 1953). "Eros is essentially and in principle self-love. . . . Agape, on the other hand, excludes all self-love" (pp. 216–17).

51. Reinhold Niebuhr, *The Nature and Destiny of Man* (London: Nisbet, 1943), p. 86.

157). Significantly, he even admits that "the relationship with the third party is an *incessant* correction of the asymmetry of proximity" (OB 158, italics added). Faced with unlimited responsibility, the self can, because my neighbor is also a third party with respect to another, "be called upon to concern itself also with itself" (OB 128). I am also another for the other and a third one. Thank God. Which is exactly what Levinas exclaims: "'Thanks to God' I am another for the others" (OB 158). In this way, "there is also justice for me" (OB 159). But, even then, he cautions that the "forgetting" of the "unlimited initial responsibility" is "pure egoism" (OB 128). Nevertheless, in this way violence and evil may be resisted "when the evil he does to me touches also a third party, one who is likewise my neighbor."[52] Thus, Levinas does allow being for oneself, but always on the basis of a prior being for the other, and only as a function of this being for the other.

A basic question that emerges is whether in Levinas's thought, for all its hallowing of the other, there is the historical possiblity of meeting an other, a neighbor, without distance or without fusion as Levinas desires. Not only is, ethically, the other always transcendent to me, but in "a history and politics," the asymmetrical ethical relation takes on "the aspect of a symmetrical relation" (TI 225). "Separation is embedded in an order in which the asymmetry of the interpersonal relation is effaced, where I and the other become interchangeable in commerce, and where the particular man, an individual of the genus man, appearing in history, is substituted for the I and for the other" (TI 226). In history, by means of the third party, the ethical priority of the other is transformed into a relation of equals. In history, it seems, we at best have the balanced exchange of reciprocity as welcome respite from the economy of war. But the exchange of "interchangeable" I's sounds more like a trading in sameness, rather than the meeting of unique, irrreplaceable I's in difference. In the end, it appears that we have a chastened or corrected asymmetry in which equality and reciprocity[53] are possible, but not genuine mutuality.[54]

Mutuality as Power-With

As an alternative to Levinas's model in which agency is inevitably and inescapably egoistic, I suggest a model of non-oppositional difference—an economy of love. Such an intersubjective model of mutual recognition, attunement, and empowerment, I believe, honors Levinas's intentions without

52. Roger Burggraeve, *Emmanuel Levinas* (Leuven, Belgium: Center for Metaphysics and Philosophy of God, n.d.), p. 56. This is an exceptionally clear and concise exposition of Levinas's thought.

53. In my view, the equality and reciprocity of justice with the emphasis on balanced exchange differs from the mutality of an ethical relationship (cf. below).

54. Levinas's recognition that there are always third parties and the necessary mediating structures again vividly raises the question of the practical viability of his ethics of priority.

some of the dangers that seem to haunt his position.[55] Here the movement of the other to myself is coincident with a simultaneous and voluntary movement of myself to the other. The desire of each evokes the desire of the other: mutual recognition, mutual yielding/receiving, mutual delighting, mutual empowering. There is the oscillating rhythm of giving and receiving, the dance of identity and intimacy called love. In giving to the other, I, paradoxically, in being received, am enlarged and enhanced—receiving, in the words of Levinas, "inspiration." In receiving the other, I expand, and paradoxically, through my receiving, give. Instead of power-over (with its corollary of power-under), or power-held-in-abeyance (to avoid domination), there is power-with and the dance of mutual empowerment.

The self is always intersubjective, either a connected or a disconnected self. Insofar as a human self is never an autonomous agent in splendid isolation, but always a connective self, the intra-psychic and the inter-psychic need not always be in opposition to each other. Indeed, the formation and nurturing of self-identity is possible only in an intersubjective matrix. It is in being seen (or not seen) that I, as an infant, come to see (or not see) myself. It is in being loved (or not loved) that I come to love (or not love) myself—and others. Since my identity is a gift I receive from and with others, my connection with others is constitutive of my identity. Community is not the sameness of fusion, but the coming-into-connection of diverse identities. We live together, in genuine community, or we strive together, in the violence of war; but in any case there is no I without a We. In other words, otherness and difference are never wholly inside or wholly outside myself. I, or, at least aspects of me, come alive and grow, or retreat and eventually die as I move in and out of relation with other selves. Mutuality assumes we cannot talk about response to and for others over and against response for and to self. In an intersubjective context of mutuality self-desires are not fundamentally desires against the other. In fear and disappointment they often become fixated in that way—and mutuality is ruptured into hostility.

Mutuality is attunement of expression, recognition, and desire, a dance in which simultaneously the differing gifts and needs of each person are honored, recognized, and often met. From our places of irreducible otherness, each of us seeks a rhythm in the other without hierarchy and without abasement—beyond considerations of duty, balance, or advantage. We recognize each other, seek each other's good, identify-with each other—in the process loving the other as we love ourselves. In this interfacing, the giving over or yielding to the other is a voluntary move in which one retains his/her own individuality and difference. The dance between staying with one's self and reaching out is the interplay of difference that is life itself. The aim is not to eradicate, accom-

---

55. Jessica Benjamin's *The Bonds of Love* (New York: Random House, 1988) is an articulate plea for "a new possibility of mutual recognition between men and women" in which both are empowered and mutually respectful.

modate, suppress, or repress difference, but to allow contact with difference to move, enhance, and change us as we become ourselves more fully. Empowered through the giving/receiving experience, a positive spiral of mutuality begins to take shape in which we are inspired to recognize, reach out, and yield more often and in deepening ways. When it happens (the difficulties and fears are many, and there are no guarantees!), we meet—graced with mutual recognition, mutual pleasure, and mutual empowerment—the fundamental ingredients of love. "The psyche is one open system connected to another, and only under those conditions is it renewable. If it lives, your psyche is in love. If it is not in love, it is dead."[56]

The dance of mutuality is always drenched in vulnerability and risk because it is a non-coerced meeting of two free subjects in the wild spaces of love.[57] Timing and spacing are of the essence. Reaching out does not guarantee being met. The timing may be off; the partner may be otherwise occupied, not at home, angry, depressed, in a different space. Venturing out but not meeting leads to impasse, and brings with it hurt, grieving—suffering. When people learn to accept that the vulnerability of mutuality always includes moments of distance, pain, and suffering, impasses may be avoided or broken, and the suffering from such non-meetings can even turn into suffering-with experiences of empathy, non-blame, and shared disappointment.

Opening to others may lead to indifference, negativity, rebuff, rebuke, assault—who knows? Indeed, it is that unknowing that makes us fearful, incessantly tempting us to try to guarantee the outcome or at least minimize the hazards through subtle or not so subtle means of control and manipulation. It is the fear of non-affirmation and disintegration, feeding the urge to take advantage of the other hidden in the recesses of every human heart, which closes our hearts, sets up defenses, and makes genuine meeting so difficult. The giving in such encounters is easily (if not consciously) counterfeit, a bribe, a come-on; the "giver" actually a taker. The receiving too becomes contaminated. Feeling a deep unworthiness but, at the same time, being desperate for a gift can lead to a feigned indifference, cloying "thankfulness," a guilt-ridden discomfort. Whether we are giving or receiving, insofar as we are deficient in self-esteem, our fears tend to get the best of us and opportunities for meeting degenerate into more or less calculated maneuvers of offense and defense, tugs-of-war of competition and resistance.

Since at every turn and in every moment the give-and-receive of mutuality threatens to degenerate into such strategies of manipulation, people often see no choice but to turn ethical relations into economic exchange relations with set demands for return and remuneration. That such degeneration is rampant in our skewed lives, however, need not mean, as is so often assumed, that all

---

56. Julia Kristeva, *Tales of Love,* trans. Leon Roudiez (New York: Columbia University Press, 1987), p. 15.

57. See my "Crossing the Threshold: Sojourning Together in the Wild Spaces of Love," ch. 1 above.

human relations are inevitably and finally only to be explained in terms of an economy of violence and sacrifice where giving necessarily implies taking from another. The mutuality model calls into question the assumption that appropriation (and the fear of expropriation) is intrinsic to human agency. Such an economy of love is not necessarily always already (although it often deteriorates into this) a zero sum game in which giving to one is always a taking from the other. There is, instead, the possibility of a giving as an overflowing to the other, which invites and often evokes (but neither demands nor coerces) a return. There is a return to the self (which would bother Levinas), but since it is not at the cost of the other, it does meet Levinas's basic concern. In neither demanding response nor being conditional upon them, mutual relations are not to be confused with or reduced to the reciprocities of market relations of exchange and contract. And there always remains the risk of violence. But in this model, as distinct from the Hegelian model of opposition, there is room for a genuine meeting of self and the other in a middle space, room for a giving in excess, without a why, which increases in its being given, transcending the economy of reciprocity and exchange. Love is the excessive gift that keeps on giving. The very possibility of betrayal and rejection—the risk of violence—is part and parcel of its "without-why"-ness, making it a "beautiful risk" (Levinas), a risk worth taking. For when, in spite of the risk, a gift is given and received, both giver and receiver experience a miracle of unmerited grace, the kind that makes all the difference in life.

In genuine mutuality it is not that the other fills up or augments myself; nor do I lose myself in the other. In both these cases, it would seem, there is no alterity, only sameness—with its suspension of genuine risk! In the first case, I ingest or dominate the other into my sameness. In the second, my otherness is assumed or subsumed into the sameness of the other.

In maintaining that ethically I can make no demand on the other, but rather that I give full priority to the other, Levinas seems to come dangerously close to this second situation despite his protestations to the contrary.[58] The problem seems to be that Levinas believes that expecting or seeking a response from the other necessarily means a tit-for-tat reciprocity, at best a contracted exchange of rights, duties, and goods, and at worst a manipulation. It is true, as I have just noted, that the risk and vulnerability of mutuality are often too much for us, so we try to regain control either through covert manipulation or overt reciprocal contract.[59] In both cases, ethical relations take on an instrumental quality. But is an ethical asymmetry (with priority of the other person) the only alternative to either manipulative relationships (with the other as object) or the balanced exchange of economic transactions (with interchangeable selves)? If it

---

58. "Contact with the other . . . is neither to invest the other and annul his alterity, nor to suppress myself in the other" (*Otherwise*, p. 86).

59. For differences between manipulative, contractual (i.e., reciprocal), and fellowship kinds of relationships, see John MacMurray, *Persons in Relation* (Atlantic Highlands, N.J.: Humanities, 1991), chs. 5–7, and Vincent Brümmer, *The Model of Love*, pp. 156–73.

is (as Levinas seems to assume), his approach would be my approach. However, as I have attempted to describe, the genuine mutuality of the ethical bears its own distinct mark, neither to be confused with or turned into the balanced exchange of reciprocal economies, nor confused with the priority of the other. Moreover, genuine mutual relations need to be clearly distinguished from their counterfeit, i.e., manipulative relations.

Genuine mutuality is not the calculation of reciprocal advantages in which I determine whether a neighbor treats me with equal regard, and then, if the conclusion is negative, I am absolved of my obligations. Levinas is right, I believe, to refuse to accept such calculation as the mark of the authentically ethical, even if, as we have observed, the difficulty of the ethical venture means that such exchange is often passed off as mutuality. In genuine mutuality both manipulation with its premium on control and reciprocity with its premium on balanced exchange are replaced with an ethics of being-with.[60] Genuine mutuality includes a self-love that is not self-aggrandizment or selfishness. It involves regard for self's own integrity, esteem for one's own worth, commitment to one's own convictions, and trust in one's own intuitions. Without such self-love, I fear, all relations with others, despite all protestations or pretenses to the contrary, will be efforts to gain a sense of belonging and worth at the expense of the other—and thereby violent. Genuine love of other is as fundamentally impossible without love of self as love of self is fundamentally impossible without love of the other. That, indeed, is the great commandment: to love my neighbor as I love myself.

This model of mutuality also calls for a revisioning of the typical selfish *eros*/altruistic *agape* contrast. *Eros* is no longer the drive to unite, dominate, or fuse, returning everything to the Same, which needs to be countermanded by an agapic drive sacrificially to give up self. *Eros* is *agape*, the intersubjective desire to connect in difference, the agapic power to interconnection (power-with) that is the meaning of life. *Eros* as be(com)ing-with is a mutual connecting that is neither indifferent nor disinterested, neither invasive nor domineering. Being-with is a power-with that respects, receives, and honors the other, and in so doing there is the mutual enrichment, mutual empowerment, and mutual pleasure of love. Without a self-other opposition, there is no longer a need to oppose *eros* and *agape*.

Suffering-With

However, as we all know too well, the mutuality of shared power—love—is too rare. *Eros* too often degenerates into selfish imperialism and defensive aggression. In fear the power of love is warped into power-over: violence, hate,

---

60. James H. Olthuis, "Being-with: Toward a Relational Psychotherapy," *Journal of Psychology and Christianity* 13, 3 (1994): 217–31.

evil. The wild spaces of love are turned into the killing fields. In such circumstances the scourges of violence mean that the give-and-receive rhythms of mutual power-with often need to become exercises in suffering-with our neighbor—and in that sense a priority of the other. Suffering-with (as distinct from suffering-from) is a voluntary, gratuitous act of standing alongside, empathic listening, affirming, speaking, and acting on behalf of.[61] It is what Levinas calls the "suffering for the useless suffering of the other person."[62]

In other words, the reality of rampant inequality, disadvantage, and outright oppression in our world means that the ethical symmetry of mutuality often calls for a priority in meeting the needs of others. Exercising mutuality means taking into account the position and circumstances of the other. When the other is "widow, orphan, stranger" (i.e., not able to be partner, whether through accident, need, impairment, lack of resources, etc.), there is what has been called in liberation theology the "preferential option for the poor." At the same time, when the other is engaged in acts of domination and injustice, an ethics of mutuality calls for acts of resistance and restraint. But this "asymmetry" is not an involuntary the-other-comes-first principle. Such "self-sacrifice" is not, I suggest, as with Niebuhr and Levinas, what it means to be quintessentially ethical. It finds its derivative place in an ethics of mutuality because of the brokenness and sinfulness of life. It is the compromise required by the breakdown of mutuality with the intention of making/restoring mutual partnerships. As Don Browning puts it, this makes "appropriate self-sacrifice as a transitional ethic on the way to restoring mutuality."[63] An ethics of being-with and suffering-with in this way also suggests that if maternity is to be the ethical metaphor *par excellence,* it would need to be recast not as the supreme emblem of self-sacrifice but (with paternity) as paradigm examples of mutuality in which life is created, given, and shared.

In the end my emphasis on "I-am-with" (power-with) instead of Levinas's "I-am-for" seems confluent with his (and my) intentions to envision a philosophy of non-violence. In his claim that the Face awakens me to responsibility, Levinas seems to assume that there is something in the ontological ego that urges or impels a journey into the exile of the "otherwise than being," giving rise to an awakening or birth of the moral self, not as "I am I," but as "I am for." Levinas stresses that this ethical "for" is not the social "with." However, "with" in my usage is not the social "being-with" of Heidegger. "With" carries the connotations of a humanity as a religious community-in-difference, gifted-with and called-to love, very similar to what Levinas calls "proximity" (OB 81–99) as the religio-ethical place of responsibility, vulnerability, and non-violence (OB 75–81).

61. See ibid., for a discussion of what this means psychotherapeutically.

62. Levinas, "Useless Suffering," in *The Provocation of Levinas: Rethinking the Other,* ed. R. Bernasconi and D. Wood (New York: Routledge, 1988), p. 159.

63. Don Browning, *Religious Thought and the Modern Psychologies* (Philadelphia: Fortress, 1987), p. 153.

Co-responsibility, care, and compassion are the key terms in a postmodern ethic. Care goes back to the old Gothic word, *Kara,* meaning "to lament, to weep with, to grieve." Compassion comes from the Latin *com* and *pati,* meaning to suffer with. Suffering love as the voluntary willingness to suffer-with another person is required to restore genuine relations of mutuality. We may even have to suffer at the hands of the other for the cause of justice. In love we are moved from the center to the margins where the lame and ill are gathered. But such sacrifice of self is not done at whatever the cost to self, but is done in tune with and at the behest of a self who, in wholeness and integrity, wants to live out its convictions. In such circumstances, doing for the other may be for the self, and doing for self may be for the other. Thank God for such possibilities. I can come face to face with difference without effacement on my part or debasement on the part of the other. Inspired and inspiring faces, shining, glowing, not fused, not distant, but connected and connecting. In this broken world where violence is so often overwhelming, disfiguring, and dismembering, we are called to suffer-with, to sojourn together.

The poignancy and urgency of this call leads me to end this essay with a spontaneous and forthright thank you[64] to Emmanuel Levinas for raising again the vision of the widow, orphan, and stranger in a world where compassion is too often in exile. May we all offer cups of cold water to the other, gifts that we offer and say, "Drink!" (*Bois*).[65]

---

64. In the mutuality model I am developing, a free, unexpected, unsolicited, and uncoerced "thank-you" escapes the economy of reciprocity and exchange. In contrast, since Derrida believes no gift can escape the economy of reciprocity and even the movement of gratitude returns to the Same, he ironically can thank Levinas only by being ungrateful and writing a faulty text. See Jacques Derrida, "At this very moment in this work here I am," trans. R. Berezdivin, in *Re-Reading Levinas,* ed. R. Bernasconi and S. Critchley (Bloomington: Indiana University Press, 1991), pp. 11–48. Simon Critchley incisively discusses Derrida's predicament in thanking Levinas in *Ethics of Deconstruction,* pp. 108ff.

65. "*Bois*" is Derrida's final word in his text of homage to Emmanuel Levinas. "At this very moment in this work here I am."

8

On Love

With Aquinas, Kristeva, Nietzsche

David Goicoechea

Throughout his career, which we are celebrating with these reflections, Jim Olthuis has tended to philosophize as a postmodernist. With his students, colleagues, and friends he has thought about life's questions with such philosophers as Levinas, Derrida, Kierkegaard, and Irigaray. But perhaps he is most at home in the world of Julia Kristeva.

As is evident in his book *The Beautiful Risk,* Jim is focused upon a new psychology of loving and being loved.[1] He is in search of this new psychology because modernity has proven to be inadequate and inconsistent even though it has made many wonderful contributions to the theory and practice of true love. Nygren's *Agape and Eros*[2] has well condensed the philosophical models from Descartes through Hegel. Like faith and reason, *agape* and *eros* are separated and set in opposition by the moderns. Jim goes to the postmoderns to let *agape* and *eros* work and play together in mutual fecundation. However, he and Kristeva seem to be working with another concept of love that is not included in the *agape-eros* distinction. To explore this third love I will here examine Jim's new psychology of love within a new, postmodern philosophy of love.

Kristeva uses the Thomist model of love for the Good as a healthy antidote to the problem of narcissism.[3] In order to clarify what she is getting at we might

1. James Olthuis, *The Beautiful Risk* (Grand Rapids: Zondervan, 2001).
2. Anders Nygren, *Agape and Eros,* trans. P. S. Watson (London: SPCK, 1953).
3. Julia Kristeva, *Tales of Love,* trans. Leon Rudiez (New York: Columbia University Press, 1987). Kristeva thinks of Ovid as first bringing to light the new insanity of Narcissus, p. 103. She thinks of Thomas Aquinas as working out an ontological formulation of the Good that provides a solution for this mad self-love by rooting natural love and love of oneself in love of the Good, pp. 170–87.

go to Frederick Crowe,[4] who, in his article on Thomist love, has distinguished between complacency and concern. Concern is either an agapeic desire for the realization of another self or an erotic desire for self-realization. Complacency is a love of delight in the goodness of the single individual. I will here show that Olthuis and Kristeva are primarily working with the love of delight which modernity has forgotten in its concern for the love of desire.

But, Jim also works constantly with the symbol of dancing in the wild spaces of love. Surely, it is Nietzsche who among philosophers most relates love to dancing in wild spaces.[5] So I will show how Jim's notion of love that is other than the concern of *agape* and *eros* is also developed according to Nietzsche's concept of *amor fati*. In order to explore Jim's thought by relating it to Kristeva, Aquinas, and Nietzsche, I will work toward explaining the relation between six dimensions of their common philosophy: (1) an ethics of true love, (2) a logic of embodied love's mixed opposites, (3) an ontology of love's wild spaces, (4) a psychology of the person's mad love, (5) a theology of love's transcendence, and (6) an epistemology of love's free wandering.

An Ethics of Delight (from Motherly Nurturing to Childish Complacency)

Jim begins his book with the story of Amanda.[6] Throughout *Tales of Love* Kristeva likewise reflects on several personal stories. Perhaps the story of "Marie and the Absence of the Mother"[7] is closest to that of Amanda. In order to conceptually think about Jim's Amanda from the angle of Kristeva's Marie we might begin, as does Jim, with ethics as first philosophy[8] and with Kristeva's use of the Freudian notion of transference.[9] Amanda came to Jim with problems of anxiety and symptoms of suffocation. Often she could get "no air." She had attacks of choking and hyperventilating. It seemed that the cause had to do with her mother and being abandoned. When her mother went to Europe she became terrified. She asked herself why she needed so much control. On Toronto's highway 401 she froze in panic. She searched for solutions. She began to say to herself: "Breathe and you'll be okay." Relief began when her mother came to a session with her and Jim and told them that she had tried to abort Amanda by sitting, when she was pregnant, in a bathtub of scalding water. At that moment

4. Frederick Crowe, *Three Thomist Studies,* ed. Michael Vertin (Boston: Lonergan Institute of Boston College, 2000).

5. Friedrich Nietzsche, *Thus Spoke Zarathustra,* trans. R. J. Hollingdale (Toronto: Penguin Books, 1969). See the two Dance Songs in the middle of part two and at the end of part 3.

6. Olthuis, *Beautiful Risk,* pp. 15–22.

7. Kristeva, *Tales of Love,* pp. 51–53. The symptom that links Amanda and Marie most clearly is Marie's "suffocation that grips her as soon as she sits at the wheel of a car."

8. Olthuis, *Beautiful Risk,* p. 37.

9. Kristeva, *Tales of Love.* Some of the best passages on transference are on pp. 13, 31, and 282.

Amanda loved her mother with a child's complacent acceptance. She was reborn. The mother's beautiful risk of telling them her secret set the three of them on a mutual quest with inspiration—with a fresh breath of childish delight.

As Jim begins to reflect on loving and healing he stresses "not curing, but caring." Amanda came to Jim with a problem and he could have seen her as a problem to be solved. But instead he saw her as a gift. He cared for her with Jesus' love as the Good Shepherd, as the good Samaritan, and as the Suffering Servant.[10] But this was not simply an *agape* that was concerned about her self-realization and the overcoming of her problems. Jim stresses that his love for her was indifferent to her abnormal differences. She does not have to be cured by fitting the norm. She can keep all her differences and be loved for them. Jesus as Jim reveals him has a love that loves abnormal persons in their differences. This is the love that delights in all that is. Amanda was loved by Jim in her very difficulties. They were for him a gift. And she began to love him.

Kristeva is a Freudian whereas Jim is not. Like Freud she is interested in a responsible transference love. Freud thought that our problems are caused by failures in loving and that they can be solved by successes in loving.[11] As a Hegelian and modernist, Freud was willing to forget about *agape* and work out everything in terms of *eros-thanatos*. Kristeva goes beyond the Hegelian logic of Freud to work with the love of delight out of which both *eros* and *agape* can grow. When you compare and contrast Kristeva's Marie with Jim's Amanda you see that the *eros-thanatos* dimensions are much greater in Kristeva's case than in Jim's. Jim does not write about Amanda's father or about any lovers. Marie is not only suffocating but is also bound up in a variety of male-female feelings. You can see how Kristeva's male patients might fall in love with her just as Freud's female patients might have fallen in love with him. But Kristeva seems to say that there is a transference love even between Marie and herself. This can transfer Marie from a realm of desire to a realm of delight. It can be Kristeva's unconditional love for Marie that Marie responds to with the intimate trust of a child. This can enable Marie to go through a transformation of self-organization even though it does not aim at that.

When Kristeva thinks of Aquinas, she sees him as having a theory of love that valorizes self-love. Because I am and I am good, I should love myself. This can defeat narcissism.[12] But because you are and you are good, I should

10. Olthuis, *Beautiful Risk.* The chapter on "Not Curing, But Caring," pp. 39–52, shows that Jim is very clear about imitating Jesus first of all in his complacent love for all.

11. Kristeva, *Tales of Love.* Kristeva's chapter on "Freud and Love: Treatment and its Discontents" already begins to indicate how Kristeva is like and unlike Freud in their quest to heal the maladies of love with caring love.

12. Ibid., pp. 113–19. Here Kristeva shows how the malady of Narcissus is a key problem for Plotinus. But by identifying the many with soul and then the dyad of *nous* and finally the monad of the one, he obliterates otherness and thus belittles concern. Thomas is critical of this approach and even sees Augustine as being too much of a Neoplatonist and of an Averroist who identifies agent intellects with one universal intellect. The divine illumination theory does not give enough power to human intelligence and effort. On p. 184 Kristeva shows how third party love that does not collapse into the monad is the way to true love.

also love you. This is what Kristeva would see as first ethics for Aquinas. She has picked out what Crowe calls Aquinas's love of complacency. The love that Jim has for Amanda and that Kristeva has for Marie is one of delight in their goodness just as they are. That lets Amanda and Marie begin to take delight in themselves and see themselves as gifts and not problems.

This is also the main point of Nietzsche's philosophy of love. In the drama of *Zarathustra*, as spirit or will to power loves with the camel of Christian Platonism or the lion of Enlightenment humanism, it is resentful.[13] It resentfully belittles this present life for eternity or for a better future. But the lioness of Romanticism challenges the lion of the Enlightenment from her standpoint of a maternal nurturing. She loves as one who is pregnant with a child and is totally loving of that child.[14] That is lovely and would not result in the rejection and abjection of Amanda and Marie. But this is still a concern. The child's love for Nietzsche will dance in a delight that even maternal nurturing in itself will not have.[15] The child loves with a Dionysian dancing joy for existence that wills its eternal return. Nietzsche, Aquinas, and Kristeva are each focusing on Jim's delightful risk. For Nietzsche this love of delight is also a risking that dances in chains and knows that if they do not kill me they can empower me.

The Logic of Delight (Embodied Love's Mixed Opposites)

In the middle of part 2 in the "First Dance Song," Nietzsche lets the gravity of Christian Platonism be revealed.[16] Zarathustra and his companions see some young girls dancing in a highland meadow. When they see him they seek to flee. But he tells them that his is not the spirit of gravity, that he loves young girls' slender ankles. He sings a song for them to which they dance. It is about two females: Life and Wisdom. The wisdom is that of Christian Platonism. It sees woman as the eternal feminine. But the girls are leery of Zarathustra's love triangle. All the females are leery of Zarathustra's singing that he loves slender female ankles. They all criticize him and he begins to learn from them. He sees that approaching the light and the heavy in terms of exclusive hierarchial opposites belittles the heavy. In the accompanying "Night Song"[17] the night too becomes light. The logic of Christian Platonism's wisdom loves only the light and not the night, only the light and not the heavy. The logic of delight deconstructs belittling light and lets there be delight in the dark and heavy

13. Nietzsche, *Thus Spoke Zarathustra*. Nietzsche writes of the three transformations as he begins part one, ch. 1. But the chapter "On Redemption" best summarizes his theory of *Ressentiment*, pp. 159–63.

14. Ibid., p. 108.

15. Ibid., p. 244. This "Second Dance Song" ends with a rhapsody about Joy that is deeper than agony.

16. Ibid., pp. 130–33.

17. Ibid., pp. 129–30.

as well. In the folly of delight the lover sees that night too is a sun and that heavy ankles too can dance.

In the "Second Dance Song"[18] at the end of part two Zarathustra is brought by Lady Life to see through the logic of opposites in their connection of dialectical implication. All things are entwined. We may get to the light through the night and to the light through the heavy. But this logic of modernity also belittles the night and the heavy by using them for the sake of an ideal future. Zarathustra discovers in his delight the logic of mixed opposites. He goes beyond the logic of good and evil to find the good even in the evil.

Kristeva also has a genius for the logic of mixed opposites. On page 51 of *Tales of Love* she begins her story of Marie with the words: "Marie exhibits all the delightful throes of hysteria." Psychiatry and psychoanalysis, as they came forth in the modernity of their birth as distinct sciences, had much to do with hysteria. When Freud went to visit Charcot in Paris and learn the talking cure of hypnosis, Charcot was caring for 3,000 hysterics. While Freud knew he could not cure alcoholics, he thought he could cure hysterics even though the analysis became interminable. But Kristeva has a new love for hysterics and for Marie. She loves them in their very hysteria. She loves the person especially insofar as she is exhibiting "the delightful throes of hysteria." She valorizes and loves the very hysteria. Marie feels loved by her and she feels that her hysteria is loved by Kristeva.

Kristeva loves each person and each reality, even feminism, with her love that has the logic of mixed opposites. In her famous article on "Women's Time"[19] she shows how she loves the women's movement with the logic of mixed opposites. She valorizes equity feminism that worked for the equal rights of men and women. That feminism wanted equity according to the male logic of the line of time. It saw the inequities of the past and present. It looked toward equity in the future. By 1968 it appreciated the equity of the present even though it was far from complete. But equity was not enough. She and others began also to valorize difference feminism. Men and women might be equal under the law and in the rights that flow from their common personhood. But they are different in their bodies and all that is embodied within them: their attitudes, priorities, feelings, thoughts, language, writing, and actions. These differences as Nietzsche shows can be affirmed in the love of eternal return. But besides affirming equity within the ethics of linear temporality and differences within the ethics of eternity there is the monumental time in which the mother brings forth the child. This is the temporality of a third ethics and of complacent love, or the love of delight, with which Kristeva loves Marie.

Difference feminism is in danger of becoming terroristic.[20] Because of a primary identification the mother has great power over the child and can use

18. Ibid., pp. 241–44.

19. Julia Kristeva, *The Kristeva Reader,* ed. Toril Moi (New York: Columbia University Press, 1986), pp. 187–213. Some key pages on Kristeva's mixed view of a mixed feminism from *Tales of Love* are: 61, 62, 64, 74, 75, 80, 87, 95–100, 112, 225, 232, 315, 363, 364, 373, and 374.

20. Ibid.

the child as a hostage. Difference feminists can join in terrorist gangs as they did in the Baader-Meinhof gang. When hysteria is affirmed by difference feminists it can become hysterically terroristic. But if it is loved as a mixed blessing and acknowledged in its dangers, even to itself, then it can be delighted in. In the monumental moment hysteria can be loved and delighted in as a worthy expression without being limited to one aspect of its being. It must also be seen as its opposite. There are the throes of hysteria. But they can be delightful throes. These throes are chains but the lover can let the beloved dance in them even with the dance of the tarantella.[21]

What Nietzsche and Kristeva are loving in Lady Life with all her delightful throes and in Marie with the delightful throes of her hysteria is a good that is simply received with affection. According to Crowe, Thomas would see the Holy Spirit as the complacent affection that proceeds from the Son for the Father. This relational process could appear paradoxical[22] or contradictory if you only had a metaphysics of substance and causality. But Thomas was already being pushed beyond that by the logic of a love within a dynamic Trinity of relating proceeding persons. The Holy Spirit is not what she is and is what she is not. She is that which proceeds from the Fatherly understanding that expresses itself in a filial saying. But she is also that which proceeds from the Son for the Father.[23] This logic of mixed opposites lets us understand the affectionate complacency that is not a desiring *eros* or a desiring *agape*. It is an appetite that is delighted in its receptivity of the other as good.

This has to be the logic of Jim's caring love also. Of course, he desires to help others. But he does that by simply loving the other for what he or she is. This is like the love of Jesus for Mary Magdalene. She could hear in the way he said her name that he loved her with an affection that was indifferent to all her differences because it loved them.

An Ontology of Childish Delight (within the Shipwrecked Space of Mad Excess)

But, what sort of logic is this logic of the mixed opposites that becomes the logic of a new ontology, psychology, and theology? This logic, in which hysteria is what it is not and is not what it is, defies the principle of identity or of noncontradiction. When Jim comes to "The Geography of Healing," the third part of *The Beautiful Risk*,[24] he uses two metaphors: that of a very turbulent journey in a ship on rough seas and that of dancing on a tightrope.

21. Nietzsche, *Thus Spoke Zarathustra*, p. 126.
22. Crowe, *Three Thomist Studies*, p. 111.
23. Ibid., p. 103.
24. Olthuis, *Beautiful Risk*, pp. 161, 169.

Nietzsche begins *Zarathustra* with the story of the tightrope dancer. What is its logic and ontology for him?

In the Prologue Zarathustra comes down from his highland cave and lake with gifts of love for the people of the lowlands. His first encounter with the people is in a town where they have gathered at the market square to watch the tightrope dancer.[25] Zarathustra tries to gift the people by getting them to move from being lower men to being higher men. He tells them of the taut rope and of the well-strung bow and asks them to discipline themselves for excellence. But they are not interested. Then he tells them to be courageous and noble like the tightrope dancer. But they only blink at him like the last man, who cares nothing for excellence. They say, give us instead the tightrope dancer. They want entertainment and not excellence.

Then the dancer appears. He begins to move high across the square. But a little devil runs out after him, taunts him and jumps over his head, and rushes along the rope. The dancer becomes flustered and falls to the ground far below. The crowd rushes away in terror. Zarathustra comes and loves him with his careful, complacent affection. The dancer becomes joyful and dies peacefully in Zarathustra's arms. Zarathustra carries him to the woods and gives him a loving burial.

Throughout the drama Zarathustra continues to meet the crowds. By part three in the chapter on "The Convalescent" he is disgusted with them and with all of existence, which is low and chaotic.[26] But then his animals teach him a new love, the love of delight for the lower men and even the higher men. The higher men are not so much higher. Zarathustra becomes the superman by becoming the child who can love them all with the child's affection of delight. The delight of this new love affirms all of existence. Its new logic knows that the low are as lovable as the high. The last are as lovable as the first. High is low and low is high. First is last and last is first.

As Jim loves Amanda with this third logic he also loves her with a third ontology. Every person, place, and thing is an Amanda, a to-be-loved in the third way. Heraclitus initiated the ethics of logocentrism and its logic of order. *Logos* was connected with the verb *legein,* which meant "to collect or to gather." This *logos* was the principle of origination (*arche*), of measured and harmonious process (*metron*), and of the goal (*telos*). The ancients sought that order for their ethics and in their science and their spirituality. The moderns sought to produce such order with the ratio of their modern science. Even Jesus would gather the people as a mother hen would gather her chicks under her wings, but they would not. People and nature are not that orderable. The lower people are falling from tightropes and so are the higher. Nature presents us with chaos and science cannot control it. But Zarathustra and Jim love the people and nature anyway because of a new ontology that goes beyond the logic of control and order.

25. Nietzsche, *Thus Spoke Zarathustra*, p. 41.
26. Ibid., pp. 232–33.

Parmenides initiated the ontology of presence at about the same time that Heraclitus initiated the ethics and logic of logocentrism. That ontology sought to love wisdom by realizing the truth of simple and stable being. Being is present to all and multiplicity and mutability are but illusory. This Parmenidean ontology belittles becoming and it is Nietzsche's chief target. The modifications of ontology by Hegel, which accept the multiplicity and flux of Heraclitus within becoming, still accepts an overarching order of *logos*. Falling off the tightrope is a fall from both the Parmenidean ontology and the Heraclitean-Hegelian logic.

Kristeva does not think of Marie as only having a tough time at sea. According to Kristeva we are all extraterrestrials whose spaceships have broken down in an alien land. In our unconscious depths we are each strangers to ourselves. We are each E.T. wandering about after shipwreck.[27] Classical philosophers imagine a harbor of order and stability. Christian philosophers had islands of safety and familiarity for Robinson Crusoe. But postmodern ontologists see us as shipwrecked at sea like Elian Gonzales. In our age of the broken family we cannot take refuge in the consolation of philosophy or the hyperbeing of Eckhart. We have fallen over the falls into a dark night of wildness and wet. But this gives affection opportunities that *eros* and *philia* never had.

Crowe shows how Aquinas is exploring a new ontology and logic of affection.[28] Plato's ontology of *eros* that flies upward toward the Parmenidean form belittles individuals as only appearances. Aristotle's ethics of friendship, while critical of that ontology, was still based on the logic of an ordered final causality of means to ends. It still trusted in the safe harbor of the Good itself, for which all goods here are but means to that end. But Thomas's new ontology of creation sees that each individual is an end in his or her own right and is to be loved as such. The ethics of affection implies an ontology that must not belittle the creature in any way, for that would belittle the creator. A creation ontology that lets creatures have a share in freedom and creativity cannot be content with a Heraclitean logocentrism or a Parmenidean ontology of pure presence.

A Psychology of Interpersonal Persons (in Process, on Trial)

Nietzsche's *Zarathustra* is most of all about giving a psychological account of his ethical ideal of receptive love. Already early in the Prologue the old saint of the forest tells him to get a love that takes rather than gives. The key chapter in part two, "The Night Song," shows why we need first of all not the active love of the light but rather the receptive love of the night.[29] Zarathustra's transformations from the active *eros* of Christian Platonism to active humanitarian love to the child's love of delight in all of existence is explained in terms of will to power,

27. Kristeva, *Tales of Love,* p. 382.
28. Crowe, *Three Thomist Studies,* p. 153.
29. Nietzsche, *Thus Spoke Zarathustra,* p. 130.

resentment, and *amor fati.* The will to power or spirit is the interplay of life forces that seek not only to survive but to prevail. These life forces can strive to grow with resentment which is a psychological attitude that has five facets: (1) suffering (2) impotence (3) brooding (4) value reversal and (5) a rewarder-punisher God. In the name of the apocalyptic Christ sufferers could become empowered and get beyond their fixed ideas if they would love the good and hate evil. Zarathustra lived through this attitude of negativity and saw its self-deceit unmasked. In resentment he had lived for the heaven of the after-life and belittled this life. But enlightenment humanists are as resentful as Christian Platonists because they are concerned about a utopian future that is not complacent with the lower men of the present. The drama of Zarathustra shows how he moves from resentful concern to a complacent *amor fati.* The child learns to receive and bless what is. How this transformation of the lion of concern to the child of complacency takes place is the multifaceted story from "The Night Song" in the middle of part two to "The Convalescent" in the middle of part three.

Father Crowe clarifies Thomist complacency by contrasting it with three modern forms of *eros:* that of Schopenhauer, that of Nietzsche, and that of the existentialists, especially Heidegger and Sartre.[30] He thinks of Nietzsche's will to power as being an active erotic force. But he identifies Nietzsche with the spirit of the lion and not with the spirit of the child. Crowe is critical of arrogant leonine aggression. But so is Nietzsche. Zarathustra as the child is the best critic there is of Zarathustra the lion. The logic of opposites that are mixed in one flow shows how this is possible. Zarathustra has a loving criticism of the lion, which at the end of part four enables the lion to be as tame as St. Francis's Wolf of Gubbio. Father Crowe also uses the image of the child to explore the receptive delight of animal affection. But he is unaware that in the chapter on "The Convalescent" Zarathustra learned from the animals how to become the very child that Crowe praises.[31]

Kristeva also is primarily critical of Nietzsche.[32] She does not know of the child's receptive love in *Zarathustra.* Neither is she aware of Nietzsche's *Anti-Christ,* in which he criticizes the resentful Christ in order to bring out by way of contrast the good news of Jesus' childlike love.[33] But Kristeva has a point in developing her psychology of interpersonal persons in relation and on trial. Nietzsche's psychology of the will to power only thinks of forces in relation and process. In his criticism of the ontology of substance and causality he takes up the position of no-self and of conditioned genesis. He is fully aware that without faith there can be no psychology of the person. Experience alone, as Buddhism shows, knows nothing of the person and develops an ethics as does Nietzsche by showing the possibility of affirmative and active forces overcoming

30. Crowe, *Three Thomist Studies,* pp. 170–82.

31. Nietzsche, *Thus Spoke Zarathustra,* pp. 236–37.

32. Kristeva, *Tales of Love,* p. 393.

33. Friedrich Nietzsche, *Twilight of the Idols and The Anti-Christ,* trans. R. J. Hollingdale (Toronto: Penguin books, 1990), pp. 159–262.

negative and reactive forces in an embodied attitude. In criticizing the little reason of modernity (Descartes, Kant, and Fichte on the ego) and emphasizing the great reason of the unconscious body, Nietzsche made his great psychological breakthrough.[34] But Kristeva, while accepting his and Freud's theory of the unconscious, which is beyond the logic of Heraclitus and the simple, stable being of Parmenides, redefines relationality and process in terms of personhood. Kristeva believes in a responsible person even though she agrees with Spinoza, Hegel, and Nietzsche that substance is not enough to account for the subjectivity of intersubjectivity. A substance is a thing in itself and a person cannot be a thing in itself.

As Jim describes the healing spirals of the affectionate bond, he works with a notion of personhood that surpasses the Thomist definition of person as "an individual substance of rational nature," which began with Boethius. In his postmodern-biblical-philosophical approach his view includes the Nietzschean criticism and the Kristevan revision.

A Theology of Delight's Transcendence (Being in Touch through the Third)

Jim and Amanda receive a breakthrough when Amanda's mother joins them and because of Jim is able to speak in a new way. This has to do with a key notion of postmodern philosophy, which we might call the logic of the triad. When the mother and the father relate to the child with such sayings as "Oh, isn't she cute!" it is very different from a relation of emotional identification between mother and daughter without the father. The mother is a subject. But if she rejects the father and he becomes an object and he rejects her so that she becomes an object, then she, as a reject, is abject. The child in the womb and later can identify with the mother as abject and become an abject child.[35] So when there is only a mother-daughter diad without the father to make a triad, then the diad becomes a monad, since love is only emotional identification. As a result Amanda and Marie go around as Narcissi caught up in an abject self-concern. But as soon as a third gets honesty going, a love of complacency that is not caught only in causes for concern can originate. Jim's complacent love for Amanda let Amanda's mother know that Amanda could love her with a complacent forgiveness and healing was underway.

Kristeva and Marie do not have the good fortune of Marie's mother joining them and offering a confession the likes of which was so helpful for Amanda. Kristeva and Marie have to work things out with the help of a third that for Kristeva is seen as a quasi transcendence. The Good that Kristeva explicates in terms of Aquinas is connected with this quasi transcendence.[36] Marie can be

---

34. Nietzsche, *Thus Spoke Zarathustra*, pp. 61–63. Part one, ch. 4 makes this key distinction.
35. Kristeva, *Tales of Love*, p. 34.

loved as good and so can her mother and so can her father. The poetic vision of this, for the poet will never belittle you, is the key step in analysis. It enables the complacent love of Kristeva for Marie to work. It puts Marie's complacent self-love into play so that it begins to free her from the concerns of narcissism.

Freudians had already worked with this in their practice and theory of transference. The patient could fall in love with the therapist and say: "I love you." The therapist could respond: "Neither do I."[37] That response has a shock value and a comic value that could begin to get the patient to see her projections and her self-love as she loves the therapist. The therapist knows that it is not only himself that she loves. But who else is it? That "Neither do I" points out the logic of mixed opposites. She loves him but she does not. She loves herself, but she hates herself, and sometimes the hate is stronger than the love.

Kristeva goes beyond these Freudians with her faith. She loves the Good in Marie and in herself and that Good is the third. Even though it is immanent in both of them and in all persons, places, and things, it also transcends them. Being, unity, truth, goodness, thinghood, and somethinghood are transcendentals according to Aquinas. They are concepts that extend to all things and even to the differences between them. But while the Good is a transcendental in all things, it is also transcendent by being more than all things. But it is a quasi transcendence insofar as it is immanent as well as transcendent. With their faith Kristeva and Aquinas believe that the Good is not only a quasi transcendence; it is also a triadic, relational process. The Trinity of Father, Son, and Holy Spirit for them keeps the third as a threefold third and never lets the dyad of Father and Son become a monad. The Trinity of three persons is the intersubjective subject of faith that guarantees otherness even with sameness and thus also guarantees the complacent love of other as other and of self as other. Belief in the personhood of the three persons of the Trinity also lets Aquinas and Kristeva believe in the personhood of humans. This belief in the third that is a trinity insofar as it is a quasi transcendence grounds complacency.

Father Crowe shows how Aquinas clarifies the Trinity in terms of complacency and complacency in terms of the Trinity.[38] The Father is the divine understanding that expresses himself in a word that is the Son. The Holy Spirit proceeds from the Son's love of the Father. God as love is a love of complacency. The Holy Spirit is the reciprocal love between Father and Son. Human beings who enter the beatific vision will also have a love of complacency with the Trinity.[39] Even in this life there is a foretaste of the beatific complacency. There is a trinitarian complacency in any complacent love. That is the delight that Amanda began to experience with Jim and her mother. It is the delight that Marie began to find with Kristeva and the Good.

36. Ibid. Key passages on the third party as a quasi transcendence are on pp. 22, 34, 42, 50, 84, 149, 184, 211, 257, 261, and 311.

37. Ibid., p. 12.

38. Crowe, *Three Thomist Studies,* pp. 102–3.

39. Ibid., pp. 109–12.

One might wonder about Nietzschean theology. Does he have the notion of the third? He does portray Zarathustra as being in a triadic relation with Lady Life and Lady Wisdom. But eventually Lady Wisdom departs as he said she would at the end of the Prologue.[40] However, he requests that she might then be replaced by Dame Folly.

Zarathustra's theology begins to become amorphous when he visits the Blessed Islands.[41] He has moved from the highlands to the lowlands and now to the islands. The highland dance of his humanistic concern proved to be too strenuous for the lowlands. The lowland dance of his romantic maternalism proved to be too ascetic for the islands. The carefree dance of the islanders proved to be nihilistic. On the Blessed Islands he sees why God has died. Since God was a rewarder-punisher God, he died.[42] Since God was a creator who did not let us create, he died. Since belief in the eternal God belittled the earth and its temporality, he died. Since God was a stopgap God of sufficient reason at the end of the chain of infinite regress that cannot be, he died. Since God was the God of pity, he died. Pity cannot be in the heart of the divine. The concerns of pity cannot be as ultimate as complacency. In part four when the old pope, who has been forced to retire because God died, explains to Zarathustra why God died, the pope says that it was because he did not love well enough. He did not even love with the love that a mother has for her child.[43] When there is the mother lion and her child and Zarathustra, there is a triad. When that happens the old pope might still keep his job because in the complacency of his concern he will let children dance with Amanda in the streets and squares of Toronto.

Nietzsche makes a case for complacency but the weakness of his philosophy has to do with his lack of faith in personhood. Because he does not have faith in the persons of the Trinity he does not believe in personhood. Without personhood he can only belittle the law and politics of concern. Thomas, Kristeva, and Jim are careful not to belittle concern even though they give the primacy to complacency. They approach concern with complacency. Jim is complacent about his concern for Amanda even though he knows that giving it the primacy will be unproductive.

An Epistemology That Embraces Uncertainty (with Wandering Metaphors That Blur Meaning)

What distinguishes the postmodern world that has not forgotten complacency from the modern world that has been content only to be concerned with concern is the postmodern retreat from the primacy of epistemology.

40. Nietzsche, *Thus Spoke Zarathustra*, p. 53.

41. Ibid., pp. 109–12.

42. Ibid., pp. 109–17. In these three chapters he gives his five existential proofs against God's existence.

43. Ibid., pp. 271–75. Here he gives his ontological argument for a more loving God.

Nietzsche and Kristeva both clearly distinguish symbols from signs.[44] They both think of semiotics as including semantics (the relation of signs with their referents), syntactics (the relation of signs with other signs), and pragmatics (the relation of signs to their users). But beyond signs there are symbols, which express the excess of force that is not reducible to subjects and predicates. At the end of part one Zarathustra departs from his friends and says that he will not return until he has a new love and a new language.[45] His new love is that of complacency and his new language is that of metaphor. Once the ethics of complacency becomes first philosophy, instead of epistemology, symbols as metaphors of excess cannot be reduced to signs. Nietzsche makes clear how our language tricks us into thinking only in terms of nouns and adjectives rather than in terms of verbal processes. We have a logic and an epistemology, as Deleuze would say, of only "the tree that is green" and not of "the greening of the tree."[46] As Zarathustra explores highlands, lowlands, and islands he becomes a wanderer. His experience of the different spiritualities and their certainties prepares him to embrace uncertainty.

Kristeva examines the history of theories of metaphor from Aristotle to Ricoeur and sees them as hermeneutical.[47] As Heidegger would say: "Leaping into the circle of thinking is a festive occasion."[48] He thinks within a triad of the thing, such as the farmer's shoes, of the artist, such as van Gogh, and of art as the third. He interprets them in terms of each other. But that triad of the hermeneutical circle is not the triad of the postmoderns. They leap out of the circle of understanding into a love without knowledge. In the excess of nonknowledge, humans can relate in complacency with each other, with animals, and with the Trinity. Kristeva's semiotic *chora* is the realm of Jim's beautiful risk. Phenomenology and hermeneutics have their place after they are added to the saying of complacent nonknowledge as the said of attempted knowledge.[49] It is not through knowledge that we can love the goodness of weakness. That is done only with a leap beyond signs into the symbols of the semiotic *chora*.

Father Crowe thinks about Aquinas exploring the complacent love of the Holy Spirit. He shows how Thomas did not create a new terminology for this

---

44. Nietzsche, *The Anti-Christ*, p. 158; Kristeva, *Tales of Love*. Kristeva's treatment of semiotics and the semiotic *chora* is based on this distinction. She also works with Lacan's distinction between the symbolic, the real, and the imaginary. Key passages are on pp. 113, 162, 201, 211, 232, and 237.

45. Nietzsche, *Thus Spoke Zarathustra*, pp. 99–103.

46. See Gilles Deleuze, *The Logic of Sense*, trans. Mark Lester with Charles Stivale. C. V. Boundas, ed. (New York: Columbia University Press, 1999).

47. Kristeva, *Tales of Love*, pp. 270–72.

48. Martin Heidegger, *The Origin of a Work of Art*, in *Basic Writings*, ed. David Farrell Krell (London: Routledge & Kegan Paul, 1978), pp. 149–50.

49. This distinction between "the saying" of immediate responsibility and "the said" of philosophical verbalization is made most strongly in Levinas, especially in *Otherwise Than Being*. The influence of Levinas on Jim is very strong, and Olthuis explains how he gets the name for his book *The Beautiful Risk* from Levinas on p. 74 of that book.

as did the Hegelians and post-Hegelians.[50] In his complacent love and friend-ship for Aristotle, Thomas would only write of a quasi friendship in order to get at the complacency prior to friendship. But as Crowe shows, Thomas kept bumping up against and exploring the symbolic realm that exceeds the Aristotelian limiting of metaphor. Aristotelian analogy of attribution and of proper proportionality tries to permit the process of metaphorical excess within signification.[51] But Thomas believed that the process of the Holy Spirit could play with a future contingency beyond any necessity and therefore beyond mere signification.[52]

The dust jacket of Jim's book *The Beautiful Risk* has a picture of a goldfish leaping out of a crowded fish bowl. It has a whole school of goldfish within it. But this fish is leaping toward another larger, freer habitat where she sees two other fish. The three of them together will be like Amanda, Jim, and Amanda's mother. They will be like Father, Son, and Holy Spirit. They will live in a love that is a metaphorical process that will blur the boundaries between them.[53] But it will not let them merge in emotional identification. The triune love will free in each of them a flourishing singularity.

---

50. Crowe, *Three Thomist Studies*, p. 155. See end of n. 9 at bottom of p. 155.

51. Kristeva, *Tales of Love*, p. 271. Kristeva explains what Crowe is getting at in terms of analogy of attribution, in which there is a causal likeness between creator and creatures.

52. Crowe, *Three Thomist Studies*, p. 164.

53. Kristeva, *Tales of Love*, p. 268. Kristeva's treatment of the relation between transference and meta-phor joins her theory of literature with her theory of psychoanalysis. Some key passages on the process of metaphor are on pp. 29, 30, 37, 268, 274, 278, 288, 330, 341, and 379–83.

9

The Good Samaritan, the Philosopher, and the Madman

Constantin V. Boundas

I should confess, as you begin to read this essay, my long-standing ambivalence toward the work of Paul Ricoeur. I have been fascinated by the scope of his research, the relentless pursuit of new and old philosophical challenges, which constantly fed his work, his resolute search for, and detection of, the exact point where they could be blended and reappear as threads of a much richer fabric—a fabric that Ricoeur has been weaving ever since his early encounters with Jean Nabert, Gabriel Marcel, and Emmanuel Mounier.[1] I have been touched by the nobility of his spirit. But I am not convinced by the ecumenical faith that sustains his labors, nor do I share the irenic attitude that motivates his hermeneutic. My allegiance to what he calls "hermeneutics of suspicion" must have been stronger than I had imagined. Ricoeur's exegesis is at its best when it registers and develops his insights just long enough to convey the intention of his agile mind and the generosity of his heart, before the saying becomes sedimented in the said. I find Ricoeur less convincing when, in the name of an allegedly robust hermeneutic rationality, he finds it tempting to show how a bend here and a twist there can prove that we are, after all, the children of the same God.

Whatever one's disposition towards Ricoeur's overall contribution to philosophy, one cannot help but be impressed by his relentless effort to think through the twin problematics of Self and Other, in a constant dialogue with

---

1. For Ricoeur's appreciation of Jean Nabert, see Paul Ricoeur, *Finitude et culpabilité: L'Homme faillible* (Paris: Aubier-Montaigne, 1960), p. 15; see also his "L'Essai sur le mal," *Esprit* (1959). For his appreciation of Gabriel Marcel, see Paul Ricoeur, *Gabriel Marcel et Karl Jaspers: Philosophie du mystère et philosophie du paradoxe* (Paris: Temps Present, 1948), and *Entretiens: Paul Ricoeur et Gabriel Marcel* (Paris: Aubier-Montaigne, 1968). On his relation to Mounier, see Paul Ricoeur, "Emmanuel Mounier: une philosophie personnaliste," *Esprit* (December 1950), reprinted in Paul Ricoeur, *Histoire et vérité* (Paris: Seuil, 1955), pp. 135–63.

all those who had already labored in this field. The published documentation of this effort reads like a well-kept archive of the most promising discussions of sameness and alterity by the best minds of the century. Having rejected the primacy of the negative and, as a result, having distanced himself from Sartre, Ricoeur undertakes the task of building a theory of intersubjectivity around three important premises: (1) Sameness and alterity cannot be left to confront each other from a distance, as if they were external to one another. The Other must be shown to inhabit the Self. (2) The Other that inhabits the Self should not be brought under the category of mere diversity, glossed over by its responsibility for disturbing and deforming the closed circuit of the Self. The Other is already always the instance that summons the Self to live with, and for, others in just institutions. Alterity is as much an ethical category as it is epistemological and ontological. (3) The summons should not hyperbolically be made to shock the unsuspecting Self to availability and to the obligation to serve. The predisposition of the Self to such an obligation and service is a necessary condition for an intersubjectivity that opens itself to ethics.

The stations that Ricoeur's meditation must traverse are, therefore, well marked on the road to ethics. The names Husserl, Heidegger, and Levinas instruct the traveler of the presence of these stations, but Ricoeur meanders along the traces of a much older pathway, one that Aristotle and the Greeks had traveled: in opposition to today's fashionable (in some circles) self-sacrificial ethics—the very idea of a non-eudaemonistic, other-regarding ethic, which considers the ethical attitude as a gesture of giving oneself to the other even unto death—Ricoeur will return to the vision of a good life for the Self and for the others. This return will require implementation of Bishop Butler's lesson on how to see the compatibility between self-regarding and other-regarding acts,[2] as well as the erection of just institutions within which to live with others, not as an afterthought but as an originary demand of the ethical. In this essay, I propose to walk, one more time, on Ricoeur's road to an ethical intersubjectivity, stopping at its stations and exploring the intersections and passageways that his sprawling work diligently fashions. My essay, besides exhibiting the pleasures of the flâneur-reader—my personal pleasures as I stroll though Ricoeur's texts—also aims to show an aporia at the center of Ricoeur's thought; an aporia that renders the passage from *bios* to *logos*, from life to reasoned reflection, or from the singular to the concept much more problematic than he himself had taken it to be. In my discussion of this aporia, I will try to bring about a face-off between the Samaritan of the biblical story, the reflective philosopher Ricoeur, and the madman—my thinly disguised reference to the demystifier-thinker of the *beyond good and evil*—Friedrich Nietzsche. My reading of the aporia will not be Derridean: I will not try to argue that the aporia is about the *cogitandum* of thought—that which we ought to think and yet can never

---

2. Joseph Butler, sermons I, V, in *Sermons* (New York : Robert Carter and Brothers, n.d.), pp. 25–36; 64–73.

think in the ordinary exercise of our faculties. My intention behind uncovering the aporia is to argue, in opposition to Ricoeur, that the passage from *bios* to *logos* cannot be negotiated in the manner that he suggests.

One of the first essays that I read of Ricoeur's—one that I never tire to reread—is "Le socius et le prochain."[3] It has, I think, in the most concise way possible, everything that must be said about someone encountering another—everything that Ricoeur has ever really said on this subject, making me doubt that his later grand detour through Husserl, Heidegger, and Levinas ever succeeded in saying it any better. "Le Socius et le prochain" is an exegesis of the parable of the good Samaritan. Jesus is asked, "who is my neighbour (πλησίον)?"[4]; and his reply frustrates the usual expectations for the neighbor to be the keen, the relative, the next-door friend, the compatriot. The Samaritan—who, while on the road, happened upon the fallen man and carried him to safety—is the answer to the question: he made himself a neighbor, attesting to the fact that one does not *have* a neighbor—one makes himself or herself the neighbor of someone. The neighbor is the attitude of making oneself present and available to the other. *Disponibilité;* availability.

Ricoeur stays with the Samaritan long enough in "Le socius et le prochain" to develop two or three more precious points. Our everydayness, he says, is not lived in the world of the neighbor; it is lived in the world of the *socius,* where relations are casual, impersonal, or, as some would say, "alienated." And this creates a longing for community and hardens the distinction between *Gesellschaft* and *Gemeinschaft,* as opposite styles of being in the world. This "hardening" is not a good thing. Ricoeur advises us not to think of them as isolated from one another, believing it is a mistake to measure all human relations according to the personal and the communal. "There is no private life," he writes, "but only to the extent that it is protected by a public order [which presumably is not *gemeinschaftliches*]; it is illusory to want to shape all human relations according to the style of communion."[5] The neighbor is not to be found necessarily in the modality "I-Thou," any more than s/he is excluded from the domain of the *socius.* S/he is marked by a dual allegiance to the near and far. And, according to Ricoeur, it is the Samaritan who exhibits this kind of allegiance: he is near because he made himself come near; but he is also distant because he is the Judean who, one day, without having anticipated or planned it, helped a stranger along the road.[6]

The seeds of a theory of intersubjectivity begin to pullulate in this essay. The later Ricoeur has insisted that to do justice to the problem of the Other requires that we place it at the point where three concerns—the epistemic, the ontological, and the ethical—intersect: How much can I know, or what can I reasonably believe, about the Other? Who is the Other that I seek to know?

3. Paul Ricoeur, *Histoire et vérité* (Paris: Aubier-Montaigne, 1956), pp. 99–111.
4. Luke 10:30–37.
5. Ibid., p. 107.
6. Ibid., p. 110.

And how should I receive or behave toward him or her? Without fanfare, these concerns are presented *in nuce* in the essay of the Samaritan, where the onto-logical point of view is already sketched out: the alterity of the other person is in the rapprochement of the far and near (the later Ricoeur will see in this rapprochement the presence of the other in the Self).[7] As for the presence of the ethical moment, it is unmistakably here, too: the characterization of the Other's position, with respect to the Self, depends on the degree of proximity or distance; and this is not the result of spatial determinations, but rather of one's attitude characterized by availability. As for the epistemic issue regarding the other person, it has also been anticipated: I do not know who my neighbor is until I make myself his or her neighbor. As I take on the role and place of the neighbor, I attest to the possibility of becoming-neighbor.

What else is there to be said? *Must* something more be said? Well, *bios,* says Ricoeur, is not *logos*—and philosophy cannot be a mere rhapsody of lived experiences. Between *bios* and *logos,* there lies the domain of conflicting inter-pretations and, consequently, reflection. There is something very Aristotelian in the way that Ricoeur contemplates the conflict of interpretations, with each rival interpretation a conflict—an Aristotelian *legomenon,* which cannot claim the epistemic certainty of a Cartesian foundation any more than it can be dis-carded as a lowly Platonic *doxa.* Each *legomenon* has a stake in the disclosure of *aletheia,* and Ricoeur, the reflective philosopher, seems to anticipate the de jure compossibility of all stakes, before the hermeneutic labor has found the time to show that they are, de facto, compossible.

Among the *legomena* of otherness that particularly impress Ricoeur, the strategies of Husserl, Heidegger, and Levinas find a place of honor.[8] They may be in conflict with one another, but, as far as Ricoeur is concerned, they are the best hope for the kind of *concordia discordata* that his hermeneutic passion projects past the conflict of interpretations. Despite his own misgiv-ings, Husserl's epistemic investigations lead to the fundamental ontology of Heidegger; and Heidegger's ontology gives way, despite itself, to the moral paroxysm of Levinas. But to the extent that the hyperbole of Levinas calls for an ontology of attestation, which, in turn, must come to rest on the epistemic achievements of the phenomenologist, Ricoeur's "theory of intersubjectivity" ends up drawing a perfect circle, whereby the epistemic, the ontological, and the ethical endlessly beckon one another.

From Husserl, Ricoeur retains the possibilities for intersubjectivity impli-cated in the phenomenological reduction, the notion of the flesh, and the analogical transfer of sense from my flesh to the flesh of the other.[9] It is in-structive to recall that Ricoeur has always maintained that the moment of the phenomenologist is irreducible: when all is said and done, the eidetic quest

---

7. See especially Paul Ricoeur, *Oneself as Another,* trans. Kathleen Blamey (Chicago: University of Chicago Press, 1992), passim.

8. See Ricoeur, "Tenth Study: What Ontology in View?" in *Oneself as Another,* pp. 297–356.

9. Ibid., pp. 319–26.

of the phenomenologist is the necessary condition for transference from *bios* to *logos*—with the following three provisos: (1) that the phenomenological theory of constitution should not be mistaken for the constructivism of the idealist; (2) that Husserl's decision to build his theory of intersubjectivity around the notion of the flesh be given the attention it deserves—indeed be developed further; and (3) that Husserl's reference to analogy be placed not in the context of syllogistics, but rather in the context of what is prereflective and prepredicative. The "idealist constructivism" is successfully countered when the phenomenological constitution becomes the practice of making the sedimented layers of meaning explicit—always already contained in the other person's presence—to one's own consciousness. The *epoche* does not end up in a tabula rasa; it rather restores the status of the transcendental clue to that which we bracket. "The presupposition of the other," writes Ricoeur, "is . . . contained in the formation of the very sense of the sphere of ownness. In the hypothesis that I am alone, this experience could never be totalized without the help of the other who helps me to gather myself together, strengthen myself, and maintain myself in my identity."[10] As for the notion of flesh, it was developed in order to make possible the pairing of one flesh with another flesh, on the basis of which a common nature can be constituted. Ricoeur, unlike Husserl, wishes to make it clear that even if the otherness of the stranger can, by some impossibility, be derived from the sphere of ownness, the otherness of the flesh would still precede it. "My flesh appears . . . as a body among bodies only to the extent that I am myself an other among all others, in the apprehension of a common nature, woven, as Husserl says, out of the network of intersubjectivity."[11] It is because Husserl thought of the "other than me" only as another I, and never of the Self as another, that he left the paradox—summed up in the question: How am I to understand that my flesh is also a body?—without answer. A more sustained attention to the passivity of "my" body than Husserl had given it would have secured this insight—an attention to the body's resistance, which is a testament to the body's knowledge of effort; an attention to the body's moods, which—Sartre notwithstanding—are not all voluntary; and an attention to the body's encounter with resisting external things, and to its ensuing suffering.

As for the third proviso, Ricoeur welcomes Husserl's decision to account for the constitution of the other person in terms of an analogical transfer of sense, provided that the contemplated analogy be prereflective and prepredicative. With this proviso satisfied, Ricoeur argues that analogy is "the ultimate and irreducible principle of constitution,"[12] the only one capable of positing the alter ego as another ego *like me*. "Husserl's analogy," he says, "is the explication of the 'like' in the ordinary expression, 'like me.' Like me, you think, you feel,

10. Ricoeur, *Oneself as Another*, p. 332.

11. Ibid., p. 326.

12. Paul Ricoeur, "Hegel et Husserl sur l'intersubjectivité," in *Du Texte à l'action* (Paris: Seuil, 1986), p. 292.

you act."[13] The transcendental and nonargumentative use of analogy rests on the description of the Other given to direct perception. This direct perception is a testament to understanding the Other as a subject for itself, which implies that the Other by itself is not continuous with my own lived experience. It is the doubling of the subject that highlights the central function of the analogy, whose careful employment prevents the ego from being thought of as a genre, since it also prevents it from becoming radically "disseminated."

In building on Husserl's discourse, Ricoeur is perfectly aware that Husserl already knew that the Other cannot to be added to the ego from outside; but he complains that Husserl's egological presuppositions did not quite secure the insight that the Other inhabits the Self. It is this task that Ricoeur gives himself in his book, *Oneself as Another,* and that announces itself in the very title of the book, because *soi* is neither the I nor the me. Ricoeur had already made this point in his essay "Ethique et morale":[14] "the term 'self' . . . should not be confused with the term 'me' (*moi*), in other words, with an egological position which would be inevitably subverted by the encounter with the other. What is worthy of a profound esteem in the self is the capacity to act intentionally and the capacity to initiate [an action]." As the agency of intentional action and of initiative, the Self is no more and no less an I than a You or a He or a She. What prevents the Self from being the ego is the fact that the Other is in the Self. Later, Ricoeur will show us how this claim is to be understood.

Heidegger is called upon to assist in this effort; especially the Heidegger of the section of *Being and Time* dedicated to conscience,[15] who shows that, far from being foreign to the constitution of selfhood, otherness is closely related to its emergence, inasmuch as, under the impetus of conscience, the Self is made capable of taking hold of itself in the very anonymity of the "they." The Self is affected by another voice—the voice of conscience—and the relationship between the agency that calls and the Self being called upon is dissymmetric. Conscience attests to this. It is true—Ricoeur well knows—that Heidegger's conscience attests to our authentic potentiality for Being, but as it attests to it, it does so from the vantage point of the Other. "Conscience attests to the power to be authentic and its verticalness belongs to the way it does the attesting: the voice of conscience hangs over me, calls and invites me from up high. In this sense, it disrupts the simple coincidence of the self to itself."[16] However indifferent to the task of elaborating a theory of intersubjectivity the Heideggerian conscience may be, it offers Ricoeur a powerful tool to move beyond Husserl. The silent call of *Gewissen* attests to and confirms the claim that the distinction between sameness (*idem*) and selfhood (*ipse*) alludes to not only two different layers of meaning, but also two different modes of Being.

13. Ibid., p. 295.

14. Paul Ricoeur, "Ethique et morale," in *Lectures 1: Autour du politique* (Paris: Seuil, 1991), p. 257.

15. Ricoeur, *Oneself as Another,* pp. 322–29, 349–53.

16. See Paul Ricoeur, "Emmanuel Levinas, penseur du témoignage," in *Lectures 3: Aux frontières de la philosophie* (Paris: Seuil, 1994), p. 85.

In the context of Heidegger's fundamental ontology, conscience—in being the Other voice or the voice of the Other—discloses the Self as being in the grips of Being ("une prise de l'être sur nous"), and witnesses the first stirrings of an ethic of the Self: the hold Being has on the Self calls for an answer; it commands the Self's engagement.

What strikes Ricoeur is Heidegger's promise of an intersection between ontology and ethics—albeit this promise is never kept. The voice of conscience never acquires the authenticity of transcendence and Ricoeur discloses in *Being and Time* that the reduction of the ethical takes place on two fronts: (1) from the point of view of the said (in Levinas's sense), conscience attests to Dasein's possibility to be (authentically) itself—rather than to any profound difference between good and evil; and (2) from the point of view of the one who does the calling, the Heideggerian reduction, even more drastically, assigns a dimension of superiority to the total immanence of Dasein to itself.[17] Neither the chapter on guilt nor the section on resoluteness would contribute anything useful to a discussion of intersubjectivity. The failing of which Dasein is said to be guilty is not a transgression against the Other; the failing lies in its being the basis for a nullity. As for resoluteness, it means to want to have a conscience—in other words, to want to be called to the appropriation of the Self by itself. It is pointless to expect anything more from these sections of *Being and Time.* In the words of Peter Kemp, Heidegger's *Eigentlichkeit* must be understood for what it is: an appropriation of the Self by the Self, whereby conscience is demoralized.[18] There is attestation in Heidegger, but there is no injunction. There is a clear understanding that alterity inhabits the Self, but the alterity contemplated is not the alterity of the other person. Despite Heidegger's reticence to go beyond *Eigentlichkeit,* Ricoeur is prepared to grant that Heidegger's important reflection on conscience creates possibilities for an ethic of self-esteem; but he adds that self-esteem, without solicitation of and by the other person, is pretty lame. Ricoeur, unlike Heidegger, is not afraid of the inevitable hominization of valuational standpoints: he makes it clear that issues surrounding the being with others must be discussed from within a horizon that is clearly ethical—one that encompasses our goal of the good life, with and for others, in just institutions.

Now, to draw self-esteem from Heidegger's *eigentlichkeit* (appropriation of the Self) may be easier said than done. Ricoeur's way will take us back to his *Time and Narrative,* and to the distinction between two senses of self-identity: identity-*idem* and identity-*ipse*—sameness and selfhood.[19] *Idem* excludes difference in the name of the repetition of the Same; *ipse* constitutes identity in the face of difference. If the Other inhabits the Self, in the sense that the Self emerges from the dialectic between Same and Other, and if the emergence

17. Ibid., pp. 85–86.

18. Peter Kemp, "Ricoeur entre Heidegger et Levinas," in *Paul Ricoeur: L'herméneutique à l'école de la phénoménologie,* ed. Jean Greisch (Paris: Beauchesne, 1995), pp. 235–59.

19. Paul Ricoeur, *Temps et Récit,* vol. 1 (Paris: Seuil, 1983); *Temps et Récit,* vol. 2 (Paris: Seuil, 1991).

implicated in this dialectic is continuous, precarious, and never guaranteed, then the passage from the ontology of the Self (which is all that one can get from Heidegger) to the ethic of the Self that Ricoeur wants may be easier to trace. Ricoeur traces it as he connects identity-*ipse* with the notion of the "maintenance of the self" and, therefore, with the promise and the temporality of the promise that grounds this preservation. Given this linkage, "maintenance of the self" is revealed as Spinoza's *conatus*—the power to be, the power to persevere in one's own existence. It is true that *conatus* is prior to conscience, understood as attestation and injunction; but, Ricoeur argues, this does not render the *conatus* indifferent or inimical to conscience (as Spinoza's *Ethics* clearly demonstrates).[20] The *conatus* is not a blind force propelling us to mere survival—or at least, it is not *only* that, because maintenance of the Self is more than one's perseverance in being. Perseverance in being can be explained in terms of drives and habit-formations, which pertain to both *idem* and *ipse;* but maintenance of the Self, to the extent that it involves and is explained by a promise to maintain the Self, pertains only to ipseity. As maintenance of the Self, the *conatus,* the desire to live and to live well, incorporates self-esteem and in self-esteem one finds the solicitation of the Other: we need other people—we need friends—in order to live well. In solicitation, the Self perceives itself as another among Others. Self-esteem is then revealed as the virtue of living well, and is intensified by self-respect, the virtue of being with and for others. The coupling of self-esteem and self-respect must be understood in the context of the distinction that Ricoeur draws between ethics (the desire to live well) and morality (the province of the norm). This is how Olivier Mongin articulates the two: "once we admit that ethics refers to self-esteem and morality refers to respect, it should be obvious that the ethics of the self is more fundamental than self-respect; that self-respect is the guise that the ethic of the self undertakes under the regime of the norm; and that the aporias of duty create situations in which self-esteem is not only the source but also the refuge of respect, when no norm offers a secure guide for the *hic et nunc* exercise of respect."[21]

Heidegger emphasizes the height from which the other voice calls; Levinas emphasizes its exteriority—its strang(er)ness.[22] An uncomprising hostility to the assimilative tendencies of representation makes the latter a foe of ontologies and of the philosophies of consciousness alike—an unlikely ally, therefore, for Ricoeur, for whom both ontology and the philosophy of consciousness have been important throughout his writings. These differences of approach in Levinas's work notwithstanding, it is the Other's call that Ricoeur heeds and the ethical responsibility that this call eo ipso imposes on the enjoined Self. In his effort to think the kind of responsibility that would be anarchic,

20. The body's *conatus,* for Spinoza, is linked to its ability to affect and be affected. Affects, in turn, are linked with adequate and inadequate ideas. See *Ethics* IV.38–39; III.9e.p.

21. Olivier Mongin, *Paul Ricoeur* (Paris: Seuil, 1991), p. 181.

22. See Ricoeur, *Oneself as Another,* pp. 335–41, 354–55; and "Emmanuel Levinas, penseur du témoignage."

nondefeasible, and nontransferable, Levinas builds the moral point of view on a commandment that cannot be universalized: "Thou shalt not kill me!" He is the thinker who, better than anyone else, formulates the problematic of the other person in the context of this injunction. We may think, at this point, that the good Samaritan has returned in Levinas; but this Samaritan is no longer the one who makes himself a neighbor, through an intentionality proper to neighborliness. He is the servant who must respond to the call—"*Me voici!*"—the one placed in a state of anarchic availability, which has nothing to do with inclinations. The epiphany of the other signals the rupture of the egocentric bliss, keeping Levinas on his guard against egology but also against phenomenology: "Epiphany expresses something other than a phenomenon . . . because the other (who calls me) . . . is not just any interlocutor but rather a paradigmatic figure of the type of a master of justice,"[23] or, as Levinas specifies in the pages of *Otherwise than Being*, "not even the master of justice but rather the offender who, as an offender, no less requires the gesture of pardon and expiation."[24]

It is clear that Levinas succeeds in foregrounding the enjoinment of the ego by the other person—the precise enjoinment that was absent from the reflections of Heidegger. But in so doing, Levinas succeeds also in obliterating all traces of the attestation of the Other in the Self. An undialectical Levinas, in Ricoeur's view, is no better than an undialectical Heidegger. Ricoeur consequently begins pointing out that the passivity necessary for the ego to answer the call of the Other (*Me voici!*) is to such an extent hyperbolic that its ability to respond remains a mystery. The shattering of the originary ego by the unsolicited force of strang(er)ness renders enigmatic the very ability of the ego to hear the call. Ricoeur's critique of Levinas, in fact, goes further. The hyperbole, he complains, deprives us of the ability to discern and to judge: for the Other is not always the poor and the needy; he may be my torturer. In the last analysis, Ricoeur doubts that Levinas has let identity-*idem* go. For suppose that we ask: Who is obsessed by the other ? Who is hostage to the other? The answer has to be that it is the same, no longer defined by separation but rather by its contrary—substitution.[25] The point of this critique is that, through the blindness and the insight of the hyperbole, Levinas shows, *malgré lui,* that there can be no contradiction between the movement from the Same to the Other and the movement from the Other to the Same: the two are dialectically complementary. Therefore, Husserl, and phenomenology, cannot be laid aside that easily: the movement from the Same to the Other is precisely Husserl's own meditation and gift. The lesson that Ricoeur learns through his meditation on Husserl and Levinas is that it is impossible to construct the dialectic in a unidirectional manner, whether one attempts, with Husserl, to derive the alter

23. Ricoeur, *Oneself as Another*, p. 337.
24. Ibid., p. 338.
25. Ibid., p. 340.

ego from the Self or, with Levinas, one reserves for the other the irreducible initiative for assigning responsibility to the Self. A two-pronged conception of otherness remains to be constructed, one that does justice in turn to the primacy of self-esteem and also to the primacy of the convocation of justice coming from the Other. One cannot think or live self-esteem and solicitude as if they were separate from one another. Solicitude makes a dialogue inherent in self-esteem explicit. The Self implies something other than itself. "The miracle of reciprocity is that persons recognize each other as insubstitutable in exchange itself,"[26] and this is precisely what solicitude is.

The circle of the *legomena*—from Husserl to Heidegger to Levinas, and then back to Husserl—has been traced. And Ricoeur holds that this hermeneutic circle subsists in a space equidistant from the hapless certitude of Descartes and the global suspicion of Nietzsche. The credits Ricoeur gives to Heidegger for having made attestation central are qualified by the recognition that attestation is a form of witnessing and, therefore, a mode of cognition between *episteme* and *doxa*. To attest is to trust, to believe. *Créance.* It is to trust my power to respond to the call of the Other in the accusative modality of the "It's me here!" Such a trust, however, demands that the Heideggerian attestation, which demoralized conscience, be replaced by the effective linkage of attestation and injunction. Only then, being-enjoined would constitute the moment of otherness appropriate to conscience. In the discussion between Ricoeur and his interlocutors (Husserl, Heidegger, Levinas), it is easy to recognize the subtlety and the strength of the mind of a seasoned hermeneutician at work. But what may be just as easily missed in this rigorous effort to reconcile conflicting interpretations is the moment Ricoeur reveals his hand (his own peculiar investment) in the orchestration of this polyphonic script. "I am called to live well," he says, "with and for others in just institutions: this is the first injunction."[27] With this statement, which is often repeated in his work, Ricoeur interjects, in hermeneutic labor, a decisively Greek-Aristotelian moment—indeed, he offers this moment as the foundation of, and also the correction to, the meditations of Husserl, Heidegger, and Levinas. The primacy of the ethical and the need to articulate a vision of the good life must be secured as the necessary condition for a creative and not oppressive meditation on the morality of the norm.[28] Ethics and morality will continue to be separated by a chasm as long as the norm of the latter is not read as the transformation of a nonnormative solicitation of the former. This nonnormative solicitation, according to Ricoeur, is a form of commandment that is not yet law: "This commandment, if it can be called such, can be heard in the tone of the *Song of Songs,* in the plea the lover addresses to the beloved: 'Thou, love me!' It is because violence taints all the relations of interaction . . . that the command-

---

26. Paul Ricoeur, "Ethique et morale," p. 258.

27. Ibid., p. 257.

28. Ricoeur's references to Aristotle as a corrective to the one-sidedness of Heidegger and Levinas are many. See, as an example, *Oneself as Another,* pp. 181–94.

ment becomes law, and the law, prohibition: 'Thou shalt not kill!'"[29] Having said this, Ricoeur seems to think that the hermeneutic circle drawn around the *legomena* on Self and Other demonstrates its fertility rather than its viciousness. Injunction is solicitude, but solicitude is now a symmetrical relation: "I call solicitude," he writes, "this movement of the self towards the other that corresponds to the interpellation of the self by the other."[30] Against Heidegger, Ricoeur presses the point that attestation is originarily injunction—otherwise it would be deprived of all ethical significance; against Levinas, he presses the point that the injunction is originarily attestation—otherwise it could not be received by, or make a difference to, the Self. Against both, he attempts to reorient thinking to the eudaemonistic ethos of the Greek origins, without which authenticity will stay empty and the injunction, blind.

The call back to the Greek ethos is one of Ricoeur's main concerns. Another is his desire to prevent the mistake of thinking that alterity may be thought solely in the context of the otherness of the other person. To discuss the problem of the other person, without placing it in the context of a broader notion of alterity, is, for Ricoeur, a mistake. Ricoeur's fidelity to the Plato of the later dialogues and to the dialectic of the *megista gene* is a testament to his determination *not* to reduce alterity to the otherness of another person. (This determination alone should have drawn the philosophers of difference out of their trenches and spurned them to an engagement with Ricoeur's sprawling oeuvre. But only the early severe critique of his interpretation of Freud by the Lacanians of the 1960s and 1970s has until now marked this spot.) Ricoeur's allegiance to Plato and to the *megista gene* is based on two considerations: (1) It is not Ricoeur's plan to inscribe the relation between one Self and another as a mere external relation; exteriority must be given its due, but it cannot have the last word. "Otherness," he writes, "is not added on to selfhood from outside. . . . it belongs instead to the tenor of meaning and to the ontological constitution of selfhood."[31] Otherness, therefore, must, in a sense, inhabit (and must be shown to inhabit) the Same. The strang(er)ness peculiar to the other person must be anticipated and, in some sense, preceded by the alterity of my flesh, by my suffering, and by the voice of conscience. (2) On the other hand, his interest in a notion of alterity, broader than that of the other person, is due to another deep conviction of his—a conviction that he announced as early as *The Voluntary and the Involuntary:* Transcendence without God, he said then, is not a real transcendence.[32] This is why alterity cannot exhaust itself in the exteriority or strang(er)ness of the other person; it needs the majestic heights to amplify the call for the voice of conscience. Ricoeur, the philosopher, is

29. Ricoeur, *Oneself as Another,* p. 351.

30. Paul Ricoeur, "Approches de la personne," in *Lectures 2: La contrée des philosophes* (Paris: Seuil, 1992), p. 205.

31. Ricoeur, *Oneself as Another,* p. 317.

32. Paul Ricoeur, *Philosophie de la volonté: Le volontaire et l'involontaire* (Paris: Aubier-Montaigne, 1967), pp. 31–32.

aware of the need for a delicate approach to these heights: the question of whether or not the abode of the Divine is at stake with alterity should, from the philosopher's point of view, be left undecidable. It is fashionable to think that alterity is coextensive with the otherness of other people. This is true for Freud's metapsychology, for which moral conscience is the affair of the superego, and the superego, the voice of the ancestor; it is also true for Heidegger, with some qualifications, to be sure, since the Dasein that calls and is called upon is not the human subject; Ricoeur thinks that it may also be true for Levinas, for whom the model of alterity is the other person. But Ricoeur does not want to be fashionable and he concludes with these words: "Perhaps, the philosopher as philosopher has to admit that one does not know and cannot say whether this Other, the source of the injunction, is another person whom I can look in the face or who can stare at me, or my ancestors . . . or God—living God, absent God—or an empty place. With the aporia of the Others, philosophical discourse comes to an end."[33]

I would like to conclude this essay with a couple of critical points, which, I hope, will address the reasons for my difficulty with Ricoeur—difficulty that I experience, despite the fact that I find his vision of living with others beyond reproach, as long as it is not entangled in philosophico-theological reflexivity.

First, recall that, in his discussion on Husserl, Ricoeur distinguishes between phenomenological description and idealist constructivism: the former, unlike the latter, makes explicit, and draws into the light, what is already present in the given. Therefore, the constitution of the Other is nothing but the methodic deployment of meaning-structures, which inhere in the Other, in the way that the Other is present in consciousness. It would then follow that everything revolves, for better or for worse, around what consciousness assumes to be given. It goes without saying that nothing prevents consciousness from refining and modifying its initial assumptions about the given; but the fact is that any explication of meaning-structures has to conform to the last assumption made.[34] It follows that Ricoeur's theory of intersubjectivity, all the way down to its eidetic underpinnings, depends on the figure of the Other that Ricoeur himself places within brackets for the sake of phenomenological elucidation—and that this figure is not presuppositionless. I realize that this point of mine reads like a retracing and a critique of the hermeneutic circle, and it is not my intention here to reopen the dispute as to whether this circle is productive or whether it is vicious. My point, rather, is that, with Ricoeur, the circle is reconstituted in the domain of the phenomenologist—and that, as a result, the question is no longer one of productivity or viciousness. It is a question of the transcendental unnecessarily duplicating the empirical and

---

33. Ricoeur, *Oneself as Another*, p. 335.

34. Certainly, one does not have to instruct Ricoeur on this subject; he himself has made this point clear for us and showed us ways of coping with this inevitability. See his *Interpretation Theory: Discourse and the Surplus of Meaning* (Fort Worth: Texas Christian University Press, 1976), pp. 75–79.

thereby claiming for itself the cognitive function that the empirical on its own could not claim.[35]

Am I unfair to Ricoeur at this point? Am I overlooking that he is the one who wishes to avoid the apodicticity of the triumphalist and the despondency of the genealogist alike? Isn't the linkage of attestation and enjoinment made with the support of credence, belief in, and trust, rather than *episteme* or *doxa?* Indeed it is. But Ricoeur must choose between the empirical supported by credence and the transcendental bolstered by epistemic apodicticity. The alterity that Ricoeur placed within the brackets of the *epoche* is the gulf between the Samaritan and the man who lay by the roadside. But then, one cannot help but riposte that the Samaritan who makes himself a neighbor may, on reflection, assert: "Here I stand; I can do no other!" He may be acting out of conviction, out of impulse, or out of sympathy; but he is not acting in accordance with an eidetic intuition of being-a-neighbor. And if what Ricoeur does in moving from the parable of the good Samaritan to the hermeneutics of *legomena*—motivated by the Aristotelian vision of the good life—is to duplicate the empirical in the transcendental, then asking analogy to solve the enigma of sense being transferred from the ego to the other ego may not be as unproblematic as Ricoeur seems to think. We may protect ourselves against thinking of analogy in the context of syllogism, we may see to it that its use is within the prepredicative and prereflective sphere, but we cannot prevent it from grasping the sense of the "like" in the expression "another like me" according to the image and the resemblance of an "alterity," which is based on our last empirical assumption. It is because we cannot prevent it from functioning in this way that Deleuze has it exactly right when he says that analogy belongs to representation.[36]

Second, it is precisely this difficulty that will affect the dialectic of attestation and enjoinment: Who attests to what? Who enjoins whom? We recall that Ricoeur chastises Heidegger for demoralizing conscience and depriving its voice of all content. By contrast, Ricoeur's conscience is loquacious. "Live well, with and for others, in just institutions" is what it whispers to him. But I ask: how am I supposed to conceptually link the "live well" with the "with and for others"? I do not dispute Ricoeur's claim that to live well requires one to have friends; but the Samaritan is not a friend—at least not in the Aristotelian sense that Ricoeur mobilizes at this point of his story. And even if we were to think of the Samaritan as a friend, how does one derive the universality of the moral norm from the relationship between friends? How does one—remembering Hume—extend his or her sympathies from kin and the intimate to those who lie by the roadside, without being kin and intimate? How does one move from self-esteem to respect for others? Or, to raise the question in the context of the *legomena*—which one is the originary call, the one that enjoins me to live

---

35. See Gilles Deleuze, *The Logic of Sense,* trans. Mark Lester with Charles Stivale, ed. Constantin V. Boundas (New York: Columbia University Press, 1990), pp. 97–99.

36. For the critique of representation and of analogy which belongs to it, see Gilles Deleuze, *Difference and Repetition,* trans. Paul Patton (New York: Columbia University Press, 1994), pp. 33–39.

with and for others? Is it the commandment that can be heard in the tone of the Song of Songs, in the plea the lover addresses to the beloved: "Thou, love me!"? Or is it the commandment having become prohibition—"Thou shalt not kill me!"—the one that resonates in the midst of the violence that taints our relations? If the plea of the lover belongs to the ethics of living well, and the prohibition belongs to the morality of the norm—and the transition from the one to the other remains as abrupt and implacable as it is in Ricoeur—how long before the sarcasm of the madman is heard again, scorning, one more time, the tender fool who, haunted by an insatiable need for love, lights the eternal fire for all those who do not return his love?

How can one fail to see that the passage from the lover's plea to normativity and responsibility is built from the bricks and mortar of *ressentiment?* How can one fail to see that the passage is not from love to the norm, but rather from spurned love to judgment? What is strange is that Ricoeur himself is quite aware of the quagmire of the dialectics of good and bad conscience: he praises Heidegger for having found a way to contemplate conscience, without making it vulnerable to Nietzsche's hermeneutics of suspicion.[37] But at the point where he himself needs to navigate with extra care around the shoals of bad conscience, he seems unable to follow the lessons of his own insight. He fails to see that there is an aporia between love and judgment; no way (*poros*) exists from the one to the other. There is (*es gibt*) love for the sake of putting norm and judgment to rest—"pour en finir avec le jugement."[38] To think of the good Samaritan in the context of normativity and judgment is to mistake him for the man of duty and to subordinate, ultimately, alterity to the norm. Perhaps, the mistake was to want to bridge the gap between *bios* and *logos,* in the first place, by sacrificing the singularity of *bios* to the generalities and equivalences of the concept. Perhaps, the singularity of Levinas's hyperbole captures the gesture of the Samaritan better than all the resources of the philosophy of reflection—which is not to say that this gesture is ineffable.

37. Ricoeur, *Oneself as Another,* pp. 341–50.
38. On the issue of judgment and the calls by Nietzsche, D. H. Lawrence, Kafka, and Artaud to have done with judgment, see Gilles Deleuze, "To Have Done with Judgement," in *Essays Critical and Clinic,* trans. Daniel W. Smith and Michael A. Greco (Minneapolis: University of Minnesota Press, 1997), pp. 126–35.

10

Religion with an Impure Heart?

Kierkegaard and Levinas on God and Other Others[1]

Jeffrey Dudiak

1. Levinas on Kierkegaard

Levinas's explicit comments on Kierkegaard, besides quite rare references elsewhere in his work—the most memorable of which is found in *Totality and Infinity* to the effect that "It is not I who resist the system, as Kierkegaard thought; it is the other" (p. 40)—are contained in two brief pieces included in his *Noms Propre* (*Proper Names*) collection, which appeared in French in 1976 and in Michael B. Smith's English translation in 1996.[2] The first of these is entitled "Existence and Ethics," and first appeared, in German, in *Schweizer Monatshefte* in 1963; and the second, which echoes in brief many of the key concerns of the first, entitled "A propos of 'Kierkegaard vivant,'" and which

---

1. In the Preface to *Totality and Infinity*, Emmanuel Levinas refers to Franz Rosenzweig's *Stern der Erlösung* as "a work too often present in this book to be cited" (Emmanuel Levinas, *Totality and Infinity: An Essay on Exteriority*, trans. A. Lingis [The Hague: Martinus Nijhoff, 1979]). Asked to contribute to a Festschrift, how does one best honor one's longtime teacher, mentor, and friend? One possibility is to write an essay specifically on the thought of the person to whom the Festschrift is dedicated (and, indeed, I have written on the thought of Prof. James Olthuis before). Another possibility is to press on with one's own ongoing work while acknowledging a debt, while gratefully acknowledging the profound influence of another's thought on one's own, to the extent that this thought is present far too often to be cited—that is, to reflect not *on* a body of work but *in and through* it. I have chosen the latter course here. I acknowledge, therefore, that I not only read and learned to read Levinas and Kierkegaard (and so much else) under the tutelage of Jim Olthuis, but, moreover, that he remains a tacit conversation partner for all of my work, and whether I am adopting, adapting, or reacting to his ideas, his influence is a formative and formidable force on every page that I write. For a greater blessing from a teacher one could not hope.

2. Emmanuel Levinas, *Proper Names,* trans. M. B. Smith (Stanford: Stanford University Press, 1996).

185

was first published in 1966, is the edited transcript of two interventions, on comments made by Jean Hyppolite and Gabriel Marcel, that Levinas made at the 1964 Paris conference celebrating the centenary of Kierkegaard.[3]

In these two reflections, Levinas both admires and disparages the power of Kierkegaard's thought, and the profound mark that it has, on his view, left on European thought up to today. Positively perceived (for the moment—as it is precisely these positives, alternately viewed, that will flip into negatives), Levinas credits Kierkegaard with two important philosophical innovations, that, Levinas claims, are the philosophical fruits of a nonphilosophical motivation or inspiration: (1) the strong notion of a separated subject, and (2) the notion of a persecuted truth, or the truth in and of faith—two ideas that are, of course, not unrelated.

It is Kierkegaard, Levinas believes, who, with incomparable force, rehabilitated the unicity and singularity of the subject against its being absorbed by Hegelian universality. This strong idea of existence, of the subject, that is, of interiority, as absolute, as separated, is based, or so Levinas claims of Kierkegaard, upon a nonphilosophical experience that permits of a delineation of the subject outside of both objectivism and idealism. For the particularity of sensibility and enjoyment, that which might have been looked to as capable of carving out on objective grounds a subject as singular, and which Kierkegaard discusses under the rubric of "the aesthetic" stage, results, after his analyses, only in a sensible dispersion leading to the impasse of hopelessness where the subject is lost. Correlatively, under idealism, where the interior life of the subject is to be translated and absorbed into the structures of external Being (be these legal, societal, institutional, communicative), and which Kierkegaard discusses as "the ethical" stage—the stage wherein the conversion from particularity to universality is the very moment of the Good, of Being, and of philosophy—the singular subject is lost altogether. For Kierkegaard, on the contrary, exteriority—whether objective or ideal—is incapable of containing the thinker. The subject has a secret, forever inexpressible, and this secret is its very subjectivity. Levinas identifies this Kierkegaardian secret, above all, with the burning of sin, that which no rational or universal truth is able to recover or extinguish. Kierkegaard's subject is a tension on itself, in tension with itself, is, Levinas claims, the son of "Christian" experience, and even of its pagan sources: "existence tensed over itself, open to the outside in an attitude of impatience and of waiting—an impatience that the outer world (of people and things), wrapped in a relaxed, impassive thought, cannot satisfy. And beyond that thirst for salvation, there is an older tension of the human soul (perhaps for this reason 'naturally' Christian) that consumes itself with desires" (EE 67). The subject received from this ancient experience, where identification is not the product of a logical tautology—I am I—but is effectuated across the tension between these terms, where being clings to its being in care, in anxiety, for itself, is

---

3. These two texts will be referred to respectively in my text by the short forms EE and AP.

precisely, Levinas maintains, the egoism, the me. But if Hegelian idealism was about the relaxation (in the form of self-consciousness) of this tension by means of a conversion of such an egoism to Being and Truth, that is, to its place in the totality, in the general law, in discourse, the first strength of Kierkegaard's position, of his Protestant protestations, according to Levinas, is to see in such a conversion the end of discourse and of philosophy in a totalitarian politics wherein humans are no longer the source of their own language, but merely reflections of an impersonal *logos*. Against all of this Kierkegaard opposes the subject—with its secret.

Kierkegaard's second innovation, according to Levinas, is the introduction of a notion of truth as a persecuted truth—as over against Hegel's triumphant truth—that emerges across "the ever recurring inner rending of doubt, which is not only an invitation to verify evidence, but part of the evidence itself" (AP 77). The faith, or belief (*la croyance*), that corresponds to this truth, that is the organon of access to it, is not then a form of imperfect knowing, not a degradation of knowing that would be perfect and triumphant in itself, and of which belief would grasp only a part. The operative opposition in Kierkegaard, according to Levinas, is not that between faith and knowledge as uncertain and certain, but between persecuted and triumphant truth. The humility of this persecuted truth, which dares not say its name, dares not present itself in the clearing, is what constitutes its transcendence, its grandeur. Never grasped, never revealed for not given over to phenomena, Kierkegaard's truth is always at the point of departure, and exists for faith in a kind of equivocation: it is "there as if it were not there"; "here with Kierkegaard something is manifested, yet one may wonder whether there was any manifestation. . . . Truth is played out on a double register: at the same time the essential has been said, and, if you like, nothing has been said" (AP 78). Kierkegaard's persecuted truth thus operates under a "permanent rending," and the value of this, for Levinas, is that this notion "allows us, perhaps, to put an end to the game of disclosure, in which immanence always wins out over transcendence; for once being has been disclosed, even partially, even in Mystery, it becomes immanent," and, as Levinas here as elsewhere insists, "there is no true exteriority in disclosure" (AP 78). Thus these two new ideas that come to philosophy through Kierkegaard, (1) that of an absolutely separated subject (2) who in faith can enter into a genuine if always tenuous relationship with a permanently transcendent truth, work together, and work together to oppose the violence imposed by an evidential and triumphant but impersonal truth. This Levinas wants too.

But there is also that which bothers Levinas in Kierkegaard. First off, Levinas finds Kierkegaard's separated subject, who rejects all form, refuses thought and discourse along with triumphant truth—presumably because it need not answer for itself in the world—to be exhibitionistic, immodest. And does this not, Levinas asks, entirely while favorably acknowledging the opposition that Kierkegaard puts up against the impersonal violence of the System, lead to other violences?

Indeed—and this is his second problem with Kierkegaard—it is the violence of Kierkegaard that "shocks" Levinas, a violence that is, Levinas claims, his very way of philosophizing. "The manner of the strong and the violent, who fear neither scandal nor destruction, has become, since Kierkegaard and before Nietzsche, a manner of philosophy. One philosophizes with a hammer" (AP 76). So, if Levinas sees the influence of Kierkegaard across "the rejection it may elicit" to his nude subjectivism in the seductiveness of the later Heidegger and the nobility of neo-Hegelianism—for, he claims, "after one hundred years of Kierkegaardian protest, one would like to get beyond that protest" (EE 71)—the "recourse to the Being of beings that reveals itself and elicits human subjectivity only in its truth and its mystery," as the "recourse to the impersonal structures of the Spirit beyond the arbitrary and imagination" that these ways of thought respectively represent, nevertheless "take on the virile and ruthless accents," the "intransigent vehemence," of the thought they oppose, "as one likes that with which one is familiar" (EE 72). This harshness and aggressivity is not, moreover, on Levinas's view, merely a rhetorical device, merely a question of literary form, but emerges "at the precise moment when, moving beyond the esthetic stage, existence can no longer limit itself with what it takes to be an ethical stage and enters the religious one" (EE 72), that is, when ethics is surpassed by faith. Thus the two new ideas that come into philosophy through Kierkegaard, that of an absolutely separated subject who in faith can enter into a genuine if always tenuous relationship with a permanently transcendent truth, that work together to oppose the violence imposed by an evidential and triumphant but impersonal truth, also collude, on Levinas's reading, in a new violence—the violence of surpassing ethics (the subject's concern for his worldly fellows, which Kierkegaard renders as consisting of general norms applicable to and for all—and thus as totalizing, as an exposure of the subject's secret), the violence of the surpassing of ethics in faith. This is what Levinas fears.

Because for Kierkegaard "the ethical means the general, . . . the singularity of the *I* would be lost in his view, under a rule valid for all." But, claims Levinas, "it is not at all certain that ethics is where he sees it" (AP 76). Indeed, for Levinas, "ethics as consciousness of a responsibility toward others . . . , far from losing you in generality, singularizes you, poses you as a unique individual, as *I*" (AP 76). "To be myself means, then, to be unable to escape responsibility" (EE 73), to be, in his famous phrase, "face to face" with the other, elected, confirmed in my ipseity, set apart by the "me and no other" of responsibility. So if "the entire polemics between Kierkegaard and speculative philosophy presupposes subjectivity as tensed on itself, existence as a care that being takes for its own existence, as a torment for oneself" (EE 72), and it is in this tension that the singularity of the subject hungry for salvation is produced, for Levinas "this putting in question of the I in the face of the Other is a new tension in the I, a tension that is not a tensing on oneself" (EE 73), but a tension, the tension of ethics, equally capable of resisting the impersonal violence of speculative thought, yet without this resistance turning into a quest that would be conducted in a clandestine relationship with a transcendence outside of the sight of my fellows and indifferent to their concerns: "It is not I who resist the system, as Kierkegaard thought; it is the other."

Levinas, against Kierkegaard, thus conceives of the ethical subject not as lost in the universal, but as diacony, that is, as one in the role of a servant, and as such as a separated subject. He seeks to draw the subjectivity of the subject not away from ethics but into it, as it. But in doing so, Levinas does not argue for the ethical as Kierkegaard defines the term (as a matter of generality and/or universality); he changes the definition of ethics.

2. A Failed Synthesis

In fact, in changing the definition of ethics to my responsibility in face of the other, a responsibility that singularizes me as the *one* called to respond, Levinas describes thereby a relationship that would seem to have far more in common with what Kierkegaard calls religion than with what Kierkegaard calls ethics. In the case of each of these relationships, I relate, as separated, as the single individual, in passivity, to an irreducible transcendence, a wholly other, across an immediate relationship that calls me to respond absolutely, with my whole and deepest self, and that I cannot turn away from without fault. The required singular response to the singular other of ethics as described by Levinas has no more to do with a reference or recourse to generality than does the religious response that Kierkegaard describes as faith. Levinas, moreover, employs, at least after *Totality and Infinity,* another term, "justice," for those general and universal norms by which I mediate between all of the human others in the world, the others of which I am one too (and this, in Levinas's phrase, "by the grace of God"),[4] those general and universal structures that Kierkegaard refers to as ethical.

One is here perhaps then tempted—and in an early graduate level paper I indeed succumbed to this temptation—to read in Levinas's protestation a merely semantic problem, and to attempt to map Levinas's employment of the term "ethics" onto Kierkegaard's use of the term "religion," to attempt to map Levinas's employment of the term "justice" onto Kierkegaard's use of the term "ethics," and to carry on an undaunted synthesizing of these two thinkers—as if any problem were merely semantic, as if any "problem" were not wholly semantic. And one can perhaps indeed collect some air miles in such an effort. But could it really be the case that Levinas, blinded by these

---

4. Emmanuel Levinas, *Otherwise than Being or Beyond Essence,* trans. A. Lingis (The Hague: Martinus Nijhoff, 1981), p. 158, hereafter abbreviated as OTB. Lingis translates Levinas's "grace à Dieu" as "thanks to God," where I am translating it as "by the grace of God." For an explanation, see Jeffrey Dudiak, *The Intrigue of Ethics* (New York: Fordham University Press, 2001), p. 254.

terminological differences, so blatantly missed the obvious? Or must we look more deeply for the source of his concerns?

A hint as to where we might begin to look for such a source comes to the fore, I think, when we note that in this roughly constructed little Kierkegaard-Levinas dictionary for translation—one that could, if one were so inclined, be to some extent expanded—there appears to be no obvious term in Kierkegaard that corresponds to what Levinas refers to as "religion." And, indeed, I will suggest, and henceforth argue, that the important difference between Levinas and Kierkegaard is not, as a cursory reading of Levinas's comments seems to indicate, on the question of ethics (since it is easy enough to translate Levinas's "ethics" by Kierkegaard's "religion" and Levinas's "justice" by Kierkegaard's "ethics," provided that Levinas's "religion" is ignored), but around the question of religion itself, in a difference between Kierkegaard's transcending religion with a pure heart and Levinas's "mundanizing" religion with an impure heart.

For despite the fact that both ethics in Levinas and religion in Kierkegaard require a singular response to the wholly other, Levinas's wholly other is not Kierkegaard's wholly other—and herein lies, perhaps, the essential point. To put simply what will turn out to be not so simple, Levinas's wholly other is the human other, whereas Kierkegaard's wholly other is God, and this is a difference that makes a huge difference, a world of difference (perhaps quite literally), and a difference that undermines the formal, and thus apparent, similarities between "ethics" in Levinas and "religion" in Kierkegaard.

I said just now that this distinction, which I will maintain holds, is not simple, and particularly not now, these days, for it is perhaps as inevitable in our contemporary philosophical climate as it is potentially helpful to inhabit, at least momentarily, the space between Kierkegaard and Levinas across Derrida's tautological/nontautological shibboleth in *The Gift of Death:*[5] "tout autre est tout autre," (GD 82ff.) for across it, in Derrida's discourse, the religion of Kierkegaard and the ethics of Levinas slip back and forth between each other—or at least seemingly. This little phrase, applicable to the thought of both Kierkegaard and Levinas, lends itself to a number of interpretations that, Derrida claims, create a slippage at the center of both of these philosophies, destabilizing them, menacing their internal borders and the borders between them. For "tout autre est tout autre" can mean, as a tautology, "the wholly other is wholly other," or nontautologically, "each other (one) is wholly other (or every bit other)," or, further, "God is wholly other," or "every other (one) is God" (GD 87).

Let us listen to a paragraph from *The Gift of Death:*

> One of them [Kierkegaard] keeps in reserve the possibility of reserving the quality of the wholly other, in other words, the *infinite other*, for God alone, or in any case

5. Jacques Derrida, *The Gift of Death*, trans. D. Wills (Chicago and London: University of Chicago Press, 1995), hereafter abbreviated as GD.

for a single other. The other [Levinas] attributes to or recognizes in this infinite alterity of the wholly other, every other, in other words, each one, for example each man and woman. Even in its critique of Kierkegaard concerning ethics and generality Levinas's thinking stays within the game—the play of difference and analogy—between the face of God and the face of my neighbor, between the infinitely other as God and the infinitely other as another human. If every human is wholly other, then one can no longer distinguish between a claimed generality of ethics that would need to be sacrificed in sacrifice, and the faith that turns towards God alone, as wholly other, turning away from human duty. But since Levinas also wants to distinguish between the infinite alterity of God and the "same" infinite alterity of every human, or of the other in general, then he cannot simply be said to be saying something different from Kierkegaard. Neither the one nor the other can assure himself of a concept of the ethical and of the religious that is of consequence; and consequently they are especially unable to determine the limit between these two orders. Kierkegaard would have to admit, as Levinas reminds him, that ethics is also the order of and respect for absolute singularity, and not only that of the generality or of the repetition of the same. He cannot distinguish so conveniently between the ethical and the religious. But for his part, in taking into account absolute singularity, that is, the absolute alterity obtaining in relations between one human and another, Levinas is no longer able to distinguish between the infinite alterity of God and that of every human. His ethics is already a religious one. In the two cases the border between the ethical and the religious becomes more than problematic, as do all attendant discourses. (GD 83–84)

Now, while I concur that Levinas's ethics is already a religious one, I am not so quick to agree that the border between the ethical and the religious is ultimately troubled here, and resisting the second conclusion will open up the thought that Levinas's ethics is already religious to a meaning that, here at least, Derrida does not suspect. However, across his translations of "tout autre" as variously "God" and "every other (one)," Derrida does open our eyes to what I, at least, take to be the key issues in maintaining the distinction between Kierkegaard's religion and Levinas's ethics, and consequently, between Kierkegaard's religion and Levinas's: first, the modalities of alterity; and, second, the number of alterity. I shall address these points consecutively.

Indeed, regarding the modalities of alterity, Derrida's point is that if we take seriously the total otherness of God and the total otherness of the other others, the human others, there must be at least an analogy of otherness between these others. Now, the capacity to analogize between things does not, in general, trouble the distinction between them. My wife has legs and our cat has legs, but I have little difficulty distinguishing between my wife and our cat. But with the analogy of total otherness we are dealing with a special case, for in total otherness we are dealing with a resistance to any application of the same, and thus to any recognition of a shared quality or attribute across which or in terms of which a difference between wholly others could be dialectically identified. If the other is truly wholly other, there is no distinguishing between one wholly other and another. The "wholly other," of which I am not able to say anything, pretty much says it all.

But for Levinas at least, otherness does not describe an ontological condition of the other, but is *produced* in my relationship with him or her across the mandate, issue of the face, "Thou shalt not commit murder." In fact, the one who issues such a command, far from being that which is ontologically furthest from me, is, ontologically speaking, the closest to me—the other human being. The category of otherness in Levinas—and it is this that Derrida in his argument seems to miss—is entirely ethical. It is the human other as susceptible to wounding and outrage, as exposed to death, and that, as such, issues to me the prohibition against murder and a call to curative help, that is the wholly other. And this is why God, for Levinas, is not the wholly other, at least not in this sense, is never for me another face. For God, the Infinite, the Eternal (after Kierkegaard's terminology), is not susceptible to wounding and death, and thus does not issue to me an ethical call, but—insofar as I could, à la Kierkegaard, enter into an immediate relationship with him—calls me to faith. To be the totally other in the sense that Levinas uses the term, someone must not be the Infinite but finite, must not be the Eternal but temporal, in a word: mortal. And if it is the case—though I am less sure of this—that it is an ontological protocol that determines the otherness of the wholly other in Kierkegaard, then Derrida could no longer expect Kierkegaard to be baffled before his shibboleth and forced to confess that the human others, my fellows, are also wholly other. Keeping clear on these diverse protocols for, or on the modalities that govern what counts for, otherness in these two thinkers helps us to clarify and honor the borders internal to the thought of each, as it helps us to be clear regarding the decisive differences between them. Kierkegaard's wholly other, again, is not Levinas's wholly other.

Now, these last couple of pages have not been presented for the sake of mounting a tirade—and perhaps a misguided one at that—against Derrida (although there is nothing inherently good or bad in tirading against Derrida), but are intended to help us, or at least help me, make some progress toward understanding the religious differences between Kierkegaard and Levinas. For this discussion leads into the other issue that I claimed emerged from Derrida's paragraph as central to the difference between Kierkegaard and Levinas, and that I called the number of alterity. For one of the decisive differences between these diverse others, and a difference that radically affects the nature of the relationship to each, is the number of other, or others, each entails. Kierkegaard's wholly other, God, in being singular (in the sense of being alone in wholly otherness), is capable of demanding of the individual an absolute fidelity, and a fidelity that must be realized in faith in a way that precludes the *partage,* the sharing of or breaking into parts, of this fidelity. God is the One. Indeed, to busy myself with every other, with every face, or any face, in the crowd, is precisely the kind of evasive doublemindedness that Kierkegaard disavows as inhibiting me, as an individual, from standing alone with myself before God, in the posture of a confessor. For him this is a temptation that the knight of faith resists.

Conversely, although for Levinas the other is also called singular (though here in the sense of not being able to be reduced to a general rule applicable to all), the other, as the human other, is not alone in being singular. For human others, the aforementioned analogy of otherness does indeed apply. In fact, for Levinas, the other of the other, the "third" in his terminology, is already present in my encounter with the first other. The other other is another other, and demands of me every bit of faithful responsibility as does the first other. And this means that the responsibility that I owe to the first other cannot be realized, that I cannot give to the first other the absolute responsibility that I do indeed owe to him or her—all of my time, all of my resources, my very self—without abandoning the third. This multiplicity of singularities, this number of others, means that I must undertake a comparison of incomparables, must betray my absolute responsibility to the one and seek justice for all, across consciousness, the generality of a reasonable law, across philosophy—read here by Levinas not as the love of wisdom so much as the wisdom of love. Justice, which (unlike ethics) must be realized (even as it is disturbed and inspired ever and again by my absolute responsibility for the singular other), keeps the absolute call coming from the other—calling me to absolute responsibility—from congealing into an absolute relationship, a relationship that would fill up and give meaning to, if it could tolerate them at all, all of my other relationships.

That there is for Kierkegaard a relationship in terms of which all other relationships sink into (at least relative) indifference (until they are filled with and made meaningful by *the* relationship), this for Levinas is violence itself. Levinas's claim, to the contrary, is that my relationship with each other is one of nonindifference, that when it comes to nonindifference there is no difference, or an indifference, between one and the other other, even if this indifference is a function of the absolute difference of and thus nonindifference to the other, and to each other. If there were only one other, Levinas tells us, there would not be a problem. And, indeed, for Kierkegaard's religion there is no problem. The task is clear: will one thing! One thing: the good, God. That God is taken as the other, as the only wholly other for Kierkegaard, corresponds to the moment of violence in Kierkegaard for Levinas. There is difficulty here according to Kierkegaard, the temptation to duplicity and multiplicity in my response to God's call as described by Kierkegaard in all of the reasons for not willing one thing in *Purity of Heart*,[6] but the call itself is univocal: no problem. As *the* wholly other, as the Holy Other, God overwhelms the other others—who by comparison are hardly others at all, but mostly the same—pushes my relationship with them to the periphery (my obligation being to leave them over

6. Søren Kierkegaard, *Purity of Heart Is to Will One Thing,* trans. D. V. Steere (New York: Harper & Row, 1938).

70,000 fathoms of water, like myself, seeking their own salvation, in fear and trembling, as we read, for example, in *Stages on Life's Way*).[7]

3. Religion with an Impure Heart

In setting forth, as I now will briefly do, what I am calling Levinas's mundanizing religion with an impure heart, it is perhaps helpful to begin by quoting Levinas's alternate interpretation of the story of Abraham and Isaac, the very tale upon which the Kierkegaardian account of faith is most powerfully based:

> In his [Kierkegaard's] evocation of Abraham, he describes the encounter with God at the point where subjectivity rises to the level of the religious, that is to say, above ethics. But one could think the opposite: Abraham's attentiveness to the voice that led him back to the ethical order, in forbidding him to perform a human sacrifice, is the highest point in the drama. That he obeyed the first voice is astonishing: that he had sufficient distance with respect to that obedience to hear the second voice—that is the essential. (AP 77)

The essential of the relationship with God, here, is a certain distance from that relationship—a distance that permits of the interruption of the relationship as absolute, the dissolution of the absoluteness of this relationship that permits of a being turned away by and to another voice, another relationship, to the face of Isaac. The essential of Levinas's account of Abraham's relationship with God is Abraham's capacity for distraction, for duplicity, his capacity to cease to will one thing. The essential of the relationship with God is, here, religion with an impure heart.

Indeed, for Levinas, God enters the human intrigue only across my relations with each, and indeed every, human other. For Levinas I never stand with myself alone, as an individual, before God. The individual, for him, is naturally atheistic, at least insofar as the individual is conceived—in what is always an abstraction—apart from others. On the contrary, the principle of individuation is a standing before the human other, and this is also the onset of a religious sensibility.

Is religion then reduced, in Levinas, to the ethical? No. On my reading, at least, the religious is the condition of possibility for the ethical. Religion, in Levinas's discourse, is the name for the unbreakable ethical bond, and God the name for the one who so binds me, and I can speak of God only as the trace that God leaves across this bond. Listen as Levinas describes the emergence of the word "God" into human discourse:

7. Søren Kierkegaard, *Stages on Life's Way,* trans. H. V. Hong and E. H. Hong (Princeton: Princeton University Press, 1988).

> There is a betrayal of my anarchic relation with illeity, but also a new relationship
> with it: it is only thanks to God that, as a subject incomparable with the other, I
> am approached as an other by the others, that is, "for myself." "Thanks to God
> [*Grâce à Dieu*]" I am another for the others. God is not involved as an alleged
> interlocutor: the reciprocal relationship binds me to the other man in the trace
> of transcendence, in *illeity*. The passing of God, of whom I can speak only by
> reference to this aid or this grace, is precisely the reverting of the incomparable
> subject into a member of society. (OTB 158)

Responsible for the other, I am responsible for the others, and so I cannot
realize my responsibility for any *one* other without injustice. And, so, with an
impure but just heart I seek to wisely distribute my diverse responsibilities
to diverse others across the norms regulative of society, a society of all of my
others, all of those to whom I am responsible. But, *voilà*—for I could not have
effectuated this myself—I am welcomed into society by the others who—and
I could not have demanded this myself—assume a responsibility for me, and,
moreover, always already have. That, claims Levinas, is the grace of God, the
human graciousness to me across which God's grace can be traced. I am, therefore, for Levinas, a graced graciousness, loved by the others as I am called to
love the others, and it is across this human intrigue that God is in the world,
that God comes to the idea.

Religious discourse, or discourse on religion, is thus conducted for Levinas
under a kind of reduction from the ethical across which its hidden horizon,
the horizon of its possibility, is traced, but since the ethical discourse, or the
discourse on ethics, is itself conducted across a kind of reduction from experience, wherein its hidden horizon, its condition of possibility that is ethics, is
traced, religion in Levinas is traced across a double reduction, at two steps away
from experience, and this not surprisingly renders his discourse on religion
immensely abstract. It is thus at the furthest reaches from religion as a direct
relationship to the Absolute, a relationship that requires that one leap over the
world, or out of the world, or against the current of responsibilities to others.
God, in Levinas, is encountered as undergirding rather than as undermining
such responsibilities, that is, in and through them. The violence that Levinas
finds in Kierkegaard is the break evinced in that thought between the absolute
relationship with God and the universality that would regulate human responsibilities, over against a universality that could be traced back to the relationship
with God—in a relationship of continuity rather than discontinuity.

Entering into an absolute relationship with the Absolute, with God, is thus,
for Levinas, as we have seen, violence. Violence, not because in terms of this
relationship everything is purportedly justified—in fact, the murder of Isaac
is precisely unjustified—but because in faith justification, and justice, does
not matter; even if to prove his faith, Isaac, if not justice, must matter very
much to Abraham, must matter more than anything, more than everything . . .
except faith. Faith believes in the promise that "all these things shall be added

unto you,"[8] but this promise is the indirect objective of faith, faith's dative case. Justification, and justice, is not the object of faith—but God, *the* Wholly Other, to whom I owe absolute fidelity, the One other that in purity of heart I am alone to will. But with a sole object of my faith, my faith is unchecked. Isaac's face may terrorize—but it does not issue a prohibition strong enough to counter God's command. There is no room for such duplicity in a pure heart willing the good—defined as the murder of Isaac if God commands it.

We can see perhaps why Levinas (and in this he is preceded by a number of perhaps not coincidentally Jewish philosophers of this century [e.g., Rosenszweig and Buber], though others too)—given the *Judenrein* policy of much of Europe that was in effect long before reaching its apogee in Germany half a century ago—fears such purity, the purity of heart that, to prove itself, must be willing to commit murder, should that—given a "religious" spin—be referred to as "sacrifice." Is it necessary at this point to pronounce the word "fanaticism," to name that almost irresistible religious temptation that is always only a turn of the head away from anyone with an agenda, which is to say, from human beings? For if, to paraphrase Karl Jaspers, the truth one would die for is the only truth worthy of the name, the truth one would kill for is another matter altogether. Another matter, but not so far from the first. Kierkegaard mocks those of his generation, whom he characterizes as everyone, who would pretend to go further than faith. Levinas fears the violence of going even as far as faith.

The violence sets in, in conclusion, to put it in Kierkegaard's own Christian idiom (for I do not believe this is a debate between Jew and Christian, but between different human orientations toward religion more generally conceived), with the disjunction between the two aspects of the greatest commandment as expressed by Jesus: the love of God and the love of neighbor—this disjunction illustrated and advocated by Kierkegaard in his evocation of the mandate of Christ that the price of discipleship is the hatred of father and mother, wife and children, brothers and sisters, that is, of human society. A Christian appropriation of the spirit of Levinas would hear these two expressions as two articulations of a single commandment—and indeed Jesus offers this in response to a question seeking after the greatest commandment, not the greatest commandments. The love of God and the love of neighbor are inseparable—to do one is to do the other. To love God and hate the neighbor is not to love God. And to love the neighbor and hate God is not to hate God, but to hate the image of a God who could be opposed to the good of the neighbor. That God, the God of Kierkegaardian faith, is, as Levinas elsewhere asserts, perhaps better off dead. It is, it seems, either him or us. But, of course, the idea of the death of God so that we might live in the spirit of God is also a Christian idea, and one at least as central as hating father and mother, wife and children, brothers and sisters, for Christ's sake.

8. Matthew 6:33; Luke 12:31.

11

The Risk of Leaving Home

Henry Isaac Venema

> "They say there is a ghost in every house,
> and if you can make peace with him
> he will stay quiet."[1]

*B*eing-at-home provides us with an interesting metaphor for exploring the "location" of selfhood. Home suggests among other things welcome, comfort, a warm bed, familiarity, freedom from the worries and pressures of work. Houses, however, are not always homes; "some are haunted by specters of loss and sorrow, pain and regret." Often our sense of self is one of dislocation and homelessness rather than one of support and comfort. Such is the difficulty of describing self-location. We are dealing with apparitions and fragments, displacement and difference, the familiar and the uncanny, all of which are part of a consideration of the comforts of home. Further, the question of self-location doubles in on itself by pointing to a differential relation between self and otherness (or alterity) that sutuates our own experience of dis/placement. As this domestic metaphor of home suggests, I am at home (or not) in my house, I am in relation to my house that may or may not be a place of welcome, I am at home or homeless, welcomed or unwelcomed, connected or disconnected. But to *whom?* To myself, to that feature of my selfhood that is other than me, an alterity that I will never be identical with, yet is always a part of me, perhaps haunting me, but always calling me beyond myself, a voice that can never stay quiet, and is silenced only at our peril.

In *The Beautiful Risk*,[2] James H. Olthuis makes significant use of this domestic metaphor. One dwells in the "place" of selfhood, yet one is neither at

---

1. *The Quiet American*, directed by Phillip Noyce, Miramax Home Entertainment, 2003.
2. James H. Olthuis, *The Beautiful Risk: A New Psychology of Loving and Being Loved*, (Grand Rapids: Zondervan, 2001).

home nor homeless within that place.[3] "Dwelling" is a temporal movement that can be arrested in the *now* or the *instance* where we will linger a while and take a moment of pause, to begin to describe this motion as one that *takes* place, *takes* location, sets up house, and *at the same time* is coupled with another movement that has *taken* us, a movement that *gives* place and opens a dwelling space in the event of passage and departure to and from the place we live.

Hence, dwelling takes place between two movements, opening and closure, sedimentation and innovation, that can also be taken *as* the difference between life (birth) and death. This is the process of *selfhood*, "me, myself, I" in relation to alterity,[4] a process that can offer hope, the possibility of growth, and freedom; but also a process that can be brought to ruin by pain, subjected to force and power beyond control, even beyond the power to endure death itself. These figures of life and death, and opening and closure, point to a quasi-structure of selfhood that requires the affirmation of life through a kind of death, or the putting to death of previous forms of life that no longer give birth to life.[5] Olthuis explains:

> Because there is a letting-go (a kind of death), there can be a letting-out (a kind of birth) and a letting-be (which is love). We are caught up in the processes of suffering love and healing connection, processes that are much bigger than ourselves. We are empowered to walk into a different future with hope—or, as Lewis Smedes puts it, free to "ride the crest of love's cosmic wave; we walk in stride with God."[6]

3. Olthuis is well aware of the ambiguity of this metaphor. A home can be lived in just as well as one can be put into a home, such as that for the elderly or mentality impaired, or one can go to the "big house," into the forced domestication of an institutional home. But this negative closure of being at home is not what Olthuis advocates, nor is recourse to a metaphysic of the *house of Being*. "This is not an encouragement to retrench and build fixed residences in the domesticity of modernity. Neither does it, in postmodern rejection of the modern, need to mean exile in the desert (expulsion and wandering), perpetual homelessness. Rather, we have an invitation to meet and sojourn together in the wild spaces of love as alternatives both to modernist distancing or domination and to postmodern fluidity and fusion. Connection rather than control is the dominant metaphor. In the interstices of love . . . mutuality can be a sojourn together in which loving self and loving other need not be in opposition but be mutually enriching." James H. Olthuis, "Sojourning Together in the Wild Spaces of Love," in *Knowing Other-wise: Philosophy at the Threshold of Spirituality*, ed. James H. Olthuis (New York: Fordham University Press, 1997), p. 248. For Olthuis's critique of the house of being as power, see pp. 236–38.

4. Olthuis, *Beautiful Risk*, pp. 88–90.

5. Olthuis, "Sojourning Together," p. 239. Olthuis gives an example of what he means by putting to death forms of death in critique of Mark C. Taylor's book *Erring*. Olthuis writes: "along with Taylor, I do not believe there is any hope of resuscitation of the Cartesian self or any of its remnants. But it is well to recognize that that is no real loss, for it never existed in the first place, but was an illusory product of reason. Put in the language of psychotherapy, the self of reason is a false self, defensively created out of fear, with my true self. This suggests that the death of the self of reason and the death of the god of reason reveal not the death of self and God, but the failure of reason. From this perspective, the death of God and now self, marks the dethronement of reason and the collapse of its house of being."

6. Olthuis, *Beautiful Risk*, p. 203.

So how can we describe this *in between place* of selfhood? That is what I will focus on in this paper, particularly with regard to Jacques Derrida's essay "To Unsense the Subjectile"[7] and Olthuis's *The Beautiful Risk*.[8] Olthuis makes a significant contribution to understanding selfhood as the relation to the other; a relation of love between self and other that is always at risk yet upheld within the matrix of God's love. However, I will argue that it is Jacques Derrida who offers an important intensification of Olthuis's notion of the *beautiful risk*. For Derrida selfhood is at *surgical risk* that *perhaps* will cut to the bone separating joint and marrow, a life and death risk that *perhaps* will bring life, *perhaps* death.

At first sight this may seem like a rather curious and puzzling project. Olthuis's work explores what he refers to as the "essence of being human," and he is not shy about declaring that "love *is* who we are,"[9] that we should "become most authentically our*selves*" in relation to others.[10] In contrast, Derrida declares that "the self does not exist. . . . There is not a constituted subject that engages itself at a given moment in writing for some reason or another,"[11] "there has never been The Subject for anyone. . . . the subject is a fable."[12] The self for Derrida is like Plato's *khôra*, without a determinate essence, without a determinate place, that is "more situating than situated, an opposition which must in its turn be shielded from some grammatical or ontological alternative between the active and the passive,"[13] a process of situating, identifying, and giving sense that is at the same time driven mad, "making her lose her sense, that is to say, her identity and her property."[14] Hence, it would appear that while Olthuis is exploring the nature of selfhood and identity, Derrida is simply deconstructing such concepts. This, however, would be a misreading of both Olthuis and Derrida.

Olthuis is quite clear that his work is indebted to contemporary figures such as Derrida, Levinas, Irigaray, and Kristeva.[15] And that reflection on the question of selfhood must turn from a modernist quest for "what" a self is (its essence), to a postmodern exploration of the singularity of "who" asks the

---

7. Jacques Derrida, "To Unsense the Subjectile," in Jacques Derrida and Paule Thévenin, *The Secret Art of Antonin Artaud*, trans. and preface by Mary Ann Caws (Cambridge, Mass.: Massachusetts Institute of Technology Press, 1998).

8. Olthuis, *Beautiful Risk*, 67.

9. Ibid., p. 69; emphasis mine.

10. Ibid., p. 70, emphasis mine.

11. Jacques Derrida, *Points . . . Interviews, 1974–94,* ed. Elisabeth Weber, trans. Kamuf et al. (Stanford, Calif.: Stanford University Press, 1995), p. 347.

12. Jacques Derrida, "'Eating Well,' or the Calculation of the Subject: An Interview with Jacques Derrida," in *Who Comes after the Subject?* ed. Eduardo Cadava, Peter Connor, and Jean-Luc Nancy, trans. Peter Conner and Avital Ronell (New York: Routledge, 1991), p. 102.

13. Jacques Derrida, "Khora," in *On the Name*, ed. Thomas Dutoit, trans. David Wood, John P. Leavey, Jr., and Ian McLoed (Stanford, Calif.: Stanford University Press, 1995), p. 92.

14. Derrida, "To Unsense the Subjectile," p. 136.

15. Olthuis, *Beautiful Risk*, p. 36.

question about his or her own selfhood. Olthuis writes that "for a postmodernist [like himself], the proper relation to the other is respect and care, not domination, repulsion, or consumption [as is the case with modernist notions of the self]. The other can be evoked, solicited, or addressed by speech, but no category or term can ever grasp the essence of a person or do justice to unique individuality."[16] To write about the *essence* of the self is for Olthuis an exploration of a phenomenological site stretched over an unfathomable mystery of alterity that dislocates the presumed stability of self-enclosed or self-grounded individuality. However, that is also Derrida's assumption. "The singularity of the 'who' is not the individuality of a thing that would be identical to itself, it is not an atom. It is a singularity that dislocates or divides itself in gathering itself together to answer to the other, whose call somehow precedes its own identification with itself."[17] It is not that Olthuis and Derrida are trying to put the self out of joint, forcing a dislocation that is unnatural to selfhood; rather, what they describe is a self-location directed beyond any and all forms of enclosure marked off from alterity, a kind of selfhood that is not identified with a modern "depersonalization" of self stripped of his or her "character, motives, history, context, interests, gender, body and worldview."[18] Describing the location of selfhood is thus dislocated by virtue of a quasi structure that is understood *as* the placing of self in the *opening* to the other. For Olthuis this *is* the opening of love, "love as gift [that] creates a space-which-is-meeting, inviting partnership and co-birthing";[19] however, for Derrida this is the space of an opening that *perhaps* will gift us with love, perhaps death.

Olthuis: The Beautiful Risk

Written in the context of developing a new ethics and approach toward psychotherapy, *The Beautiful Risk* develops a description of the "place" of selfhood by means of a

> genuine embrace of difference, both in others and in ourselves . . . that begins not with freedom but with responsibility . . . that Emmanuel Levinas calls "first philosophy." Such an ethics and psychology begins with a recognition of difference—not as deviance or deficit, but as otherness to connect with, cherish, celebrate, and embrace. Genuine community in this view begins with difference and consists of staying together amid difference and diversity—in, through, and despite adversity. Difference as invitation and evocation calls us to

16. Olthuis, *Beautiful Risk,* p. 36.
17. Derrida, "Eating Well," pp. 100–101.
18. James H. Olthuis, "Face-to-Face: Ethical Asymmetry or the Symmetry of Mutuality?" in *Knowing Other-wise: Philosophy at the Threshold of Spirituality,* ed. James H. Olthuis (New York: Fordham University Press, 1997), p. 134.
19. Olthuis, "Sojourning Together," p. 247.

responsibility and mutual empowerment in which power-with replaces power-over or power-under.[20]

The *essence* of selfhood is a differentiated dynamic interconnected place, a "space-between" oneself and alterity that refuses the permanence of identity, metaphysical or otherwise. What Olthuis pursues is the intersubjective site of selfhood where the word

> *with* underlines the relational nature of life; it indicates connection between things, beings, creatures (identities), without fusion and without isolation. With has the force of a healthy (that is, loving) connection. To be-with is to be in-love-with or in-care-with. To be without love is to be in a poor painful, unhealthy state of broken connection. It is to be disconnected, dismembered. It is to be in-enmity-against, in-hate-to, care-less. *With* connotes vulnerability, mutuality, respect, and honor rather than domination or shame. It is the opposite of *under, above,* and *against,* all of which speak of control, mastery and independence.[21]

Undetermined and unformed space without place, selfhood is barren until formed in the "wild spaces of love."[22] Wild spaces are "not voids or vacuums, but spheres alive with love's coursing, the place and resource for healing, the matrix of love; and 'wild' because they are uncharted, and therefore venturing into them is to take the beautiful risk."[23] Hence, Olthuis's phenomenological description of the site of selfhood differentiated from within and without by alterity is coupled with a discourse of passionate love lived in and through a testimony to love that "witnesses to the radical interconnectedness of all things" held together by the gift of love from God the giver of love. What Olthuis describes is a location of interconnected *"withing,"* a dynamic relational "mysticism of the ordinary life,"[24] where phenomenological discourse gives way to a profound trust that, at the end of the day, lives in love as both a gift and call, a living response to a call to live, a call that calls us to life, a calling without which there is no life to be lived.[25]

20. Olthuis, *Beautiful Risk,* p. 37.
21. Ibid., pp. 47–48. Olthuis, "Face-to-Face" p. 151; Olthuis explains that "'with' in my usage is not the social 'being-with' of Heidegger. 'With' carries the connotations of a humanity as a religious community-in-difference, gifted-with and called-to love, very similar to what Levinas calls 'proximity' as the religio-ethical place of responsibility, vulnerability, and non-violence."
22. Olthuis, *Beautiful Risk,* pp. 12, 14, 48. Also see Olthuis, "Sojourning Together," pp. 235–57.
23. Olthuis, *Beautiful Risk,* p. 48.
24. Ibid., p. 49.
25. I too share a similar belief with Olthuis, and I also share the assumption that the testimony of/in faith is inseparable from the description of self-location. However, for the purposes of this paper my primary focus will not deal with the particularities of the relation between phenomenology and testimony; rather, what I will explore in more detail is this "in-between place" of difference where death and birth fold into each, where the self can be "betrayed" and at the same time give birth to passion so deep that we suffer with suffering others and ourselves. Even though Olthuis beautifully interweaves these two fields of discourse

Taking his clue from Ricoeur, Levinas, and Derrida, Olthuis understands selfhood as a decentered process "open-to what is beyond us."[26] In contrast to modernist notions of the ego-self, selfhood is for Olthuis a "gift/call" that is *structurally* and originally open to the other. Hence, "the *gift* of being human and the *call* to become human" are "quintessentially *to be and to become* a lover—a lover of God, neighbor, self, and world."[27] The openness of selfhood is an agency "of love called *to* love, and called *by* love."[28] In fact, Olthuis asserts that "love is who we are, as gift and call, as passion to be lived out. It is in loving (or not loving) that we are (or are not) human. It is in heeding the call of love—in making life-affirming connections—that we become human. . . . Loving is of the essence of being human, the connective tissue of reality, the oxygen of life."[29]

What becomes clear in Olthuis's understanding of selfhood is that the "center" of selfhood is not rooted in a solitary ego, nor in a self open to the other simply by virtue of voluntary will. We are "relational" individuals; that is how we are structured. "*I* is not a separate, preformed, enclosed human self that enters into relationships unable to affect its very essence. *I* is itself a relational entity that continually forms and reforms its unique shape in terms of its network of relations and its claims."[30] This kind of openness makes it possible to "become who we are through relationships with other persons (intersubjectivity), with creation and its creatures (caring solidarity), and with God (spirituality)."[31] Hence, as Olthuis claims, "to be a self-in-relation is to be centered in relation—that is, oriented outward, toward others."[32] This is where we find our home, where our "authentic" self is located: *with* the other beyond me, *dislocated* from a center within myself.

However, if our authentic selves are found "when we are authentically with others,"[33] and the other is that which is beyond me, then it would seem that authentic selfhood is impossible on its face. If as Olthuis claims "my identity forms in confluence with and under the influence of other persons,"[34] who, then, is identified when I say "self"? If my self is rooted in a relation to the other who is beyond me, then this in-between relational space doesn't simply "constitute . . . who I become," but must be a constitut*ing* process of some

in such a way that one flows into the other without clearly marking their boundaries, it should be kept in mind that the separation of the life of faith and the structure of the self is artificial, a descriptive strategy, which only provisionally brackets this relation in order to explore the "wild spaces" of differential selfhood with greater care.

26. Olthuis, *Beautiful Risk*, p. 70.
27. Ibid., p. 68.
28. Ibid., p. 68.
29. Ibid., p. 69.
30. Ibid., p. 70.
31. Ibid., pp. 70–71.
32. Ibid., p. 71.
33. Ibid., p. 70.
34. Ibid., p. 72.

kind that leaves every attempt to identify myself necessarily open to constant revision, and infinitely so. Therefore, Olthuis's relational understanding of self and identity must have an indefinite or quasi-structure that is forever forming and unforming itself, forever becoming, forever responding to a call to become a self in relation to the other, and cuts short every attempt to say this *is* the self.

According to Olthuis, the open process of selfhood is part and parcel of the "mystery of God's gift of love,"[35] part of the rhythmic breath of life, which breathes in the gift of love to become a self in relation to the other, and breathes out the ego/self cut off from the other.

> There is the oscillating rhythm of giving and receiving, the dance of identity and intimacy called love. In giving to the other, I, paradoxically, in being received, am enlarged and enhanced—receiving, in the words of Levinas, "inspiration." In receiving the other, I expand, and paradoxically, through my receiving, give. Instead of power-over (with its corollary of power-under), or power-held-in-abeyance (to avoid domination), there is power-with and the dance of mutual empowerment.[36]

Only by living in the opening *to* the other do we find authentic life that can let go of the kind of identification and ownership that has been cut loose from its relational matrix. "What is most deeply myself is *more than* I am at present, *more than* the me that I have forged in the past."[37] Openness of this sort is an "identity in process."[38] We never *find* ourselves. If that were the case we would be in search of substantive fixed and immobile self, underlying the process of becoming. What Olthuis is describing is the *risk* of a "fragile" self "exposed" and "vulnerable" to what can never be my own: the other beyond yet in relation to me, the other in me, the other that I am to myself, the other that calls and haunts me. Therefore, the process of selfhood "lives on the cusp of the present, constantly negotiating the transition between the past and future."[39] Far more complex than a simple opposition between a passive involuntary other and active will,[40] selfhood is the site of a difficult negotiation between what is given me and what I project onto the given surface of my life; a negotiation between the conditions of my existence that I have been thrown into, and my life that I am responsible for, which I throw onto my conditioned existence.

Olthuis further elaborates this complex dialogue by employing a model of the "three faces of the self . . . *me-myself-I*": the surface, the depth, and "who I am today."[41] This model is used to understand *me* as a "character style" in

35. Ibid., p. 73.

36. Olthuis, "Face-to-Face," 146.

37. Olthuis, *Beautiful Risk*, p. 76; emphasis mine.

38. Ibid., p. 76.

39. Ibid., p. 89.

40. See Paul Ricoeur, *Freedom and Nature: The Voluntary and the Involuntary*, trans. with introduction by Erazim V. Kohák (Evanston, Ill.: Northwestern University Press, 1966).

41. Olthuis, *Beautiful Risk*, p. 88.

relation to my history and life story. This face of selfhood is on the surface as a history of response, as the way in which I have "adapted" to the conditions of life, the way I have structured the givenness of my personality, the patterned responses to others and circumstances that either "mask" my true self or make *myself* open and available to others. That is what my face implies: *myself*, "the authentic self, the inner self that I am gifted to be and am in the process of becoming . . . that deep 'place,' the heart of and for connection (and disconnection) with self, God, others, and creation."[42] But we must be careful here to see that *me* and *myself* are not things, but features of selfhood that take shape in the "agency [of the history and life of] the existential I,"[43] in the instant of the process that I am now living but never complete.

This is "who" I am. Not three things, but a quest for health and wholeness that struggles to get me-myself-I "in sync with each other" in relation *to* the other.[44] "Who am I?" is a passionate desire for love that drives us to the other to become a self. The other puts me into question in the instant of my response. I am always in question; I am always the question "Who am I?" There is no essential me-myself-I; how could there be if selfhood is a relation to other that infinitely recedes my grasp? The question of "essential" selfhood arrives late, after the fact, if at all, and then needs to be asked again, and again. . . . It is not the first word, but neither is it the last. In that regard, Olthuis is very close to Blanchot's assertion that we shouldn't substitute "the openness of a 'Who?' without answer for the closed and singular 'I'; not that this means that [we have to simply ask ourselves,] '*What is this I that I am?*' but much more radically to recover self without reprieve, no longer as 'I' but as a 'Who?,' the unknown and slippery being of an indefinite 'Who?'"[45]

Why an indefinite being, why an open question of a self without reprieve? Because *I* can never be a "me, master of myself," master of a response to a call, an infinite call, which precedes every event of its hearing. How can I be identical to myself when the voices that call me to selfhood come from somewhere else, from another, from all the other others, from the wholly other, all of which, as Olthuis suggests, comes from only God knows where![46] Postmodern selfhood is then an open response *to the other*, or discipleship of the other.[47]

42. Olthuis, *Beautiful Risk*, p. 89.

43. Ibid., pp. 88–89.

44. Ibid., p. 90.

45. Maurice Blanchot, *Friendship*, trans. Elizabeth Rottenberg (Stanford, Calif.: Stanford University Press, 1997), p. 291.

46. Also see John D. Caputo, *On Religion* (London and New York: Routledge, 2001), p. 9. Here Caputo leaves the question even more indefinite, suggesting that it is not "only" God who knows where, but literally, God knows where?

47. Here I paraphrase and combine Paul Ricoeur's phrase "I exchange the *me, master* of itself, for the *self, disciple* of the text," "Phenomenology and Hermeneutics," in *Hermeneutics and the Human Sciences*, ed. John B. Thompson (Cambridge, U.K.: Cambridge University Press, 1981), p. 113, with Jacques Derrida's reinterpretation of Levinas's understanding of the experience of self *to* the other, as "*A-Dieu*," *to*-God, *to* the other, in *Adieu: To Emmanuel Levinas*, trans. Pascale-Anne Brault and Michael Naas (Stanford, Calif.: Stanford University Press, 1997), pp. 80–81, 102–5.

What response, then, can I, can "one," give to such a question: "Who?" How can I even offer a response to such a question when I am uncertain as to what I am, and unclear as to "who" it is that responds to this question of selfhood in the first place? Yet this inescapable and difficult question calls *for* a response, we cannot not respond, we are required to take the risk of self *in* response to the other, and that risk defines selfhood *as response* to the other. As Derrida explains,

> I would say that for me the great question is always the question *who.* Call it biographical, autobiographical or existential, the form of the question *who* is what matters to me, be it in, say, its Kierkegaardian, Nietzschean, Heideggerian form. *Who? Who asks the question who? Where? How? When? Who arrives?* It is always the most difficult question, the irreducibility of *who* to *what,* or the place where between *who* and *what* the limit trembles, in some way.[48]

But where then is this *in between place* of selfhood that both Olthuis and Derrida concern themselves with? Is it the case, as Derrida suggests, that this place of selfhood is an emptying place, the kenosis of place that *saves* the place[49] in which "singular existence, even if it is given over to non-self-presence, dislocation, and the non-reappropriation of the a present, is for all that no less singular?"[50] Or is it as Olthuis suggests a place of connection and embrace held together by the gift and call of God's love? Perhaps it is both?

Derrida: To Unsense the Subjectile

Self-location is indeed difficult *placing* to describe. What is asked of us, as Derrida points out, is to engage a "phenomenal system of nonphenomenality" that conditions the possibility of such description on its impossibility.[51] No language, metaphor, or model can grasp alterity within ourselves, others, or the wholly other. All we can do, as Derrida suggests, is "dream" of describing the placing of selfhood "because it must vanish *at daybreak,* as soon as language awakens."[52] This is a "dream of an inconceivable process of dismantling and

48. Jacques Derrida and Maurizio Ferraris, *A Taste for the Secret,* trans. Giacom Donis, ed. Giacome Donis and David Webb (Cambridge, U.K.: Polity, 2001), p. 41.

49. For a parallel development of this logic of place without place, Derrida suggests that the name of God can only be saved by losing the name. Jacques Derrida, "Sauf le nom (Post-Scriptum)," in *On the Name,* ed. Thomas Dutoit, trans. David Wood, John P. Leavey, Jr., and Ian McLoed (Stanford, Calif.: Stanford University Press, 1995), p. 58.

50. Derrida and Ferraris, *Taste,* p. 13.

51. Jacques Derrida, "Violence and Metaphysics: An Essay on the Thought of Emmanuel Levinas," in *Writing and Difference,* trans. with intro. by Alan Bass (Chicago: University of Chicago Press, 1978), pp. 124–25.

52. Derrida, "Violence and Metaphysics," p. 151; Jacques Derrida, "Khora," in *On the Name,* ed. Thomas Dutoit, trans. David Wood, John P. Leavey, Jr., and Ian McLoed (Stanford, Calif.: Stanford University Press, 1995), pp. 90, 126; Derrida, "To Unsense the Subjectile," p. 135.

dispossession"[53] that understands selfhood as a movement to the other (*a-Dieu*), "to me as to an other,"[54] a phenomenology of subjectivity as the "naked opening" to the other, which is nevertheless the "unsurpassable necessity" for "nonviolent respect for the secret" of the absolute singularity of myself and others.[55] For Derrida openness to alterity is a gift that can only arrive as the interruption of phenomenological systems of description. The other is a shore that I do not reach, that I must respect as that which I am not, and therefore is "*le pas au délà*: the step (*pas*)/not (*pas*) beyond, the beyond that is never reached but always pursued."[56] What Derrida asks us to think about is the

> question of designating a space or hollow within naked experience where this eschatology [the coming of the Other] can be understood and where it must resonate. This hollow space is not an opening among others. It is opening itself, the opening of opening, that which can be enclosed within no category or totality, that is, everything within experience which can no longer be described by traditional concepts, and which resists every philosopheme.[57]

Derrida listens and looks for a "kind of unheard of *graphics*,"[58] a "voiceless voice [*la voix blanche*],"[59] an as yet unheard voice of the other beyond the economies of language that have already determined *who* or *what* will arrive. Such a voiceless voice interrupts self-enclosure in a "strange dialogue of speech and silence"[60] and instills a desire to "exit"[61] or "leap"[62] beyond the death of self-containment in hope of new birth and arrival of the unexpected. Not that we can avoid closure and self-identification for continual natality and renewal, but we find ourselves in process between this kind of birth and death, opening and closure, where we forge, in defiance of death, an identity for ourselves that must itself constantly be put to death.

> Each time this identity announces itself, each time a belonging circumscribes me, if I may put it this way, someone or something cries: Look out for the trap, you're caught. Take off, get free, disengage yourself. Your engagement is elsewhere. . . . Identification is a difference to itself, a difference with/of itself.

53. Derrida, "Violence and Metaphysics," p. 82.

54. Ibid., p. 126.

55. Ibid., pp. 124–26, 128.

56. Maurice Blanchot, *The Step Not Beyond,* trans. Lycette Nelson (Albany: State University of New York Press, 1992), quoted in John D. Caputo, *Deconstruction in a Nutshell: A Conversation with Jacques Derrida* (New York: Fordham University Press, 1997), p. 163.

57. Derrida, "Violence and Metaphysics," p. 83.

58. Ibid., p. 111. Also see Olthuis, "Sojourning Together," pp. 240–41, where he critiques Derrida's appropriation of negative theology as silence and speech.

59. Derrida, "Sauf le nom," p. 35.

60. Derrida, "Violence and Metaphysics," p. 133.

61. Jacques Derrida, *Given Time, 1: Counterfeit Money,* trans. Peggy Kamuf (Chicago: University of Chicago Press, 1991), p. 8.

62. Derrida, "Sauf le nom," p. 48.

Thus *with, without,* and *except* itself. The circle of the return to birth can only remain open, but this is at once a chance, sign of life, and a wound. If it closed in on birth, on plenitude of the utterance or the knowledge that says "I am born," that would be death.[63]

To be at home with closed doors that try to shut out and silence alterity only creates the illusion of self-mastery and life, when in fact it is death. Rather,

the other is in me before me: the ego (even the collective ego) implies alterity as its own condition. There is no "I" that ethically makes room for the other, but rather an "I" that is structured by the alterity within it, an "I" that is itself in a state of self-deconstruction, of dislocation. . . . the other is there before me, that comes before [*prévient*], precedes and anticipates me. . . . I am not a proprietor of my "I," I am not proprietor of the place open to hospitality.[64]

Hence any description of selfhood requires a kind of *expropriation*[65] and *dis-ownership* that takes its point of departure from "there where this belonging has broken."[66]

This is a curious yet illuminating understanding of selfhood. The "I" is never the proprietor of its own home, of its own self. The "I" is *structured* by an openness to the other that precedes any and every movement of self-identification. I am incommensurate with any description of myself because the otherness that structures me is beyond me, beyond description; it is a shore that I cannot reach, and a future that I cannot know.[67] Hence, the site of selfhood as a hospitable opening and passage *to* the other is differentiated

63. Derrida, *Points,* p. 346.

64. Derrida, *Secret,* pp. 84–85; Olthuis, "Face-to-Face," p. 147. Olthuis also claims this to be true: "otherness and difference are never wholly inside or wholly outside myself. I, or, at least aspects of me, come alive and grow, or retreat and eventually die as I move in and out of relation with other selves."

65. Derrida, "To Unsense the Subjectile," pp. 93–94. "Through all the passion or pathology to which his suffering submits him, his truth exhibits, *in his name,* the truth of the truth, that is to say that every 'self' in its own self is *called to* this familial expropriation of the newly born, constituted, properly instructed by that expropriation, that imposture, that forfeit, at the moment when, very simply, a family declares a child born and gives it its name, in other words, takes it from him. This expropriating appropriation, this legitimation can only be a violence of fiction, it can never be natural or true by its structure."

66. Derrida, *Secret,* p. 85.

67. Derrida, "To Unsense the Subjectile," p. 130: "And yet. What remains to come and announces itself here in labor, in travail [in birth], will no longer have the name of being: it will be something else, whose future will not longer be the reconstituted, restored, redressed, resuscitated presence of the 'beingness' of being [*l'êtreté de l'être*]. Neither theology nor ontology for this *êtreté,* for this *être T* of *l'être.* (Twice in the proper noun.) The future will be what it must be, *absolute,* thus beyond any present-being-to-come, thus beyond being. To be what it must be, the future, *it must not be,* but rather, go (*ira*), be about to come. *Ne pas être, naître.* [Not to be, to be born.] That supposes another *labor,* another apocalypse, another martyrdom, another *suffering.* As we will see later, the subjectile must be made to suffer and to labor differently. The classic subjectile, that of fine arts, of theology, of ontology, apparently supports without suffering, without gestation, without incubation, without this travail of labor from which the other of true being will be born. It lies recumbent [*gît*], but without being in confinement [*gésiner*]. We know that the old word of lying-in [*gésine*], coming from 'to lie helpless' [*gésir*], signifies the birthing of a woman."

by an *infinite break*. I can never grasp or own the other—that would be the
very definition of violence; therefore, to attempt to own myself, to identify
and establish the "I am" as the null point around which the world turns, would
require horrific self-destructive violence. The other and otherness that constitute the quasi structure of selfhood cannot be silenced and closed off, cannot
be mastered, cannot be owned by reason. The kind of selfhood that Derrida
urges us to consider is one where reason and unreason belong together, where
the economies of rationality that wish to identify and nail things down need
to be broken open not by nonsense, but by *un*sensing the strategies of identity
that enclose life in the repetition of the same, namely death.

One way of reading Derrida here is to draw a parallel with Olthuis's existential *I* situated between surface (me) and depth (myself). However, the
problem with such a comparison is that it suggests the *I* is static and neatly
placed between a dialectically mediated surface and depth, located "there"
between two other things. But that is true of neither Derrida nor Olthuis.
The Derridian notion "self" proceeds from a "mobile or nonmarked place"[68]
that "is called . . . a subjectile."[69]

Derrida borrows this unusual term from Antonin Artaud. In his essay "To
Unsense the Subjectile," Derrida reads Artaud's paintings, texts, and pictograms
as a way to develop a "sort of subject without subject"[70] that combines the
"subjective, subtle, sublime" together with the "projectile." This he claims "is
Artaud's *thought*. The body of his thought working itself out in the graphic
treatment of the subjectile is a dramaturgy through and through, of a surgery
of the projectile,"[71] but this as we will see is Derrida's thought as well.

Explaining that "the word 'subjectile' is itself a subjectile,"[72] untranslatable
like Plato's *khôra* in the *Timaeus*,[73] Derrida writes that "the subjectile is nothing
other than the empty placing of the place, a figure of the *khora*, if not the *khora*
itself,"[74] that is, the placing of a differentiated "I" that is always without a place.
The subjectile is a place without place because it "remains between these [two]
jetées,"[75] between two movements that are forever in process of placing. This is a
"drama of its own becoming [that] always oscillates between the intransitivity of
jacere and the transitivity of *jacere* . . . the intransitivity of *being*-thrown and the
transitivity of *throwing*," one folding into the other, and the other into its fold,[76]
so that "being-thrown or the being-founded founds in its turn. And I cannot

68. Derrida, "Sauf le nom," p. 109.
69. Derrida, "To Unsense the Subjectile," p. 63.
70. Ibid., p. 67.
71. Ibid., p. 62.
72. Ibid., p. 65.
73. Ibid., p. 132.
74. Ibid., p. 123.
75. Ibid., p. 75.
76. See Jacques Derrida, "Living On," trans. James Hulbert, in *Deconstruction and Criticism*, ed. Harold
Bloom, Paul De Man, Jacques Derrida, Geoffrey H. Hartman, and J. Hillis Miller (New York: Continuum,
1990), pp. 99–101.

throw [*jeter*] or project [*projeter*] if I have not been thrown myself, at birth."⁷⁷ This is a process that takes place on the surface, on the face of the opening "between sense and non-sense [unsense]," and thus "driving meaning to madness,"⁷⁸ to what is "*outside of sense*,"⁷⁹ to the other beyond the economies of sense.

Perhaps some further clarification is in order. The original French meaning of the term subjectile belongs

> to the code of painting and designates what is in some way lying below [*sub-jectum*] as a substance, a subject, or a succubus. Between the beneath and the above, it is at once a support and a surface, sometimes also the matter of a painting or a sculpture, everything distinct from form, as well as from meaning and representation, not representable. Its presumed depth or thickness can only be seen on a surface, that of the wall or of wood, but already also that of paper, of textiles, and of the panel. A sort of skin with pores.⁸⁰

Hence the subjectile *as both* surface and support is akin to the page and the ink where the two can be differentiated but as a text they cannot. In fact, Derrida says, "the textile is always, along with paper, the best paradigm of the subjectile."⁸¹ Why is this case? Because the paper supports the ink thrown and projected upon it, but both are effaced in the birth of the text. So the subjectile is two movements at once and a third, yet none of them. It is the "border that it forms between *beneath* and *above* (support and surface), *before* and *behind*, *here* and *over there*, *on this side* and *on that*, *back* and *forth*, the border of a textile, paper, veil, or canvas, but between what and what?"⁸²

Through these figures of ink and paper, and elsewhere with mother, father, child,⁸³ Derrida is trying to describe a sense of self, of the existential "who"⁸⁴ that resists description and, at the same time, appears on and as the surface of a resistance⁸⁵ to the incessant movement of becoming, to the departure or partition beyond the "geological" sedimentations⁸⁶ of what has been thrown

77. Derrida, "To Unsense the Subjectile," p. 77.

78. Ibid., p. 147.

79. Ibid., p. 146.

80. Ibid., p. 64.

81. Ibid., p. 142.

82. Ibid., p. 71.

83. Ibid., p. 139: "The subjectile is never literally what it is. We always speak of it by figures."

84. Derrida, *Secret,* p. 41.

85. Derrida, "To Unsense the Subjectile," pp. 76–77: "The subjectile resists. It has to resist. Sometime it resists too much, sometimes not enough." We have to resist and "pass beneath the one that is already beneath," resist the one that resists, resist the inertia of sedimentation. "Its inert body must not resist too much. If it does, it has to be mistreated, violently attacked. We will come to blows with it. The *neither/nor* of the subjectile (*neither* subservient *nor* dominating) situates the place of a *double constraint:* this way it becomes unrepresentable."

86. Ibid., pp. 145–46: "There is then the bed of the subjectile (we also speak of a bed in geological code), the bed that stretches out under the bodies, for sleep or love, the *cubile* or *cubitum*, the couch, the nuptial bed, the bedroom, nest niche, and animal *lair*. These beds have privileged hosts or parasites, the incubi and the succubi. Then there are the diapers of the newborn (a subjectile is not only a place and a

and projected as "a self, *and myself,* the newborn."[87] By leaving a "trace of traversal" the self "tries to gather [itself] into the signature [and identity] of its proper name."[88] Like Olthuis, Derrida understands the complexity of this process of becoming as birth and death, a simultaneous holding on to oneself and a letting go, which involves an incalculable maddening risk of betrayal and hospitality.[89] The self must be born and reborn, it must be *given* or *give* birth to itself by breaking through the closed economies of identity and sense.[90]

> You have to make it frenetically desire this birth, and to unsense it from the outset in making it come out of itself to announce this next proximity. . . . Such a proximity confines you to madness, but the one that snatches you from the other madness, the madness of stagnation, of stabilization in the inert when sense becomes a subjectivized theme, introjected or objectivized, and the subjectile a tomb. But you can force the tomb. You can unsense the subjectile until—unsensed from birth—it gives way to the innate which was assassinated there one day.[91]

Birth of course signifies incubation and new life, the "production of a 'new reality,' its violent coming to be, its *expulsion at birth*, by the act of birth,"[92] the singularity of every birth that breaks from the womb, "tomb." Here Derrida is playing with complexity of the nonmarked place between the two movements of the subjectile and projectile: the support, bed, foundation for life that can also be a deathbed; birth can be botched, stillborn, or aborted.[93] This is a process where everything could go right or wrong, but in either case it is

---

birthing bed, a *clinic,* a *maternity ward,* is also a self, *and myself,* the newborn). . . . Whether he is standing or lying down, whether he is walking or sleeping, a subjectile is *under him,* a receptacle of the most aggressive or the most precious deposits."

87. Ibid., p. 145.

88. Ibid., pp. 147, 136.

89. Olthuis, *Beautiful Risk,* p. 69. Olthuis writes: "If we fail to love, if we fail to find our passion, then we squander our humanity, lose our souls, and betray our inmost selves." This is similar to Derrida. A subjectile can betray and "commit treason" in the sense that to betray is "to fail in one's promise, belittle the project, remove oneself from its control, but in so doing to reveal the project as it is thus betrayed." Translating it and dragging it out to broad daylight." The subjectile can also betray it calling, "not come when it is called, or call before even being called, before even receiving it name." Derrida, "To Unsense the Subjectile," pp. 61–62, 63.

90. Claiming that "I am Henry Venema," and that I can sign my name as a legal and proper form of identity, is undone and betrayed by the failure of any signature and name to identify myself. As Olthuis has explained, I am always more than the past, more than any proper form of identification (*Beautiful Risk,* p. 76).

91. Derrida, "To Unsense the Subjectile," p. 74.

92. Ibid., p. 102.

93. Ibid., pp. 106, 107. Such birth can also be at the same time an abortion, a sending of writing/drawing, a missive, a "hand-to-hand fight where a sort of *abortion* at once repeats and counterfeits itself, in self-imitation by simulacrum, controlling itself and contradicting itself through a kind of formal argument toward another birth, that of an expression. . . . The subjectile, place of treason, always resembles a device of abortion, it gives rise to a deflection first deforming by precipitation and causing a headfirst fall ('stubbing'). A premature fall, lapsus, prolapsus, expression, excrement, a newborn supplanted, deformed and detoured, mad form birth from then on, made with the desire to be reborn."

always a difficult place of blood, sweat, and tears, of pain, pushing, force, and intense labor that *gives* birth.[94] This is where life begins, in a "place of travail and of birthing, lying down and lying in at the same time. . . . Fragile, gracile, docile, the slight weakness of what is more gracious than powerful, the aerial, the ethereal, the subtle or the volatile, even the futile. The subjectile *breathes and flies*."[95] Life, "Being," begins with the push "starting with the *jetée,* not the inverse."[96]

But which movement gives life? There are two that double in on themselves: the subjectile and the projectile. Who can tell the difference? Life can give death, and death life. "Everything will play itself out from now on in the critical but precarious difference, unstable and reversible, between these two. Such at least would be our working hypothesis."[97] The self is "a place, separation and receptacle, difference, interval, interstice, spacing, as the *khora,*"[98] "the emptying placing of the place,"[99] passionate suffering and patient waiting, expecting that the newborn who breathes will also be able to take flight.[100] Perhaps even a departure from within and into the "wild spaces of love."

Impossible Conclusion: Perhaps?

Does Derrida leave us in an *impossible* position? It would seem so. How can selfhood be a *kenotic* place when the place of selfhood is the support for the movement of self toward the other? Without the subjectile womb there can be no birth, no new reality, and no invitation, no invention, no *in*coming of the other. The movement of selfhood is one of expectation and labor that

94. Ibid., p. 112: "At once a place of combat, the meadow for a duel, a ground, a bed, a bedding down, even a tomb: you give birth there, you abort there, or you die there. Birth and death, the origin or abortion can be simultaneous there. It isn't enough to say that a subjectile is stretched or lies out *beneath*. War takes place between several *underneaths*. The parergonal support of the work, the subjectile sustains also the whole system of a culture marked by evil."

95. Ibid., p. 133.

96. Ibid., pp. 75–76: "We don't even have to speak of pulsion or compulsive interest in the direction of the spurt. The thought of the throwing is the thought of pulsion itself, of the jet of pulsional [like a beating heart] *force*, of compulsion and expulsion. Force before form . . . a spurt of blood . . . We have to wash literature off ourselves. We want to be human before anything else. There are no forms or any form. There is only the gushing forth of life. Life is like a spurt of blood." This also picks up on a number of themes in "Circumfession: Fifty-nine Periods and Periphrases," in Geoffrey Bennington and Jacques Derrida, *Jacques Derrida* (Chicago: University of Chicago Press, 1993). Most notably, Derrida's "hemophiliac panic," that giving birth to life, to a new reality, is also the loss of one's life blood, hence the beginning of death.

97. Derrida, "To Unsense the Subjectile," pp. 78–79: "But what we will surely verify is that, hypothetically, the subjectile always has the function of a *hypothesis*, it exasperates and keeps you in suspense, it makes you give out of breath by always being *posed beneath*. The hypothesis has the form here of a conjecture, with *two* contradictory motifs in one. Thrown throwing, the subjectile is nothing, however, nothing but a solidified interval *between* above and below, visible and invisible, before and behind this side and that."

98. Ibid., p. 134.

99. Ibid., p. 123.

100. Ibid., p. 133.

pushes the newborn out in the open; a womb opens and gives birth to the arrival of an absolutely irreplaceable other. Such is possible, it happens all the time, the womb empties and the other arrives. But in the case of selfhood the arrival of the other is the arrival of the other-in-me that releases the self from the sedimentation of the same, frees it in response to the other. Selfhood then is a discontinuous continuity, an impossible possibility, a naked opening to the other in which I might become new through the event of the *in*coming of the other. But does Derrida ask us to give new birth to our self, to push the self out into being, and, *at the same time,* become transformed by the opening, invitation, the interruption and call of the other who has pulled us out into new life? Are we to expect and prepare for the arrival of what has been incubating and gestating in the womb only to find that in the *event* of birth we are required to file adoption papers for the other who we never expected to arrive?

Yes! But this isn't bad news. Derrida wants us to expect the unexpected, to expect an interruption of our horizon of expectation. The self doesn't give birth to itself, it doesn't call itself into being; it is called into being by the other.[101] However, the arrival is *at the same time* a push toward the other. While expectation always falls within the economy of the possible, what Derrida hopes for is the arrival of what can never be expected: *the impossible,* "an impossible that would not be negative";[102] not a logical impossibility, rather it is the *possibility of the impossible,* the possibility that the impossible could *perhaps* arrive.[103] This according to Derrida is "one of the possible definitions of deconstruction [which] might perhaps be 'the experience of the impossible'" and the experience of selfhood par excellence.[104]

101. In Olthuis, "Sojourning Together," pp. 245–46, Olthuis expresses a similar belief: "A self is born not only in and through (receiving) love, but equally, reciprocally, in and through (giving) love to others. The two sides belong inextricably together. In this understanding of identity and agency, not as self-creation or self-certification, but as a received empowerment, a call to live out and fulfill, it remains important to talk (in contrast to postmodernism) of a core self of continuity, coherence and agency."

102. Jacques Derrida, "As If It Were Possible, 'Within Such Limits' . . . ," in *Negotiations: Interventions and Interviews, 1971–2001,* ed., trans., and with introduction by Elizabeth Rottenberg (Stanford, Calif.: Stanford University Press, 2002), p. 357.

103. Derrida, "As If It Were Possible," p. 357. What Derrida is introducing here is the limit of philosophical reflection "in the face of questions like *hospitality* (*invitation/visitation,* and a whole chain of associated topics: the *promise, testimony,* the *gift, forgiveness,* etc.), [that is] also capable of withstanding [*à l'épreuve de*] an impossible that would not be negative. Such a test implies another thinking of the event, of the *avoir-lieu:* only the impossible takes place. The deployment of a potentiality or a possibility that is already there will never make an event or an invention. What is true of the event is also true of the decision, therefore of responsibility: a decision that I *am able* to make, the decision that is *in my power* and that indicates the passage to the act or the deployment of what is *already possible* for me, the actualization of my possible, a decision that only depends on me: would this still be a decision? Whence the paradox without paradox that I am trying to accept: the responsible decision must be this impossible possibility of a 'passive' decision, a decision of the other-in-me who will not acquit me [*qui ne m'exonère*] of any freedom or any responsibility."

104. Ibid., p. 352.

Hence selfhood for Derrida is both the possible and the noncalculable experience of the impossible, where we are both patient and obstetrician at once, caught up in a *surgical risk* that requires that the

> subjectile subjects itself to the surgery it is subjected to: the subjectile is this, that, that again, *and me*. And let's not hesitate to say it: the subjectile is all that and Antonin Artaud. And me. And as all that holds together "under my hand," the surgery resembles a manual demiurge *at once* aggressive *and* repairing, murderous *and* loving. The Thing is reconstituted; the cicatrisation comes to it from the very gesture that wounds it.[105]

The push of the patient and the pull of forceps exerted by the doctor,[106] the loss of blood in a hemophiliac panic,[107] the suffering, sweat, pain, and joy give birth to the incoming other, which the subjectile could never expect. However, we still need to work, plan, and pray, do all we can to prepare our life to live in the opening to the other, to open ourselves for the *in*coming other by softening the subjectile,[108] digging out from under the sedimentations that cover us in death, doing all that is possible for the impossible to come, the impossible gift "to me as to an other,"[109] of "letting-go (a kind of death), [so that] there can be a letting-out (a kind of birth), and a letting-be (which . . . love[s])" myself and others.[110]

Olthuis and Derrida are remarkable close here. Olthuis directs us to negotiate the difference between *me-myself-I* and become a *self-in-sync with others.* Likewise, Derrida describes the place of selfhood as the "summons [to] these two contradictory projects . . . gestures, or gestations [departure and trace]. Between these two adverse tensions. Adversely, they provoke the maddening, driving meaning to madness. But insofar as they balance out, offer a place to the birthing and its traces, *interrupting the fire,* they have made a work—and kept the subjectile softened," ready to invite and invent the other.[111] Additionally, both Olthuis and Derrida describe the experience of self and other as a relation at constant risk. In fact, it would be quite fair to say that for both Olthuis and Derrida to be a self *is* to be at risk for the other. However, what differentiates Olthuis from Derrida on this point is the kind of risk that selfhood involves. For Olthuis we have seen that the risk of selfhood is *beautiful,* an adventure taken within the wild spaces of love. But for Derrida it is an unpredictable *surgical risk* caught in "an irreducible modality of the 'perhaps.'"[112] Perhaps I will negotiate well. Perhaps I will "let go" and "let be" with you in love. Perhaps

105. Derrida, "To Unsense the Subjectile," p. 138.
106. Ibid., 74, 93, 105.
107. See above, n. 96.
108. Derrida, "To Unsense the Subjectile," p. 147.
109. Derrida, "Violence and Metaphysics," p. 126.
110. Olthuis, *Beautiful Risk,* p. 203.
111. Derrida, "To Unsense the Subjectile," p. 147.
112. Derrida, "As If It Were Possible," p. 344.

today I will give birth to beauty and tenderness. Yes, perhaps! But perhaps my gift will be stillborn. Perhaps my risk of love will be a disaster and die. Perhaps I will betray myself and others, or "the subjectile will betray me."[113]

I think Derrida's *surgical risk* offers an important intensification of Olthuis's notion of risk. It's not that Olthuis would object to Derrida's description of the place of selfhood as multiple itineraries and movements, layer upon layers and within layers, effort on top of effort, active passivities and passive activities, separations and connections, reversals and retrievals, incubation and birth, outside and inside, up and down, back and forth, all of these and more; rather, the objection would be that such an incalculable differential quasi-structure of selfhood is by definition a beautiful risk that is situated within the matrix of God's love. Olthuis's understanding of selfhood doesn't rest in the logic of the *perhaps;* it rests in the claim of a primordial goodness of connection (creational intention), which must be distinguished from the lived experience of disconnected dislocation (misdirection and loss) associated with failed modes of selfhood that trade in counterfeit dysfunctions. It is not the case that Olthuis doesn't understand that the risk of self is always on the brink of disaster, one step away from slipping into the grave; rather, for Olthuis the possibility of disaster is countered with a belief that the goodness of God's love precedes, and will never recede from, the pain of broken connections. Olthuis sees how life is indeed bound up in ambiguity, and never comes with guarantees (hence the risk), but for him life is not *structured* by the *perhaps:* it needs to be released from the *bondage of the perhaps* that forestalls connection and embrace with others.

Olthuis complains that "Derrida remains poised on the threshold: although he wants to *come home* and tell his story, he cannot. He remains on the outside, an exile, displaced, wanting to break through."[114] Yes, that is true! Derrida remains on the threshold of the "experience of the 'perhaps,'"[115] but so does Olthuis in spite of his complaint. We are always on the threshold of the differential space between self and otherness, others, and the wholly other. Although Olthuis wants to cross the threshold and be welcomed home with arms of loving embrace, such hospitality requires the space between. Stepping beyond the threshold is impossible. However, the dream of the *impossible,* the desire to exit and leap beyond the *possible,* beyond the repetition of the self-same, is a dream of meeting at the threshold. This should never be the desire to *break through* the other and close the differential space between, but a desire to break through the inertia of the subjectile, with all its comforts of home, *to the other.* Such dreams are lived at the threshold where we meet the other, where perhaps we will begin the "dance of mutuality [that] is always drenched in vulnerability and risk because it is a non-coerced meeting of two free subjects in the wild spaces of love."[116]

113. Derrida, "To Unsense the Subjectile," p. 61.
114. Olthuis, "Sojourning Together," p. 244; emphasis mine.
115. Derrida, "As If It Were Possible," p. 344.
116. Olthuis, "Face-to-Face," p. 147.

Meeting the other is not so much a home*coming* as it is a departure *from* home, from where we are placed, from where we hope and pray we'll find a gracious hand to take us *from* home on a wonderful sojourn of love. We have been placed before we take place, and take our place. We have been placed into a world already traced, inscribed, and signed by the texts of others. This is where we start, the home from where we depart, "[a]nd we are unable to do otherwise than *take our departure in texts insofar as they depart* (they separate from themselves and their origin, from us) *at the departure* [*dès le départ*]. We could not do otherwise even if we wished to do so or thought to do so."[117] This is the aporia of our departure, "the impasse in which I find myself paralyzed. This is the aporia in which I have placed myself. I find myself placed here, in truth, even before installing myself here."[118] We depart with projectile force trying to break through the surface the subjectile, only to be reinscribed once again on the surface from where we depart. It is only in faith that we hope the impossible event of the incoming of the other will *perhaps* take place.

But this experience of the "perhaps" would be that of the possible *and* the impossible *at the same time,* of the possible *as* impossible. If only what is already possible arrives, what can be thus anticipated and expected, it does not make an event. An event is only possible when it comes from the impossible. It arrives *as* the coming of the impossible, where a "perhaps" deprives us of all assurance and leaves the future to the future.[119]

What else can we do but depart *to the other* from where we are inscribed by the other. Will we take flight, will our risk be beautiful? Perhaps! That is our hope, which for Derrida

names a suffering or a passion, an effect that is both sad and joyous, the instability of an anxiety proper to all possibilization. Possibilization allows itself to be haunted by the specter of its impossibility, by its mourning for itself: a self-mourning carried within itself that also gives it its life or its survival, its very possibility. This *im*possibility opens its possibility, it leaves a trace—chance and threat—*within* that which it makes possible. Torment signs this scar, the trace of this trace.[120]

117. Derrida, *Given Time,* p. 100.
118. Derrida, "As If It Were Possible," p. 347.
119. Ibid., p. 344. Derrida continues: "The 'perhaps' is necessarily allied to a 'yes': yes, yes to whatever (whoever) arrives [(*ce*) *que vient*]. This 'yes' would be common to the affirmation and the response; it would even come before and question. A *peut-être* like 'perhaps' (*it may happen,* rather than the insubstantial *vielleicht,* rather than the call to being or the ontological insinuation, the *to be or not to be* of a *maybe*) is perhaps that which, exposed to an event like the 'yes,' that is, to the experience of what arrives (*happens*) and of *who* then arrives, far from interrupting the question, allows it to breath. . . . The 'perhaps' keeps the question alive, and perhaps ensures its survival [*sur-vie*]. What does 'perhaps' mean, then, at the disarticulated juncture of the possible and impossible? Of the possible *as* impossible?"
120. Ibid., p. 359.

This too is Olthuis's passion and hope, but with one significant difference. The risk of selfhood is not signed with torment; it is signed with love and grace. Even though this passion is located in the uncertainty of risk, in an experience of the perhaps, Olthuis believes that such a risk is rooted in a God of love who in fear and trembling risks everything, including God's own self, to find our hands as we sojourn together in the wild spaces of love. But is such love possible: a meeting at the threshold that embraces difference without fusion, without coercion, and without a reciprocal calculated exchange?

Here we see the overlap of Olthuis's and Derrida's thought. Selfhood is the opening to the other, a process of departure that hopes to receive the other beyond the economies of the same. Olthuis's *me-myself-I* and Derrida's sub-jectile are incomplete projects of invitation and birth, sweat, and tears, which are called beyond the closure of death. For both Olthuis and Derrida, what is at stake is the profound and deep ethic that calls us to respect the infinite fragility and singularity of the other, of every other. This is a call to meet the other *as* other, the call to step beyond the closure of the self-same that can never step beyond the other as such. Olthuis's and Derrida's descriptions of selfhood are structured by an infinite break in the openness to the other, which paradoxically creates the possibility for connection. This is the aporia they both share: selfhood as openness to the other structured by the impasse of departure to the other. This is the aporia of describing selfhood, "of thinking both its possibility and its impossibility, one *as* the other" at the same time.[121] Think-ing the possibility of impossible love and living in love at the opening to the other, is this really the impossibility of loving possibilities, or the possibility of impossible love itself? Perhaps this is the very love of God for whom nothing is impossible, even the impossible possibility of love at the threshold open to the other. This is the risk of selfhood that *perhaps* will fail; but *perhaps* it might also be a beautiful gift of love.

121. Ibid., p. 356.

12

The Call as Gift

The Subject's Donation in Marion and Levinas

James K.A. Smith

> "Loving—receiving and giving love—is not something, first of all, that
> we do. Love is who we are, as gift and call, as passion to be lived
> out. . . . It is in heeding the call of love—in making life-affirming
> connections—that we become human."[1]

In Ingmar Bergman's cinematic masterpiece, *Persona,* the central character is the subject of a *gaze*—finding herself subject *to* a voyeuristic exhibition, which is, at the same time, that which makes possible the construction of an "identity." Like the adolescent boy in the prefatory sequences,[2] in which Bergman explores the themes of voyeurism and the implication of his own camera in such subjugation, Sister Alma/Elisabeth Vogler finds herself subject to a gaze that is at the same time a *call*—a call to be subject. The "observation" of this gaze is at the same time a command, a decree, a call to respond by gathering oneself into a subject. The gaze as call thus grants subjectivity—the subjectivity of a respondent, perhaps even a "devoted one" [*l'adonné*].[3]

1. James H. Olthuis, *The Beautiful Risk: A New Psychology of Loving and Being Loved* (Grand Rapids: Zondervan, 2001), p. 69.

2. The young boy finds himself the subject of a gaze but from an other who cannot be constituted or brought into focus—the gaze comes from a sort of shifting other who remains anonymous. This is part of an opening montage of what might be described as "case studies" in which Bergman places the viewer as the subject of a question: To what extent do I, like the director's camera, participate in such a voyeuristic gaze? And in what sense am I also subject *to* such a gaze? To what extent is my own "subjectivity" constructed out of response to a call that perhaps even the film evokes, and which is troubled by its breakdown (when the celluloid becomes tangled in the projector)?

3. Jean-Luc Marion, *Étant donné: Essai d'une phénoménologie de la donation* (Paris: Presses Universitaires de France, 1998), pp. 369-72. The word can also carry the connotation of an "addict," one who is

But who is looking? What calls? What gives [*ce que cela donne*]?[4] The play of the film leaves this ambiguous: Is she the subject of her own gaze? Is the care of Sister Alma for Elisabeth in fact a concern for herself? Is Elisabeth's supposed "study" of Sister Alma in fact a case of self-reflection and hence exhibition for an audience of the same? Is this gaze and call circulating only within a closed economy, in which case the only one "calling" is in fact oneself? If that were the case, according to Marion and Levinas, what we would have is a simply Heideggerian account[5] of subjectivity, which, despite its critique of the transcendental subject, nevertheless remains within a horizon of immanence where no one *other* calls to Dasein—Dasein simply calls to itself. Being self-constituted, the "autarky" of Dasein remains intact.[6] As Levinas earlier observed, in Heidegger "Being is already an appeal to subjectivity," but this is always already an "egoism"—Dasein calling unto itself, never escaping the swirling eddy of the same, never interrupted by an exteriority.[7]

But in the play of *Persona*—and the play of personas within *Persona*—there remains the possibility for another account, what we might describe as a Levinasian thesis: the possibility that the gaze is neither Elisabeth's nor Sister Alma's—that the gaze, and hence the call, comes from outside, from another, an Other. Our focus here is not the film per se, but this warrants further consideration. Any account of the evidence would have to consider the role of the fiancé and the lover—as well as the son (both the son who is and the son who was not permitted to be)—as instances of exteriority that constantly call upon Elisabeth/Sister Alma and, in the end, are perhaps the occasion for her gathering herself up into a responsible subject. These matters would be considered in light of Levinas's account of the domestic scene of fecundity, and in particular the child who is "the stranger" par excellence.[8] On this reading, the call is haunting but nevertheless *welcomed*, received as a gift that *gives* the subject *of* responsibility.[9] Rather than a constituting

---

obsessed, which comes to characterize Sister Alma in *Persona*. Unfortunately, I don't think either sense is denoted by Jeffrey Kosky's translation of *l'adonné* as "the gifted." See Jean-Luc Marion, *Being Given: Toward a Phenomenology of Givenness*, trans. Jeffrey L. Kosky (Stanford, Calif.: Stanford University Press, 2002), pp. 268 and 369, n. 22.

4. Jean-Luc Marion, *La croisée du visible* (Paris: Presses Universitaires de France, 1996), pp. 80–81.

5. This, of course, would be no surprise, given Bergman's (deeply Lutheran) debts to existentialism.

6. Jean-Luc Marion, "The Final Appeal of the Subject [*L'interloqué*]," trans. Simon Critchley, in *Deconstructive Subjectivities,* ed. Simon Critchley and Peter Dews (Albany: State University of New York Press, 1996), pp. 90–92.

7. Emmanuel Levinas, *Totality and Infinity,* trans. Alphonso Lingis (Pittsburgh: Duquesne University Press, 1969), pp. 45–48. In other words, and here Marion merely echoes Levinas, Dasein is *self*-constituted. What both Marion and Levinas's account of the "subject" shares is the sense that the subject is constituted by the Other.

8. Ibid., pp. 267–71.

9. Ibid., pp. 27, 84. For discussion, see Jacques Derrida, "A Word of Welcome," in *Adieu to Emmanuel Levinas,* trans. Pascale-Anne Brault and Michael Naas (Stanford, Calif.: Stanford University Press, 1999), pp. 15–123.

subject whose intentional gaze dominates its "world," the called-self is a constitut*ed* self, subject *of* a gaze. And as such, the call is a gift that gives the subject.[10]

My goal in this paper is to first consider the way in which Jean-Luc Marion's account of the "subject" repeats this Levinasian thesis, insofar as both Levinas and Marion provide an "analytic"[11] of the "subject" who comes "after the subject"—a subject *of* donation (including the sense in which the subject is both called and donated, both obligated and *graced*).[12] The second part of the paper will then consider an important point of departure in Marion's account that, perhaps, grants a richer account of the postmetaphysical subject. Here I want to address the question of reciprocity, in dialogue with James Olthuis and John Milbank, suggesting that Levinas operates on the basis of an oppositional notion of difference (or "differential ontology"), which means that an "ontology of violence" continues to undergird his project, even if it is offered in the name of peace.[13] In contrast, I think Marion's account of the gifted subject is (or *should* be) undergirded by an "ontology of peace," which conceives of differential relations in a harmonious (i.e., analogous), rather than oppositional, way.[14]

I

While the question of Marion's unpaid debts to Levinas remains a legitimate avenue of inquiry, my concern in this paper is not one of attempting to sort out genealogical filiations. Instead, I want to first outline the parallels in Levinas and Marion regarding the subject.[15] Like Levinas, Marion reverses the intentional arrow of the Husserlian ego,[16] arguing that, prior to the intentionality of consciousness (as well as prior to the *Anspruch des Seins*), the subject is the subject *of* and subject *to* a "claim" [*revendication*] and a "call" [*appel*]:[17] "the human being should thus be named *der Angesprochene*—the one who is claimed

10. See, for instance, Levinas, *Otherwise Than Being, or Beyond Essence*, trans. Alphonso Lingis (The Hague, Netherlands: Martinus Nijhoff, 1981), p. 10.

11. Marion remarks: "while *Dasein* indeed received an analytic [*Daseinanalytik*], the one who is claimed [*le revendiqué*] does not, explicitly at least, receive any" ("Final Appeal of the Subject," p. 93).

12. The "claim" *gives* ("the claim imparts," ibid., p. 94); "I receive *myself* from the call or appeal which gives me to myself" (p. 97).

13. In suggesting this, I am invoking the language of John Milbank's critique of Nietzsche, Foucault, Lyotard, and Derrida in *Theology and Social Theory* (Oxford, U.K.: Blackwell, 1990), ch. 10. Interestingly, Levinas is not dealt with extensively there; this is corrected in his more recent "The Soul of Reciprocity, Part One: Reciprocity Refused," *Modern Theology* 17 (2001): 341–43. My reading of Levinas (and especially the theme of "peace") owes much, even in disagreement, to Jeffrey Dudiak's masterful reading in *The Intrigue of Ethics* (New York: Fordham University Press, 2001).

14. On an "ontology of peace," see Milbank, *Theology and Social Theory*, pp. 279–311.

15. Given space constraints, I will largely assume an understanding of the Levinasian "paradigm."

16. Marion, *Étant donné*, p. 367.

17. Ibid., pp. 366–69.

[*le revendiqué*]."[18] With this suggestion, Marion sets up a contrast between the analytic of Dasein in *Sein und Zeit* and the later Heidegger's account of the call of Being. Indeed, "anticipatory resoluteness" marks the way in which Dasein, far from coming "after" the metaphysical subject (Descartes, Kant, Husserl), is rather the culmination of the modern subject—its "last heir."[19] For the call that beckons Dasein in *Sein und Zeit* is merely an echo of Dasein's own voice. To the "they-self," the caller is "*something like* an alien voice"[20]—but it is not *really* alien, because in the end, "the caller is Dasein."[21] As such, Dasein is never opened up to alterity; as Marion puts it, "Dasein does not comport itself towards anything other, to any being, and therefore comports itself towards nothing."[22] Never opened up to any exteriority, Dasein is never ruptured by any alterity; as such, Dasein "no longer admits any extrinsic relation."[23] The result is an obfuscation of Being rather than a revealing.

But precisely "[s]ince anticipatory resoluteness, as a self-calling or auto-appeal, fails through neutralizing the question of Being," Marion comments, "it must be opened, *from the outside,* to an appeal or call that it no longer controls, decides, or performs."[24] We find this irruption of an *outside,* Marion argues, in the later Heidegger (particularly the postface to *What Is Metaphysics?* and in the *Letter on Humanism*).[25] It is in these later analyses of the "appeal of Being" that Marion launches his own analysis of the original "claim" [*la revendication*] of/upon the human being as an "analytic" of "the one who is claimed."

"The claim, then," he continues, "interpellates me. Before I have even said 'I,' the claim has summoned me, named me, and isolated me as myself."[26] Rather than a constituting *je,* I already find myself a constituted *me:* the nominative gives way—"provisionally at least"—to the accusative. I am at the same time both recipient and subject of a call that makes me subject.[27] While this "dis-

18. Marion, "Final Appeal of the Subject," p. 93. This subject is also designated "the interlocuted" (*l'interloqué*) and later, in *Étant donné,* "the devoted" (*l'adonné*). In fact, in *Étant donné,* Marion tends to use the word "subject" to describe *the phenomenon,* in contrast to the "receiver" [*l'attributaire*] who "per/re-ceives" the phenomenon. Indeed, he argues that the phenomenon must be a kind of "self." See *Étant donné,* pp. 343–44; *Being Given,* pp. 248–49.

19. Ibid., p. 91. Earlier he remarks that "[t]he shadow of the ego falls across *Dasein*" (p. 90). This analysis of the Heideggerian subject is paralleled in *Étant donné,* pp. 355–61; *Being Given,* pp. 257–62. I think Marion would level the same charge against the Nietzschean "subject." See Jean-Luc Marion, "The End of the End of Metaphysics," *Epoché* 2, 2 (1994): 1–22.

20. Martin Heidegger, *Being and Time,* trans. John Macquarrie and Edward Robinson (New York: Harper & Row, 1962), §57, p. 321 [H. 277], emphasis added.

21. Ibid., p. 322 [H. 277].

22. Marion, "Final Appeal," p. 89.

23. Ibid., p. 92.

24. Ibid., p. 93, emphasis added.

25. In Martin Heidegger, *Basic Writings,* ed. David Farrell Krell (San Franciso: HarperSanFransisco, 1977), pp. 189–242

26. Ibid., p. 94.

27. "[S]i j'ai à en répondre, j'ai aussi à lui répondre, j'ai donc reçu (et subi) un appel" (Marion, *Étant donné,* p. 368).

possession"[28] marks the "disaster of the I,"[29] it also signals another event: the *birth* of the subject as receiver, as gifted, as the *interloqué*.[30] Thus, in contrast to the Cartesian (or Husserlian) ego, the subject as receiver is an inherently *relational* self; its identity is constituted by a relation whereby it is identified.[31] As Marion summarizes:

> the relation precedes and produces individuality. And moreover, individuality loses its autarkic essence by being derived from a relation which not only is more originary than it, but is half unknown; for the claim delivers up to evidence only one of its two poles—*myself* or rather *me*—without necessarily or for the most part delivering up the other pole, namely, the origin of the call or appeal.[32]

So in a manner that echoes Levinas, Marion emphasizes the anonymity of that which calls.[33] The alterity of the other, which alters the identity of the receiver, comes *je ne sais d'où*. This anonymity of the convocation entails a surprise for the interlocuted one: contradicting intentionality, the *interloqué* is called out of itself, "covered over (taken over [*sur*-prise]) by an extasis."[34] But this extasis is "a more originary affection which precedes metaphysical subjectivity."[35] As soon as I awake, I find myself called—a called one. My "subjectity"[36] [*sic*] is a matter of donation.

II

When Marion moves on to consider the nature of the interlocution, we begin to detect a divergence from Levinas—or at least a moment in which Marion intentionally marks a distinction between his account and that of

---

28. Ibid., p. 344; *Being Given*, p. 249.

29. Marion, "Final Appeal," p. 95.

30. Marion, *Étant donné*, pp. 361, 367; *Being Given*, pp. 262, 266, cf. pp. 289–90. This metaphor of *birth* marks a development, I think, between the earlier "Final Appeal" and *Étant donné*. This should be considered in relation to Olthuis's consideration of the "matrix" and "womb" of love and perhaps the way in which birth is a product of *love*.

31. Marion, "Final Appeal," p. 95. However, even the Cartesian subject's "isolation" is interrupted at its origin by its relationship to the Infinite (*Meditations*, III): "I am not alone in the world," he concludes. For a critical discussion, see Marion, "Does the *Ego* Alter the Other? The Solitude of the *Cogito* and the Absence of the *Alter Ego*," in *Cartesian Questions* (Chicago: University of Chicago Press, 1999), pp. 118–38.

32. Ibid., p. 95.

33. This anonymity, akin to the slippage between *Il* and *il y a* in Levinas, is important for Marion, since he believes it preserves the properly "phenomenological" (rather than "theological") parameters of his account. This is also emphasized in his account of the "gift" in *Étant donné*, §10.

34. Marion, "Final Appeal," p. 96.

35. Ibid., p. 96.

36. I use this phrase to try to indicate a sense of identity that is not a (Cartesian) subjectivity. We might also appeal to Kristeva's account of a self in-process/on trial. For a discussion in a Levinasian context, see Olthuis, *Beautiful Risk*, pp. 76–77.

Levinas. For Marion, "interlocution"—the interlocutionary appeal[37]—effects a *reduction:* "the ultimate phenomenological reduction,"[38] or what he elsewhere describes as a "third reduction" to the pure givenness of a claimed self.[39] When describing such, he contrasts such a reduction with the reductions of Husserl, Heidegger, *and Levinas:*

> To determine the given as pure given demands the suspension [hence a "reduction"] within the *I* of everything which does not directly result from the claim itself, and therefore to reduce the *I* to the pure giving or donation of a *myself/me.* It is no longer a question of comprehending this giving according to the nominative case (Husserl) or according to the genitive case (of Being: Heidegger) *nor even according to the accusative case* (Levinas), but rather according to the dative case—I receive *myself* from the call or appeal which gives me to myself.[40]

In a later formulation of this point, Marion continues by again invoking the metaphor of *birth:* "Receiving himself from the call that summons him, the gifted is therefore open to an alterity, from which the Other can be lacking, but who thus appears all the more. . . . Thus the gifted is delivered straightaway—with its birth—from solipsism."[41] So we clearly have the elements a Levinasian structure here: a primordial relationality that is the condition of a call that makes me subject—which calls forth my "identity," not as a solipsistic individual but as a responsible "called one." Alterity is at the heart of identity, for Marion.

But what are we to make of this evaluation of and departure from Levinas? What does Marion mean to indicate by suggesting that the Levinasian subject is understood according to the *accusative* (my identity is *given*), whereas the interlocuted subject is understood according to the *dative* (my identity is given *to me*)? I want to (tentatively) argue that here Marion may be calling into question the thesis of *substitution* in Levinas; that is, I believe that we might see Marion as here rejecting the Levinasian axiom regarding nonreciprocity.[42] In contrast, Marion's account of the interlocuted subject, while still maintaining some element of asymmetry, also tries to (or *ought* to) provide an account of *reciprocity* in intersubjective relationships.[43] While my identity is given *for* the Other, it is nonetheless given *to* me.

37. Marion notes the legal universe of this metaphor ("Final Appeal," pp. 96–97).

38. Ibid., p. 97.

39. It is named such in Marion, *Reduction and Givenness: Investigations of Husserl, Heidegger, and Phenomenology,* trans. Thomas A. Carlson (Evanston, Ill.: Northwestern University Press, 1998), p. 204. For my reservations regarding the possibility (or even desirability) of an "unconditional givenness," see my "Respect and Donation: A Critique of Marion's Critique of Husserl," *American Catholic Philosophical Quarterly* 71 (1997): 523–38.

40. Marion, "Final Appeal," p. 97, emphasis added. Cf. *Étant donné,* p. 371; *Being Given,* p. 269.

41. Marion, *Étant donné,* pp. 371–72; *Being Given,* p. 269.

42. The project thus is related to Brian Treanor's paper offering a critique of Levinas following Marcel. See Treanor, "*Apres Vous:* Levinas, Marcel, and Intersubjective Reciprocity" (unpublished).

43. On this score, John Milbank's project echoes Olthuis's concerns. As Milbank puts it, "what I have been trying to promote is an asymmetrical reciprocity, which implies not a fixed circle, but an unending spiral, in which each response only completes the circle by breaking out of it to re-establish it" (in "Soul of Reciprocity Part Two: Reciprocity Granted," *Modern Theology* 17 (2001): 486.

My thesis rests on a particular reading of Levinas, which I should at least briefly lay on the table.[44] While I could concede that Levinas understands the relationship with the Other to be "primordial," it seems to me that it is at best *co*primordial with egoism, which makes it *co*-originary. In other words, even if, as Levinas asserts, infinity is "as primordial as totality,"[45] this seems to still entail that totality is primordial. Hence, there is a way in which relationality is always already inscribed with war. Even if the swirling eddy of egoistic enjoyment is a kind of "second" moment, it seems to be one that grows out of this primordial war. (In other words, there is a sense in which "Cartesian dualism" is "rigorously preserved" by Levinas.[46]) It is against this backdrop that I understand the language and descriptions of *Otherwise Than Being, or Beyond Essence*[47] pertaining to substitution, persecution, and hostage-taking. Don't we simply have here the inversion of egoism?[48]

While I have tried to note obvious echoes of Levinas in Marion's account of the postmetaphysical subject (which stems from their parallel accounts of a phenomenology of absolute revelation divined so well by Janicaud),[49] what are we to make of some obvious differences? First, let's note the striking difference in language, especially the notable absence in Marion of the Levinasian language of guilt and persecution, and the (intentional?) avoidance of a violent paradigm that construes the relation as one of hostage-taking. I think we need to do justice to this absence, since it is certainly not just a matter of "semantics."

Second, we need to return to our earlier question regarding Marion's own suggestion that the devoted or gifted one (*l'adonné*) is to be understood not in the accusative sense of Levinas, but rather in terms of the dative. What does Marion mean to suggest by this? If we begin with this question, we'll be in a place to account for the first set of questions regarding language.

If we look at Marion's suggestion carefully, we note that what distinguishes the accusative from the dative is the direction or telos of the giving, not the object given. In the dative conception, "I receive *myself*"; the call or appeal "gives me to myself."[50] He goes on to suggest that perhaps "this strange dative case was not here distinguished from the ablative case (as in Greek), since the *myself/me* accomplishes, insofar as it is the first gift which derives from the appeal

44. I have articulated my concerns about Levinas's account in more detail in *The Fall of Interpretation: Philosophical Foundations for a Creational Hermeneutic* (Downers Grove, Ill.: InterVarsity, 2000), pp. 123–26.

45. See Levinas, *Totality and Infinity,* p. 23.

46. Milbank, "Soul of Reciprocity," p. 341.

47. Levinas, *Otherwise Than Being, or Beyond Essence,* trans. Alphonso Lingis (Pittsburgh: Duquesne University Press, 1998).

48. I have suggested this in *Fall of Interpretation,* p. 125. Milbank suggests the same ("Soul of Reciprocity," p. 342).

49. I take up Janicaud's critique of Marion and Levinas (and basically take his side) in my *Speech and Theology: Language and the Logic of Incarnation,* Radical Orthodoxy (London and New York: Routledge, 2002).

50. Marion, "Final Appeal," p. 97.

or call, the opening of all other donations or gifts and particular givens, which are possibly ethical."[51] In *Étant donné*, this last aspect is further developed:

> Fully offering himself to givenness, to the point that he delivers it as such, the gifted finally attains his ultimate determination—to receive himself by receiving the given unfolded by him according to givenness. Consequently, the gifted is defined entirely in terms of givenness because he is completely achieved as soon as he surrenders conditionally to what gives itself—and first of all to the saturated phenomenon that calls him.[52]

For Marion, the gifted, while recipient of subjectivity, is nevertheless also a certain giver—an "unfolder" of the givenness of phenomena. In other words, I hear in Marion a sense in which the call to be subject is a call to responsibility, which at the same time affirms a certain *reciprocity* of giving—stemming from an iconic[53] paradigm in which the gaze of the Other is an invitation to relation. I think Marion recognizes that our conception of this relation is rooted in an ontology—more specifically, in how we conceive *difference*.[54] While I would concede that Marion is somewhat ambiguous on this score, there are at least suggestions in his corpus of an ontology that conceives of difference, not as opposition (as in Levinas's differential ontology),[55] but as participatory—engendering an account of intersubjective relation that provides a positive account of mutuality.[56] If this is not immediately evident in *Being Given*,[57] I think we see the rudimentary lines of such an ontology in the early work, *Idol and Distance*. There, in the context of a critique of Levinas, Marion notes that when trying to think the "relation" with the Other, we need to think difference differently—a thinking that would "free itself . . . by ceasing to play on the field and with the terms of ontological difference, in order to reinterpret it, in situating it on another terrain of difference."[58] What we would

51. Ibid.

52. Marion, *Being Given*, pp. 282–83.

53. I allude, of course, to Marion, *God without Being* (trans. Thomas A. Carlson [Chicago: University of Chicago Press, 1991]); but see, in this immediate context, *Being Given*, pp. 318–19.

54. See Marion's discussions of different notions of "difference" in *Étant donné*, pp. 405–8; *Being Given*, pp. 294–96.

55. Though I would concede that at times he appears to (and perhaps *does*) buy into the logic of oppositional differnce and a differential ontology. See, for instance, Marion, *Prolegomena to Charity*, trans. Stephen Lewis (New York: Fordham University Press, 2002), pp. 80–81.

56. Following Jim Olthuis, one could think of *relation* not only as "analogical" or "participatory," but also *covenantal*, in which case the marital relationship could be a model for thinking about difference. See James H. Olthuis, *I Pledge You My Troth* (New York: Harper & Row, 1975; rev. ed., 1989) and idem., *Keeping Our Troth* (San Francisco: Harper & Row, 1986).

57. I am leaving open a dialogue that must take place regarding Milbank's reading of Marion in "The Soul of Reciprocity," pp. 344–55.

58. Jean-Luc Marion, *Idol and Distance*, trans. Thomas A. Carlson (New York: Fordham University Press, 2001), p. 220. He goes on to conclude that like Levinas, Derrida's *différance* really does not escape the problem: "One perhaps escapes the ontological difference as little through *différance* as through the Other" (p. 231).

ultimately need is what we might call a "Chalcedonian" *difference*, an account of analogical difference "without confusion or separation."[59] The Chalcedonian understanding of the Incarnation—what I have elsewhere described as the "logic of incarnation"—provides an alternative way for understanding difference, or better, the *relation* between differences. In the Chalcedonian model we see a certain mutuality—a play of differences that permits relation without either reducing the terms to the Same or asserting a radical incommensurability that precludes connection. In his phenomenology of the icon, one finds Marion taking this Chalcedonian model seriously and we see hints of it spilling over into his anthropology—enough traces of an alternative to mark a difference between the philosophical anthropologies of Levinas and Marion.

Let me conclude by trying to get at this intuition of a difference between Levinas and Marion in another way. As Jeffrey Dudiak has amply demonstrated, there is a (very qualified!) moment of reciprocity in Levinas's account, commenting on a passage celebrated by our common mentor, Jim Olthuis. In *Otherwise than Being*, Levinas remarks: "It is only thanks to God that, as a subject incomparable with the other, I am approached as an other by the others, that is, 'for myself.' 'Thanks be to God,' I am an other for the others."[60] As Dudiak comments, this is not a relation that is "deducible" from my asymmetrical relationship, as though we were dealing with a kind of Kantian kingdom of ends; rather, *if* it happens that I am respected as an other by the other, it happens as a matter of *grace*. In this way, "[j]ustice as a society of equals, wherein I too am a citizen, already presupposes this grace."[61]

Marion also appeals to a role for grace; indeed, the very notion of being "gifted" entails a being "graced." "What do we have that we have not *received?*" Augustine would often ask, echoing St. Paul (1 Cor. 4:7). So too in Marion: our identity itself, as gift, is a matter of grace. Thus he concludes that "[g]race gives the *myself* to *itself* before the *I* even notices itself. My grace precedes me."[62] In light of this role of grace in both Levinas and Marion, my concluding question is this: Is grace *original?*[63] I would put the question to both. It seems to me that for Levinas, grace, in a way, supervenes upon nature. I am trying to argue for an *original* grace, perhaps not so common, which is more primordial than violence.

If Marion would consistently follow the logic of Chalcedon and Nicea,[64] then I would argue that he should adopt an ontology that accounts for difference (or "distance")—not oppositionally, yielding a paradigm of violence—but

59. I concede that my argument might be normative, not descriptive: that perhaps Marion does *not* articulate an "ontology of peace," but that, given other commitments of his thought, he *should.*

60. Levinas, *Otherwise than Being,* p. 158.

61. See Dudiak, *Intrigue of Ethics,* pp. 329–30.

61. Marion, "Final Appeal," p. 104.

63. This demands a correlate question: "Is sin original?" What is the nature of this originality?

64. Marion does so in *The Crossing of the Visible,* trans. James K.A. Smith (Stanford, Ca.: Stanford University Press, 2004), ch. 4.

analogically or *incarnationally,* yielding an ontology of peace that undergirds an account of originary intersubjectivity. If this connection is not explicitly made in Marion, I would at least return to our earlier question regarding *language:* perhaps the absence of the language of violation (persecution, hostage-taking) can be explained in these terms. In that case we might suggest that Marion's account of intersubjectivity inscribes grace into the structure of creation. When we begin with this graced creation, the relationships of intersubjectivity need not be construed as acts of violence (as in Levinas), but rather can be described as a "dance"—a being-with that involves an erotics of mutuality, a giving-and-receiving that is an-economic. Olthuis describes this as "with-ing": "With-ing is a healing dance in the wild spaces of love, a meeting-in-the-middle to mark out space together."[65] It seems to me that Levinas's model of relations cannot account for the space where such with-ing is possible. Thus Olthuis emphasizes not just the *gift,* but also the *call* to identity and relation:

> God is love, and humans are made in God's image. Love, then, is who we are—love's agents. God is the giver, we are the gifted, love is the gift. God is the caller, we are the called, love is the calling. This is what I mean by the *gift/call* structure of humankind. Being and becoming lovers—the *gift* of being human and the *call* to become human—happen together, inextricably, simultaneously in a process of being and becoming.[66]

This is why Olthuis criticizes Levinas's "ontologizing" of egoism such that the other always comes to me as a violent interruption. In Levinas, Olthuis concludes, "there seems to be no room, ontologically, for the possibility of a self, of its own initiative, to reach out, attentive and open to the other."[67] Resisting the oppositional notion of difference that funds Levinas's understanding of *relation,* Olthuis also rejects the notion of asymmetry for a model of an-economic but nevertheless reciprocal *mutuality.*

I mean to suggest that Marion's account of intersubjectivity, unlike Levinas's, at least glimpses this reality of an originary grace, a primordial love, which is then free to see relations as otherwise-than-violent (even if, in a broken world, all relations are susceptible to such violence). The genius of Olthuis's contribution to philosophical anthropology has been his consistent refusal to inscribe structures of violence into the fabric of creation.[68] For Olthuis, the advent of the Other can be an invitation to dance.

63. Olthuis, *Beautiful Risk,* p. 130.
66. Ibid., p. 68. Cf. Idem., "Be(com)ing: Humankind as Gift and Call," *Philosophia Reformata* 58 (1993): 153–72.
67. James H. Olthuis, "Face-to-Face: Ethical Asymmetry or the Symmetry of Mutuality?" in *Knowing Other-wise: Philosophy on the Threshold of Spirituality,* ed. James H. Olthuis (New York: Fordham University Press, 1997), p. 141, reprinted as chapter 7 above. Olthuis attributes this to Levinas's acceptance of the traditional understanding of power as necessarily power-*over* (pp. 143–44).
68. This refusal, far from making him blind to the realities of violence, has in fact been the impetus for real, concrete concern about relational violence. See, for example, his research on family abuse in Olthuis,

But here a final key theme comes to the fore: the deep eschatology of Olthuis's account, which recognizes the fallenness of creation,[69] both requires and engenders a hope for the final banquet, with lots of wine, where the dance of mutuality will no longer be tinged with the risk of refusal or exclusion. We hope to find ourselves dancing in the kingdom of love—in its redeemed wild spaces. The hope for this final dance, however, is not utopian; it is eschatological, and we are called to both occasion and testify to its inbreaking—its *ad-venire*—in the dances we find ourselves in. We are called to be subjects of responsibility and love, dancing agents of the kingdom who are gifted and called to be image bearers of the God who is love.

"Rethinking the Family: Belonging, Respecting, and Connecting," in *Towards an Ethics of Community: Negotiations of Difference in a Pluralist Society,* ed. James H. Olthuis (Waterloo, Ont.: Wilfrid Laurier University Press, 2000), pp. 127–49.

69. It is crucial to recognize that Olthuis's "dance" model in no way expects all of our intersubjective being-in-the-world to be a party. Indeed, no one more than Olthuis emphasizes the dangers, risk, and vulnerability of relationships and love. But at the same time, for Olthuis this risk and danger is the product of the fall—of sin—not the constitutive structures of finitude. See Olthuis, *Beautiful Risk,* pp. 74–75, 78–79.

13

With and Without Boundaries

Christian Homemaking amidst Postmodern Homelessness

Brian J. Walsh and Steven Bouma-Prediger

"Home . . . hard to know what it is if you've never had one
Home . . . I can't say where it is but I know I'm going home
That's where the hurt is"

U2, "Walk On," from the album *All That You Can't Leave Behind*
© 2000 Universal International Music

On the Problem of Boundaries

"Secret video exposes plight of homeless" So read the headline in the *Toronto Star* on May 21, 2002. And there on the front page of the newspaper were pictures of body-to-body conditions in one of Toronto's homeless shelters. While the United Nations stipulates that refugee camps should allow for at least 4.5 to 5 square meters per person, here in this shelter as many as four people could be found lying in such a space. The problems here are complex and they go to the very heart of the character of our society. But they are also fundamentally problems of boundaries.

While notions of "personal space" are culturally constructed and differ throughout the world, it seems to be a universal human requirement that some sense of personal space is necessary for all people. Invasion of that space, transgression of such boundaries, invariably causes tensions, often violence, and sometimes the spread of disease (especially tuberculosis in Toronto shelters). Indeed, one of the tragedies of homelessness is precisely the stripping of homeless people of all sense of boundaries so that "they have no stabilizing walls against which they can lean for the identity and security so critical for personal and family dignity."[1]

Boundaries, it would seem, are constitutive to life. Clear boundaries need to be established in order to determine the distinction between friendliness and sexual harassment. Churches and volunteer organizations working with children need to establish clear behavioral boundaries in the relation between adults and children. Professors must either have windows on their office doors, or those doors need to be kept open when they are alone with a student. Conflict of interest rules need to be established for the ethical conducting of our affairs in business, politics, the church, and the academy. And any family knows that rules of the household—agreed or, if necessary, imposed boundaries—are indispensable if the home is to be a place of security and comfort for all.

But how do we talk about boundaries in a post–September 11, 2001, context of a xenophobic "war on terrorism" and the American "Homeland Security Act"? When borders and boundaries are guarded with a fortresslike vigilance, fueled by an ideological demonization of the "other," and when that other—"outside" our borders, "outside" the bounds of our civilization—is seen to be a force of "chaos" that would undermine the well-constructed and self-serving "order" established "inside" our geopolitical, economic, and cultural boundaries, then how can we meaningfully speak of boundaries and borders as necessary and good dimensions of human life together?

While these problems have been heightened since the tragic events of September 11, 2001, they are not new to anyone paying attention to postmodern discourse. Boundaries require categories of in and out and that means boundaries necessarily marginalize. An "other" who is not "in" is relegated "out"—on the margins of the space constructed by these boundaries.[2] And the ethical impulse of postmodernity is to overcome this allergic reaction to alterity, this violent marginalization, and bring an end to this homogenizing terrorism.[3] But since the other is constituted as other by the imposition of someone else's notion of boundaries, something has to be done about boundaries. And the postmodern turn is to recognize the constructed character of all such boundaries and therefore their inherent deconstructability. In his book *Wittgenstein and Derrida*, Henry Statten argues that "deconstruction is not a defense of formlessness,

---

1. Caroline Westerhoff, *Good Fences: The Boundaries of Hospitality* (Boston: Cowley, 1999), p. 15. It is for this reason that folks who work with street people are careful to recognize and respect what little boundaries they are able to erect around themselves—whether it be their grocery cart, doorway, park bench, or squat in the woods.

2. A quintessentially American metaphor for all of this is provided by baseball. This is the game about leaving home and trying to find one's way back to home. If one is ruled "out" then there is no path back home. To be "safe" then is to be "in"—still on the path home, if not already "safe at home."

3. Michael Purcell speaks of a "non-allergic relation with alterity," in "Homelessness as a Theological Motif: Emmanuel Levinas and the Significance of Home," *Scottish Journal of Religious Studies* 15, 2 (Autumn 1994): 89. Walter Truett Anderson speaks of postmodernism as "the age of overexposure to otherness." *The Truth about the Truth: De-confusing and Re-constructing the Postmodern World* (New York: G. P. Putnam's Sons, 1995), p. 6.

but a regulated overflowing of established boundaries." Statten's point "is *not* that we can get along without demarcating boundaries, but rather that there is no 'boundary fixing,' that cannot itself be questioned."[4] And the questions that will be raised will come from the perspective of the marginal—those who are relegated to the outside. But there is another question that remains begged here. If we still need some sort of demarcated boundaries, then how will they be drawn? What are the criteria by which people draw up boundaries, even if these boundaries are never finally fixed? This is, we suggest, a deeply theological question to which we will return at the end of this essay.[5]

In a postmodern context, then, we find frequent employment of the discourse of boundary or border crossing. The boundaries that have kept various academic disciplines in an apartheidlike arrangement of separation are being dismantled by interdisciplinary discourses such as semiotics. The borders that distinguished cultures are transgressed in the production of "hybrid" art forms, music, styles, and even identities.[6] These shifting borders undermine and re-territorialize different configurations of culture, power, and knowledge. Since sociocultural borders, together with ethnic, sexual, and behavioral boundaries, map our existence in monolithic, homogenizing, and exclusionary ways, Henry Giroux calls for a pedagogy and cultural criticism that engage in a praxis of border crossing. He argues that we need "forms of transgression in which existing borders forged in domination can be challenged and redefined."[7] Indeed, Giroux argues that modernity—and its economic muscleman, capitalism—is a culture dedicated to the colonization of difference by creating "borders saturated in terror, inequality and forced exclusions."[8] In these terms, postmodernism "constitutes a general attempt to transgress the borders sealed by modernism, to proclaim the arbitrariness of all boundaries, and to call attention to the sphere of culture as a shifting social and historical construction."[9]

4. Cited by Richard Bernstein, *The New Constellation: The Ethical-Political Horizons of Modernity/Postmodernity* (Cambridge: Massachusetts Institute of Technology Press, 1992), p. 184. From Henry Statten, *Wittgenstein and Derrida* (Lincoln: University of Nebraska Press, 1984), p. 34.

5. Mark C. Taylor expresses the deconstructive spirit well when he says, "Settling inevitably unsettles. Since every place presupposes a certain displacement, there can be no settlement(s) without neglect." "Unsettling Issues," *Journal of the American Academy of Religion* 62, 4 (Winter 1994): 949. Our question is whether it might be possible to settle, indeed be placed, without neglect—or at least without malicious neglect.

6. In his collection of essays, *Border Crossings: Christian Trespasses on Popular Culture and Public Affairs* (Grand Rapids: Brazos, 2000), Rodney Clapp employs such a metaphor to suggest the fruitful interchanges that happen when such disciplinary, cultural—and religious—borders are crossed.

7. Henry Giroux, *Border Crossings: Cultural Workers and the Politics of Education* (New York and London: Routledge, 1992), p. 28.

8. Ibid., p. 33.

9. Ibid., p. 55. In *Truth Is Stranger Than It Used to Be: Biblical Faith in a Postmodern Age* (Downers Grove, Ill.: InterVarsity, 1995), Richard Middleton and Brian Walsh make the point that postmodern critique attends to both the constructed and the oppressive character of home. See also Brian J. Walsh, "Homemaking in Exile: Homelessness, Postmodernity, and Theological Reflection," in Doug Blomberg and Ian Lambert, eds., *Reminding: Renewing the Mind in Learning* (Sydney: Centre for the Study of Australian Christianity, 1998).

This does not mean, however, that Giroux's pedagogy of border crossings leaves us in a borderless wasteland with no identity or citizenships. In a world of "lived homophobia, racial oppression, and escalating economic inequality" an apolitical postmodern aestheticism of bricolage and pastiche will not do.[10] Rather, Giroux says that we need a pedagogy that enables students "to be border-crossers in order to understand Otherness on its own terms, and . . . to create borderlands in which diverse cultural resources allow for the fashioning of new identities within existing configurations of power."[11] If all we have is border crossing and boundary blurring in a postmodern context of radical pluralism, then we have no place from which to make ethical/political judgements, no borders or boundaries the transgression of which constitutes oppression, and no ability to discern between the cry of the oppressed and the arrogant exclamations of the powerful. We need to cross borders, says Giroux, and create new borderlands. Again, the question is begged as to what the criteria of the borders of those new borderlands will be and on what basis they will be erected.[12]

Boundaries, we are saying, are constitutive to life (all of life, not just human life), but they are deeply problematic. Let's investigate their ambiguity more deeply by returning to the themes of poverty and homelessness.[13]

Mary Douglas describes "patterning" in a culture as the imposition of a symbolic order "whose keystone, boundaries, margins and internal lines are held in relation by rituals of separation" in which the defiling pollution on the outside of the boundary is kept from infecting the inside.[14] While this anthropological observation has its origins in ancient texts (like Leviticus) and so-called "primitive tribes," postmodern critical geographers and urbanists discern similar patterning going on in the modern city. David Sibley calls this a "geography of exclusion."

> There is a history of imaginary geographies which cast minorities, "imperfect" people, and a list of others who are seen to pose a threat to the dominant group in society as polluting bodies or folk devils who are then located "elsewhere." This "elsewhere" might be nowhere, as when genocide or the moral transfor-

10. Ibid., p. 240.

11. Ibid., p. 245.

12. Interestingly, Giroux's postmodern critical pedagogy espouses a discourse that is "multiaccentual and dispersed and resists permanent closure" (p. 29) because it is rooted in no "master narratives" that are "monolithic" and "timeless" (p. 76). Such a pedagogy is to be preferred, he insists, because such multiplicity creates "more democratic forms of public life" (p. 76). It seems to us, however, that his own affirmation of radical democracy is nothing less than a "master narrative" that would appear to carry "timeless authority."

13. The literature on homelessness in Canada and the United States is voluminous. We bring to the reader's attention to four books: Jack Layton, *Homelessness: The Making and Unmaking of a Crisis* (Toronto: Penguin, 2000); John Sewell, *Houses and Homes: Housing for Canadians* (Toronto: Lorimer, 1994); Gerald Daly, *Homeless: Policies, Strategies, and Lives on the Street* (London and New York: Routledge, 1996); and Doug A. Timmer, D. Stanley Eitzen, and Kathryn D. Talley, *Paths to Homelessness: Extreme Poverty and the Urban Housing Crisis* (Boulder, Colo., San Francisco, and Oxford: Westview, 1994).

14. Mary Douglas, *Purity and Danger* (London: Routledge & Kegan Paul, 1966), p. 41.

mation of a minority like prostitutes is advocated, or it might be some spatial periphery, like the edge of the world or the edge of the city.[15]

The boundaries between the rich and the poor are erected by the powerful in order to reduce the threat of their own defilement. Slums are *down*town as opposed to the suburbs, which are *up*town. The topography of the poor is identified with filth, disease, excrement, and foul odors.[16] And all of this legitimates the ideological rhetoric of "cleanup campaigns."[17] The unhomogenized other is identified with the forces of chaos that threaten from outside the well-ordered homes of cleanliness and purity of the inside. Boundaries are then violently exclusionary, especially for the most vulnerable—those who do not have the resources to erect their own boundaries and to overcome the boundaries of domination that oppress them.

And so we return to the homeless shelter in which the most basic boundaries of personal space cannot be respected. We could say that these people find themselves in this situation for various reasons, not the least being that the racist boundaries of our society (most of the men in the picture were aboriginal), combined with economic boundaries imposed by a neoconservative political regime (which abandoned progressive housing and social policy in favor of tax breaks) and not-in-my-backyard geocultural boundaries (which has limited the ability of social service and volunteer agencies to provide shelters spread throughout the city), have all conspired in this geography of exclusion to keep these people out of sight and out of mind in disease-ridden shelters in the inner city. Boundaries put these people in this situation, and yet it is

15. David Sibley, *Geographies of Exclusion: Society and Difference in the West* (New York and London: Routledge, 1995), p. 49. Rosemary Haughton makes a similar point, though without the geographical specificity of Sibley. She says that homeless people are objects of fear and suspicion because "they don't fit in and their 'not belonging' is a threat to the sense of stability everyone wants. It could happen to us: perhaps if we can blame them and remove them we shall feel more secure." "Hospitality: Home as the Integration of Privacy and Community," in Leroy Rouner, ed., *The Longing for Home* (Notre Dame, Ind.: University of Notre Dame Press, 1996), p. 213.

16. James Duncan and David Ley make this point well: "Topography is also therefore a science of domination—confirming boundaries, securing norms and treating questionable social conventions as unquestioned social facts." "Introduction: Representing the Place of Culture," in James Duncan and David Ley, eds., *Place/Culture/Representation* (London and New York: Routledge, 1993): p. 1.

17. Sibley graphically makes his point by citing the character Travis Bickle from Martin Scorcese's film *Taxi Driver*. Speaking to a presidential hopeful in his cab, Bickle says, "You should clean up this city here because this city here is like an open sewer, it's full of filth and scum and sometimes I can hardly take it. Whoever becomes the president should just really clean it up, you know what I mean. Sometimes I go out and I smell it. I get headaches, it's so bad, you know, they just like never go away, you know. It seems like the president should just clean up the whole mess here, should just flush it down the . . . toilet." Ibid., p. 61. A further comment on Sibley: While Sibley's book powerfully unpacks the oppressive dynamics of a geography of exclusion, he has precious little to say about geographies of inclusion. This is the question we have raised in relation to both the deconstructive demarcation of new boundaries and Giroux's notion of new borderlands and it returns in relation to Sibley. If geographies of exclusion are to be rejected, but boundaries are constitutive to human life (a point that Sibley grants), then how do we make space, which is bounded, more hospitable? What are the characteristics of boundaries that do *not* violently exclude?

precisely the unconscionable transgression of boundaries of personal space that brought public attention to their plight. So, recognizing the profound ambiguity of all boundary construction, we need to reflect further on the necessity of boundaries.

The Necessity of Boundaries

"Strangers," Walter Brueggemann writes, "are people without a place." They are "displaced persons" because the "social system . . . has . . . assigned their place to another and so denied them any safe place of their own."[18] In ancient Israel they are often people whose "boundary stones" have been moved.[19] To be placeless is to live in the tenuous vulnerability of life without the bounded security of home and shelter.[20] Boundaries that demarcate in and out, mine and yours, ours and theirs, my body in distinction from other bodies, private and public, are necessary if life is to be secure. Strangers are people who have been stripped of such boundaries.

A boundary, writes Caroline Westerhoff, is "that which defines and gives identity to all kinds of systems." Such boundaries can be concerned with "physical borders and property lines, as well as names and stories, traditions and values." Boundaries are constitutive to identity and "unless we can draw a line—a boundary—and say that something lies outside its domain, then we can speak about nothing that lies inside with deep meaning."[21] Westerhoff continues:

> Boundaries are lines that afford definition, identity and protection—for persons, families, institutions, nations. . . . A boundary gives us something to which we can point and ascribe a name. Without a boundary, we have nothing to which we can invite or welcome anyone else.[22]

18. Walter Brueggemann, "Welcoming the Stranger," in *Interpretation and Obedience: From Faithful Reading to Faithful Living* (Minneapolis: Fortress, 1991), p. 294. For groundbreaking and integrative work on the notion of welcoming the stranger and its implication for foreign language teaching from a Christian perspective, see David I. Smith and Barbara Carvill, *The Gift of the Stranger: Faith, Hospitality, and Foreign Language Learning* (Grand Rapids and Cambridge: Eerdmans, 2000).

19. Deut. 19:14; Prov. 22:28: 23:10–11; Isa. 5:7–10; 10:13; Amos 2:7; 5:12.

20. This is why Ed Loring argues that housing—that is, bounded and secure space for living in—is foundational to life. Reflecting on years of ministry amongst the homeless, Loring argues that housing is foundational to life and therefore precedes employment, sobriety, education, health, evangelization, and even the struggle for justice. His provocative article, "Housing Comes First," was published in *The Other Side* 38, 3 (May–June, 2002): 32–33. In the wilderness, shelter is second only to air in the priorities for survival. You can live three minutes without air, three hours without shelter (in difficult conditions), three days without water, and three weeks without food.

21. Westerhoff, *Good Fences*, p. xi.

22. Ibid., p. 7. All italicized in the original. Providing a phenomenological description of the inhabitation of a room, Edward Casey makes a similar point: "Indeed, to be in an intimately inhabited room is not merely to tolerate but to *require* boundaries." *The Fate of Place: A Philosophical History* (Berkeley: University of California Press, 1997), p. 294.

Without boundaries there can be no sense of "place" as home, as site of hospitality, security, and intimacy with local knowledge. Without boundaries there is no locality, and therefore no sense of membership in a particular community, family, or neighborhood that has an identity in distinction from other communities, families, and neighborhoods.[23] Without boundaries identity is impossible.

Christine Pohl's historical/theological discussion of hospitality makes the same claim. "Hospitality," Pohl writes, "is fundamentally connected to place—to a space bounded by commitments, values, meanings."[24] Boundaries are necessary conditions for hospitality because they provide definition of the space being entered, and identity to both host and guest. They also provide "the kind of ordering necessary to life."[25] Homemaking, like world-building, is, of course, a nomic enterprise.[26] To turn space into place, to transform space into what Michael Walzer calls the "dense moral culture" of home,[27] is to establish normative boundaries that bring a certain kind of order to the life lived within those boundaries. Sallie McFague reminds us that ecology has to do with discerning and obeying the "house rules" of the planet.[28] What is true of the *oikos* known as planet Earth is true of any home, any "oikonomic" structure. To be home is to be a site where certain kinds of rules are obeyed, certain kinds of order are constructed.[29]

Of course we are now back to where we started. Boundaries provide

23. Interestingly, the agenda of global consumerism is precisely the eradication of such borders—such cultural, political, economic, and communal boundaries—in favor of a borderless homogeneity of global consumers who have no attachments to place and no distinct identities. That such an economic/cultural consumerist agenda bears striking similarity to the decentred pluralism of postmodern discourse has been noted by Nicholas Boyle, *Where Are We Now? Christian Humanism and the Global Market: From Hegel to Heaney* (Edinburgh: T & T Clark, 1998); Mark McLain Taylor, "Vodou Resistance/Vodou Hope: Forging a Postmodernism that Liberates," in David Batstone et al., eds., *Liberation Theologies, Postmodernity, and the Americas* (New York: Routledge 1997); Stanley Hauerwas, "The Christian Difference: Or Surviving Postmodernism," in Susan and Gerald Biesecker-Mast, eds., *Anabaptists and Postmodernity* (Telford, Pa.: Pandora, 2000); and Middleton and Walsh, *Truth Is Stranger Than It Used to Be.*

24. Christine Pohl, *Making Room: Recovering Hospitality as a Christian Tradition* (Grand Rapids: Eerdmans, 1999), p. 134.

25. Ibid., p. 139. Pohl goes on to say that "Boundaries are an important part of making a place physically and psychologically safe. Many needy strangers (e.g., refugees, homeless people, abused women and children) come from living in chronic states of fear. A safe place gives them a chance to relax, heal, and reconstruct their lives. If hospitality involves providing a safe place—where a person is protected and respected—then certain behaviors are precluded and certain pragmatic structures follow" (p. 140).

26. Peter Berger, *The Sacred Canopy: Elements of a Sociological Theory of Religion* (Garden City, N.Y.: Doubleday/Anchor, 1969), pp. 19–24.

27. Michael Walzer, *Interpretation and Social Criticism* (Cambridge and London: Harvard University Press, 1987), p. 16.

28. Sallie McFague, *The Body of God: An Ecological Theology* (Minneapolis: Fortress, 1993), p. 5.

29. Kimberly Dovey also describes "home" in terms of the ordering or patterning of environmental experience and behavior: "Being at home is a mode of being whereby we are oriented within a spatial, temporal and sociocultural order that we understand." "Home and Homelessness," in I. Altman and C. Werner, eds., *Home Environments* (New York: Plenum, 1985), p. 35.

nomic ordering to experience and space and that ordering renders certain people and certain behaviors as defiled, polluted, threatening. Some are ruled out of order. So boundaries are constitutive to life, yet also invariably an ideological legitimation of our geographies of exclusion. Edward Said, who knows something about the reality of exilic homelessness of his own Palestinian people, describes well the ambiguity of boundaries and borders: "Borders and barriers, which enclose us within the safety of familiar territory, can also become prisons, and are often defended beyond reason or necessity."[30] Rosemary Haughton concurs: "the impregnable home where the only comers are clones of the hosts becomes not a home but a fortress and a prison combined."[31]

Boundaries used to erect fortresses of self-protection, then, can never be refuges of hospitality. The walls are simply too thick, the barriers too impenetrable. But boundaries that demarcate definite spaces and identities need not be exclusionary. Borders need not create prisons. Heidegger evocatively suggests that "a boundary is not that at which something stops but . . . the boundary is that from which something *begins in its essential unfolding.* That is why the concept is that of *horismos,* that is, the horizon, the boundary."[32] Boundaries can be horizons that provide a sense of orientation, yet are dynamic. Boundaries are not there so much to stop something from coming in—though that remains part of the safety-producing function of boundaries—as to provide a context for a certain kind of unfolding, or opening up, that happens within those boundaries.

Emmanuel Levinas puts it this way. "The privileged role of the home does not consist in being the end of human activity but in being its condition, and in this sense its commencement."[33] Human cultural engagement within the world has, as its ontological condition, the dwelling, security, and refuge that is the bounded space of home. But this "retreat home within oneself as in a land of refuge . . . answers to a hospitality, an expectancy, a human welcome."[34] What unfolds within the horizon of home—Heidegger's essential unfolding—is, for Levinas, a cosmic gentleness and intimacy characterized by welcome. "The possibility for the home to open to the Other," Levinas argues, "is as essential to the essence of the home as closed doors and windows."[35] Home, as bounded space, must have windows and doors that can be closed. But those are not sealed doors and windows. They

30. Edward Said, "Reflections on Exile," in R. Ferguson et al., eds., *Out There: Marginalization and Contemporary Cultures* (New York: New Museum of Contemporary Art; Cambridge, Mass., and London: MIT Press, 1990), p. 365.

31. Haughton, "Hospitality," p. 215.

32. Martin Heidegger, "Building, Dwelling, Thinking," in *Basic Writings,* ed. David Farell Krell (San Francisco: HarperSanFrancisco, 1992), p. 356.

33. Emmanuel Levinas, *Totality and Infinity: An Essay on Exteriority,* trans. Alphonso Lingis (Pittsburgh: Duquesne University Press, 1969), p. 152.

34. Ibid., p. 156.

35. Ibid., p. 173.

can, and must, be opened.[36] An open door is a liminal reality, a threshold both for those entering and those departing. It is the place between places, fraught with anxiety and danger (for people moving in both directions).[37] But whether those departing leave with a spirit of embrace and service to the world and whether those entering feel that they are coming into a safe place of welcome depends on the kind of unfolding, the emerging character, of the bounded place that is here identified as home.[38] A deepening of our analysis of boundaries, then, requires some further phenomenological reflection on home.[39]

On Home and Boundaries: A Phenomenological Description

What does it mean to be at-home? What is it that homeless people do not have that renders them homeless? And how would the jet-setting, global-consumerist, postmodern nomad recognize home if she ever found one? Recognizing the dangers inherent in any kind of phenomenological description of such a clearly constructed reality as "home," and not wanting to crash on either the constructivist shores of Scylla or the essentialist shores of Charybdis,[40] we nonetheless need to reflect on the basic phenomenological contours of what might count as "home."[41] And at the risk of sounding overly schematized, we offer seven characteristics of home.

36. Jürgen Moltmann describes boundaries as living, moving, and open frontiers. "Once they are closed, exclusive and self-isolating communities grow up." "Shekinah: The Home of the Homeless God," in Rouner, ed., *Longing for Home,* p. 172.

37. See Beldon C. Lane, *Landscapes of the Sacred: Geography and Narrative in American Spirituality* (Baltimore and London: Johns Hopkins University Press, 2002), pp. 187–88; and Victor Turner, *The Ritual Process* (Chicago: Aldine, 1969).

38. Westerhoff employs the analogy of the cell membrane to describe boundaries that are open, yet still function as boundaries that provide identity and life: "Like a cell membrane, a boundary must be semi-permeable: admitting and containing what is necessary for sustaining and enriching life, discharging and excluding anything that does not belong within its borders. A membrane that allows for anything and everything to enter and leave is a membrane that is no longer functioning. The cell—the system—is now dead or dying. A healthy boundary is firm enough to hold, but not so tight that it binds, confines and cuts. It is flexible enough to allow movement and change within time and circumstance, but not so loose that it encourages sloppiness and aimless wandering. A boundary that is too rigid fosters stiff and brittle attitudes; it is always in danger of freezing and cracking. One that is too porous encourages attitudes of carelessness and disorder; it will rot and crumble." *Good Fences,* p. 83.

39. The phenomenological description that follows was first developed by Steven Bouma-Prediger in "Yearning for Home: The Christian Doctrine of Creation in a Postmodern Age," in Merold Westphal, ed., *Postmodern Philosophy and Christian Thought* (Bloomington: Indiana University Press, 1999).

40. Beldon Lane attempts to steer the same treacherous course in his discussion of "sacred space" in *Landscapes of the Sacred,* p. 5.

41. By "phenomenology" we are not referring to the exact science of apodictic certainty found in the early Husserl. Rather, following the hermeneutical turn in phenomenology identified with Heidegger, Merleau-Ponty, and Ricoeur, we mean by phenomenology a mode of philosophical reflection, in the words of Merold Westphal, whose "central point has to do with noticing what is too obvious to be seen, with

First, home is a place of permanence and familiarity. To be at-home some-where is more than simply having a place to stay. We can also stay in motels and hotels, but these are sites of transience. Home, by contrast, signifies a certain degree of spatial permanence, a kind of enduring presence or residence. Edward Casey's phenomenology of place is instructive here:

> To lack a primal place is to be "homeless" indeed, not only in the literal sense of having no permanently sheltering structure but also as being without any effective means of orientation in a complex and confusing world. By late modern times, this world had become increasingly placeless, a matter of mere sites instead of lived places, of sudden displacements rather than perduring emplacements.[42]

In a dromocratic, speed-bound culture, every highly mobile person is a victim of at least some form of homelessness because there is no time or stability to foster a sense of perduring emplacement.[43] Indeed, even traditionally nomadic peoples do not live in a world of sudden displacements. They too function within a context of a permanently sheltering structure of tribe and environment. Remove an aboriginal child from her tribe, strip the people of their traplines, transport them to a different landscape and you will render them homeless.[44]

For home to be a place of permanence and familiarity, however, there must be boundaries that distinguish permanence from transience, familiarity from unfamiliarity. These are spatial and geographical boundaries that are constructed from the fabric of family, tribe, and culture.

Second, a home is not merely a house, a domicile, or an abode. While the occupation of space is foundational for there be an experience of at-homeless, home transforms space into place. As Brueggemann argues, "place is space which has historical meanings, where some things have happened which are now remembered and which provide continuity and identity across genera-

---

finding the glasses we've been wearing." *God, Guilt, and Death* (Bloomington: Indiana University Press, 1984), p. 13. This task of noticing the familiar, of seeing the overlooked, "is not motivated by the desire to be rigorously scientific, but rather by a passion for self-understanding that is itself neither detached nor disengaged" (ibid., p. 22). This phenomenology, as Langdon Gilkey puts it, "seeks to interpret the latent *meanings*, i.e., unveil the implicit structures of man's being in the world." *Naming the Whirlwind: The Renewal of God-Language* (Indianapolis and New York: Bobbs-Merrill, 1969), p. 280. Such a method is certainly not a matter of offering decisive proofs of its conclusions, but rather a disciplined descriptive proposal for intuitive recognition. In Heideggerian terms, this is an exercise in disclosure.

42. Edward S. Casey, *Getting Back into Place: Toward a Renewed Understanding of the Place-World* (Bloomington: Indiana University Press, 1993), p. xv.

43. Deborah Tall rightly comments that "Individualism and mobility are at the core of American identity." "Dwelling: Making Peace with Space and Place," in William Vitek and Wes Jackson, eds., *Rooted in the Land* (New Haven, Conn., and London: Yale University Press, 1996), p. 107. In *Staying Put: Making a Home in a Restless World* (Boston: Beacon, 1993), Scott Russell Sanders resists the "vagabond wind" of his culture (p. xv), and says, "Only by knocking against the golden calf of mobility, which looms so large and shines so brightly, have I come to realize that it is hollow. Like all idols, it distracts us from true divinity" (p. 117).

44. See Keith Basso, *Wisdom Sits in Places: Landscape and Language among the Western Apache* (Albuquerque: University of New Mexico Press, 1996).

tions. Place is space in which important words have been spoken which have established identity, defined vocation and envisioned destiny."[45] A domicile becomes a dwelling place, a house becomes a home, when it is transformed by memories into a place of identity, connectedness, meaning, order, appropriation, and care. Heidegger says that "genuine building" is "dwelling" and to dwell is "to cherish and protect, to preserve and care for."[46] And to bring Brueggemann and Heidegger together we could say that care-ful and protective dwelling is itself always rooted in and directed by those memories, those historical meanings that made this space into the dwelling-place of being at-home. Another way to say this is that the boundaries that make this home the home that it is and give it the character that it has as this kind of home are the stories that have shaped the memories of life lived here. The boundaries of homemaking are narratively formed.[47] Home is a storied place and without stories, without particular memories, there is neither home nor identity.[48] That is why Elie Wiesel says that forgetfulness is always the temptation of exile. "The one who forgets to come back has forgotten the home he or she came from and where he or she is going. Ultimately, one might say that the opposite of home is not

45. Walter Brueggemann, *The Land: Place as Gift, Promise, and Challenge in Biblical Faith* (Philadelphia: Fortress, 1977), p. 5.

46. Heidegger, "Building, Dwelling, Thinking," p. 325. Heidegger reverses the simplistic relation that temporally places building before dwelling by saying that "to build is not merely a means and a way toward dwelling—to build is already to dwell" (p. 324). Levinas also insists on the priority of dwelling to building when he says, "Concretely speaking, the dwelling is not situated in the objective world, but the objective world is situated in relation to my dwelling." *Totality and Infinity,* p. 153. Or, as Casey would put it, "the priority of dwelling to building holds *only if building itself is cultivational in character. . . .* Only fully cultivational acts of building will carry cosmic dwelling into the focused dwelling that we call "houses" and above all "homes." *Getting Back into Place,* p. 177.

47. John Berger talks about the homebuilding of the homeless, of the displaced, in terms of memory. "The mortar which holds the impoverished 'home' together—even for a child—is memory. . . . To the underprivileged, home is represented, not by a house, but by a set of practices. . . . Home is no longer a dwelling but the untold story of a life being lived." *And Our Faces, My Heart, Brief as Photos* (New York: Vintage, 1991), p. 64. Charles Winquist makes a similar point, though not with reference to the socioeconomically displaced: "Storytelling can be allied with homecoming because homecoming is more than the collection of actuality. Homecoming is a re-collection of experience. Our remembrance is an interpretation. We tell a story about the actuality of experience to lift it into a context of meaning that speaks out of the reality of possibility as well as actuality." "To come home to the self we must be able to tell the story of our lives with a memory for reality." *Homecoming: Interpretation, Transformation, Individuation,* AAR Studies in Religion 18 (Missoula: Scholars Press, 1978), p. 108.

48. "The home is a space replete with pasts and memories." M. Cooper, cited by Sibley, *Geographies of Exclusion ,* p. 93, from "Making Changes," in T. Putnam and C. Newton, eds., *Household Choices* (London: Futures, 1990), pp. 37–42.

Memory, however, is ambivalent, for some homes are precarious, or worse, painful. A home that is rooted in stories of conflict with others becomes a fortress of protection against those demonized others (we think of tribal/ethnic conflicts from Bosnia to Northern Ireland to Rwanda). The narrative foundation functions here to make home a deeply ambivalent reality. Conversely, homes are as precarious as the narratives upon which they are founded. What happens to the identity of a home, or a homeland, when it becomes clear that the narratives which were taken to be stories of bravery, fidelity, and discovery are revealed to be narratives of cowardice, broken trust, and conquest?

distance but forgetfulness. One who forgets forgets everything, including the roads leading homeward."[49] Once the stories are forgotten, there is no home to return to because there is no place, or even potential place, that could be shaped by those stories.

Third, and again following Heidegger, to dwell is "to be set at peace."[50] Home is a place of rest. Beyond the insatiability of restlessness, home can be a place of "enough," of satisfaction, of contentment.[51] When a space becomes a dwelling-place of homemaking, it is received as a gift, not an anxious accomplishment. Edith Wyschogrod says that the metaphor of home as bed or lodging "suggests that home is a milieu of safety, that at home one can drop one's wariness, allow oneself to fall asleep."[52] Or as Bruce Cockburn sings, "Make me a bed of fond memories / make me to lie down with a smile."[53] Home is a place that is constructed in such a way that we are safe to rest. Rest, then, is another boundary marker for homes.

Fourth, if homes are to resist the temptation to become self-enclosed fortresses—that is, if homes are to have windows and doors that are open—then homes must be sites of hospitality. For Levinas, to dwell requires "the non-aggressive and non-allergic advent of the other into my dwelling, 'not in a shock negating the I, but as the primordial phenomenon of gentleness,' which affirms my place (*lieu*) precisely as a home (*maison*)."[54] And just as rest is founded in a sense of home as gift, so is hospitality—arising in grateful response to the gift—its own giving. Indeed, Levinas says that such welcome—such extraterritoriality that is necessarily constitutive of the interiority of the home, such intimacy with the other—is nothing less than "an event in the oecumenia of being," the coming together of the household in the *oikos* of the home.[55] It is in the welcome of the other that the home does not degenerate into self-

49. Elie Wiesel, "Longing for Home," in Rouner, ed., *Longing for Home*, pp. 24–25.

50. Heidegger, "Building, Dwelling, Thinking," p. 327.

51. It needs to be said that this is a normative statement that is hardly descriptive of most "homes" in an upwardly mobile, economically driven society of insatiable affluence. See Paul Wachtel, *The Poverty of Affluence: A Psychological Portrait of the American Way of Life* (Philadelphia: New Society, 1989); David Myers, *The Pursuit of Happiness* (New York: William Morrow, 1992); David Myers, *The American Paradox: Spiritual Hunger in an Age of Plenty* (New Haven, Conn.: Yale University Press, 2000); and Alan Durning, *This Place on Earth: Home and the Practice of Permanence* (Seattle: Sasquatch Books, 1996).

52. Edith Wyschogrod, "Dwellers, Migrants, Nomads: Home in the Age of the Refugee," in Rouner, ed., *Longing for Home*, p. 189.

53. Bruce Cockburn, "Joy will find a way," from the album, *Joy Will Find a Way* © 1975, Golden Mountain Music. Brian Walsh has discussed the metaphors of home and homecoming in the lyrics of Bruce Cockburn in "One Day I Shall Be Home," *Christianity and the Arts* 7, 1 (Winter 2000): 28–32.

54. Purcell, "Homelessness as Theological Motif," p. 96; citing Levinas, *Totality and Infinity*, p. 150. Purcell sums up Levinas's contribution well: "Securing the home does not result in the emptiness and coldness of shelter, but in the interiority and intimacy of welcome, for the dwelling refers essentially beyond itself to an other person, who, while remaining absolutely other and transcendent with respect to me, beyond my acquisitive grasp, and while contesting my happy possession of the world, yet always draws me in intimacy, inviting my response and actually rendering me *responsible* subjectivity" (p. 96).

55. Levinas, *Totality and Infinity*, p. 150.

protective isolation.[56] Haughton notes that "hospitality means a letting go of certainty and control—and paradoxically it's only this letting go that allows the richness of growth and change that makes real and not pretended continuity possible."[57] Or we could say that hospitality is the unique boundary that constitutes home as home, yet keeps that home open, keeps the boundaries suffused with welcome and protection, not exclusion.[58]

A fifth characteristic of home could be called inhabitation. Following David Orr, we distinguish between a resident who is "a temporary occupant, putting down few roots and investing little," and an inhabitant who "dwells . . . in an intimate, organic, and mutually nurturing relationship with a place." "Good inhabitance," Orr says, "is an art requiring detailed knowledge of a place, the capacity for observation and sense of care and rootedness."[59] Inhabitation is a matter of being "not merely *at* our destination but fully *in* it."[60] Home, we have said, requires care and cultivation, but that care and cultivation is always located in a particular place.[61] Inhabitation requires an attention, intimacy, and even love of a particular place—only then are we at-home in that place and only then do we respect the integrity of that place.[62] The place itself, then, functions as another boundary for homemaking.[63]

The sixth characteristic of home is that it is a point of orientation. This has been our theme all along. Home is a nomic structure that provides order

---

56. Such hospitality was, of course, at the heart of Dorothy Day's vision for the Catholic Worker communities. Day was dependent in her views on the philosopher Emmanuel Mounier, who argued that property was an extension of the body of a human being. In capitalist societies, however, "the tendency is for property (or place) to be used simply as the physical extension of one's sphere of control. It becomes a protective shell, making oneself less vulnerable to the intrusion of the world." "By using property (or space) in a protective, defensive manner, one becomes unavailable to the outside world. His property insulates and isolates him." Mounier, cited by Beldon Lane, *Landscapes of the Sacred*, p. 206.

57. Haughton, "Hospitality," in Rouner, ed., *Longing for Home*, 214.

58. These themes are discussed in greater depth by Miroslav Volf, *Exclusion and Embrace: A Theological Exploration of Identity, Otherness, and Reconciliation* (Nashville: Abingdon, 1996).

59. David Orr, *Ecological Literacy* (Albany: State University of New York Press, 1992), p. 130. We have discussed the implications of inhabitance further vis-à-vis higher education in our article, "Education for Homelessness or Homemaking? The Christian College in a Postmodern Culture," *Christian Scholar's Review* 32 (3): 281–95. Bouma-Prediger has discussed Orr's views further in *For the Beauty of the Earth: A Christian Vision for Creation Care* (Grand Rapids: Baker, 2001), esp. ch. 1.

60. Edward Casey, *Fate of Place*, p. 121.

61. Ibid., p. 175.

62. See Wes Jackson, *Becoming Native to the Place* (Washington, D.C.: Counterpoint, 1994); Wendell Berry, *The Gift of Good Land* (San Francisco: North Point, 1981) and *Home Economics* (New York: North Point, 1987).

63. One could say that the sin of Ahab's power grab of Naboth's vineyard did not just transgress the boundaries of covenantal law and inheritance rights—though it certainly did that!—but also failed to respect the integrity of *this* place in distinction from other places. This was a vineyard and Ahab wanted a market garden. These are two very different uses of land, and it would seem that for Ahab one piece of land is as good as another. That it would have taken several generations to nurture this place into a vineyard, as opposed to the overnight mechanical tiller job that it would take to convert it to a market garden (a sort of vegetable 7-11 store for the royal household), means nothing to the acquisitive king. See 1 Kings 21.

and direction for life. It functions, as Eliade has put it, as an *axis mundi* for life.[64] Bringing together themes from our discussion of inhabitation with this question of orientation, Edward Relph says that "home in its most profound form is an attachment to a particular setting, a particular environment, in comparison with which all other associations with places have only a limited significance. It is the point of departure from which we orient ourselves and take possession of the world."[65]

Finally, home is a locus of belonging, acceptance, and affiliation. Moltmann states it well: "I am 'at home' where people know me, and where I find recognition without having to struggle for it."[66] Home is "a place where you feel you belong, and which in some sense belongs to you."[67] In homemaking a process of appropriation takes place in which the place and the relationships within that place are taken as one's own. And this appropriation seems to go both ways. The place somehow belongs to us and yet we belong to the place. We belong to the web of interconnected relationships that make up this place, and yet they belong to us. And herein there are, again, boundaries to be erected and respected. To belong here is to not belong elsewhere. To be on the inside of this locus of affiliation necessarily entails that there are others who are on the outside of this home, who do not "belong" in the same way.

And, again, we return to the problem with which we began. While it is worthwhile to suggest a phenomenology of home that focuses on placed permanence, dwelling, rest, hospitality, inhabitation, orientation, and belonging, all of this amounts to little more than what David Sibley calls a "happy phenomenology of home,"[68] which is too cozy, romantic, and benign unless we take seriously the realities of home as exclusionary space in which "a fear of difference is projected onto the objects and spaces comprising the home or locality which can be polluted by the presence of non-conforming people, activities or artefacts."[69] Or, as Cockburn would put it: "O sweet fantasia of the safe home / where nobody has to scrape for honey at the bottom of the comb / where every actor understands the scene / and nobody ever means to be mean / catch it in a dream, catch it in a song / seek it on the street you

64. Mircea Eliade, *The Sacred and the Profane* (New York: Harcourt Brace Jovanovich, 1959).

65. Edward Relph, *Place and Placelessness* (London: Pion, 1976), p. 40. Relph connects such orientation to the notion of "roots": "To have roots in a place is to have a secure point from which to look out on the world, a firm grasp of one's own position in the order of things, and a significant spiritual and psychological attachment to somewhere in particular" (p. 38). See also Simone Weil, *The Need for Roots* (London: Routledge & Kegan Paul, 1952).

66. Jürgen Moltmann, *God in Creation* (San Francisco: Harper and Row, 1985), p. 46. Bouma-Prediger has discussed Moltmann's theology of creation as the home of God further in "Creation as the Home of God: The Doctrine of Creation in the Theology of Jürgen Moltmann," *Calvin Theological Journal* 32, 1 (1997). See also Brian J. Walsh, "Theology of Hope and the Doctrine of Creation: An Appraisal of Jürgen Moltmann," *Evangelical Quarterly* 59, 1 (January 1987).

67. Frederick Buechner, *The Longing for Home* (San Francisco: HarperCollins, 1996), p. 7.

68. Sibley, *Geographies of Exclusion*, p. 94.

69. Ibid., p. 91.

find the candy man's gone / I hate to tell you but the candy man's gone."[70] A mere glance at the street or the homeless shelters, indeed a mere glance into the heart of family violence and alienation, and we discover that home often degenerates into a precarious site of deception, anxiety, violent enclosure, disrespect, disorientation, and alienation. Even if our phenomenology does disclose real and normative dimensions of homemaking, we are still left with a culture of homelessness with little or no resources, it would seem, to begin a process of rebuilding that might construct a life hospitable to all and therefore a home for all.

For anyone literate in biblical literature, this might sound familiar. Indeed, the condition in which we find ourselves bears some parallel to that of the returning Jewish exiles after the Babylonian captivity. Perhaps by listening to one of their prophets we might find resources, at least within a Christian community and perhaps also with our Jewish and Muslim neighbors, for a rebuilding project that would address our homeless predicament.

Story, Sabbath, and Streets for Dwelling in Isaiah

Home, we have suggested, is always storied place. Stories, however, are plural and therefore contested. Which stories will shape the construction of space into home, and whose home will this be? Exilic Jews returning to Jerusalem after the Babylonian exile found themselves in a context in which there was debate about which stories would serve as foundations for their reconstruction projects and their praxis. We could say that the postexilic community was attempting to construct a nomic framework, a sacred canopy, a home as *axis mundi*, in the face of the anomic deconstruction and decentering of their lives. If home is a matter of living in a place of permanent familiarity, a dwelling place embedded in memory, where one can rest, offer hospitality, live in a way that respects the integrity of the place, and find a grounding point of orientation and a profound sense of belonging, then in a postexilic context nothing is familiar anymore, memories are broken, things are too tenuous to be able to rest, life is too dangerous to risk hospitality, one is alienated from place, and one is disoriented while struggling to reconstruct relationships of affiliation and belonging. All of the nomic structures of home that had served to provide identity, vision, and hope before 587 B.C.E. had collapsed. The sacred canopy of temple, monarchy, and land inheritance that had given cultic, political, economic, agricultural, and societal order to their lives was buried under the rubble of Babylonian conquest. And now, they were in the midst of that rubble and beginning the reconstruction. But where to start? Which nomic

---

70. Bruce Cockburn, "Candy Man's Gone," from the album *Trouble with Normal* © 1983 Golden Mountain Music Corp. Used with permission of True North Records.

structures ought to have priority? What stories can be life-giving memories upon which to rebuild home?[71]

If it is home that you need, it was reasoned, and if your fundamental identity is that of the chosen people of the God of Jacob, then the first priority must be to engage in a repentant mourning for the loss of God's house. And so Israel instituted fast days to mourn the destruction of the temple and the fall of Jerusalem. The center did not hold. The city of the great king, the seat of David, the house of God—indeed the very center of the universe—is in ruins. That memory must be painfully kept alive if the community is to rebuild.

But a prophet who stands in the tradition of Isaiah of Jerusalem begs to differ. This prophet is unimpressed with this fast because he is unimpressed with the kind of nomic structures and practices it nostalgically remembers and seeks to reinstall.

> Shout out, do not hold back!
>   Lift up your voice like a trumpet!
> Announce to my people their rebellion,
>   to the house of Jacob their sins.
> Yet day after day they seek me
>   and delight to know my ways,
> as if they were a nation that practiced righteousness
>   and did not forsake the ordinance of their God;
> they ask of me righteous judgments,
>   they delight to draw near to God.
> "Why do we fast, but you do not see?
>   Why humble ourselves, but you do not notice?" (Isa. 58:1–3a)

Employing language that echoes the blowing of the trumpet on the day of atonement (Lev. 23:23–32) and the advent of the Jubilee year (Lev. 25:8–12), and which recalls the only day of fasting commanded in the Torah, the prophet proclaims that this fasting in memory of the temple and monarchy is not a practice that can reconstruct life in the ruins because it is rooted in a memory that is not liberating. The repressive, domesticating domicile of a God who served as the ideological legitimation for the imperial aspirations of the monarchy is a memory—a narrative—that was the cause of Jerusalem's collapse and therefore cannot be part of the solution. This is a fast, says the prophet, that functions as a boundary marker and ritual of identity formation, but which (by the people's own admission) has not succeeded in re-creating a sense of the presence of God in their midst. And that is because they are a people who offer a cheap immitation of the Torah requirements of righteousness (*tsedekah*) and justice (*mishpat*) while the praxis on the street bears witness to something else.

---

71. That such images bear striking similarity to the rubble of the World Trade Center after September 11, 2001, and to the serious questions of what might rise from that rubble, is here noted, though not developed.

> Take a look! You serve your own interests on your fast day,
>   and oppress all your workers.
> Take a look! You fast only to quarrel and fight
>   and to strike with a wicked fist. (Isa. 58:3b–4a, authors' translation)

Fast in nostalgic remembrance of a regime of violence, long for the good old days of royal oppression under temple sanction, and you will reinscribe the same boundaries of exclusion, regardless of your piety. You call this a fast, asks the prophet? You think that *this* is an acceptable day of the Lord?

An alternative praxis, an alternative fast, an alternative way of inscribing the boundaries of the covenant people, rooted in an alternative memory, is necessary. And this reconstruction project is rooted in the deepest memories of Torah and directed by the most radical traditions of a hospitality infused by justice.

> Is not this the fast that I choose:
>   to loose the bonds of injustice,
>   to undo the thongs of the yoke,
> to let the oppressed go free,
>   and to break every yoke?
> Is it not to share your bread with the hungry,
>   and to bring the homeless poor into your house;
> when you see the naked, to cover them,
>   and not to hide yourself from your own kin? (Isa. 58:6–7)

If the constructed home that has collapsed was indeed a home that objectified the other and violently suppressed her when she raised her voice of dissent against the terror-saturated boundaries that had been imposed upon her, then any home-rebuilding project that would be healing must see her face, be confronted by her otherness, and hear her cry. What the prophet is saying is that those bonds, those boundaries, that enslave, marginalize, and keep silent must first be loosened. This was a form of homemaking that was too constricted. But beyond just untying the yoke, beyond adjusting the nomic structure so that it is less oppressive, the prophet even more radically calls the community to break such yokes, to dismantle the societal, cultic, political, and economic structures that oppress, and to deconstruct such nomic constructions.

This is not, however, a call for indiscriminate border crossing just for the postmodern fun of it. Rather, the prophet calls for the most radical structure of hospitality—Jubilee. Blow the trumpet! The day of atonement has arrived! And fast. But this is a Jubilee fast. This is an atonement, a fast of return and repatriation, of emancipation of slaves and economic redistribution. This, he proclaims, is the nomic structure—the home-constituting boundary—that transforms the rubble of Jerusalem into a home of covenantal renewal. Subject to the orientation provided by such Jubilee-shaped hospitality, home can be reconstituted as a place of belonging for the most vulnerable, a secure dwelling place of permanence. Indeed, under such conditions, and in response to such homemaking praxis, the home-grounding presence of God can replace the devastating absence that has characterized Israel's life since the Shekinah departed from the temple (Ezekiel 10). The glory (*kabod*) of God will return, but not to sanctify and legitimate our sacred canopies, our temples for exclusionary domestication. Rather, this glory will be our "rear guard" (Isa. 58:8). This, of course, is an exodus image. Isaiah will not countenance a conservative homemaking of settled arrival. This is a homemaking under the sign of sojourn. A sojourning community will be home because God's glory accompanies them. They will, like their forebears in Egypt, call for help and the God who liberates slaves will answer (58:9).[72] They will be hungry in the wilderness and God will feed them (58:11).[73] Indeed, they will "be like a watered garden, like a spring of water, whose waters never fail." (58:11) They will inhabit a covenanted world of rest and sustenance and refreshment.

We see, then, that the prophet counters the ideological memory of temple and monarchy with more ancient memories of Torah, Jubilee, exodus, and creation.[74] If place is always a site of conflicting stories, then the prophet enters into the reconstruction projects of Jerusalem and proclaims which stories are normative for Israel and which stories are not. Practice jubilee, reinscribe such liberating structures, reconstruct home on such nomic foundations, rooted in such deep memories, says the prophet, and

> Your ancient ruins shall be rebuilt;
>   you shall raise up the foundations of many generations;
> you shall be called the repairer of the breach,
>   the restorer of streets to live in. (Isa. 58:12)

The cultural, economic, and political ruins must be rebuilt and the breach in the boundaries of life must be repaired because otherwise life is too precarious and too dangerous for the most vulnerable amongst us. But the walls of Jerusalem—the constructed boundaries of our communities, churches, nations, families, and identities—are not rebuilt with bricks and mortar, but with justice-directed hospitality rooted in life-giving and home-constituting memories. Only then, says the prophet, will the streets be secure enough to be sites of dwelling. Only then will we construct a "city of homes, a city for people to feel at home in, a city where no one is hungry because we are nourished by the practice of justice, and where no one is thirsty because our thirst

72. Exod. 2:23–25; 3:7–10.

73. Exod. 16:1–21.

74. That the older critical dichotomy between exodus and creation is untenable has been convincingly demonstrated by Terence Fretheim in his commentary, *Exodus* (Louisville: John Knox, 1991); and two of his articles, "The Reclamation of Creation: Redemption and Law in Exodus," *Interpretation* 45, 4 (1991); and "The Plagues as Ecological Signs of Historical Disaster," *Journal of Biblical Literature* 110, 3 (1991).

for righteousness has been met."[75] Only then will we no longer need secret videos recording body-to-body conditions in Toronto shelters. And only then will people be able to lie down in safety to take their rest.

This prophet's vision is rooted, we have argued, in narratives of exodus and creation. This is a Torah-shaped vision of homemaking. Not surprisingly, then, he concludes with Sabbath.

> If you refrain from trampling the sabbath,
>   from pursuing your own interests on my holy day;
> if you call the sabbath a delight
>   and the holy day of the LORD honorable;
> if you honor it, not going your own ways,
>   serving your own interests, or pursuing your own affairs;
> then you shall take delight in the LORD,
>   and I will make you ride upon the heights of the earth;
> I will feed you with the heritage of your ancestor Jacob,
>   for the mouth of the LORD has spoken. (Isa. 58:13–14)

The God who orders space for hospitality orders the rhythms of time by Sabbath.[76] Richard Lowery puts it this way: "Creation climaxes and finally coheres in sabbath rest. It is the glue that holds the world together."[77] "Sabbath is the final piece of the creative process by which the world comes into being. It is the crowning touch, the cosmic sign that God's universal and benevolent dominion is fully extended and secure."[78] Those who "trample the sabbath" will necessarily also trample the poor because they will never grant to the poor the rest from their labors that Sabbath requires.[79] Nor will they ever countenance the restoration of the poor to their own bounded space called home that the Sabbath year, and the Sabbath of Sabbaths—Jubilee—requires of covenantal people. Therefore, Lowery argues that Sabbath rejects the "natural law of scarcity, poverty and excessive toil for the laboring majority alongside luxury, leisure and excessive consumption for the court-connected few. It assumes instead a divinely sanctioned social and cosmic order characterized by social solidarity, natural abundance, and self-restraint."[80] Brueggemann puts it this way:

> Sabbath observance is understood as a deep rejection of imperial patterns of exploitation. It is the dramatic act whereby this people asserts to itself and announces to a watching world that this is Israel, a different people with a different way in the world, who will not behave according to the expectations

75. Sylvia Keesmaat, "Talman's Story" (unpublished paper, Toronto, 2000).
76. Jürgen Moltmann, "Shekinah: The Home of the Homeless God," in Rouner, ed., *Longing for Home*, p. 176.
77. Richard H. Lowery, *Sabbath and Jubilee* (St. Louis: Chalice, 2000), p. 82.
78. Ibid., p. 89.
79. See Amos 8:4–6.
80. Lowery, *Sabbath and Jubilee*, p. 102.

of the imperial world. In the purview of covenant, the stability of political life and the effectiveness of worship depend on sabbath, an act that hands life back to God in trusting obedience. If life is not handed over to God regularly, with discipline and intentionality, then the entire political-religious system will end in destruction.[81]

In radical contrast to all homemaking rooted in autonomous self-construction and anxious labor, Sabbath proclaims that the world is a "creational gift, and as such nurtures an attitude of basic trust."[82] Trust in such a gift, and deep trust in the Giver, frames all of our homemaking activities, for Sabbath insists that the world ultimately depends not on our striving but on God's generous world-sustaining love. Moreover, Sabbath is a boundary marker, which itself is a curb on the propensity of boundaries to privilege the powerful. Sabbath is a radically egalitarian ordering of time and culture that is "the alternative to a restless, aggressive, unbridled acquisitiveness that exploits neighbor for self-gain."[83] The Creator's generosity celebrated in Sabbath calls us to construct homes of generosity, borders of welcome, dwelling-places of love.

With and without boundaries. Boundaries, we have said, are necessary. They are constitutive to life. And yet certain boundaries exclude, imprison, oppress. Neither postmodern celebration of border-crossing nor modernist retrenchment into walled fortresses of fear will make streets for dwelling. Only sojourning homes of hospitality shaped by a Sabbath-vision of trust in a gift-giving God will repair the breach.[84] Only such homes of generosity, welcome, and love can be a healing balm for where the hurt is.

81. Walter Brueggemann, *Interpretation and Obedience*, p. 159.
82. Sylvia Keesmaat, "Sabbath and Jubilee: Radical Alternatives for Being Human," in Canadian Ecumenical Jubilee Initiative, *Making a New Beginning: Biblical Reflections on Jubilee* (Toronto: Canadian Ecumenical Jubilee Initiative, 1998), p. 15.
83. Walter Brueggemann, *Isaiah 40–66* (Louisville: Westminster/John Knox, 1998), p. 193.
84. Isa. 58:12.

Part Three

THE WORK
OF JAMES H.
OLTHUIS

14

Olthuis and the Project
of Integral Christian Scholarship

A Narrative by a Friend[1]

Hendrik Hart

Dear Jim,

The occasion of your retirement is an opportunity for me to reflect, in gratitude, on your labors as a Christian scholar. The chorus of voices collected here have engaged the themes that have long characterized your work. I hope that this brief narrative will give some insight into the formation *behind* those theoretical results. In some ways, your own story is a microcosmic narrative about the cause of integral Christian scholarship in North America.

Student Years: 1956–1968

We met in Grand Rapids, Michigan, at Calvin College, the liberal arts college of the Christian Reformed Church of North America. It was 1956, a year before our parents' generation set up the Association for Reformed Scientific Studies, which would later be renamed the Association for the Advancement of Christian Scholarship. The AACS would later, in 1967, establish the Institute for Christian Studies (ICS) with the hope that a small graduate institute would develop in time into a Christian university in Canada on the model of the Free University in Amsterdam.

---

1. With many thanks to another friend, Bob Sweetman, without whose substantial help this project would have lacked the appropriate boundaries.

We had not yet named what we were looking for at Calvin College, but already we knew that having religious exercises on a college campus did not, in and of itself, affect the scholarship done on that campus. Nor did we think that the role of faith could be limited to the ethical dimensions of learning. We were persuaded from the beginning that, to merit the name, scholarship could be Christian only if faith would constitute the orienting perspective for the entire academic enterprise, permeating every nook and cranny.

I say "we" but I am running ahead of myself. In 1956 you were skeptical, maybe even cynical, about students like me and about our enthusiasm for the charismatic philosophy professor H. Evan Runner and the student club he mentored. There, students like me were given a cultural and intellectual context for the things we intuitively knew but could not name. Runner inspired us with a vision of the world of "neo-Calvinism." We learned of its early beginnings in the early-nineteenth-century Dutch Awakening and the work of Guillaume Groen van Prinsterer, its swift elaboration under Abraham Kuyper into a political movement with its own party, an academic movement with its own university, and an ecclesiastical movement with its own denomination. Runner was himself a product of the Free University in Amsterdam that Kuyper had founded. He had studied a recognizably neo-Calvinist approach to philosophy under the direction of its founders, Herman Dooyeweerd and Dirk H. T. Vollenhoven. It was this philosophical approach that Runner taught at the college and it was the neo-Calvinism that lay behind it that he promoted among the students of the "Groen Club" he mentored.

As I said, during your undergraduate years you held back from joining the Groen Club. You did not, however, hold back from conversations with students like me. We became friends and later roommates. Our enthusiasm finally drew you in. By the time you began your theological studies at Calvin Theological Seminary, you had joined the club and you even served as its president during your seminary years. The experience was immensely formative for your career. For in that context you began to consider that academic work of all kinds had its roots in philosophical assumptions—and that a distinctively Christian approach to scholarly work would require assumptions rooted in Christian faith.

In those early years, within our very conservative Christian Reformed Church, we were regarded as conservatives; that is, our attempts to move classroom discussion away from the atmosphere of scholarly neutrality and toward the idea of Christian scholarship were perceived as conservative, because these attempts seemed to fit with the conservative segments of the Christian Reformed Church and their battle for "purity of doctrine" and against the general culture's pervasive spirit of secular liberalism. Only years later would we come to think of ourselves in different terms, and to think of the idea of integral Christian scholarship as a *radical* and not a conservative one. And it was only in the era of the counterculture of the late 1960s and early 1970s that our changed sense of ourselves and of our project became clear to others, causing tension between us and our conservative allies in the Christian Reformed Church.

In those early years we had no idea of our future at ICS. Still, there was talk about students doing graduate work to create a pool for future ICS faculty. Upon graduating from seminary you came to the Free University in Amsterdam to join the rest of us who had been encouraged to undertake graduate study with a future ICS in mind. It was here that the sense of our task as radical, not conservative, became clear to us. You were radical in your own way, weaving different fields, emphases, and angles together, crossing and recrossing the boundaries between philosophy and theology in order to explore ethics. Your cross-disciplinary eye even extended to your choice of a mentor, a philosopher of technology who had a secondary interest in cultural studies.

We former Groen Club members of Grand Rapids also formed a Groen Club in Amsterdam. There we were mentored by people like the philosopher J. P. A. Mekkes, who like our college mentor Runner taught philosophy in the tradition of Dooyeweerd and Vollenhoven. I think it was Mekkes who really gave shape to our conviction that the idea of Christian scholarship as integrally faith-oriented scholarship was a radical idea, because it went to the root (*radix*) of things. This view of scholarship as faith-oriented we took to be true not only in our own work but also in the work of others. Your thesis on the ethical thought of G. E. Moore was a typical example of what we were about, namely, showing how to understand other scholars via the most basic assumptions underlying their thought. We identified such assumptions as religious in nature.

We understood religion, of course, in a broad sense; we meant far more than cultic worship. We saw religion as an entire way of life—even among secular people—that has a fundamental orientation to an ideology, a faith tradition, an ultimate perspective, or whatever else people call a fundamental position. If we had learned anything from our Groen club years, it was that "life is religion."

Mekkes clarified for us what most philosophers take for granted nowadays. Reason without prejudice or with only those assumptions that can be rationally justified is self-referentially incoherent. Such an idea cannot itself be established in the desirable rational manner, because rational justification cannot be applied to itself without losing one of its essential components, its objectivity. Consequently, the ultimacy of rational justification is, as Mekkes taught us, an article of faith. And that, of course, was a very radical approach, which would not gain wide adherence until postmodern thinkers began to expose the inner contradictions of what Gadamer described as the "Enlightenment prejudice against prejudice," or what Derrida would call later "logocentrism." When we began to read Derrida on logocentrism, he spoke to us, because we intuitively understood logocentrism to be his name for traditions that have—quite nonrationally—posited Reason (*logos*) as their spiritual center. We could say, if we were minded to boast, that our tradition had long "been there." In fact, Dooyeweerd had opposed what he called "the dogma of the autonomy of reason" as early as the 1920s.

Thinking back, I have pondered why our work initially had such a strong appeal among conservatives within the Christian Reformed world. My guess is that we shared a rejection of neutrality, which both of us understood as an attempt to justify the whole notion of secularity. In short, we were both articulating what we knew as the "antithesis" between Christian faith and secular worldviews. We accepted that faith and reason were different, but not that the one could do without the other. So our conservative friends took the challenge we posed to the neutrality of scholarship as a challenge to the spirit of secularity (liberalism). Later our friends would discover that our philosophical work had spiritual consequences that they hadn't foreseen. For example, our criticism of rational autonomy could also feed criticism of a propositionalist understanding of biblical revelation.

ICS's Beginnings: 1968–1972

The Institute for Christian Studies opened its doors in 1967, and by 1968 we were both there on staff. There we confronted an academic culture grappling with the counterculture touched off by the war in Vietnam. We struggled to place our radicality with respect to this. We noted that the counterculture also seemed to challenge the deepest assumptions of established forms of culture, including assumptions of objectivity and neutrality in scholarship. Moreover, its style was primarily confrontational, as was ours. We focused on opposing trends we considered unacceptable to Christians. We encouraged our students to challenge the secular establishment, but also to question churches that did not engage the culture, and Christian student organizations that expressed their faith merely in piety rather than in academic work. This confrontational engagement of culture was what we had learned from our mentors but it seemed to become a strategy that promised real success. We listened sympathetically to much of the rhetoric of the day and found that our own approach had appeal in that climate.

In these years we came to think of the Christian tradition at its best as not so much a set of assumptions but more a "spirit" embodied differently by different communities. Of course, we also thought that our own community embodied that spirit more truly than others. Still, this more dynamic understanding led to an emphasis upon the continuous need for reform rather than the preservation of earlier achievements. This orientation has marked our work ever since.

The focus of your work was more recognizably theological than it would later become. You debated theological colleagues who viewed revelation as propositional, confronting them with principles of hermeneutics that demanded a much more differentiated approach to texts. You were tireless in exposing the characterization of the Scripture as propositional, seeing such a characterization as a capitulation to the autonomy of reason. This turn to hermeneutics is an early indication of your later concerns. There were other indications as well: your insistence on interdisciplinary focus, your ecumenical orientation (I think of your collaboration with Gustav Wingren), and your creative adaptation of Vollenhoven's work to gain a deeper sense of the literature you were reading (many a former student will smile at the mere mention of the term "contradictory monism").

In these years you modeled the combination of a radical orientation in your work with a pastoral and irenic approach. You forcefully criticized theologians, but your style did not alienate. That same joining of pastoral and radical elements is to be seen in your work today. You are a postmodern scholar with a distinctively Christian outlook. You share much of the postmodern criticism of modernity, especially where that was an expression of human autonomy. But you also continue to expose and correct continuations of such autonomy in the revolt against boundaries or the suspicion of meaning among postmoderns. The way you do this inspires both your critics and those you criticize to acknowledge the fruitfulness and integrity of your work.

The Search for Scholarly Identity: 1972–1985

By the early 1970s the faculty at ICS began to focus its energies in a new, less polemical, way. We spent less time writing and speaking against what we opposed, and more time developing our own academic positions. This newer emphasis bore fruit in your work in hermeneutics. Challenging a propositionalist understanding of biblical revelation receded to the background. You disliked the acrimony such challenges occasioned and were determined to develop a positive approach in hopes of forging connections with a broader community of Christian scholars. Working on this project with a number of talented students, your "certitudinal hermeneutics" was the result of your efforts and collaborations—a theory that was published in *A Hermeneutics of Ultimacy.*

As the faculty of ICS turned from a strategy of confrontation to the development of positive alternative positions, a diversity of views emerged. This sometimes gave rise to tensions, particularly when some of the emerging positions challenged our own tradition's assumptions. We all realized that our work had to form a concretely recognizable body of scholarship, fitting our time even as we were critical of it. But, would we align ourselves with some scholarly traditions more than others? What were our research priorities? Would analyses of philosophical assumptions continue to be justifiable in their own right or would a positive orientation to politics, economics, psychotherapy, or education (to name a few examples) provide a necessary context for our criticism? Where would we come down in discussions surrounding theory and practice? Could we restrict our focus to theory or did our theorizing require close ties to activist organizations? In supporting the call for justice that was heard everywhere, would we support people whose lives seemed out of sync with traditionally accepted norms? What were we to do with the enormous influence of Marxism?

In resolving these common issues for yourself, you made a number of important decisions. First and foremost, you chose a practical orientation in scholarship. You were persuaded that, in order to be redemptively Christian, scholars needed concrete ties to lived practice. Your conviction led you to train yourself and establish a practice in psychotherapy. I remember that I disagreed with you in subsequent discussions. Even today I am skeptical about the ability of theoreticians to speak persuasively about the implications of their views for practice. Let me put it this way: contrary to what theoreticians think, theory is a prime example of what Derrida has called an "undecidable" text. Hence the practical evaluation of a theory seems, to me, better left, as a rule, to practitioners. But maybe my view of the matter is too theoretical? What is undeniable is that, over the years, you have demonstrated the winsomeness of your approach. Students certainly seemed to tune in to what you were trying to do and have continued to do so to this day. No one has had more students at ICS than you.

Slowly, in these years, your mature identity as a scholar emerged. You became a strong advocate for links between ICS and Christian activist organizations involved in labor relations, political policy formation, the arts, curriculum development, and the like. Your publications were never exclusively academic. Many were intended for a broader public and explored the practical sides of the matters you theorized about in an academic setting. *I Pledge You My Troth* is an eloquent example of this kind of publication. In it, you made core insights of the theoretical work done at ICS available to people struggling with issues in their relationships. You brought together the modal theory you learned from Herman Dooyeweerd's philosophy and practical issues in ethics. Your analysis is built on the assumption that particular areas of human experience have their own specific point of orientation and their own peculiar norms. Family, friendship, and marriage need, in your view, to be focused on and integrated by a concern for troth or faithful love. On that basis you provided fresh treatments of traditional ethical quandaries such as the structure of authority in families, divorce, and parental discipline.

Looking back today, I can see just how deeply influential your choice of practical orientation was for you. The only monographs you have written, *I Pledge You My Troth, Keeping Troth,* and *The Beautiful Risk,* are all exercises in putting hard-won theoretical insight to work in the area of pastoral care and therapy. Your books of a more purely theoretical character have all been cooperative ventures and as such demonstrate how you believe an academic community ought to work. Not surprisingly, however, even your academic publications, like *A Hermeneutics of Ultimacy, Knowing* Other-*wise,* or *Towards an Ethics of Community,* are visibly connected to a practical need.

But you did not just become an advocate for theory's necessary tie to lived practice. In *A Hermeneutics of Ultimacy,* you used Dooyeweerd's modal theory to come to a novel perspective on faith, giving it its own character not as a clone of reason but as a source of certitude. After all, modal theory requires the acknowledgment of fundamental distinctions in the different kinds of experience there are, thus precluding views of faith as some sort of supernatural cognition. In the Reformed and evangelical communities to which ICS faculty belonged, your approach to hermeneutics evoked suspicion. But the thrust of your moves was to link hermeneutics with the practical needs of the faithful, particularly those most perplexed and straitened by their situation. Here we see the effect of your second choice in these years: your (leftlike) focus upon fostering freedom and justice toward burdened and marginalized persons.

Of course, the emergence of a recognizable identity did not lead immediately to a flood of publications. This was not because your thinking was stagnant; quite to the contrary, you made significant progress in developing a philosophy of psychotherapy. You moved first to examine the body therapy of Alexander Löwen, later focusing upon theories of developmental stages. You redesigned stage theory into spiral theory, thereby transforming developmental theories from preoccupation with overly static pictures of successive stages into a spiraling conception in which stages could be understood to repeat themselves on new and deeper levels, reflecting the never finished process of redemption, while at the same time making room for progress. In my view all of your concerns came together in the emergence of a postmodern climate. It too fostered criticism of abstraction from the issues of the day and an eye for the burdened and the marginalized. Your computer began to hum; articles and books followed in due course.

Honoring Difference: 1985–1994

Until the mid-1980s the ICS faculty had assumed that a community of any kind would be known by its unity. And unity in an intellectual community seemed inconceivable without fundamental agreements within a shared general conceptual framework, a philosophy in point of fact. What were we then to make of the fairly distinct positions taken by different faculty members? How would differences affect our experience of community? In the mid-1980s our sense of how to name our differences began to change. They came to be named less in terms of the left/right model we had been using to that point, and more in terms of the tensions between modernity and postmodernity, or between realism and antirealism, between the nexus of truth, logic, order, and reason and marginalized realities, between sameness and difference, and so on.

As already noted, Dooyeweerd's criticism of autonomous reason seemed to have strong resemblances to the postmodern criticism of logocentrism and to parallel developments in feminism and neopragmatism. Dooyeweerd stressed as early as the 1920s the relativity of all created reality, the dogmatism characteristic of the doctrine of rational autonomy, and the unidentifiable nature of the self except in the context of religious community. These themes had their analogies in the work of contemporary authors. But these authors interpreted the themes in ways that seemed novel and suggestive to some of us. And so it was in the years between 1985 and 1994 that we started to listen closely to the voice of Emmanuel Levinas, who showed a marked tendency to listen, in turn, to Old Testament prophets and to attract the attention of secularized thinkers like Jacques Derrida. It became clear to us that such authors opened up new possibilities within the development of typically neo-Calvinist philosophical themes. In particular, they demonstrated that the doctrine of the autonomy of Reason undermined social justice, curtailed Christian love, promoted inequality, and in many other ways did its damage far beyond the realm of theory.

Your response to our shared situation was reinforced by your work in psychotherapy, which introduced you to the value of unique identities. Difference, you began to argue, was a gift to be treasured. Community was less dependent on agreement in thought and sameness in behavior than had been assumed. The ensuing variety in scholarship, for example, could contribute to the good of all. Your long-standing ecumenical impulse had already moved you far in this direction, but the postmodern thematizations of sameness and difference provided you a current vocabulary in which to articulate and develop your impulses. Thus, you came to retranslate the prominent Dooyeweerdian theme articulated as the demand of God's Word of order for creaturely obedience as God's gift that comes with a call, a formulation more amenable to difference.

It was at this time that I learned in dialogue with you to connect my criticism of realistic conceptions of order and reason with your positive explorations of love as a more centrally important focus than order. For it was also then that you conceived the all-important concept of "the wild spaces of love." I judge that in that concept you have combined a biblical focus on love that is not found in postmodern theory with the postmodern insight that our world does not exhibit what I would call "a known, eternal order." I like to think that you took an Augustinian turn in a postmodern context: "Love and do what you will" made the wildest places of postmodern thought habitable for Christians, wherever the love in question is embodied as the love of God in Christ. I can articulate what I learned with your help during these years in another way. By decentering order and moving love to the center it became possible to acknowledge the centrality of love in the Gospels, while at the same time allowing the spaces of love to be wild, that is, uncharted by an eternal order, though not without structure. Your and my essays published in *The Order of Creation and an Ethos of Compassion* represented firstfruits of the changes our thinking underwent in the late 1980s. Of course, our essays were controversial, and we paid a price for them. Nevertheless, I read their eventual inclusion within the ICS's anniversary conference proceedings as a sign that the ICS community as a whole was prepared to take seriously the need to adapt its philosophical tradition to the up-and-coming climate of postmodern thought.

Coming into Your Own: 1995–

In the last decade you have come into your own. Your work has gained an ever-wider hearing in the academy, far beyond the Reformed and evangelical communities in which it was first nourished. You belong within a circle of prominent Christian scholars who have become known for the care with which they engage postmodern thought. Your appreciation is both a reading with and a reading against that thought. You are sensitive to postmodernism's criticism of modernity without falling prey to a certain conceptual logic that would bar us from celebrating positive achievements. In your work on self and ethics, for example, you show that what may seem to flow with an iron logic from certain abstract conceptual arguments, namely, the impossibility of actual, real, and positive achievements in this life, does not help people live with one another in their flesh-and-blood communities. In other words, you take to heart valid criticism of modernity while encouraging people yet to have confidence in future achievements that will be concretely redemptive. You preserve the Gospel's call to love neighbor as self and not at the cost of self. You show that to reflect on oneself in the face of the other is healthy; to let the face of the other efface oneself is not.

In my view, your present work shows that both Levinas and Derrida retain unnecessary traces of logocentric thinking. Their philosophical work at times remains constrained by their assumption of a certain kind of abstract logic. Nor do they seem aware that *logos* remains dominant in their analyses insofar as they both continue to espouse some version of an "autonomous" philosophy. Moreover, their work has implications for selfhood and achievement that creates pessimism. This pessimism does not result from the appraisal of concrete life situations, but because they follow a logic of criticism to its logical conclusions.

Your own position within the modern/postmodern struggle is robustly positive and practical. It is informed by your work in theology, philosophy, and psychotherapy as well as by your long participation in the intellectual community of ICS. Your dance, as you call it, in the wild spaces gives you the room you need to speak to postmodern discussion partners. But your orientation to the love we see in the crucified Jesus allows you to work out positions that give people hope. In other words, the love you embrace is a robust following of Christ, not an ever-receding ideal, though it is certainly marked by failure. Faith gives you a "hold" on life that differs from the grasp of reason. But even without the grasp of reason, you are not left empty-handed.

One final mention of your many students is in place before I close—perhaps your most fitting legacy. You have had more students than anyone else at ICS. Many of these are now teaching in colleges across North America, and several are widely published in their own right. Their interaction with what they have received from you is unfailingly appreciative but never slavish. They show that what you have done can be carried on. They also show that what you have done can be reinterpreted to fit the needs of new worlds, rather than just copied. They together make up one of the weightiest arguments for the worth of your academic career.

With love and respect,
Henk

A Poetic Adieu

Call to Prayer

Julie Robinson

i.
At dawn, minutes before terra-cotta tiles
again glow by the fire that grows
creativity and forgetfulness,
an unearthly invitation
calls slumber from my inner eye,
draws a bath of light and music
to cleanse my soul.
This light that dims the sun,
guides the living to eternity,
waits on the far side of a dream
I'm not yet ready to relinquish.

The need for earth when finally
you weigh too much,
when I've carried you here and finally
plant you like a pocketed bulb,
heavy and misplaced,
I need earth to welcome the overflow
of sorrow and longing,
to cool me in shadow,
soothe the burn when rough winds
spark energies of what might have been.

ii.
At noon the heat alters my surface
like tightly packed painted tiles
in the fires of underground kilns
at Iznik.

The hours spent together
mark my skin like pigment on stone-paste—
not erasable but perhaps forgettable.

Faint with the disappearing of you,
I dip my hands my face and feet
in ancient complexities of the Bosphorus,
attempt to clear what the heat drew out
and left in a thin film
at the edge of my pores.

iii.
Late afternoon and still caught in currents
of watery confusion.
The muezzin rings a harmony of light
that splinters and garbles
under the surface.
In this liquid place
you seep through openings,
soak my dreams with a need for you,
an unquenchable thirst
these salty waters cannot heal.
Desire will not drown,
total immersion not enough.
Your name repeats
like a canyon echo
as if uttered
somewhere deep.

iv.
Early evening at Eminonu,
passengers spill onto docks
like rising tide over beach,
voices crash against a jut of yellow taxis,
gulls cry for fish and garbage
as plentiful as sand crabs after
water recedes.
Fourth call of the day,
though I bury burn and wash you away,
grief remains caught in my throat.
Smog lingers after the fact,
my breath short as haze begins to fold you
into gentler memory.

v.
Before sleep, before midnight,
when darkness has bled through the city
staining everydayness the colour of mystery,

when I've run you round my mind,
ground my sorrow like fine grain
that tomorrow I may return to the earth,
when my feet can no longer bear
a body burdened with sadness
I slip off my shoes,
place them with other worn witnesses
of difficult journeys
and enter.

Carpets floral and calligraphic
welcome my bones as if lowered
into paradise.
The sky, visible again in blue and white tiles,
beckons unto the bosom of heaven.
Here the promise of invitation
may be fulfilled.

Bibliographies

The Work and Legacy of James H. Olthuis

Compiled by Michael DeMoor

I. Publications

"Federal Aid for Private Schools." *Stromata* 7 (1961): 8–9.

"The University and Its Basis." *Christian Vanguard* 4 (November 1962): 6–7.

"Guarding the Universal Office of Believer (1)." *Christian Vanguard* 4 (December 1962): 6–8.

"The Universal Office of Believer and Individualism." *Christian Vanguard* 5 (January 1963): 4–5.

"The Universal Office of Believer and Collectivism." *Christian Vanguard* 5 (March 1963): 8–10.

"Letter to the Editors." *Reformed Journal* 14, 6 (July–August 1964): 19–20.

"Must—A Reply to Mr. Helm." *International Reformed Bulletin* (July 1967): 22–26.

"Must the Church Become Secular?" *International Reformed Bulletin* (January 1967): 14–31. Reprinted, in revised form, in: *Out of Concern for the Church.* Toronto: Wedge, 1970: 105–25.

"Values and Valuation: With Particular Attention to Ethical Thought in Twentieth Century Britain." *Philosophia Reformata* 32 (1967): 37–54.

Facts, Values, and Ethics: A Confrontation with Twentieth Century British Moral Philosophy, in Particular G. E. Moore. Assen, Netherlands: Van Gorcum and Comp. N.V., 1968; Doctoral Dissertation: Vrije Universiteit te Amsterdam.

"Ambiguity Is the Key (Remarks on H. M. Kuitert's View of Scriptures)." *International Reformed Bulletin* 38 (July 1969): 6–16.

Facts, Values, and Ethics: A Confrontation with Twentieth Century British Moral Philosophy, in Particular G. E. Moore, 2d edition. Assen, Netherlands: Van Gorcum and Comp. N.V., 1969.

"Confessing Christ in Education." Written together with Bernard Zylstra. *International Reformed Bulletin* 42 (1970): 36–44.

"Family Values—A Ping Pong Game." *Vanguard* (November 1970): 8–10, 14.

"Must the Church Become Secular?" *Out of Concern for the Church: Five Essays.* Toronto: Wedge Publishing Foundation, 1970: 105–125.

"The Reality of Societal Structures." Unpublished mimeograph. Toronto: Institute for Christian Studies, 1970. Association for the Advancement of Christian Scholarship Academic Papers. *Tydskrif vir Christelike Wetenskap* 13 (1977): 198–207.

"America—Walking the Way of the WASP." *Vanguard* (July–August 1971): 7–11, 21–22.

"Confessing Christ in Education." Written together with Bernard Zylstra. *Christian Educator's Journal* 10 (April 1971): 4–8.

"'Bunglers and Visionaries': Past and Future of the CLAC." *Bunglers and Visionaries: Christian Labour at the Crossroads,* by James H. Olthuis and Gerald Vandezande. Toronto: Wedge, 1972: 1–17.

"An Educational Creed." Written together with Bernard Zylstra. *To Prod the Slumbering Giant: A Christian Response to the Crisis in the Classroom.* Toronto: Wedge, 1972: 167–70.

"To Prod the 'Slumbering Giant.'" *To Prod the Slumbering Giant: A Christian Response to the Crisis in the Classroom.* Toronto: Wedge, 1972: 15–41.

"Worship and Witness." *Will all the King's Men . . . . Out of Concern for the Church, Phase II.* Toronto: Wedge, 1972: 1–27.

"The Word of God and Hermeneutics." Unpublished mimeograph. Toronto: Institute for Christian Studies, 1973.

"The Word of God and Science." Unpublished mimeograph. Toronto: Institute for Christian Studies, 1973.

"The Word of God." Unpublished mimeograph. Toronto: Institute for Christian Studies, 1974.

"Friendship: Trust and Congeniality." *Vanguard* (March–April 1975): 18–19.

"God, Word, Creation: A Reply to Professor Frame." *Vanguard* (January–February 1975): 9–11.

I Pledge You My Troth: A Christian View of Marriage, Family, and Friendship. New York: Harper & Row, 1975.

"The Word of God and Creation." Unpublished mimeograph. Toronto: Institute for Christian Studies, 1975. Published in *Tydskrif vir Christelike Wetenskap* 25 (1989): 25–37.

"Review of: *Intimate Friendships* by James Ramey." *Vanguard* (November–December 1976): 25–26.

"The Unique Certitudinal Focus of the Scriptures: Towards a Certitudinal Hermeneutic." Unpublished mimeograph. Toronto: Institute for Christian Studies, 1976.

The Word of God and Biblical Authority. Potchefstroom, South Africa: Wetenskaplike Bydraes van die Potchefstroom University for Christian Higher Education, 1976.

"The Reality of Societal Structures." *Tydskrif vir Christelike Wetenskap* 13 (1977): 198–207.

"Models of Man in Theology and Psychology." Written together with Arnold H. De Graaff. Unpublished mimeograph. Toronto: Institute for Christian Studies, 1978.

Toward a Biblical View of Man: Some Readings. Edited with Arnold H. De Graaff. Toronto: Institute for Christian Studies, 1978.

"Visions and Ways of Life: The Nature of Religion." *Toward a Biblical View of Man: Some Readings.* Edited with Arnold H. De Graaff. Toronto: Institute for Christian Studies, 1978: 162–90.

"Sense and Non-Sense of Self." *Vanguard* (May–June 1979): 13–17.

"Theses on Science and Revelation." Written together with Hendrik Hart. Unpublished mimeograph. Toronto: Institute for Christian Studies, 1979.

"Towards a Certitudinal Hermeneutic." *Hearing and Doing: Philosophical Essays Dedicated to H. Evan Runner*, ed. John Kraay and Anthony Tol. Toronto: Wedge, 1979: 65–85.

"People in Development: A Life-Span Appoach." Written together with Stephen Bouma-Prediger and Jeff Sloan. Unpublished Mimeograph. Toronto: Institute for Christian Studies, 1982.

"Review of: *Testaments of Love: A Study of Love in the Bible* by Leon Morris." *Calvin Theological Journal* 18 (1983): 109–12.

"Self or Society: Is There a Choice?" *Your Better Self: Christianity, Psychology, and Self Esteem*, ed. Craig W. Ellison. New York: Harper & Row, 1983: 202–14.

"Dooyeweerd on Religion and Faith." *The Legacy of Herman Dooyeweerd: Reflections on Critical Philosophy in the Christian Tradition*, ed. C. T. McIntire. Lanham, Md.: University Press of America, 1985: 21–40.

"Faith Development in the Adult Life Span." *Studies in Religion/Sciences Religieuses* 14 (1985): 497–509.

"On Worldviews." *Christian Scholar's Review* 14 (1985): 153–64. Reprinted in: *Stained Glass: Worldviews and Social Science*, ed. Paul A. Marshall, Sander Griffioen, and Richard J. Mouw. Lanham, Md.: University Press of America, 1990: 26–40.

"Straddling the Boundaries Between Theology and Psychology: The Faith-Feeling Interface." *Journal of Psychology and Christianity* 4 (1985): 6–15.

"Evolutionary Dialectics and Segundo's *Liberation of Theology*." *Calvin Theological Journal* 21 (1986): 79–93.

Keeping Our Troth: Staying in Love through the Five Stages of Marriage. San Francisco: Harper & Row, 1986.

A Hermeneutics of Ultimacy: Peril or Promise [Primary author, with responses by Donald G. Bloesch, Clark H. Pinnock, and Gerald T. Sheppard]. Lanham, Md.: University Press of America, 1987.

"Review of: *What Is Living, What Is Dead in Christianity Today?* by Charles Davis." *Calvin Theological Journal* 22 (1987): 321–24.

"The Family: God's School of Compassion." *Banner* 123 (November 21, 1988): 12–13.

"Review of *Men and Marriage* by George Gilder." *Banner* 123 (March 14, 1988): 20.

"The Covenanting Metaphor of the Christian Faith and the Self Psychology of Heinz Kohut." *Studies in Religion/Sciences Religieuses* 18 (1989): 313–24.

"The Word of God and Creation." *Tydskrif vir Christelike Wetenskap* 25 (1989): 25–37.

"A Cold and Comfortless Hermeneutic or a Warm and Trembling Hermeneutic: A Conversation with John D. Caputo." *Christian Scholar's Review* 19 (1990): 345–62.

"An Ethics of Compassion: Ethics in a Post-Modernist Age." *What Right Does Ethics Have?* ed. Sander Griffioen. Amsterdam: Vrije Universiteit Press, 1990: 125–46.

"The Fashion of Spirituality." *Banner* 125 (February 26, 1990): 8–9.

"Response to André Droogers." *Norm and Context in the Social Sciences*, ed. Sander Griffioen and Jan Verhoogt. Lanham, Md.: University Press of America, 1990: 123–128.

"Undecidability and the Impossibility of Faith: Continuing the Conversation with Professor Caputo." *Christian Scholar's Review* 20 (1990): 171–73.

"God as True Infinite: Concerns about Wolfhart Pannenberg's Systematic Theology v. 1." *Calvin Theological Journal* 27 (1992): 318–26.

"Review of: *By Way of the Heart: Toward a Holistic Christian Spirituality* by Wilke Mahwah." *Calvin Theological Journal* 27 (1992): 111–13.

"Be(com)ing: Humankind as Gift and Call." *Philosophia Reformata* 58 (1993): 153–72.

"A Spirituality of Mutuality or a Spirituality of Domination." *Newsletter of the Canadian Theological Society* (1993): 2–5.

"Being-With: Towards a Relational Psychotherapy." *Journal of Psychology and Christianity* 13 (1994): 217–30.

"God-With-Us: Toward a Relational Psychotherapeutic Model." In *Journal of Psychology and Christianity* 13 (1994): 37–49.

"Review of: *Habermas, Modernity, and Public Theology*, edited by Don S. Browning and Francis Schussler Fiorenza; and *Negation and Theology*, edited by Robert P. Scharlemann." In *Calvin Theological Journal* 29 (1994): 550–53.

"Crossing the Threshold: Sojourning Together in the Wild Spaces of Love." *Toronto Journal of Theology* 11 (1995): 39–57. Presidential address to the Canadian Theological Society, 1993. Reprinted in: *Knowing Other-Wise: Philosophy at the Threshold of Spirituality*. New York: Fordham University Press, 1997. Perspectives in Continental Philosophy 4: 235–57.

"When Is Sex Against Nature?" *An Ethos of Compassion and the Integrity of Creation*, ed. Brian J. Walsh, Hendrik Hart, and Robert E. Vander Vennen. Lanham, Md.: University Press of America, 1995: 188–205.

"Face-to-Face: Ethical Asymmetry or the Symmetry of Mutuality?" *Studies in Religion/Sciences Religieuses* 25 (1996): 459–79. Reprinted in: *Knowing Other-Wise: Philosophy at the Threshold of Spirituality*. New York: Fordham University Press, 1997. Perspectives in Continental Philosophy 4: 131–58.

"A Hermeneutics of Suffering Love." *The Very Idea of Radical Hermeneutics*, ed. R. Martinez. New York: Humanities, 1996: 149–65.

"The Inner Work of a Happy Marriage." *Banner* (February 12, 1996): 12–15.

Editor, *Knowing Other-Wise: Philosophy at the Threshold of Spirituality*. New York: Fordham University Press, 1997. Perspectives in Continental Philosophy 4.

"Love / Knowledge: Sojourning with Others, Meeting with Differences: Introduction." *Knowing Other-Wise: Philosophy at the Threshold of Spirituality*. New York: Fordham University Press, 1997. Perspectives in Continental Philosophy 4: 1–15.

"Review of: *Trance Zero: Breaking the Spell of Conformity* by Adam Crabtree." *Connections: Newsletter of the Ontario Society of Psychotherapists* 3 (1997): 4–5.

"Review of: *Figuring the Sacred: Religion, Narrative, and Imagination* by Paul Ricouer." *Toronto Journal of Theology* 14 (1998): 307–8.

"Dancing Together in the Wild Spaces of Love: Postmodernism, Psychotherapy, and the Spirit of God." *Journal of Psychology and Christianity* 18 (1999): 140–52.

"Feature Review Article: *Deconstruction in a Nutshell;* and *The Prayers and Tears of Jacques Derrida*, by John D. Caputo." *International Philosophical Quarterly* 34 (1999): 347–53. Reprinted as: "The Test of Khora: Grace à Dieu," in *Religion With/out Religion: The Prayers and Tears of John D. Caputo*. London: Routledge, 2002: 110–19.

Editor, *Towards an Ethics of Community: Negotiations of Difference in a Pluralist Society*. Waterloo, Ont.: Wilfred Laurier University Press, 2000. Comparative Ethics Series 5.

"Exclusions and Inclusions: Dilemmas of Difference." *Towards an Ethics of Community: Negotiations of Difference in a Pluralist Society*. Waterloo, Ont.: Wilfred Laurier University Press, 2000. Comparative Ethics Series 5: 1–10.

"Of Webs and Whirlwinds: Me, Myself, and I." *Contemporary Reflections on the Philosophy of Herman Dooyeweerd*, ed. D. F. M. Strauss and Michelle Botting. Lewiston, N.Y.: Edwin Mellen, 2000: 31–48.

"Otherwise than Violence: Towards a Hermeneutics of Connection." *The Arts, Community, and Cultural Democracy*, ed. Lambert Zuidervaart and Henry Luttikhuizen. New York: St. Martin's, 2000: 137–64.

"Rethinking the Family: Belonging, Respecting, Connecting." *Towards an Ethics of Community: Negotiations of Difference in a Pluralist Society*. Waterloo, Ont.: Wilfred Laurier University Press, 2000. Comparative Ethics Series 5: 127–49.

The Beautiful Risk: A New Psychology of Loving and Being Loved. Grand Rapids: Zondervan, 2001.

Editor and "Introduction," *Religion With/Out Religion: The Prayers and Tears of John D. Caputo*. London: Routledge, 2002.

"The Test of Khora: Grace à Dieu." In *Religion With/out Religion: The Prayers and Tears of John D. Caputo*. London: Routledge, 2002: 110–19. Reprinted with new title from *International Philosophical Quarterly* 34 (1999): 347–53.

"Introduction: Philosophy as Spiritual Exercise." *Philosophy as Responsibility: A Celebration of Hendrik Hart's Contribution to the Discipline*, ed. Ronald A. Kuipers and Janet Catherina Wessalius. Lanham, Md.: University Press of America, 2002: xi–xxiii.

"Review of: *Ethics, Exegesis, and Philosophy*, by Richard Cohen." *Religious Studies* 21 (2002): 84–87.

Forthcoming

"Donner la Mort/Donner l'Amour: From Derrida's Pure Giving to Irigaray's Mutual Loving." *Heretical Offerings: On the Question of Religion*. Chicago: University of Chicago Press, forthcoming.

"God as May-Be: Richard Kearney's Metaxology." *Transversing the Imaginary*. Bloomington: Indiana University Press, forthcoming.

"The Miracle of Mutual Love: Luce Irigaray and the Ethics of Sexual Difference." *Ways of Knowing*, ed. John Kok. Sioux Center, Iowa: Dordt College Press, forthcoming.

II. Theses Supervised

AMPhil and MPhilF Theses

1975

Breems, Bradley. One Man's God . . . Another's Demon: A Study into the Relativity of Value and the Remoteness of Science in the Sociology of Max Weber.

Fernhout, Harry. Man, Faith, and Religion in Bavinck, Kuyper, and Dooyeweerd.

Miyazaki, Masuo. A Basic Pattern in Zen Buddhism: The Logic of Sokuhi.

Sinnema, Donald. Reflections on Theology at the University of Leyden Before the Synod of Dordt.

1977

Tollefson, Terry. Paul Tillich: The Usefulness of Anthropological Typology in Grasping His Thought.

1979

Valk, John. The Concept of the *Coincidentia Oppositorum* in the Thought of Mircea Eliade.

Walsh, Brian J. Futurity and Creation: Explorations in the Eschatological Theology of Wolfhart Pannenberg.

1981

Malarkey, Robert. Eros and Agape in the Sexual Ethics of Helmut Thielicke.

1984

Bouma-Prediger, Steven. Bonhoeffer and Berkouwer on the World, Humans, and Sin: Two Models of Ontology and Anthropology.

Shahinian, Gary. The Problem of Evil in Griffin's Process Theology.

1985

Chapko, John. Faith in Search of a Focus: An Internal Critique of the Faith Development Theory of James Fowler.

Gousmett, Chris. The Miracle of Nature and the Nature of Miracle.

Shaw, Steven. Evolutionary Monism: The Continuity of John Hick's Thought.

Wilson, Gordon. Towards an Integral Anthropology: An Examination of Donald Evans' Philosophy of Religion.

1986

Venema, Henry. Philosophical Anthropology: An Interpretive Analysis of Paul Ricouer's Philosophy of Will.

1987

Dudiak, Jeffrey. Philosophy and Faith: A Critical Examination of Karl Jaspers' Philosophy of Religion.

Pearcey, J. Richard. Yes & No: Carl F. Henry and the Question of Empirical Verification.

Wells, Jeffrey John. Being and Being Known: The Place of Revelation in a Marcellian Ontology.

1988

Hildebrand, Glenda. Imaginatively Constructing God Concepts: Exploring the Role of Imagination in Gordon Kaufman's Theological Method.

1989

Lysander, Nesamoni. Natural Healing in Biblical Perspective: Its Contribution to Health Care.

1990

Ansell, Nicholas John. The Woman Will Overcome the Warrior: A Dialogue with the Feminist Theology of Rosemary Radford Ruether.

Fauquex, Jacques Albert. Victimized by Bad Accusation but Set Free in the Light of Hope: An Introduction to Paul Ricoeur's Thinking with a Difference in his Anthology Titled *The Conflict of Interpretations* (1969).

1992

Martin, Stephen W. Decomposing Modernity: Images of Human Existence in the Writing of Ernest Becker.

1995

Smith, James K. A. In or After Eden? Creation, Fall, and Interpretation.

1996

Cudney, Shane. Philosophy, Deconstruction, and the Im/Possibility of Faith: An Exploration of the Relationship Between the "Tragic" and the "Religious" in the Writings of John D. Caputo.

1997

Robinson, Julie. Revealing/Reveiling the Sacred: The Atheology of Mark C. Taylor.

Smith, David Ian. Power and Mutuality in Modern Foreign Language Education: The Possibility of a Christian Orientation.

1998

Kerkham, Ruth H. Renegotiating Body Boundaries at the Dawn of a New Millennium.

Lai, Anthony Der-Lin. Tracing Ruth in the Straits and Islands of Im/Emigrant Blood: Be/Longing in Rootedness and Routedness.

1999

Erickson, Timothy M. Faith and Doubt: A Socratic Alliance of Religion between Kierkegaard and Derrida.

2000

Friesen, Henry. Phronesis, Tradition, Logos, and Context: A Reading of Gadamer's Philosophical Hermeneutics.

Lie, Joshua. The Hermeneutic Spiral as the Hermeneutics of Reconciliation: The Significance of a Hermeneutics of Connection for Biblical Hermeneutics.

Park, Weon-Cheol. Is There an Illusion in the Text? Deconstruction, Meaning, and Hermeneutics.

2002

VanderBerg, James. Forgiveness: The Gift and Its Counterfeit.

B. Doctoral Dissertations Supervised:

1998

Dudiak, Jeffrey. The Intrigue of Ethics: A Reading of the Idea of Discourse in the Thought of Emmanuel Levinas.

In Progress

Ansell, Nicholas John; Bonzo, Matthew; Cudney, Shane; Middleton, J. Richard.